Readings in
Personality Psychology

JOHN D. MAYER

University of New Hampshire

PEARSON

Boston • New York • San Francisco

New Mexico • Montreal • Toronto • London • Madrid • Munich • Paris
Hong Kong • Singapore • Tokyo • Cape Town • Sydney

To my family . . .

Editor in Chief: *Susan Hartman*
Production Supervisor: *Karen Mason*
Editorial Production: *Tom Scalzo, Sylvie Scholvin, and Lauren Houlihan*
Project Manager: *Steve Simpson*
Manufacturing Buyer *JoAnne Sweeney*
Cover Administrator *Joel Gendron*

For related titles and support materials, visit our online catalog at
www.ablongman.com.

Library of Congress Cataloging-in-Publication Data
Mayer, John D.
    Readings in personality psychology / John D. Mayer
        p. cm.
    Includes bibliographical references.
    ISBN 0-205-43098-8
    1. Personality.   I. Title.
    BF698.M23665 2007
    155.2—dc22

                                        2006048387

Printed in the United States of America

10 9 8 7 6 5 4 3 2 1   11 10 09 08 07 06

Contents

A Systems Organization

Alternative Contents

A Theoretical Perspectives Organization

PSYCHODYNAMICS AND SOCIAL COGNITION

Acknowledgments

I deeply appreciate the people who have helped me develop and complete this book. Without their assistance, the book, *Readings in Personality Psychology*, would not have been possible, nor would it be as good as it is. Karon Bowers helped get the project started by acquiring the publication rights to the book for Allyn & Bacon in 2003.

Karon encouraged the initial release of the book as a classroom-test edition, to be used with students in a few select courses before the final version was prepared. To assist with that project, my editors at Pearson Custom Publishing, including Kim Brugger, Rebecca Faber, and Scott Salesses, acquired, printed, and distributed a version for classroom testing in 2004. Feedback from that edition allowed me to improve the quality of the present edition substantially.

Robin Scholefield and Anne Kendal generously gave their time and skills to (re)type many of the works reprinted in this book. Their painstaking and meticulous efforts were essential to making the text professional and accurate.

Claudine Bellanton, Deb Hanlon, and Therese Felser helped guide the book's development for Allyn & Bacon, answering myriad questions regarding its form and gently encouraging me to keep the book on schedule (or close to it). Robert Tonner assisted with issues of copyright permissions.

I am especially grateful to Steve Simpson, who agreed to serve as the book's project manager in the final stages of its development for Allyn & Bacon. Steve single-handedly planned the initial design and layout of the book, and coped with everything from copyediting to permissions lines.

The production team at Allyn and Bacon, consisting of Karen Mason, Tom Scalzo, Lauren Houlihan, and Sylvie Scholvin, worked tirelessly to create the print-ready version of the manuscript, proofing the manuscript again, making further design suggestions, and otherwise enhancing the final version of the book you now are holding. The group welcomed my own and Steve Simpson's input during this time, and it was a pleasure working with them all.

My wife, Deborah, provided helpful suggestions and feedback regarding several aspects of the book. She, along with my daughter, exhibited great patience during the time I developed and completed the work; I am very thankful for their forbearance, interest, and support.

To all of them and to anyone inadvertently omitted, I express my sincere gratitude for their support, assistance, and many talents, that collectively helped make this book far better than anything I might have created alone.

Instructor's Preface

This is a book of—and about—readings in personality psychology. The book, *Readings in Personality Psychology* contains both reprinted primary sources for students to read, and also original commentary on how to read the selections. The book is intended for both undergraduate lecture and seminar courses on personality psychology. It is equally appropriate for theory-by-theory (or perspective-by-perspective) approaches to the personality course, research topics approaches, or systems approaches. It also may be suitable for some graduate seminars in personality.

Readings in Personality Psychology is designed to strengthen the abilities of students in personality psychology by, first, exposing students to a wide variety of primary source material that is relevant to personality psychology, and second, by providing pedagogical support that can help students better understand and more fully appreciate the readings that are included.

Students often find reading primary sources quite challenging. The book addresses such challenges by providing students with carefully planned support in relation to reading primary source material in general, and in relation to each individual reading.

The book also is smaller and more focused in scope, and as a consequence, it places a relatively modest time demand on students, and also is relatively economical when compared to other books of readings.

A Wide Variety of Primary Source Materials

Readings in Personality Psychology exposes students to 16 chapters of key readings. The readings represent a diversity of sources in the field. Included among them are contemporary theoretical articles, contemporary empirical studies, historical theoretical articles, reviews of important books and tests, opinion pieces from *Dialogue* (the newsletter of the *Society of Personality and Social Psychology*) and humorous writings. Most readings involve just one selection, but a few readings are made up of one or two short selections.

Providing Support for the Student

At the time they take their first course in personality psychology, most undergraduates will be unfamiliar with the primary source materials of the discipline, and lack experience in reading them. *Readings in Personality Psychology* provides those students with both global and reading-specific support for their studies.

The book's first chapter, written by the editor, provides global support for beginning readers of personality psychology by explaining to students why it is useful to read the psychological literature. The chapter explains what primary sources are and provides general pointers about how to read the literature and the challenges involved in doing so.

Further global support is provided in the opening essay of each subsequent chapter, which often speaks to general issues of reading psychology as well as to the specific material being introduced. This supporting material consists of the following:

An Introduction to the Type of Reading. Each chapter introduces students to the type of reading that is to be encountered. From this, students are prepared ahead of time for whether the reading is historical or contemporary, theoretical or empirical, and whether it appeared in a journal, book, or other medium. The chapter introductions serve to educate students as to what the available sources in the field are like.

The Significance of the Reading. The next section of each readings chapter examines the reasons the specific selection was chosen for the book and why it is of importance for psychology students to read. In the case of historical articles, for example, the context of the article will be discussed, sometimes with a brief discussion of the field's response to a given article, with documenting scholarship.

The Watch List. The watch list provides students with specific, section-by-section preparation for reading the article. The list explains special technical vocabulary the student might encounter, provides background on any psychological tests mentioned in the article, discusses any historical context useful to understanding what is going on, and comments on statistical techniques where useful.

Concluding Comments. At the end of the selection, brief comments are provided to help students reflect on the material they have just encountered.

Study Questions. Finally, each article concludes with a review section that contains four or more review questions that students can use to further integrate and synthesize what they have read.

Fewer, Often Better, Readings, with More Support

Providing more support across a smaller number of readings than is typical creates several advantages: It allows for a few key readings that are a bit longer than those found in a typical readings book, and allows students to spend more time with each reading so as to develop a greater appreciation for what it can teach them.

Books of readings sometimes compromise their selections by including shorter but less accessible articles in place of genuine classics. Thus, Erikson's "Eight stages of man" which is very readable and accessible—is sometimes replaced by far shorter and less accessible articles such as "Identity and the life cycle," or "The life-cycle: Epigenesis of identity." Here, the longer pieces are used when that makes sense (cf. Frick, 1995). Shorter readings are also included, of course, and help to balance the longer ones.

The smaller number of readings also keeps costs down, a benefit passed along to students in the form of a less-expensive, but high-quality, book.

Flexible Organization for Use with a Variety of Course Approaches

The book is designed to be used with a number of approaches to the personality course. The main table of contents organizes the readings according to whether they pertain to (a) defining personality and the discipline, (b) personality's parts, (c) personality's organization, or (d) personality development. This is a systems approach (Mayer, 2005) employed by several textbooks (e.g., Cloninger, 1996; Mayer, 2007; Pervin, 2002).

Another widely-used organization for the course is to introduce the major theoretical perspectives on the field, including (a) Biological, Trait and Dispositional, (b) Humanistic/Developmental, and (c) Social/Cognitive. The book can be used with this organization as well, by shifting the order of chapters in the book, as shown in the second alternate table of contents. A reordering of these readings also can accommodate still other organizations, such as those based on major research topics.

Editorial Treatment of the Selections

For the most part, articles are reproduced exactly as they were in the original. The following exceptions and qualifications apply, however.

First, to create a uniform look for this book of readings, many of the selections were reformatted slightly. For example, the headings of all articles were made parallel such that their first- and second-level headings were parallel across readings. Headings always were capitalized in these reprints, although this practice varied across the original selections. Similarly, the titles of tables always were capitalized in these reprints, although there was some variability in that practice in the original sources as well. References are reproduced here in APA style, although the original selections contained small deviations from that practice (for example, volume numbers were sometimes in bold type in the originals; these were revised in italics here). In the selection from Freud's *Introductory Lectures,* the footnotes were renumbered consecutively.

Regarding the text of the selections, article abstracts and most author notes were omitted. Longer reprinted selections occasionally were abridged somewhat to focus the argument and in order to allow students to skip over material of narrower interest. In such instances, the first deletion point is marked with a shaded box, and later deletions are marked by ellipses (...), or by additional shaded boxes explaining what was omitted.

Finally, in many sources, minor corrections were made in those instances where errors of spelling, grammar, or formatting clearly were present in the original.

1

Reading Personality Psychology:
Frequently Asked Questions

What Does It Mean to Read
Personality Psychology?

People sometimes encounter a description or claim about personality psychology and want to know more about it. Perhaps the description raises a matter of personal concern—something that might help a person understand his or her own psychology, for example. Or, perhaps it supports (or violates) their beliefs and they want to know more about it for that reason. Or, perhaps, it simply piques their curiosity. If you have ever wanted to know more about personality psychology, it probably has occurred to you to read some of the theoretical and research reports in the area.

The collected knowledge of a discipline—the sum of its intellectual accomplishments—is recorded in large part in its written literature. Being able to read personality psychology means being able to find the articles and books you are interested in, understand the literature when you read it, and benefit from that information. This book introduces some articles, chapters, and other works in personality psychology, and provides some context and support to help make the experience of reading these works—and others you may encounter later—an easier, richer experience.

The literature of personality psychology is a broad, constantly expanding network of articles, book chapters, books, and other written sources, including book and test reviews, newsletter articles, and more. Whereas in 1957 there were about half a million accumulated scientific articles in psychology journals alone, the number had risen to nearly 4 million by 1997. According to one estimate, psychologists publish articles at the rate of about 100 per day, or one article every 15 minutes (Thorngate, 1990).

An interested individual can learn a great deal from looking at those articles, chapters, and other sources. As the variety of publications and their number suggest, however, it is easy to become overwhelmed. Searching out the exact article one needs can be a challenging task—and then, many articles can be slow going, even for those experienced in the field. Other articles can be just right, and even fun to read. Whatever the case, reading this material is critical to independent learning in this and other fields—as well as a critical objective of many courses (Steuer, 1996). But where should one start?

How Can This Book Help Me Read
the Scientific Literature?

Often, students are asked to read material and are given little support for the reading—that is, a student is asked to read some material without being told where it comes from, why it is written as it is, or what to pay attention to within it. This book of readings is designed to support you as you read. The book will provide you with useful information to help you understand what you are reading before and after you encounter challenging material. Before the article, you will find an introductory essay that sets the stage for the reading. It concludes with a "Watch List" which explains some of the vocabulary and other specifically challenging content you may encounter. After the article, there are study questions. That doesn't mean you will understand everything in these readings, but it will provide you with some support so that you can get more out of them than is often the case for students.

In this book, I'll often define a term in a reading, or explain that 'N' in an empirical report stands for the number of participants in a study, even though some readers will assume it is fairly clear from the context. I expect most readers to exclaim (to themselves) "Everyone knows that!" from time to time, in response to my comments. But not everyone does know, and not everyone remembers, and that is why some comments are there. If they seem obvious, please remember that someone, somewhere, didn't learn it, or has forgotten it since. I'm not trying to insult your intelligence. Far from it, I am trying to marshal your intelligence and challenge you to learn through reading. This is particularly crucial as you approach primary sources.

What Are Primary Sources?

In personality psychology, *primary source* material can be considered any piece of the literature that is a direct record of an experiment, or an original explanation of a theory, or an original opinion piece of some other sort. Primary sources also include most editorials in journals, or letters or e-mails from one scientist to another. These can be contrasted with *secondary sources*.

What Are Secondary Sources?

Secondary sources are materials that organize, present portions of, and/or comment on, primary sources. A standard textbook in personality psychology is a secondary source. Such textbooks cover the primary sources in the psychological literature, such as basic research reports and original theoretical writing, and then summarize their ideas and findings in a narrative designed to be used in the classroom.

"Gray areas" exist, however, between primary sources, represented by a single research report or journal article that describes a theory, and secondary sources, represented by textbooks. For example, some journal articles are themselves scientific reviews that summarize a series of original research reports published in other scientific journals. These reviews, which are mostly written by researchers, could be considered primary sources, as they are found in scientific journals. Alternatively, they could be considered secondary sources, as they summarize and integrate earlier-published research reports.

Perhaps it is stretching matters too far to suggest that another example of this gray area would be book reviews. For example, there are book reviews published by scientists in *Contemporary Psychology: The APA Review of Books.* These book reviews are probably best considered secondary sources discussing a primary source (i.e., the book the author is reviewing). Still, it might be possible to consider the reviews as primary source material under some circumstances, as they are themselves primary sources of book reviews.

Don't worry too much about the gray area sources for now. Rather, concentrate on what is clear: experiments and theories in journal articles are primary; textbooks, secondary.

Why Read Primary and Secondary Source Material?

A textbook, no matter how good, filters the material you learn about through the eyes of its author. When you read a textbook, you are dependent upon the viewpoint and interpretation of the author. There may come a time, however, when you truly want to understand a research report in greater detail than what is reported in the textbook. For example, you might happen to encounter a study that makes a controversial claim as you are reading a textbook. (Or, you might read an article on the web or in a newspaper that makes a controversial claim). You might want to understand the logic of the original article itself and the evidence on which it is based. That can best be done by reading the original article itself.

Another reason to read primary source material is to obtain first-hand knowledge of a historical or contemporary figure in which you are interested. For example, most people alive today have heard of Sigmund Freud and his theories, but fewer people have actually read something written by Freud or have experienced his written style directly. Reading Freud directly provides a sense of his work that reading an account of it simply cannot approach.

Will Reading Primary Sources in Personality Psychology Help Me Read Primary Sources in Other Fields?

Whether you are reading to better understand a controversy or to acquaint yourself with the thoughts and style of a historical or contemporary figure who interests you, learning to read primary source material will improve your reading skills in personality psychology—and in other fields as well. Reading primary source material in personality psychology should help you read primary source material, not only in other areas of psychology, but also in other natural and social sciences, particularly in allied fields such as biology, medicine, nursing, education, anthropology, sociology, and economics. That is because many of the same conventions—how an empirical study is reported, and even some of the mathematics—are the same across fields.

What Kinds of Readings Will I Encounter in This Book?

Depending upon which readings your professor assigns, you will find in this book at least one reading, and often more, representing each of the following types: (a) contemporary theories, (b) original experiments, (c) discussions in professional newsletters, (d) editorials, (e) reviews of books, (f) reviews of tests, (g) reviews of research literature, (h) historically classic theories, and (i) others. Each of these has its own styles, pleasures, and challenges to read.

Are There Some General Pointers for Reading the Selections in This Book?

Yes. Literature inside a scientific field is often a specialized form of literature you are already familiar with. So, editorials in a journal are like editorials in the newspaper, except, of course, that they are editorializing about the field of personality psychology rather than other matters. Similarly, book reviews are like book reviews in a magazine, except the book reviews here deal with books on psychology.

Journal articles reporting empirical studies are a bit different than anything else you may have read. Still, they all follow a fairly consistent pattern: Each begins with (a) an introduction that explains the significance of the research, and proceeds to (b) a background section which ideally fills you in on some prior scientific research. After that, the (c) study or studies themselves are reported. Those are followed by the (d) results of the study, (e) a discussion of the results, and sometimes (f) a conclusion. Almost all empirical reports follow this pattern precisely, so each one you read will familiarize you with the pattern.

Theoretical papers are a bit more creative in their design than research reports. The theoretical paper's form is governed by the author's decision of how to best get across the ideas of the theory. Therefore, each such work is a bit different. Still, like research articles, most theory papers have an introduction that presents a problem, a middle section that develops the ideas, and a conclusion.

Beyond these general characterizations, it is probably best to refer to the introduction of a particular article for its form. In this book, each introduction to an article explains the significance of the article, and then helps prepare you for what you will encounter when you read the article. That introduction will also explain to you the reading's context—that is, the type of source material it is (e.g., original experiment, book review, etc.). Be sure to read the introduction as a way of preparing yourself for reading the source. Instructors of psychology have recommended that this is the best way to support students through such literature (Steuer, 1996).

There is one other matter that concerns many of the readings here, however, and that is citations.

What's the Problem with Citations?

Citations are mentions of earlier-published works in a scientific article. These can be in the form of footnotes, or mentions of an author and date (e.g., Freud, 1920). For instance, an author might want to discuss the ancient Greek idea of catharsis (Aristotle, 350 BCE/1961). Catharsis concerns the idea that expressing a feeling releases it, and therefore reduces the amount of feeling a person has. The citation to Aristotle just connected the idea to its ancient Greek origins. The first date after Aristotle's name, 350 BCE, is that of his original work. The second date, 1961, indicates a reprint of the original. The idea of catharsis has been discussed in contemporary research as well (e.g., Pennebaker, 1997). So, Pennebaker's article of 1997 was just cited so that the interested reader can examine a recent article that discusses the importance and evidence for the idea of catharsis. Most articles, like Pennebaker's, are denoted by just one date, as the original is still available.

One feature that distinguishes scientific (and scholarly writing, more generally) from less formal writing is the use of citations. Citations allow the reader to check the references section of the article for connections to other parts of the literature. (The citation to Pennebaker, like all others in the introduction, can be found in the references list at the end of the book).

You have seen citations in your personality textbook, and your introductory psychology book. As the scientific literature is growing, the number of citations in a typical article is increasing (Adair & Vohra, 2003). On the one hand, that means more evidence (and more credit) is being given where evidence and credit are due. On the other hand, it tends to interrupt sentences a bit more as you read.

The typical article in the *Journal of Personality and Social Psychology* had 18 references to the scientific literature in 1974. Twenty-five years later, the number had more than tripled, to 66. Citations in another journal, *Personality and Social Psychology Bulletin,* rose nearly tenfold from an average of 6 in 1974 to 50 in 2000 (Adair & Vohra, 2003, Table 1). When you see the citations, be awed at all the research that has taken place; try not to be too frustrated by the interruption of the sentences. If you are frustrated, though, know that the problem is one that professionals in the field experience as well! A similar comment can be made about understanding statistics.

What about Understanding Statistics?

Statistical techniques, like scientific articles themselves, have been proliferating in number and type. Few people anymore—if anyone—can knowledgeably read and understand all the statistical procedures in use today. Few of the articles in this book are heavily statistical, and supporting comments will be offered in places where they are. Know, however, that when picking up empirical pieces, the statistics can often be quite challenging.

Will It Be on the Test?

Exactly what part of the reading your professor asks you about on a quiz, test, or writing assignment will be up to your professor. Be sure to check with your professor as to what is expected. Whatever is expected, however, review questions and issues are offered after each article to help you consolidate what you are reading.

Concluding Comments

The Choice of Articles

Each source reading here has its own joys and peculiarities. I read a great number of articles in order to choose the ones included here. Some are included because of their tremendous importance, some because they illustrate an important point, and others because they were representative of an article of a particular kind. Each reading has some enjoyable or important quality to it. I hope you enjoy reading what you find here.

Review Questions

1. There were nearly 4 million published scientific articles across disciplines by 1997. How frequently are psychologists publishing new articles?
2. Primary sources are said to be any direct report of an experiment, or original statement of a theory in the literature. How does this compare with secondary sources in psychology? Is one type of source more important than the other?
3. Citations are critical because they connect a piece of scientific information with earlier articles on the same topic. Why can they also become a problem?
4. Papers in psychology that report empirical studies follow a fairly fixed order of coverage. Can you say what that order is?

2

Teaching Personality Psychology:
The Professors' Debate

Reading a Professional Newsletter

Professional organizations of scientists have a variety of outlets for written articles. The scientists' most central mission is to investigate psychology and psychological phenomena, and to communicate the central findings of their research to others. Scientists most frequently report their research in peer-reviewed scientific journals. These journals contain the most important scientific research and theory of the field.

Surrounding this most central mission of scientific research, however, are additional, crucial activities without which scientific research could not proceed. These activities include teaching the field and training the next generation of scientists, and maintaining scientific societies and organizations to oversee these processes.

Scientific societies are organizations of scientists who have banded together because they investigate common questions using similar methods. In the case of personality and social psychologists, one central organization is the *Society for Personality and Social Psychology (SPSP)*. This society (and other, similar ones) are typically composed of psychologists in college and university settings, and also in corporate, governmental, and non-profit settings such as foundations and medical centers. The scientists in these diverse settings need a means of communicating with one another and of staying in touch.

The *Society* fosters more flexible, informal communications among members, in several ways. For example, there exist e-mail and web-based communication of various sorts among members. In addition, the professional society issues a newsletter. *Dialogue: The Newsletter for the Society of Personality and Social Psychology* has been the main newsletter of the Society of Personality and Social Psychology for two decades now. It is published twice a year and all members of the society receive it. The newsletter's contents vary from the humorous to serious news about the association, to opinion pieces about what is going on (or failing to go on) in the field. In recent years, an issue of the newsletter *Dialogue* has typically been about 8 or 12 pages long. It is printed on plain, non-glossy paper; that is, it is a low tech, informal sort of newsletter.

One function *Dialogue* serves is to publish informal opinion statements; that is, professors' opinions on controversial or important topics related to the field. Because they are informal exchanges, the articles themselves are fairly accessible and easy to read. In contrast to a typical journal publication, newsletter opinion pieces are not expected to be heavily documented. Nor are they peer-reviewed—that is, the author receives little or no feedback on them before they are published. Basically, newsletter pieces are just the ideas of the experienced professionals who write them. They allow you, as a student, to basically eavesdrop on some professional communication.

The Significance of This Reading

The following selections represent a discussion that occurred in *Dialogue* among professors about the best way to teach the course in personality psychology. When professors are thinking about their courses, like you, they are often trying to figure things out: What are students thinking? How should the class be managed? And how could the material be taught most effectively? Sometimes, they express their frustration or new ideas with their colleagues.

In 1993, Mark Leary, a well-known personality and social psychologist, wrote a brief article in *Dialogue* expressing his frustration about teaching personality psychology in the traditional "theories" way. In the traditional way, instructors began with Freud's theories and psychodynamics, and moved the course through other theoretical approaches such as the humanistic, trait, and social cognitive. In the next issue of *Dialogue,* (which appeared half-a-year later), four other psychologists replied, expressing their own thoughts about teaching the personality psychology course. Those who replied were Robert Hogan, Robert J. Wheeler, Randall E. Osborne, and John Mayer (this author). Roy Baumeister and Dianne Tice, although not mentioned by name, wrote an editorial summary and response.

These articles are significant in that they represent a wide range of opinion about how the personality course should be taught, suggest a number of good ideas, and accurately describe alternative courses in personality psychology that could be taught. The articles also foreshadow developments in teaching the course that have taken place since the exchange. By understanding some of the diverse aims in teaching the personality course, you may better benefit from taking it.

The Watch List

Here are some things to watch for as you read the articles. Each of the several pieces below is by a different author. Each one has a different background and raises different points. Mark Leary starts off the debate by criticizing how personality psychology was taught at the time (and is often still taught): in a theory-by-theory fashion. Professor Leary teaches personality psychology at Wake Forest University in North Carolina. He has published widely on self-esteem, rejection, and social self-presentation, among other areas. Professor Leary went on to become the founding editor of *Self and Identity,* a new journal of importance to the discipline, and has written numerous books in the area.

John D. Mayer (this editor) responded in the next issue. I teach personality psychology at the University of New Hampshire and have published widely on personality theory, emotional intelligence, and related areas. My article outlined a (then) new framework for the field of personality psychology, called the "systems-topics framework," which later became the "systems framework for personality," and described the basis for an alternative type of textbook. The *Dialogue* article discusses three topics of the framework: personality's parts, organization, and development. Soon thereafter, a new first topic was added: defining personality, which made four topics in all.

Robert Hogan came to the defense of the theories approach. Professor Hogan has been editor of the prestigious *Journal of Personality and Social Psychology: Personality and Individual Differences* (JPSP: PID), and is widely published in personality psychology. He last taught the course at the University of Tulsa, in Oklahoma. Hogan makes reference to a then-recent cover of *Time* magazine. *Time* (June 6, 1992) had a cover story on Freud entitled "Is Freud Finished?" suggesting that Sigmund Freud's influence had, perhaps, come to an end. Perhaps thinking twice about it, *Time* ran a second cover story (November 29, 1993) called "The Assault on Freud," discussing various criticisms of Freud. Remarkably, more recently, *Time* has had two further cover stories on Freud: in 1999, and again in 2003. Apparently, Freud wasn't as finished as they thought in 1992.

Hogan further brings up a textbook *Theories of Personality* that he refers to by the authors' names: "Hall & Lindzey." That book was the first theory-by-theory textbook in the area, and provided an authoritative and highly balanced survey of all the theories of the field. First published in 1957, it was the reigning textbook of the field through the early 1970's. Textbook publishers were indeed inclined to imitate it.

Robert J. Wheeler argues for a question-based approach to the field. Professor Wheeler teaches personality psychology at St. Louis University in Missouri. His research interests include well-being and job satisfaction, among other areas.

Randall Osborne focuses on students' experiences and the growth of self-knowledge in such courses. Professor Osborne teaches personality psychology at Indiana University East.

The final editorial on the exchange was unsigned though it is credited here as Roy Baumeister and Dianne Tice, who then edited *Dialogue* from Case Western Reserve University in Cleveland. They explain their own approach to the course. Professors Baumeister and Tice are widely published researchers who now teach at Florida State University.

How Should We Teach Undergraduates about Personality?

by Mark Leary

Source: Leary, M. (1994). How should we teach undergraduates about personality?
Dialogue: The Newsletter of the Society of Personality and Social Psychologists (SPSP),
9 (1), 8–9.

Undergraduate courses in personality fall roughly into two general types. The first ("Theories") focuses primarily on the grand theories of personality. Some instructors organize the course by specific theories or theorists, others by theoretical approaches, such as the psychodynamic, humanistic, cognitive, behavioral, and trait perspectives. Textbooks for these courses are similarly organized by specific theories, general conceptual approaches, or theorists.

The second type of personality course ("Personality Psychology") is organized around major topics, such as personality structure, self and identity, self-regulation, motivation, unconscious processes, and biological bases of personality. Classic personality theories are covered, but alongside more recent theoretical and empirical work. The textbooks for these courses either are organized around those same topics, or they devote some chapters to major theoretical orientations and other chapters to specific topics.

Traditionally, the main undergraduate personality course has tended to be in the "Theories" category. However, I think it is time for instructors to consider the relative merits of the two types. My purpose here is to suggest that students who take a single course in personality are better served by the second type.

The classic theories course does not adequately reflect contemporary personality psychology in content, perspective, or methodology. Students who take only a "Theories" course may receive inadequate exposure to important lines of work and may not have an inkling of the rich theoretical and empirical work going on in personality. In fact, a pure theories course may give students a distorted view of the present state of knowledge and may fail to prepare students to understand the research they encounter in journals and elsewhere. In contrast, the personality psychology course exposes students to both classic and contemporary theories, perspectives, findings, and methods.

Of course, many courses (and textbooks) in theories of personality discuss research that is relevant to each theory or school, thereby exposing students to work in contemporary personality psychology. However, many important areas of investigation in contemporary personality psychology are not directly relevant to any of the classic theories, and little of the work being published in the primary journals in personality emerges from or bears upon traditional theories. As a result, much recent research simply does not fit easily into a course that is organized around theoretical approaches.

A second reason for my position is that many of the central ideas covered in the standard "Theories" course are unsubstantiated. Specifically, many of these theoretical positions are known to be inaccurate or inadequate, empirically untested, or simply untestable. Of course there is nothing wrong with teaching theoretical positions that do not yet have empirical support; the absence of support for an otherwise viable idea does not mean that it is wrong. However, many textbooks in theories of personality present the material as if it is known to be valid or do not adequately inform the students regarding which ideas are and are not accepted within the field. Furthermore, some instructors seem to assume that all of each theorist's ideas are worthy of students' attention regardless of their viability. Consequently, students spend time learning the details of theoretical conceptualizations of questionable validity—time that might be better spent learning about what we do know about the psychology of personality. Many of the influential theorists' ideas have been supported by research or are widely accepted even in the absence of direct support, and these should be covered. But we should ask ourselves why we expect our students to learn the details of theoretical orientations of unknown or even questionable validity except, perhaps, for historical reasons.

A third argument for my position is that the organization of the typical theories course is not optimal for teaching students about personality (although it may be appropriate for teaching about theorists or schools of thought). It strikes me as pedagogically more defensible to organize courses by content rather than by theoretical orientation, instead of spreading material regarding, for example, unconscious processes across sections about several different theories or theorists. Is it not more reasonable to integrate all of that material within a single section of the course? The contributions of various theoretical orientations, including the classic theories, can be presented, contrasted, and examined in light of empirical research. Students will develop a richer, more coherent understanding of a particular psychological process if all of the material on a particular topic is presented together and integrated.

I am not suggesting that the classic theories of personality have no place in the undergraduate curriculum. Rather, my point is that the traditional theories course may not be the course of choice as the first or only personality course that a student takes. Furthermore, departments that currently do not offer a course in personality psychology should consider implementing one.

Classic theories of personality fit into the undergraduate curriculum in at least three places. First, every course that surveys personality psychology should include the major theories, as historical background and in discussing specific topics. Second, "Theories of Personality" is a legitimate course in its own right, assuming that students also have the opportunity to be exposed to contemporary personality psychology and that students aren't inadvertently misled to confuse classic theories with the latest findings. The theories course is perhaps best regarded as a second-level personality course that students take after obtaining a survey of personality psychology. Students who have had such a general survey are in a better position to appreciate a course on theories. Third, the classic personality theorists deserve considerable attention in courses in the history and systems of psychology, as well as in discussions of the historical underpinnings of more specific content courses.

I hope that in the not-too-distant future all psychology departments will offer a course in personality psychology alongside the traditional theories course. Such a move toward modernization of the personality course would have obvious benefits for the education of our students.

A System-Topics Alternative

by John D. Mayer

Source: Mayer, J. D. (1994). A systems-topics alternative. *Dialogue: The Newsletter of the Society of Personality and Social Psychologists (SPSP), 9* (2), 7.

Last issue, Leary argued that the theory-by-theory personality course provides students with an outmoded introduction to the field of personality psychology. Theory-by-theory courses are those that sequentially expose students to the viewpoints of such theorists as Freud, Jung, Adler, Horney, and Maslow. Leary argued that such courses can no longer adequately integrate contemporary problems in research. He and others (Craik, 1993) have described an alternative course, here termed a *research topics* course, that sequentially reviews major research areas of personality such as the unconscious, the self, and traits. This discussion about how to teach personality psychology is perhaps more deeply a discussion of how to think about the field of personality psychology itself. In this deeper sense, both the theory-by-theory and research-topics conceptualizations of personality can be viewed as *frameworks* for the field.

The framework of an academic field can be defined as an outline for how the work in that field is to be presented. What makes such a framework sublime is that it includes and organizes all the field's important theory and research. As Leary and others have noted, the research findings of today do not always fit well within the theories of yesterday—or even within the theories of today. The research-topics framework solves this problem by covering multiple research areas (e.g., the unconscious, the self, traits) and discusses each area's theories, research, and integrative conclusions. The research-topics approach is extremely flexible because it covers a series of topics that have no particular beginning, middle, or end. As such, it can be extended as needed. But its drawbacks include that it offers no definition of personality and fails to present the person as an integrated, functioning whole.

A third alternative is the system-topics framework (Mayer, 1993). This framework defines personality as a system and sequentially describes (a) its components, (b) how those components are organized, and (c) how those components and their organization function over time. In the systems-topics framework, the components topic covers such parts of personality as faculties (e.g., memory, motives), traits (e.g., extraversion, emotionality), and control mechanisms (e.g., ego, id). The organization topic describes outside control of personality (e.g., situationism), distributed control (e.g., id-ego conflicts), and hierarchical control (e.g., self-regulation). The last, developmental topic covers personality stability (e.g., cross-temporal correlations), cycles (e.g., mood swings), and stages (e.g., identity vs. role confusion). In the system-topics approach, each section builds on earlier sections in a cumulative fashion—from pieces to whole to the growth of wholes—and discussion of more complex topics is commensurately richer and more complete.

Variants of this set of three topics (i.e., components, organization, and development) were proposed by several psychologists who made earlier attempts to reorganize the field. For example, Sears (1950) employed a version of the three topics in his *Annual Review* chapter on personality, where he treated the topics as essentially self-explanatory. For a few years thereafter, some reviewers of personality for the *Annual Review* followed Sears's outline; later reviewers, however, discarded Sears's outline because they said it was unclear. More recently, Pervin (1990, p. 12) suggested that the three topics might form the core of personality psychology, and that the field would benefit from a greater recognition of this possibility. The present, system-topics framework is an explicit clarification and development of the three topics that can be used to represent the field of personality psychology as it exists today. The developed framework integrates the best personality theory and research in such a way as to depict people as whole, dynamic organisms. Because of its many advantages, the system-topics framework may be among our most promising alternatives for conceptualizing, teaching, and researching in the field of personality psychology.

References

Craik (1993). APA symposium.
Mayer (1993). A system-topics framework for the study of personality. *Imagination, Cognition, and Personality, 13,* 99–123.
Pervin (1990). In Pervin, *Handbook of Personality,* Guilford.
Sears (1950). Personality. *Annual Review, 1,* 105–118.

Heritage Has Value

by Robert Hogan

Source: Hogan, R. (1994). Heritage has value. *Dialogue: The Newsletter of the Society of Personality and Social Psychologists (SPSP), 9*(2), 8.

Mark Leary's essay in the last issue inspired the following response in defense of "traditional" personality psychology.

First, psychology has, over the years, demonstrated a remarkable talent for squandering its patrimony, and the consequence is that no one with authority in government or industry takes us seriously. Economists and historians dictate the terms of the national debate on issues that rightfully belong to psychology. For example, economists put together the educational agenda that is being pushed by the Dept. of Labor, and historians are leading the public discussion about how to manage a diverse society. In both cases the answer depends on assumptions about human nature, and ideas about the nature of human nature are an essential part of our patrimony—especially in personality psychology.

Second, the articles that appear in JPSP are of interest primarily to other people who publish in JPSP. They are a fraction of the membership of Division 8 and a teeny fraction of the smart people in American society. Moreover, the articles that appear in JPSP are

written more to advance someone's career than they are to advance our knowledge of human nature. Thus, by directing students' attention to recent issues of JPSP, they will learn little about our true patrimony.

Third, as the recent cover article on *Time* magazine indicates, Freud is, and will remain, news for the educated public. Consider Freud for a moment; he is the only person who has anything interesting to say about prejudice, and that immediately brings our attention to Bosnia, Rwanda, Northern Ireland, etc. Jung is the only person who has something interesting to say about the recent events in Waco, Texas. Adler invented the notion of self-handicapping as a way of understanding how people deal with deficient self-esteem. Karen Horney is essential for understanding the psychology of women. Then think of Erik Erikson and the recent lamentations of V. S. Naipaul.

My guess is that the primary problem with current theories texts is that they simply aren't very good, because they don't establish the relevance and enduring legitimacy of the ideas. And that is so primarily because they take Hall and Lindzey as their model. As you know, the textbook publishing industry won't allow for much deviation—hence the long series of Hall and Lindzey clones of a book that was only okay at the outset.

I would like to suggest that each of the major theories of personality began as a topic, an effort to understand a single problem. For Freud, the problem was individual differences in relations to authority, for Jung the problem was the role of religious belief in mental health, for Adler the problem was how people deal with their feelings of inadequacy, and so on. It was only later that their musings were expanded into full-blown and not very adequate theories.

It seems to me that the question today is, to what degree has the analysis of reactions to authority advanced significantly since Freud, and so on for the rest of them? In a surprising number of cases, the analysis hasn't gone very far—take prejudice or religion as examples. More importantly, what we see in JPSP is people reinventing the wheel—most famously, perhaps, Leon Festinger rediscovering Anna Freud's defense mechanism of undoing—because they aren't very well grounded in the history of their own discipline.

Applying Theories

by Robert J. Wheeler

Source: Wheeler, R. J. (1994). Applying theories. *Dialogue: The Newsletter of the Society of Personality and Social Psychologists (SPSP), 9* (2), 8–9.

The Spring 1994 issue of Dialogue contained an interesting and important article by Mark Leary entitled "How should we teach undergraduates about personality?" That article bears on the role of personality psychology, an issue summarized last summer at the annual APA meeting in a symposium chaired by Kenneth Craik. Major personality psychologists voiced concern at that time about the dwindling relevance of personality theory courses and of personality as an academic field.

Personality is typically taught at both the undergraduate and graduate levels as a theory course based on history and emphasizing comparisons of conflicting theories. This not only seems of relatively little importance to most students, but it fails to reflect the current activities in personality psychology and derogates the field as a whole. By stimulating the non-paradigmatic prescientific aspects of psychology, personality is losing its role as the integrator of psychological information and proponent of the scientific view of human nature.

Academic advisors and students tend to see the typical personality course as having little applied value and to be taken only as a requirement.

The time has come for the teaching of personality to be reorganized to reflect the role of personality psychology as the foundation upon which applied fields are built. Experience in critical analysis of conflicting theories is academically valuable, however, an introductory or only course in personality would better use the time to survey scientific information about human characteristics that have demonstrated usefulness and validity for health, well-being, and performance. This would be an approach that is functional rather than theoretical or topical.

I have used this approach and found it worked well for an undergraduate personality theory course, and for a human factors course for student pilots. It started with the question, "What is personality and what are the human characteristics important for health, well-being, and performance?" The theories started by Allport, Cattell, Eysenck, Murray, and Costa and McCrae were presented with a comprehensive survey of habits, traits, types, and attitudes currently in use. Then the question was asked, "How does personality work and what influences it?" The second section of the course concerned the physiological influences: psychobiology. The third concerned unconscious influences and the "divided self" which involve Freud and the psychodynamic theories. The fourth concerned environmental influences involving learning theories. And the final section concerned cognitive influences including expectancy, existential, personal construct, and actualization theories. By using the time to focus on the portions of theories that have been supported scientifically or demonstrated usefulness, the students left the course with a picture of human nature as being complex and requiring differ-

ent approaches for different aspects. The emphasis was on synthesis and unification of theories rather than separation and conflict.

Most psychologists now agree that human behavior and cognition are complex, sophisticated, complicated, diverse, situational, and interactional. But most recent personality textbooks disparage synthesis and eclecticism as discouraging competitive advancement or encouraging a lukewarm ambivalence. Patterns are emerging from the prolific, rich, and scattered findings of empirical research that have the potential of providing a scientifically based explanation of human nature. By emphasizing the situational complementarity of various "sub-theories," personality psychology could help fill the philosophical vacuum that is of concern in our society.

A Collage of Self-Discovery

by Randall E. Osborne

Source: Osborne, R. E. (1994). A collage of self-discovery. *Dialogue: The Newsletter of the Society of Personality and Social Psychologists (SPSP), 9* (2), 9–10.

As a college educator who teaches courses in both personality and social psychology I have found myself faced with the dilemma of helping students to understand the development of their own personality as well as the development of individual differences within others. Many colleagues have asked me, "How do we help students to experience their own personality without giving them a battery of personality tests?" The answer, it seems, is to aid them in discovering exactly who they think they are. In a related area, it is also useful to help students to appreciate that there may be a large difference between how they see themselves and how others view them. But why would such an exercise be beneficial?

First, I think it is crucial that students be allowed to explore who they are. Anyone who has ever taught the personality psychology class knows that student questions often attempt to bring the material back to understanding themselves better. Whether we teach the personality psychology course as a theories course or as a personality psychology course (as Mark Leary suggested last issue), students will question who they are as they learn more about this thing called personality and all the things that come together to mold and shape the person. If students are engaging in this kind of self-analysis regardless of how we teach the course, it would be helpful for us to give them some guidance in doing so.

Second, students often work from the assumption that "what you see is what you get." The cliché I mention is meant to illustrate the students' assumption that everyone sees them exactly as they see themselves. The fact that others see us differently than we see ourselves can be a humbling experience. But it can be a profound learning experience as well. The fact that we are not perceived exactly as we had hoped, intended, or feared, can teach us a lot about our values and beliefs about who we are. This point also illustrates the importance of "subjective reality." The concept of subjective reality is based on the fact that individuals see their own unique version of reality. If an individual looks at a door and yells "Mom!" and then runs to hug the door, it does him little good for me to challenge his assumption that the door is his mother. Instead, I should be asking myself why he has come to view the door this way. Only if I put aside my own subjective view of reality will I truly be in a position to understand or appreciate how others come to be the unique persons that they are.

In order to aid students in such a learning experience, I suggest using a personality collage. With such a technique, students are asked to take newspaper and magazine photos, comic strips, cartoons, advertisements, headlines, and such and make a collage that shows the world who they are. Students are instructed to make a collage that reflects who they are on the inside, not just how they look. A second part of the assignment involves students asking someone who they think "knows them quite well" to make a collage of the student's personality. In a short paper (3–5 pages) students are instructed to reflect on the collages and address 7 questions: What are the major themes of self-depicted in your collage? What are the major similarities between the two collages? What are the major differences between how you see yourself and how the partner views you? How did these differences make you feel? Would you want to eliminate these differences, and, if so, what would you do to eliminate them? What did these differences teach you about the other person that you didn't already know? What did these differences teach you about yourself that you didn't already know?

Finally, students are told that their collages will be given a certain number of points just for being completed. After all, I tell them, how can I grade the quality of how you depict your own personality? The paper, then, is graded for quality, complexity, and such. In the end, students often incorporate many of the theories and principles covered in the personality course within their papers. In this fashion, students are allowed to experience their own personalities and discover the importance of subjective reality and other important concepts from the course. Perhaps as Mark Leary suggested, then, we can find ways such as this to integrate an understanding of personality theories into the personality psychology course that also involves the student as an active participant in his or her own learning.

Editorial

Source: Baumeister, R. & Tice, D. Editorial. *Dialogue: The Newsletter of the Society of Personality and Social Psychologists (SPSP), 9* (2), 10.

Over the years we have edited *Dialogue,* the greatest volume of responses has come in response to columns about teaching, and the present batch of comments on Leary's column is no exception. It is clear that issues of teaching are extremely important to the membership of SPSP and that they are heartened to see that the new journal (PSPR) has taken as one of its missions, the providing of a valuable resource for lecturers.

We cannot resist adding our own thoughts to the debate on how best to teach personality, having spent several years teaching it ourselves and exploring several alternatives. The conclusion we reached about the ideal plan differs from all existing textbooks, unfortunately, but it combines key features raised in Leary's column and the commentaries.

To be precise, we think that a first course in personality psychology should begin with an extended, detailed coverage of Freud and then should leap to the present and cover current research, with some discussion of applications. Clearly this plan is unsightly, in that it begins with one man's theory and then spends the rest of the semester working by topics. Several reasons speak in favor of this plan, however.

In the first place, Freud still represents the point of departure for much current research (and, not incidentally, much clinical work). Moreover, Freud's influence extends beyond psychology itself. Freud is probably the only psychologist whom nonpsychologists expect to know and discuss, and the only one about whom it can be said that an undergraduate education is deficient if his work was omitted.

We also think that exploring Freud in depth and detail is worth more than a superficial treatment of a half dozen theories. Jung, Adler, Erikson, and the rest do have ample merit, of course, but they do not need to be covered in a first course in personality, whereas Freud does. (Actually, we do like to follow Freud with a quick tour of Sullivan, as a contrast and as a transition.) To appreciate Freud's thought, including individual dynamics, social theory, and critical reassessment, takes several weeks and offers the student a valuable foundation. Some genuine understanding, rather than a superficial list of terms, can be reached in that time.

Apart from Freud, however, we agree with Leary and several of the commentators that it is important to teach students what the field of personality encompasses today: individual differences, personality processes, and assessment, along with the debates such as over situationism, the Big Five, and personality change. Covering current research gives students a useful insight into what the field has to offer and should provide some basis for applying research findings to social problems, practical dilemmas, and self-knowledge.

Presenting current research also helps students understand the change in the way the field is approached. A pure theories course leaves many students with the impression that the field of personality is constructed by spinning introspection and personal opinions into grand theories of human nature. The discipline of having to prove one's points is itself a useful lesson.

Concluding Comments

When reading the articles above, could you identify the type of personality course that you are taking? Is the course organized in the way you would prefer, or do you think some other arrangement would be better? Ultimately, a lot depends not only on the organization of the course, but on the nature of your instructor—and equally on you. I hope you enjoy and learn from whatever type of course you are taking.

Review Questions

1. The introduction to this exchange of papers discusses publishing in a newsletter. How are articles in a newsletter different from those in a professional journal?
2. Leary makes a distinction between a course on theories and a personality psychology course; Mayer suggests a systems approach. Can you describe the difference?
3. Osborne suggests a different kind of learning process involving personality psychology that involves the student's self-concept. Can you describe what that is about?
4. What would your ideal course in personality psychology be like? What would it teach you?

3

Thinking Big about Personality Psychology

Encountering the Big Picture

Some scientific writing concerns the field of personality psychology as a whole; other writing is concerned with details, for example, of a specific research finding. A person can gain a lot from examining personality in its detailed particulars. William Blake wrote at the outset of his *Auguries of Innocence* (c. 1803), that a person can "… see a world in a grain of sand; And a heaven in a wild flower…." Much of scientific writing deals with—what sometimes seems like—grains of sand: small details, behavior under one or two conditions, interactions between several personality traits. As Blake's poetry foretells, such detailed observations can give rise to a world of understanding. On the other hand, without the poet's imagination, it is also possible to become frustrated with the amount of detail in scientific writing.

Sometimes, in other words, we want the big picture—to look, with a guide, not at the sand grain, but at the whole beach, and maybe even the land and water around it. For those times when we prefer to see a larger picture, the scientific literature contains many relevant articles. For example, literature reviews of an individual research topic draw together individual articles to examine an overall pattern of findings. Theoretical reviews compare theories as to their logic and empirical support, in search of the best theory.

At an even higher, broader level, field-wide frameworks are, essentially, outlines of the entire discipline of personality psychology. A field-wide framework for a discipline tries to identify the field's major questions and to organize them into an appealing whole. The field of personality psychology is so vast and far-reaching, however, that more than one type of organization is possible, and none is all-encompassing or perfect.

So there is often more than one sensible way to organize a field, although it is a challenging task. To be successful, after all, a field-wide framework must be clear and concise, and yet include much of what people agree constitutes the field of personality psychology in a logical, meaningful fashion. For that reason, framework articles form a very, very small class of articles in the field of personality psychology. Discussions of frameworks occasionally appear in the prefaces to textbooks, or as part of a chapter in a book. Entire articles devoted to a framework of personality psychology

19

arose in the 1990's, in part because the field of personality psychology was searching for a new way to organize itself.

During the late 1980's and 1990's, several frameworks were discussed for the field, including one that organized the field according to multiple theoretical perspectives (e.g., Emmons, 1989), one that used a systems approach (Mayer, 1993–1994; 1998; 2005), and one that organized topics according to how much it involved a sense of knowing another (McAdams, 1996).

Significance of the Reading

Dan McAdams is a personality psychologist whose work spans many different articles and studies. A central theme of his work involves the stories people tell about themselves and the lives they lead. So, perhaps, it is not surprising to learn that McAdams' framework is based on understanding what it is we know when we know someone. McAdams' article, "What Do We Know When We Know a Person?" presents a framework for organizing the field of personality psychology based on knowing another. McAdams's framework serves as a means for organizing his own contemporary textbook on personality psychology. Others have also used his framework to distinguish among different ways of knowing or understanding personality (which he refers to as "Level 1, Level 2, and Level 3").

McAdams' article is captivating and provocative from the first. Many people are worried that, if they talk to a psychologist on an informal basis, the psychologist will analyze them in some fashion. When meeting a psychologist at a party or in some other situation, they exclaim, "Don't analyze me!" or "You'll probably think poorly of my saying this…" Dan McAdams owns up to analyzing others—as he indeed analyzes a party-goer, Lynn, who spoke to him.

One of McAdams' points is that everyone analyzes others, but personality psychology can help present a fairer, more considered view of another person. That is, using the methods and knowledge of personality psychology can—and should—help us to get to know another person better. But what kind of knowing does the personality psychologist strive to develop? Would you like to be subject to McAdams' analysis? What do we ultimately learn about personality psychology from the analysis? Do you think all personality psychologists do this? To form your own opinion, read on!

The Watch List

McAdams' article is divided into several sections. The following comments are similarly divided by section, and can help to smooth the reader's way.

For example, a bit of supportive commentary on some of the vocabulary employed in the opening passages can be of help. McAdams uses the term *personology*. Personology is an alternative term for personality psychology. It was used by a psychologist of the early 20th century named Henry Murray, and McAdams follows in Murray's footsteps; hence, his use of the term *personological*…

A second possibly unfamiliar term in this section is *idiographic.* Idiographic is a term introduced by the trait theorist Gordon Allport; the general sense of the term is that, to some extent, each individual is uniquely organized and simply cannot be compared to other individuals.

A further note on the introduction is the number of strings of citations that sometimes occurs in the introduction (and elsewhere). As you become more experienced in the field, more and more of these names carry the weight and meaning of a body of work. A beginning reader can skip over most of them—although, note the citation to someone named Henry Murray, who I have already mentioned is the person who coined "personologist."

The next section of the article is "Making Sense of Persons." In the middle and toward the end of that section, McAdams describes some important alternative frameworks for the discipline in very abbreviated terms. It is probably necessary to consult the original works to fully appreciate the early frameworks he is discussing here. Do the best you can with this part of the article, but don't give up.

In the section, "The Power of Traits," McAdams repeatedly employs the word *non-contingent,* to refer to traits. By this, McAdams means personality qualities that are independent of the situation. That is, qualities that Lynn would exhibit almost anywhere.

In the section, "The Problem with Traits," the repeated reference to *linear dimensions* reminds the reader that, in addition to other limits described, the mathematical models used to represent traits assume that traits influence one another and other variables in a linear manner—that is, the relation can be represented as a straight line: as one variable rises, so does the other. The linear model works fairly well, of course, but there also exist non-linear relations.

In the section, "Going Beyond Traits: Time, Place, and Role," *temporal* refers to issues and variables concerning time or development. "Attributional schemes" refers to the ways the person understands what causes his or her behavior. In that same section, you will run across this citation: "(Demorest, this issue)." McAdams' article was part of a special issue of the *Journal of Personality* devoted to organizing and understanding personality psychology. Using "this issue" rather than a date is customary when referring to other articles in the same issue of a journal in which one's article appears.

In the section, "Misunderstandings about Level III," McAdams uses the term *imago* to refer to an idealized image of oneself as a central character in one's own life story. In the following section, "What Else Is There?" McAdams refers to *depth psychologists.* Depth psychology is a loose term designating theoretical interest in what lies beneath the surface of personality, particularly the unconscious. Depth psychologists typically include psycho-dynamically oriented psychologists and others interested in the unconscious.

What Do We Know When We Know a Person?

by Dan McAdams

Source: McAdams, D. P. (1995). What do we know when we know a person?
Journal of Personality, 63, 365–396.

One of the great social rituals in the lives of middle-class American families is "the drive home." The ritual comes in many different forms, but the idealized scene that I am now envisioning involves my wife and me leaving the dinner party sometime around midnight, getting into our car, and, finding nothing worth listening to on the radio, beginning our traditional post-party post-mortem. Summing up all of the personological wisdom and nuance I can muster at the moment, I may start off with something like, "he was really an ass." Or adopting the more "relational" mode that psychologists such as Gilligan (1982) insist comes more naturally to women than men, my wife may say something like, "I can't believe they stay married to each other." It's often easier to begin with the cheap shots. As the conversation develops, however, our attributions become more detailed and more interesting. We talk about people we liked as well as those we found offensive. There is often a single character who stands out from the party—the person we found most intriguing, perhaps; or the one who seemed most troubled; maybe the one we would like to get to know much better in the future. In the scene I am imagining, let us call that person "Lynn" and let us consider what my wife and I might say about her as we drive home in the dark.

I sat next to Lynn at dinner. For the first 15 minutes, she dominated the conversation at our end of the table with her account of her recent trip to Mexico where she was doing research for an article to appear in a national magazine. Most of the people at the party knew that Lynn is a free-lance writer whose projects have taken her around the world, and they asked her many questions about her work and her travels. Early on, I felt awkward and intimidated in Lynn's presence. I have never been to Mexico; I was not familiar with her

articles; I felt I couldn't keep up with the fast tempo of her account, how she moved quickly from one exotic tale to another. Add to this the fact that she is a strikingly attractive woman, about 40 years old with jet black hair, dark eyes, a seemingly flawless complexion, clothing both flamboyant and tasteful, and one might be able to sympathize with my initial feeling that she was, in a sense, "just too much."

My wife formed a similar first impression earlier in the evening when she engaged Lynn in a lengthy conversation on the patio. But she ended up feeling much more positive about Lynn as they shared stories of their childhoods. My wife mentioned that she was born in Tokyo during the time her parents were Lutheran missionaries in Japan. Lynn remarked that she had great admiration for missionaries "because they really believe in something." Then she remarked: "I've never really believed in anything very strongly, nothing to get real passionate about. Neither did my parents, except for believing in us kids. They probably believed in us kids too much." My wife immediately warmed up to Lynn for this disarmingly intimate comment. It was not clear exactly what she meant, but Lynn seemed more vulnerable now, and more mysterious.

I eventually warmed up to Lynn, too. As she and I talked about politics and our jobs, she seemed less brash and domineering than before. She seemed genuinely interested in my work as a personality psychologist who, among other things, collects people's life stories. She had been a psychology major in college. And lately she had been reading a great many popular psychology books on such things as Jungian archetypes, the "child within," and "addictions to love." As a serious researcher and theorist, I must confess that I have something of a visceral prejudice against many of these self-

Source: McAdams, D. P. (1995). What do we know when we know a person? *Journal of Personality, 63*, 365–396. Reprinted with permission from Blackwell Publishing, Ltd.

help, "New Age" books. Still, I resisted the urge to scoff at her reading list and ended up enjoying our conversation very much. I did notice, though, that Lynn filled her wine glass about twice as often as I did mine. She never made eye contact with her husband, who was sitting directly across the table from her, and twice she said something sarcastic in response to a story he was telling.

Over the course of the evening, my wife and I learned many other things about Lynn. On our drive home we noted the following:

1. Lynn was married once before and has two children by her first husband.

2. The children, now teenagers, currently live with her first husband rather than with her; she didn't say how often she sees them.

3. Lynn doesn't seem to like President Clinton and is very critical of his excessively "liberal policies"; she admires his wife, Hillary, who is arguably more liberal in her views; we couldn't pin a label of conservative or liberal to Lynn because she seemed to contradict herself on political topics.

4. Lynn hates jogging and rarely exercises; she claims to eat a lot of "junk food"; she ate very little food at dinner.

5. Lynn says she is an atheist.

6. Over the course of the evening, Lynn's elegant demeanor and refined speech style seemed to give way to a certain crudeness; shortly before we left, my wife heard her telling an off-color joke, and I noticed that she seemed to lapse into a street-smart Chicago dialect that one often associates with growing up in the toughest neighborhoods.

As we compared our notes on Lynn during the drive home, my wife and I realized that we learned a great deal about Lynn during the evening, and that we were eager to learn more. But what is it that we thought we now knew about her? And what would we need to know to know her better? In our social ritual, my wife and I were enjoying the rather playful exercise of trying to make sense of persons. In the professional enterprise of personality psychology, however, making sense of persons is or should be the very raison d'etre of the discipline. From the time of Allport (1937) and Murray (1938), through the anxious days of the "situationist" critique (Bowers, 1973; Mischel, 1968), and up to the present, upbeat period wherein we celebrate traits

(John, 1990; Wiggins, in press) while we offer a sparkling array of new methods and models for personality inquiry (see, for example, McAdams, 1994a; Ozer & Reise, 1994; Revelle, 1995), making sense of persons was and is fundamentally what personality psychologists are supposed to do, in the lab, in the office, even on the drive home. But how should we do it?

Making Sense of Persons

One of the downsides of attending dinner parties is telling people I am a psychologist and then hearing them say things such as "I bet you're trying to figure me out" or "Oh, good, maybe you can tell me what makes my husband (wife, son, daughter, friend, etc.) tick." "Figuring out" a person, trying to determine "what makes her tick"—these well-worn cliches do indeed refer to personologists' efforts to make sense of persons. The figuring out seems to involve the two separate but related procedures of description and explanation. Epistemologically, description seems to come first. One must be able to describe the phenomenon before one can explain it. Astute social scientists know, however, that what one chooses to describe and how one describes it are influenced by the kinds of explanations one is presuming one will make. Thus, describing persons is never objective, is driven by theory which shapes both the observations that are made and the categories that are used to describe the observations, and therefore is, like explanation itself, essentially an interpretation. Despite the subjective, interpretive nature of description and despite the fact that descriptions and explanations are not neatly separable, scientists of all stripes must still make sense of phenomena by offering a detailed description of events—so that others may know *what is*—and then offering a causal explanation for what has been described—so that others may know *why it is*. In studying persons, the "what is" refers to personality structure ("what it looks like") and function ("how it works"). The "why it is" (or "what makes it tick") often translates into "how it came to be," urging the psychologist to discern the causes, origins, roots, determinants, and reasons for the "what is," be those reasons nature or nurture, be they internal or external, be they biological, social, cultural, economic, or whatever.

I am mainly concerned in this article with the "what is" rather than the "why it is." This is not to suggest that personality description is more important or more exciting than explaining why. But I will submit that good explanation depends upon good description, whereas the reverse is not necessarily true, and that personality psychologists are sometimes too eager to explain away phenomena before they have adequately identified the phenomena they are trying to explain. If I am going to know Lynn well (realizing, of course, that one never "truly" knows another in full, perhaps not even oneself), I must first be able to offer a full description of her personality. My speculations about how that personality came to be (which orients me to the past in some sense) or, if I am a clinician, how that personality may be changed (which orients me to the future) depend on a good understanding of what the personality is—here and now. To know Lynn well, then, is first and foremost to describe her fully to another. A great deal of "sense making" in personality psychology, and in life, takes place in the description.

Description is a translation of observations into communicable form, typically in our society into the form of words. In the drive home, my wife and I are translating our observations into words. The translation serves the dual purpose of enabling us to communicate with each other and of sharpening, modifying, and organizing our observations so that they can be made more sensible. The making sense of Lynn began when I first met her, as I suspect the making sense of Dan did for her, but it is given a tremendous boost when words are found and exchanged in the car to depict the evening's events. The personologist, too, must find the right words to depict the observations that have been made, to make sense of the data. But what the personologist does in making sense of people differs in two important ways from what my wife and I do at and after the party. First, the observations that the personologist makes are likely to be more systematic and structured, via standardized questionnaires, laboratory citings, ethnographic inquiries, content analysis, etc. Second, the personologist will or should push much harder than my wife and I will to organize the observations and measurements into a meaningful system or framework.

How should this organization take place? Allport (1937) proposed an organizational scheme emphasizing traits. He distinguished among cardinal, central, and secondary traits as the main structural units of personality, while arguing that a comprehensive understanding of the person must ultimately incorporate noncomparative, idiographic information about the particular person in question. Cattell (1957) offered a more complicated but scientifically conventional system, distinguishing between surface and source traits for starters and then dividing source traits into ability, temperament, and dynamic traits. Dynamic traits were further decomposed into biological ergs, attitudes, and sentiments. Assessments of these various sorts of traits could be combined with measurements of a person's momentary "states" and customary "roles" into a "specification equation" in order to predict the person's behavior. By contrast, Murray (1938) seemed less interested in predicting behavior per se and more concerned with providing a conceptual framework that could cut the widest possible swath across the conscious and unconscious terrain of personality. At minimum, an adequate personological portrait in Murray's terms should encompass descriptions of the well-known psychogenic needs for sure, but it should also describe complexes, proceedings, serials, durances, and recurrent need—press themata that characterize a particular life in time (McAdams, 1994a). For Murray, there were many different levels upon which personality might be observed and described, and the different levels were not necessarily commensurate with each other.

Since the time of Allport, Cattell, and Murray, personality psychologists have offered a number of different schemes for describing persons. For example, McClelland (1951) proposed that an adequate account of personality requires assessments of stylistic traits (e.g., extraversion, friendliness), cognitive schemes (e.g., personal constructs, values, frames), and dynamic motives (e.g., the need for achievement, power motivation). In the wake of Mischel's (1968) critique of personality dispositions, many personality psychologists eschewed broadband constructs such as traits and motives in favor of more domain-specific variables, like "encoding strategies" "self-regulatory systems and plans," and other "cognitive social learning person variables" (Mischel, 1973). By contrast, the 1980s and 1990s have witnessed a strong comeback for the concept of the broad, dispositional trait, culminating in what many have argued is a consensus around the five-factor model of personality traits (Digman, 1990; Goldberg, 1993; MacDonald, this issue; McCrae & Costa, 1990). Personality psychologists such as A. H. Buss (1989) have essentially proclaimed that personality is traits and only traits. Others are less sanguine, however, about the ability of the Big Five trait taxonomy in particular and the concept of trait in general to provide all or even most of the right stuff for personality inquiry (Block, in press; Briggs, 1989; Emmons, 1993; McAdams, 1992, 1994b; Pervin, 1994).

Despite current popularity of the trait concept, I submit that I will never be able to render Lynn "knowable" by relying solely on a description of her personality traits. At the same time, a description that failed to consider traits would be equally inadequate. Trait descriptions are essential both for social rituals like the post-party postmortem and for adequate personological inquiry. A person cannot be known without knowing traits. But knowing traits is not enough. Persons should be described on at least *three separate* and, at best, *loosely related levels* of functioning. The three may be viewed as levels of comprehending *individuality* amidst otherness—how the person is similar to and different from *some* (but not all) other persons. Each level offers categories and frameworks for organizing *individual differences* among persons. Dispositional traits comprise the first level in this scheme—the level that deals primarily with what I have called (McAdams, 1992, 1994b) a "psychology of a stranger."

The Power of Traits

Dispositional traits are those relatively nonconditional, relatively decontextualized, generally linear, and implicitly comparative dimensions of personality that go by such titles as "extraversion," "dominance," and "neuroticism." One of the first things both I and my wife noticed about Lynn was her social dominance. She talked loudly and fast; she held people's attention when she described her adventures; she effectively controlled the conversation in the large group. Along with her striking appearance, social dominance appeared early on as one of her salient characteristics. Other behavioral signs also suggested an elevated rating on the trait of neuroticism, though these might also indicate the situationally specific anxiety she may have been experiencing in her relationship with the man who accompanied her to the party. According to contemporary norms for dinner parties of this kind, she seemed to drink a bit too much. Her moods shifted rather dramatically over the course of the evening. While she remained socially dominant, she seemed to become more and more nervous as the night wore on. The interjection of her off-color joke and the street dialect stretched slightly the bounds of propriety one expects on such occasions, though not to an alarming extent. In a summary way, then, one might describe Lynn, as she became known during the dinner party, as socially dominant, extraverted, entertaining, dramatic, moody, slightly anxious, intelligent, and introspective. These adjectives describe part of her dispositional signature.

How useful are these trait descriptions? Given that my wife's and my observations were limited to one behavioral setting (the party), we do not have enough systematic data to say how accurate our descriptions are. However, if further systematic observation were to bear out this initial description—say, Lynn were observed in many settings; say, peers rated her on trait dimensions; say, she completed standard trait questionnaires such as the Personality Research Form (Jackson, 1974) or the NEO Personality Inventory (Costa & McCrae, 1985)—then trait descriptions like these, wherein the individual is rated on a series of linear and noncontingent behavior dimensions, prove very useful indeed. This optimistic spin on trait assessment is a relatively recent development in personality psychology. In the midst of the situationist critique of the 1970s, traits were virtually constructs non grata among personality psychologists. As recently as 1980, Jackson and Paunonen wryly observed that "trait theorists" seemed to be viewed "like witches of 300 years ago.... [T]here is confidence in their existence, and even possibly their sinister properties, although one is hard pressed to find one in the flesh or even meet someone who has" (p. 523).

No longer witches, trait psychologists now publicly proclaim the cross-situational consistency and longitudinal stability of personality dispositions. Looking over the past 20 years of research on traits, one can see at least five reasons that the concept of trait has emerged from the situationist critique as a powerfully legitimate mode of personality description (McAdams, 1994a):

1. *Traits are more than mere linguistic conveniences.* Standard situationist rhetoric of the 1970s had it that traits are in the mind of the observers rather than in the behavior of the people they observe (Nisbett & Ross, 1980). Similarly, Shweder (1975) argued that trait ratings simply reflect observers' biases about how different words are associated with each other in language. A significant body of research, however, shows that these critiques were probably more clever than true (Block, Weiss, & Thorne, 1979; Funder & Colvin, 1990; Moskowitz, 1990). Trait attributions based on careful observations reflect real differences in behavior and personality of the people being rated.

2. *Many traits show remarkable longitudinal consistency.* Longitudinal studies of the 1980s demonstrate that individual differences in many traits, such as extraversion and neuroticism, are quite stable over long periods of time (Conley, 1985; McCrae & Costa, 1990). Stability has been demonstrated when trait scores come from self-ratings, spouse ratings, or peer ratings. Some have suggested that longitudinal stability in traits is partly a result of a substantial genetic underpinning for dispositional differences. Twin studies consistently estimate that as much as 40% to 50% of the variance in trait scores may be attributed to genetic factors (e.g., Bouchard, Lykken, McGue, Segal, & Tellegen, 1990; Dunn & Plomin, 1990).

3. *Aggregation shows that traits often predict behavior fairly well.* Beginning with Epstein (1979), studies consistently show that individual differences in personality traits are often strongly correlated with individual differences in theoretically related behavior when behavior is aggregated across situations. Individual differences in traits can often account for a substantial amount of variance in aggregated behaviors (Kenrick & Funder, 1988).

4. *Situational effects are often no stronger than trait effects.* Funder and Ozer (1983) reexamined some of the most well-known laboratory studies of the 1960s and 1970s demonstrating significant effects for *situational variables* in predicting behavior. They found that the statistical effects obtained in these studies were typically no higher than those obtained in studies employing personality traits. Funder and Ozer argued that while trait scores may sometimes account for only modest amounts of variance in behavior, it appears that carefully measured situational variables often account for no more.

5. *Trait psychologists have rallied around the Big Five.* The most important development in trait psychology of the 1980s was the emergence of the Big Five model. Factor-analytic findings from many recent studies converge on a five-factor model of personality traits. The broad five factors may be labeled Extraversion (E), Neuroticism (N), Openness to Experience (O), Conscientiousness (C), and Agreeableness (A). The Big Five scheme appears to be the first truly comprehensive and consensual description of the trait domain to appear in the history of personality psychology (Digman, 1990). This is not to say that the Big Five is the last word on traits. But the model is an impressive achievement, and it has substantially enhanced the position of trait psychology in the eyes of the scientific community.

The Problem with Traits

It is easy to criticize the concept of trait. Trait formulations proposed by Allport (1937), Cattell (1957), Guilford (1959), Eysenck (1967), Jackson (1974), Tellegen (1982), Hogan (1986), and advocates of the Big Five have been called superficial, reductionistic, atheoretical, and even imperialistic. Traits are mere labels, it is said again and again. Traits don't explain anything. Traits lack precision. Traits disregard the environment. Traits apply only to score distributions in groups, not to the individual person (e.g., Lamiell, 1987). I believe that there is some validity in some of these traditional claims but that traits nonetheless provide invaluable information about persons. I believe that many critics expect too much of traits. Yet, those trait enthusiasts (e.g., A.H. Buss, 1989; Digman, 1990; Goldberg, 1993) who equate personality with traits in general, and with the Big Five in particular, are also claiming too much.

Goldberg (1981) contended that the English language includes five clusters of trait-related terms—the Big Five—because personality characteristics encoded in these terms have proved especially salient in human interpersonal perception, especially when it comes to the perennial and evolutionary crucial task of sizing up a stranger. I think Goldberg was more right than many trait enthusiasts would like him to be. Reliable and valid trait ratings provide an excellent "first read" on a person by offering estimates of a person's relative standing on a delimited series of general and linear dimensions of proven social significance. This is indeed crucial information in the evaluation of strangers and others about whom we know very little. It is the kind of information that strangers quickly glean from one another as they size one another up and anticipate future interactions. It did not take long for me to conclude that Lynn was high on certain aspects of Extraversion and moderately high on Neuroticism. What makes trait information like this so valuable is that it is comparative and relatively nonconditional. A highly extraverted person is generally more extraverted than most other people (comparative) and tends to be extraverted in a wide variety of settings (nonconditional), although by no means in all.

Consider, furthermore, the phenomenology of traditional trait assessment in personality psychology. In rating one's own or another's traits on a typical paper-and-pencil measure, the rater/subject must adopt an observational stance in which the target of the rating becomes an object of comparison on a series of linear and only vaguely conditional dimensions (McAdams, 1994c). Thus, if I were to rate Lynn, or if Lynn were to rate herself, on the Extraversion-keyed personality item "I am not a cheerful optimist" (from the NEO), I (or Lynn) would be judging the extent of Lynn's own "cheerful optimism" in comparison to the cheerful optimism of people I (or she) know or have heard about, or perhaps even an assumed average level of cheerful optimism of the rest of humankind. Ratings like these must have a social referent if they are to be meaningful. The end result of my (or her) ratings is a determination of the extent to which Lynn is seen as more or less extraverted across a wide variety of situations, conditions, and contexts, and compared to other people in general. There is, therefore, no place in trait assessment for what Thorne (1989) calls the conditional patterns of personality (see also Wright & Mischel, 1987). Here are some examples of conditional patterns: "My dominance shows when my competence is threatened; I fall apart when people try to comfort me; I talk most when I am nervous" (Thorne, 1989, p. 149). But to make traits into conditional statements is to rob them of their power as nonconditional indicators of general trends.

The two most valuable features of trait description—its comparative and nonconditional qualities—

double as its two greatest limitations as well. As persons come to know one another better, they seek and obtain information that is both noncomparative and highly conditional, contingent, and contextualized. They move beyond the mind-set of comparing individuals on linear dimensions. In a sense, they move beyond traits to construct a more detailed and nuanced portrait of personality, so that the stranger can become more fully known. New information is then integrated with the trait profile to give a fuller picture. My wife and I began to move beyond traits on the drive home. As a first read, Lynn seemed socially dominant (Extraversion) and mildly neurotic (Neuroticism). I would also give her a high rating on Openness to Experience; I would say that Agreeableness was probably medium; I would say that Conscientiousness was low-to-medium, though I do not feel that I received much trait-relative information on Conscientiousness. Beyond these traits, however, Lynn professed a confusing set of political beliefs: She claimed to be rather conservative but was a big fan of Hillary Clinton's; she scorned government for meddling in citizens' private affairs and she paid too much in taxes to support wasteful social programs, while at the same time she claimed to be a pacifist and to have great compassion for poor people and those who could not obtain health insurance. Beyond traits, Lynn claimed to be an atheist but expressed great admiration for missionaries. Beyond traits, Lynn appeared to be having problems in intimate relationships; she wished she could believe in something; she enjoyed her work as a free-lance writer; she was a good listener one-on-one but not in the large group; she expressed strong interest in New Age psychology; she seemed to think her parents invested too much faith in her and in her siblings. To know Lynn well, to know her more fully than one would know a stranger, one must be privy to information that does not fit trait categories, information that is exquisitely conditional and contextualized.

Going beyond Traits: Time, Place, and Role

There is a vast and largely unmapped domain in personality wherein reside such constructs as motives (McClelland, 1961), values (Rokeach, 1973), defense mechanisms (Cramer, 1991), coping styles (Lazarus, 1991), developmental issues and concerns (Erikson, 1963; Havighurst, 1972), personal strivings (Emmons, 1986), personal projects (Little, 1989), current concerns (Klinger, 1977), life tasks (Cantor & Kihlstrom, 1987), attachment styles (Hazan & Shaver, 1990), conditional patterns (Thorne, 1989), core conflictual relationship themes (Luborsky & Crits-Cristoph, 1991), patterns of self-with-other (Ogilvie & Rose, this issue), domain-specific skills and talents (Gardner, 1993), strategies and tactics (D.M. Buss, 1991), and many more personality variables that are both linked to behavior (Cantor, 1990) and important for the full description of the person (McAdams, 1994a). This assorted collection of constructs makes up a second level of personality, to which I give the generic and doubtlessly inadequate label of personal concerns. Compared with dispositional traits, personal concerns are typically couched in motivational, developmental, or strategic terms. They speak to what people want, often during particular periods in their lives or within particular domains of action, and what life methods people use (strategies, plans, defenses, and so on) in order to get what they want or avoid getting what they don't want over time, in particular places, and/or with respect to particular roles.

What primarily differentiates, then, personal concerns from dispositional traits is the contextualization of the former within time, place, and/or role. Time is perhaps the most ubiquitous context. In their studies of the "intimacy life task" among young adults, Cantor, Acker, and Cook-Flanagan (1992) focus on "those tasks that individuals see as personally important and time consuming at particular times in their lives" (p. 644). In their studies of generativity across the adult life span, McAdams, de St. Aubin, and Logan (1993) focus on a cluster of concern, belief, commitment, and action oriented toward providing for the well-being of the next generation, a cluster that appears to peak in salience around middle age. Intimacy and generativity must be contextualized in the temporal life span if they are to be properly understood. By contrast, the traits of Extraversion and Agreeableness are easily defined and understood outside of time. They are not linked to developmental stages, phases, or seasons.

The temporal context also distinguishes traits on the one hand from motives and goals on the other. Motives, goals, strivings, and plans are defined in terms of future ends. A person high in power motivation wants, desires, strives for power—having impact on others is the desired end state, the temporal goal (Winter, 1973). To have a strong motive, goal, striving, or plan is to orient oneself in a particular way in time. The same cannot be readily assumed with traits. Extraversion is not naturally conceived in goal-directed terms. It is not necessary for the viability of the concept of extraversion that an extraverted person strive to obtain a particular goal in time, although of course such a person may do so. Extraverted people simply *are* extraverted; whether they try to be or not is irrelevant. The case is even clearer for neuroticism, for the commonsense assumption here is that highly neurotic people do not strive to be neurotic over time. They simply are neurotic. While dispositional traits may have motivational properties (Allport, 1937; McCrae & Costa, in press), traits do not exist in time in the same way that motives, strivings, goals, and plans are temporally contextualized. To put it another way, I cannot understand Lynn's life in time when I merely consider her dispositional traits. Developmental and motivational constructs, by contrast, begin to provide me with the temporal context, the life embedded in and evolving over time.

Contextualization of behavior in place was a major theme of the situationist critique in the 1970s (Frederiksen, 1972; Magnusson, 1971). The situationists argued that behavior is by and large local rather than general, subject to the norms and expectations of a given social place or space. Attempts to formulate taxonomies of situations have frequently involved delineating the physical and interpersonal features of certain kinds of prototypical behavioral settings and social environments, like "church," "football game," "classroom," and "party" (Cantor, Mischel, & Schwartz, 1982; Krahe, 1992; Moos, 1973). Certain domain-specific skills, competencies, attitudes, and schemas are examples of personality variables contextualized in place. For example, Lynn is both a very good listener in one-on-one conversations, especially when the topic concerns psychology, and an extremely effective storyteller in large groups, especially when she is talking about travel.

When she is angry with her husband in a social setting, she drinks too much. The latter is an example of a conditional pattern (Thorne, 1989) or perhaps a very simple personal script (Demorest, this issue).

Some varieties of personal scripts and conditional patterns are contextualized in place and space: "When I am at home, I am unable to relax"; "When the weather is hot, I think about how miserable I was as a child, growing up in St. Louis"; "If I am lost in Chicago, I never ask for directions." To know a person well, it is not necessary to have information about all of the different personal scripts and conditional patterns that prevail in all of the different behavioral settings he or she will encounter. Instead, the personologist should seek information on the most salient settings and environments that make up the ecology of a person's life and investigate the most influential, most common, or most problematic personal scripts and conditional patterns that appear within that ecology (Demorest & Alexander, 1992).

Another major context in personality is social role. Certain strivings, tasks, strategies, defense mechanisms, competencies, values, interests, and styles may be role-specific. For example, Lynn may employ the defense mechanism of rationalization to cope with her anxiety about the setbacks she has experienced in her role as a mother. In her role as a writer, she may excel in expressing herself in a laconic, Hemingway-like style (role competence, skill) and she may strive to win certain journalistic awards or to make more money than her husband (motivation, striving). In the role of student/learner, she is fascinated with New Age psychology (interests). In the role of daughter, she manifests an insecure attachment style, especially with her mother, and this style seems to carry over to her relationships with men (role of lover/spouse) but not with women (role of friend). Ogilvie (Ogilvie & Ashmore, 1991; Ogilvie & Rose, this issue) has developed a new approach to personality assessment that matches personality descriptors with significant persons in one's life, resulting in an organization of self-with-other constructs. It would appear that some of the more significant self-with-other constellations in a person's life are those associated with important social roles. Like social places, not all social roles are equally important in a person's life. Among the most salient in

the lives of many American men and women are the roles of spouse/lover, son/daughter, parent, sibling, worker/provider, and citizen.

For personality psychologists who like order and clarity in their conceptualizations, Level II would appear to be an ill-defined, bulky, and disorderly domain at present. It is, therefore, tempting to try to simplify it by linking it with something that is elegant and well-defined. Thus, one may sympathize with the efforts of McCrae and Costa (in press) to link personal concerns (Level II) directly to the Big Five traits (Level I). McCrae and Costa distinguish between the "basic tendencies" of personality (Level I: dispositional traits) and "characteristic adaptations," which consist of learned skills, habits, attitudes, and relationships that are the ultimate results of the interaction of personality dispositions with environments. Characteristic adaptations would appear to cover some of the same terrain as Level II. McCrae and Costa argue that characteristic adaptations are essentially derivatives of the interaction between basic tendencies and environmental press. In other words, characteristic adaptations stem ultimately from traits; they are the contextualized manifestations of a person's dispositional signature.

In a further brief section, McAdams continued as to the ways people might view the relation between his Levels II and I.

What Is Missing?

As we move from Level I to Level II, we move from the psychology of the stranger to a more detailed and nuanced description of a flesh-and-blood, in-the-world person, striving to do things over time, situated in place and role, expressing herself or himself in and through strategies, tactics, plans, and goals. In Lynn's case, we begin our very provisional sketch with nonconditional attributions suggesting a high level of extraversion and moderately high neuroticism and we move to more contingent statements suggesting that she seems insecurely attached to her parents and her husband, strives for power and recognition in her career, wants desperately to believe in something but as yet has not found it in religion or in spirituality, holds strong but seemingly contradictory beliefs about politics and public service, employs the defense of rationalization to cope with the frustration she feels in her role as mother, has interests that tend toward books and ideas rather than physical health and fitness, loves to travel, is a good listener one-on-one but not in groups, is a skilled writer, is a good storyteller, tells stories that are rambling and dramatic. If we were to continue a relationship with Lynn, we would learn more and more about her. We would find that some of our initial suppositions were naive, or even plain wrong. We would obtain much more information on her traits, enabling us to obtain a clearer and more accurate dispositional signature. We would learn more about the contextualized constructs of her personality, about how she functions in time, place, and role. Filling in more and more information in Levels I and II, we might get to know Lynn very well.

But I submit that, as Westerners living in this modern age, we would not know Lynn "well enough" until we moved beyond dispositional traits and personal concerns to a third level of personality. Relatedly, should Lynn think of herself only in Level I and Level II terms, then she, too, as a Western, middle-class adult living in the last years of the 20th century, would not know herself "well enough" to comprehend her own identity. The problem of identity is the problem of overall unity and purpose in human lives (McAdams, 1985). It is a problem that has come to preoccupy men and women in Western democracies during the past 200 years (Baumeister, 1986; Langbaum, 1982). It is not generally a problem for children, though there are some exceptions. It is probably not as salient a problem for many non-Western societies that put less of a premium on individualism and articulating the autonomous adult self, although it is a problem in many of these societies. It is not equally problematic for all contemporary American adults. Nonetheless, identity is likely to be a problem for Lynn, for virtually all people attending that dinner party or reading this article, and for most contemporary Americans and Western Europeans who at one time or another in their adult lives have found the question "Who am I?" to be worth asking, worth pondering, and worth working on.

Modern and postmodern democratic societies do not explicitly tell adults who they should be. At the same time, however, these societies insist that an adult should be someone who both fits in and is unique (Bellah, Mad-

sen, Sullivan, Swidler, & Tipton, 1985). The self should be defined so that it is both separate and connected, individuated and integrated at the same time. These kinds of selves do not exist in prepackaged, readily assimilated form. They are not passed down from one generation to the next, as they were perhaps in simpler times. Rather, selves must be made or discovered as people become what they are to become in time. The selves that we make before we reach late adolescence and adulthood are, among other things, "lists" of characteristics to be found in Levels I and II of personality. My 8-year-old daughter, Amanda, sees herself as relatively shy (low Extraversion) and very caring and warm (high Agreeableness); she knows she is a good ice skater (domain-specific skill); she loves amusement parks (interests); and she has strong feelings of love and resentment toward her older sister (ambivalent attachment style, though she wouldn't call it that). I hazard to guess that these are a few items in a long list of things, including many that are not in the realm of personality proper ("I live in a white house"; "I go to Central School"), that make up Amanda's self-concept. A list of attributes from Levels I and II is not, however, an identity. Then again, Amanda is too young to have an identity because she is probably not able to experience unity and purpose as problematic in her life. Therefore, one can know Amanda very well by sticking to Levels I and II.

But not so for Lynn. As a contemporary adult, Lynn most likely can understand and appreciate, more or less, the problem of unity and purpose in her life. While the question of "Who am I?" may seem silly or obvious to Amanda, Lynn is likely to see the question as potentially problematic, challenging, interesting, ego-involving, and so on. For reasons that are no doubt physiological and cognitive, as well as social and cultural, it is in late adolescence and young adulthood that many contemporary Westerners come to believe that the self must or should be constructed and told in a manner that integrates the disparate roles they play, incorporates their many different values and skills, and organizes into a meaningful temporal pattern their reconstructed past, perceived present, and anticipated future (Breger, 1974; Erikson, 1959; McAdams, 1985). The challenge of identity demands that the Western adult construct a telling of the self that synthesizes synchronic and diachronic elements in such a way as to suggest that (*a*) despite its many facets the self is coherent and unified and (*b*) despite the many changes that attend the passage of time, the self of the past led up to or set the stage for the self of the present, which in turn will lead up to or set the stage for the self of the future (McAdams, 1990, 1993).

What form does such a construction take? A growing number of theorists believe that the only conceivable form for a unified and purposeful telling of a life is the story (Bruner, 1990; Charme, 1984; Cohler, 1982, 1994; Hermans & Kempen, 1993; Howard, 1991; Kotre, 1984; Linde, 1990; MacIntyre, 1984; Polkinghorne, 1988). In my own theoretical and empirical work, I have argued that identity is itself an internalized and evolving life story, or personal myth (McAdams, 1984, 1985, 1990, 1993, in press). Contemporary adults create identity in their lives to the extent that the self can be told in a coherent, followable, and vivifying narrative that integrates the person into society in a productive and generative way and provides the person with a purposeful self-history that explains how the self of yesterday became the self of today and will become the anticipated self of tomorrow. Level III in personality, therefore, is the level of identity as a life story. Without exploring this third level, the personologist can never understand how and to what extent the person is able to find unity, purpose, and meaning in life. Thus what is missing so far from our consideration of Lynn is her very identity.

Misunderstandings about Level III

Lynn's identity is an inner story, a narration of the self that she continues to author and revise over time to make sense, for herself and others, of her own life in time. It is a story, or perhaps a collection of related stories, that Lynn continues to fashion to specify who she is and how she fits into the adult world. Incorporating beginning, middle, and anticipated ending, Lynn's story tells how she came to be, where she has been and where she may be going, and who she will become (Hankiss, 1981). Lynn continues to create and revise the story across her adult years as she and her changing social world negotiate niches, places, opportunities, and positions within which she can live, and live meaningfully.

What is Lynn's story about? The dinner party provided my wife and me with ample material to begin talking about Lynn's personality from the perspectives of Levels I and II. But life-story information is typically more difficult to obtain in a casual social setting. Even after strangers have sized each other up on dispositional traits and even after they have begun to learn a little bit about each others' goals, plans, defenses, strategies, and domain-specific skills, they typically have little to say about the other person's identity. By contrast, when people have been involved in long-term intensive relationships with each other, they may know a great deal about each others' stories, about how the friend or lover (or psychotherapy client) makes sense of his or her own life in narrative terms. They have shared many stories with each other; they have observed each other's behavior in many different situations; they have come to see how the other person sees life, indeed, how the other sees his or her own life organized with purpose in time.

Without that kind of intimate relationship with Lynn, my wife and I could say little of substance about how Lynn creates identity in her life. We left the party with but a few promising hints or leads as to what her story might be about. For example, we were both struck by her enigmatic comment about passionate belief. Why did she suggest that her parents believed too strongly in her and in her siblings? Shouldn't parents believe in their children? Has she disappointed her parents in a deep way, such that their initial belief in their children was proven untenable? Does her inability to believe passionately in things extend to her own children as well? It is perhaps odd that her ex-husband has custody of their children; how is this related to the narrative she has developed about her family and her beliefs? And what might one make of that last incident at the party, when Lynn seemed to lapse into a different mode of talking, indicative perhaps of a different persona, a different public self, maybe a different "character" or "imago" (McAdams, 1984) in her life story? One can imagine many different kinds of stories that Lynn might create to make sense of her own life—adventure stories that incorporate her exotic travels and her considerable success; tragic stories that tell of failed love and lost children; stories in which the protagonist searches far and wide for something to believe in; stories in which early disappointments lead to cynicism, hardheartedness, despair, or maybe even hope. We do not know Lynn well enough yet to know what kinds of stories she has been working on. Until we can talk with some authority both to her and about her in the narrative language of Level III, we cannot say that we know her well at all. On the drive home, my wife and I know Lynn a little better than we might know a stranger. Our desire to know her much better than we know her now is, in large part, our desire to know her story. And were we to get to know her better and come to feel a bond of intimacy with her, we would want her to know our stories, too (McAdams, 1989).

There are numerous indications in the scientific literature that personality psychologists—like their colleagues in developmental and social psychology and in certain other branches of the social sciences (e.g., Denzin & Lincoln, 1994)—are becoming increasingly interested in narrative and life stories—the stuff of Level III. At the same time, there appears to be considerable confusion and misunderstanding about just what stories are about and how they relate to lives and personality. From the standpoint of my own life-story theory of identity and its relation to multiple levels and domains in the study of persons, let me comment upon four of the more common misunderstandings and confusions:

1. *A story can be a method or a construct, but the two are not the same.* Recent years have witnessed a proliferation of the narrative methods in personality psychology, whereby psychologists obtain data from study participants by asking them to tell stories (e.g., Josselson & Lieblich, 1993; McAdams & Ochber, 1988; Singer, this issue; Thorne, this issue). Such methods can be used to obtain information from persons pertaining to any of the three levels of personality I have identified above. For example, one can learn about defense mechanisms, self-schemas, personal strivings, motives, or even traits by asking a person to tell some kind of story, though story methods work much better for some constructs (e.g., Thematic Apperception Test [TAT] stories for motives) than they do for others (e.g., traits). What is important is that the stories obtained are not the constructs themselves. A TAT story about success is not achievement motivation itself; rather it is a measure of the construct achievement motivation. Similarly, when an interviewer asks a person to tell the story of his or her own life, the narrative account that is obtained is not

synonymous with the internal life story that is assumed, more or less, to provide that person's life with some semblance of unity and purpose. As in the TAT example, the data obtained from a story method may be interpreted to shed light on the life story itself. A person's life story is "inside" him or her in the same sense that a trait, motive, or striving is. The life story is a psychological construct—a dynamic, inner telling or narration, evolving over time—that may be assessed through storytelling methods. Arguably, other methods might be employed as well.

2. *Identity is a quality of the self; it is not the same thing as the self.* The terms "self" and "identity" are often used interchangeably, both by laypersons and psychologists (e.g., Banaji & Prentice, 1994). Following Erikson (1959), however, I believe it is advisable to save the term identity for a rather specific aspect or feature of self. If what James (1892/1963) called the "self-as-object" is all that a person considers or claims to be "me" and "mine," then identity refers to a particular way in which the self may be arranged, constructed, and eventually told. Identity, then, is the quality of unity and purpose of the self. Selves do not need to be unified and purposeful in order to be selves. But, as I argued above, contemporary Western adults tend to demand that their selves be unified and purposeful. In other words, adults demand that their own selves be endowed with identity. How might the self be arranged and told in such a way as to provide it with unity and purpose? By formulating it into a story. Therefore, identity is the *storied self*—the self as it is made into a story by the person whose self it is.

3. *If identity is a story, it must be understood in story terms.* The language of identity is the language of stories, narrative, drama, literature. The language comes from what Bruner (1986) terms the narrative mode of human cognition, rather than the paradigmatic mode of argument, logic, and causal proof. Therefore, identities are best comprehended in such terms as "imagery," "plot," "theme," "scene," "setting," "conflict," "character," and "ending" (McAdams, 1985, 1993). A well-formed, well-functioning identity in contemporary Western society is a "good story," exhibiting such traditionally valued features of Western narrative as coherence, credibility, richness, openness, and integration (McAdams, 1993). Personologists who seek to explore Level III must become comfortable with the language of stories. They must resist

attempts to taxonomize and evaluate identities in the traditional terms of traits, types, syndromes, stages, and other well-worn scientific nomenclatures. At the same time, however, they should continue to uphold social-scientific aims of systematic description and explanation, scientific discovery and proof. Contrary to the claims of some social constructivists (e.g., Rosenwald & Ochberg, 1992) as well as died-in-the-wool positivists (e.g., Fiske, 1974), life stories are not so fuzzy, so literary in nature, and so culturally embedded that they cannot be systematically observed, classified, categorized, quantified, and even subjected to hypothesis-testing research. It probably does not make sense to factor-analyze stories, or to think of narrative accounts in terms of split-half reliabilities (e.g., does the content of the first half of the story match that of the second?). But creative personologists should be able to undertake systematic, high-quality research employing narrative methods and dealing with narrative constructs if they are sensitive to the grammar of stories and if they are willing to see stories as ends in themselves, rather than as means for investigating other ends.

4. *The three levels of personality description are conceptually and epistemologically independent.* The wrong way to think about the three levels is to imagine a tight hierarchy in which traits give rise to more specific personal concerns, which ultimately coalesce to form a life story. The wrong way suggests that traits are the raw stuff of personality, that personal concerns are contextualized derivatives of traits, and that stories represent a fashioning of personal concerns into a meaningful life narrative. The wrong way suggests that stories are ultimately derived from traits. As I suggested above, I believe it is premature and unwise to view any of the three levels of personality as derivative of another. There are at least two reasons for my caution.

First, whereas the trait domain of Level I appears to be well-mapped at present, Levels II and III are relatively uncharted. The kind of geography that can be said to exist at these levels is simply unknown. As 40 years of trait psychology now attests, a given domain requires a great deal of time and considerable scrutiny before researchers can determine an indigenously adequate structure. Thus, Levels II and III need to be explored on their own terms, for a very long time. Second, the levels do not need to exist in meaningful relation to each other in order to exist as meaningful levels.

There is no holy writ dictating perfect hierarchy for conceptions of personality, that is, neat levels feeding into neat levels according to general laws of consistency. Lynn's internalized life story may reflect her traits in a very general sort of way and it may organize some of her values and strivings into a more coherent form than is obvious at Level II. Then again, her life story may not do much of this at all. Whether the life story is more or less consistent with traits and personal concerns or not, one cannot know Lynn well until one has explored her personality at all three levels. A full knowledge of her traits would tell me virtually nothing about her identity. A full airing of her life story is likely to provide me with virtually no valid data on her traits. Thus, each of the three different levels has a unique legitimacy and "range of convenience," to borrow a term from Kelly (1955). Each may have its own logic and rhetoric; each may require its own methods of inquiry and measurement; and each may inspire its own theories, models, frameworks, and laws.

What Else Is There?

I have argued that in order to know a person well a personologist must obtain data from three distinct and nonoverlapping levels or domains—dispositional traits, personal concerns, and life stories. The three levels provide three very different formats and frameworks for describing a person. Good description is necessary for good explanation. Once the personologist has a full description of "what is," she or he may then proceed to inquire into *why* the "what is" indeed *is,* how it came to be, and how it may be changed. Like description, it is likely that explanation may be specific to level. Explaining the origins of traits may be a very different matter from explaining the origins of a life story. Explanations for personality typically invoke a blend of biology, family, and culture. Current explanations for individual differences in personality traits (Level I) tend to emphasize genetic predispositions over and against shared environments (Dunn & Plomin, 1990; McCrae & Costa, in press). Little is known or even speculated about the origins of constructs to be found in Levels II and III. Given the significant contextualization of personal concerns and life stories in culture and society, it seems likely that viable explanations at these levels would emphasize environmental factors to a greater extent than has proven to be the case with decontextualized, noncontingent personality traits.

There is, of course, more to understanding a person than providing a full description of characteristics residing at the three levels delineated in this article. In both science and social life, description may and often should lead to attempts at explanation. Beyond describing Lynn's traits, concerns, and stories, therefore, I may be able to know her even better if I am fortunate enough, for example, to explain why she has such a strong trait of social dominance or why her life story, should it turn out to be this way, contains so many villains and no heroes, is punctuated by scenes of contamination (good things turn suddenly bad) rather than redemption (bad things turn suddenly good), portrays recurrent conflicts between themes of power and love, accentuates imagery of darkness (usually bad) and movement (usually good), and, despite its gloomy narrative tone, holds out the hope of a happy ending in the chapters to come.

To explain personality, the investigator must typically summon forth concepts and phenomena that reside outside the realm of personality proper. For example, one may explain the trait of hostility as a manifestation of a particular genetic endowment. While the trait is an aspect of personality, the genetic endowment is typically viewed as the "determinant" of the trait, the explanation for the personality feature rather than the feature itself. To use a parallel example invoking the environment, a disorganized attachment pattern may be explained as the result of repeated physical abuse at the hands of parents. The attachment pattern is an aspect of personality (Level II) whereas the abuse itself exists outside of personality proper, as a cause or reason for a personality feature rather than as the feature itself. The distinction between what is (personality proper) and why it is (determinants of personality) blurs a bit at the level of narrative, for a person may choose to interpret events from his or her past as part of a causal story concerning how he or she came to be. In the case of abuse, therefore, one might incorporate recollections of the negative events into a particular kind of story ("How I triumphed over the past"; "How I was ruined by my family") to provide life with unity and purpose. The events themselves remain outside the realm of personality proper, but the narra-

tion of the events within the life story now becomes part and parcel of personality itself, at Level III. One can now proceed to explain why the individual has created one kind of identity story rather than another.

Therefore, one answer to the question "What else is there?" beyond the levels of dispositional traits, personal concerns, and life stories is that there exists a great deal to know in the realm of explanation, and explanation requires a consideration of biological, environmental, cultural, and other sorts of factors that reside outside the realm of personality proper. Within personality proper, however, one may still imagine other kinds of constructs and phenomena that may not fit readily within my tripartite scheme.

For example, one might argue that the three levels do not leave enough room for what psychoanalysts and other depth psychologists have variously understood to be the unconscious. Should there exist a Level IV wherein reside the deeper and more implicit characteristics of the person? Recently, Epstein (1994) has synthesized some very old ideas and some very new research to argue vigorously for the existence of two parallel information processing systems that appear to link up with two corresponding systems of personality—one rational and conscious and the other implicit, experiential, and unconscious. A reasonable response to this argument may be to view each of the three levels of personality as containing an assumed gradient of consciousness upon which various kinds of constructs might be found. Thus, some traits may be more accessible to consciousness than others, and whereas some personal concerns (e.g., strivings) may be objects of everyday conscious thought, others (e.g., defense mechanisms) may operate outside awareness.

Gradients of awareness may have especially interesting implications at the level of narrative. As Wiersma (1988) has pointed out, some life narrations may be akin to "press releases" in that they provide superficial and socially desirable stories for "public" consumption. Others may probe more deeply and offer more discerning and revealing information about the self. The development of mature identity in adulthood may involve the narration of progressively more discerning self stories over time, as the person moves to transform that which was implicit or unconscious into an explicit narration that defines the self more fully than it was defined before. At any given time, furthermore, there may exist in personality a hierarchy of self-defining narratives, from the most consciously articulated but potentially superficial press releases to the deeper and more revealing life narrations whose existence as integrative stories of the self is only vaguely discerned by the narrator who has created them.

If Freud's conscious/unconscious distinction, therefore, informs our understanding levels and domains, a second distinction, made famous by James (1892/1963), offers another challenge to the tripartite scheme. The distinction is between the self-as-subject (the "I" or "ego") and the self-as-object (the "me" or "self-concept"). To the extent that "self" and "personality" are overlapping realms, the personality itself may be endowed with certain "I" features and certain "me" features. Traits, concerns, and life stories are more easily understood as potential features of the "me"—of the "self-concept"—in that most of the constructs that we can identify or imagine in these levels seem to be potential objects of the "I's" reflection. In a sense, the "I" (subject) "has" its own traits, acts in accord with its own personal concerns, and narrates its own stories (Cantor, 1990; McAdams, 1994c). But what can be said of the "I" itself?

While some have argued that the "I" is a redundant or unnecessary concept in personality and others have suggested that whatever the "I" is it cannot be known without transforming it into the "me" (making the subject into an object of reflection), still others suggest that the "I" or "ego" is the basic agential process in personality that is responsible for synthesizing human experience (Blasi, 1988; Loevinger, 1976). As such, the "I" is more a verb than a noun—the process of "selfing," of approaching human experience as an agential, synthesizing self. This process may in turn be described and analyzed, as Loevinger (1976) proposes in describing stages of ego development. Research has shown that certain stages of ego development are related to particular personality traits (higher ego stages are correlated with higher scores on Openness to Experience; McCrae & Costa, 1980), to personal concerns (middle-stage individuals value conformity in social settings; higher stage individuals strive for reciprocal interpersonal communication; Rosznafszky, 1981). Nonetheless, the ego stages do not appear to be conceptually reducible to either traits, concerns, or stories themselves, nor to a combina-

tion of the three. Instead, each stage seems to specify how the basic "I" process of meaning-making works, how the "I" is and does, how it engages in the fundamental enterprise of selfing. In the same sense that the "me" results from the "I," traits, concerns, and stories may be, among other things, results of that process, but they are not the process itself.

It is not altogether clear, therefore, how certain constructs that emphasize process (the "I") over content (the "me") fit into the three levels of personality description that I have set forth. The three levels relate most directly to those features of personality that are potential candidates for inclusion within a person's self-concept—the self as "me." These are characteristics of a person that are potential objects of the person's reflection and sources for the personality descriptions that persons typically develop to portray themselves and others to themselves and others. Dispositional traits, personal concerns, and life stories together provide a full description of a person. While the three levels may not contain the answers to all the questions a personality psychologist might raise about a person, they nonetheless provide explicit guidelines for determining just how well we know a person and, when that knowledge is inadequate, what else we need to know to make our knowledge better.

References

Allport, G.W. (1937). *Personality: A psychological interpretation.* New York: Holt, Rinehart & Winston.

Banaji, M.R., & Prentice, D.A. (1994). The self in social contexts. In L.W. Porter & M.R. Rosenzweig (Eds.), *Annual review of psychology* (Vol. 45, pp. 297–332). Palo Alto, CA: Annual Reviews.

Baumeister, R.F. (1986). *Identity: Cultural change and the struggle for self.* New York: Oxford University Press.

Bellah, R.N., Madsen, R., Sullivan, W.M., Swidler, A., & Tipton, S.M. (1985). *Habits of the heart.* Berkeley: University of California Press.

Blasi, A. (1988). Identity and the development of the self. In D.K. Lapsley & F.C. Powers (Eds.), *Self, ego, and identity: Integrative approaches* (pp. 226–242). New York: Springer-Verlag.

Block, J. (in press). A contrarian view of the five-factor approach to personality description. *Psychological Bulletin.*

Block, J., Weiss, D.S., & Thorne, A. (1979). How relevant is a semantic similarity interpretation of personality ratings? *Journal of Personality and Social Psychology, 37,* 1055–1074.

Bouchard, T.J., Jr., Lykken, D.T., McGue, M., Segal, N.L., & Tellegen, A. (1990). Sources of human psychological differences: The Minnesota Study of Twins Reared Apart. *Science, 250,* 223–228.

Bowers, K.S. (1973). Situationism in psychology: An analysis and critique. *Psychology Review, 80,* 307–336.

Breger, L. (1974). *From instinct to identity: The development of personality.* Englewood Cliffs, NJ: Prentice-Hall.

Briggs, S.R. (1989). The optimal level of measurement for personality constructs. In D.M. Buss & N. Cantor (Eds.), *Personality psychology: Recent trends and emerging directions* (pp. 246–260). New York: Springer-Verlag.

Bruner, J.S. (1986). *Actual minds, possible worlds.* Cambridge, MA: Harvard University Press.

Bruner, J.S. (1990). *Acts of meaning.* Cambridge, MA: Harvard University Press.

Buss, A.H. (1989). Personality as traits. *American Psychologist, 44,* 1378–1388.

Buss, D.M. (1991). Evolutionary personality psychology. In M.R. Rosenzweig & L.W. Porter (Eds.), *Annual review of psychology* (Vol. 42, pp. 459–491). Palo Alto, CA: Annual Reviews.

Buss, D.M., & Canton, N. (Eds.). (1989). *Personality psychology: Recent trends and emerging Directions.* New York: Springer-Verlag.

Cantor, N. (1990). From thought to behavior: "Having" and "doing" in the study of personality and cognition. *American Psychologist, 45,* 735–750.

Cantor, N., Acker, M., & Cook-Flanagan, C. (1992). Conflict and preoccupation in the intimacy life task. *Journal of Personality and Social Psychology, 63,* 644–655.

Cantor, N., & Kihlstrom, J.F. (1987). *Personality and social intelligence.* Englewood Cliffs, NJ: Prentice-Hall.

Cantor, N., Mischel, W., & Schwartz, J.C. (1982). A prototype analysis of psychological situations, *Cognitive Psychology, 14,* 45–77.

Cantor, N., & Zirkel, S. (1990). Personality, cognition, and purposive behavior. In L. Pervin (Ed.), *Handbook of personality theory and research* (pp. 135–164). New York: Guilford.

Cattell, R.B. (1957). *Personality and motivation structure and measurement.* New York: Harcourt, Brace, and World.

Charme, S.T. (1984). *Meaning and myth in the study of lives: A Sartrean perspective.* Philadelphia: University of Pennsylvania Press.

Cohler, B.J. (1982). Personal narrative and the life course. In P. Blates, & O.G. Brim, Jr. (Eds.), *Life span development and behavior* (Vol. 4, pp. 205–241). New York: Academic Press.

Cohler, B.J. (1994, June). *Studying older lives: Reciprocal acts of telling and listening.* Paper presented at annual meeting of the Society for Personology, Ann Arbor.

Conley, J.J. (1985). Longitudinal stability of personality traits: A multitrait-multimethod-multi-occasion analysis. *Journal of Personality and Social Psychology, 49,* 1266–1282.

Costa, P.T., Jr., & McCrae, R.R. (1985). *The NEO Personality Inventory.* Odessa, FL: Psychological Assessment Resources.

Cramer, P. (1991). *The development of defense mechanisms.* New York: Springer-Verlag.

Demorest, A.P., & Alexander, I.E. (1992). Affective scripts as organizers of personal experience. *Journal of Personality, 60,* 645–663.

Denzin, N.K., & Lincoln, Y.S. (Eds.). (1994). *Handbook of qualitative research.* London: Sage.

Digman, J.M. (1990). Personality structure: Emergence of the five-factor model. In M.R. Rosenzweig & L.W. Porter (Eds.), *Annual review of psychology* (Vol. 41, pp. 417–440). Palo Alto, CA: Annual Reviews.

Dunn, J., & Plomin, R. (1990). *Separate lives: Why siblings are so different.* New York: Basic Books.

Emmons, R.A. (1986). Personal strivings: An approach to personality and subjective well-being. *Journal of Personality and Social Psychology, 51,* 1058–1068.

Emmons, R.A. (1993). Current status of the motive concept. In K.H. Craik, R. Hogan, & R.N. Wolfe (Eds.), *Fifty years of personality psychology* (pp. 187–196). New York: Plenum.

Epstein, S. (1979). The stability of behavior: 1. On predicting most of the people much of the time. *Journal of Personality and Social Psychology, 37,* 1097–1126.

Epstein, S. (1994). Integration of the cognitive and the psychodynamic unconscious. *American Psychologist, 49,* 709–724.

Erikson, E.H. (1959). Identity and the life cycle: Selected papers. *Psychological Issues, 1* (1), 5–165.

Erikson, E.H. (1963). *Childhood and society* (2nd ed.). New York: Norton.

Eysenck, H.J. (1967). *The biological basis of personality.* Springfield, IL: Thomas.

Fiske, D.W. (1974). The limits of the conventional science of personality. *Journal of Personality, 42,* 1–11.

Frederickson, N. (1972). Toward a taxonomy of situations. *American Psychologist, 27,* 114–123.

Funder, D.C., & Colvin, C.R. (1991). Explorations in behavioral consistency: Properties of persons, situations, and behaviors. *Journal of Personality and Social Psychology, 60,* 773–794.

Funder, D.C., & Ozer, D.J. (1983). Behavior as a function of the situation. *Journal of Personality and Social Psychology, 44,* 107–112.

Gardner, H. (1993). *Creating minds.* New York: Basic Books.

Gilligan, C. (1982). *In a different voice.* Cambridge, MA: Harvard University Press.

Goldberg, L.R. (1981). Language and individual differences: The search for universals in personality lexicons. In L. Wheeler (Ed.), *Review of personality and social psychology* (Vol. 2, pp. 141–166). Beverly Hills: Sage.

Goldberg, L.R. (1993). The structure of phenotypic personality traits. *American Psychologist, 48,* 26–34.

Guilford, J.P. (1959). *Personality.* New York: McGraw-Hill.

Hankiss, A. (1981). On the mythological rearranging of one's life history. In D. Bertaux (Ed.), *Biography and society: The life history approach in the social sciences* (pp. 203–209). Beverly Hills: Sage.

Havighurst, R.J. (1972). *Developmental tasks and education* (3rd ed.). New York: McKay.

Hazan, C., & Shaver, P. (1990). Love and work: An attachment-theoretical perspective. *Journal of Personality and Social Psychology, 59,* 270–280.

Hermans, H.J.M., & Kempen, H.J.G. (1993). *The dialogical self.* New York: Academic Press.

Hogan, R. (1986). *Hogan Personality Inventory manual.* Minneapolis: National Computer Systems.

Howard, G.S. (1991). Culture tales: A narrative approach to thinking, cross-cultural psychology, and psychotherapy. *American Psychologist, 46,* 187–197.

Jackson, D.N. (1974). *The Personality Research Form.* Port Huron, MI: Research Psychologists Press.

Jackson, D.N., & Paunonen, S.V. (1980). Personality structure and assessment. In M.R. Rosenzweig & L.W. Porter (Eds.), *Annual review of psychology* (Vol. 31, pp. 503–552). Palo Alto, CA: Annual Reviews.

James, W. (1963). *Psychology.* Greenwich, CT: Fawcett. (Original work published 1892.)

John, O.P. (1990). The "Big Five" factor taxonomy: Dimensions of personality in the natural language and in questionnaires. In L. Pervin (Ed.), *Handbook of personality theory and research* (pp. 66–100). New York: Guilford.

Josselson, R., & Lieblich, A. (Eds.). (1993). *The narrative study of lives.* Newbury Park, CA: Sage.

Kaiser, R.T., & Ozer, D.J. (in press). The structure of personal goals and their relation to personality traits. *Journal of Personality and Social Psychology.*

Kelly, G. (1955). *The psychology of personal constructs.* New York: Norton.

Kenrick, D.T., & Funder, D.C. (1988). Profiting from controversy: Lessons from the person-situation debate. *American Psychologist, 43,* 23–34.

Klinger, E. (1977). *Meaning and void.* Minneapolis: University of Minneapolis Press.

Kotre, J. (1984). *Outliving the self: Generativity and the interpretation of lives.* Baltimore: Johns Hopkins University Press.

Krahe, B. (1992). *Personality and social psychology: Toward a synthesis.* London: Sage.

Lamiell, J.T. (1987). *The psychology of personality: An epistemological inquiry.* New York: Columbia University Press.

Langbaum, R. (1982). *The mysteries of identity: A theme in modern literature.* Chicago: University of Chicago Press.

Lazarus, R.J. (1991). *Emotion and adaptation.* New York: Oxford University Press.

Linde, C. (1990). *Life stories: The creation of coherence 60,* (Monograph No. IRL 90–0001). Palo Alto, CA: Institute for Research on Learning.

Little, B.R. (1989). Personal projects analysis: Trivial pursuits, magnificent obsessions, and the search for coherence. In D.M. Buss & N. Cantor (Eds.), *Personality psychology: Recent trends and emerging directions* (pp. 15–31). New York: Springer-Verlag.

Loevinger, J. (1976). *Ego development.* San Francisco: Jossey-Bass.

Luborsky, L., & Crits-Cristoph, P. (1991). *Understanding transference: The core conflictual relationship theme method.* New York: Basic Books.

MacIntyre, A. (1984). *After virtue.* Notre Dame: University of Notre Dame Press.

Magnusson, D. (1971). An analysis of situational dimensions. *Perceptual and Motor Skills, 32,* 851–867.

McAdams, D.P. (1984). Love, power, and images of the self. In C.Z. Malatesta & C.E. Izard (Eds.), *Emotion in adult development* (pp. 159–174). Beverly Hills: Sage.

McAdams, D.P. (1985). *Power, intimacy, and the life story: Personological inquiries into identity.* New York: Guilford.

McAdams, D.P. (1989). *Intimacy: The need to be close.* New York: Doubleday.

McAdams, D.P. (1990). Unity and purpose in human lives: The emergence of identity as a life story. In A.I. Rabin, R.A. Zucker, R.A. Emmons, & S. Frank (Eds.), *Studying persons and lives* (pp. 148–200). New York: Springer.

McAdams, D.P. (1992). The five-factor model in personality: A critical appraisal. *Journal of Personality, 60,* 329–361.

McAdams, D.P. (1993). *The stories we live by: Personal myths and the making of the self.* New York: Morrow.

McAdams, D.P. (1994a). *The person: An introduction to personality psychology* (2nd ed.). Fort Worth: Harcourt Brace.

McAdams, D.P. (1994b). A psychology of the stranger. *Psychological inquiry, 5,* 145–148.

McAdams, D.P. (1994c). Can personality change? Levels of stability and growth in personality across the life span. In T.F. Heatherton & J.L. Weinberger (Eds.), *Can personality change?* (pp. 299–314). Washington, DC: American Psychological Association.

McAdams, D.P. (in press). Narrating the self in adulthood. In J. Birren, G. Kenyon, J.E. Ruth, J.J.F. Schroots, & T. Svensson (Eds.), *Aging and biography: Explorations in adult development.* New York: Springer.

McAdams, D.P., Booth, L., & Selvik, R. (1981). Religious identity among students at a private college: Social motives, ego stage, and development. *Merrill-Palmer Quarterly, 27,* 219–239.

McAdams, D.P., de St. Aubin, E., & Logan, R.L. (1993). Generativity among young, midlife, and older adults. *Psychology and Aging, 8,* 221–230.

McAdams, D.P., & Ochber, R.L. (Eds.). (1988). *Psychobiography and life narratives.* Durham, NC: Duke University Press.

McClelland, D.C. (1951). *Personality.* New York: Holt, Rinehart & Winston.

McClelland, D.C. (1961). *The achieving society.* New York: D. Van Nostrand.

McCrae, R.R., & Costa, P.T., Jr. (1980). Openness to experience and ego level in Loevinger's Sentence Completion Test: Dispositional contributions to developmental models of personality. *Journal of Personality and Social Psychology, 39,* 1179–1190.

McCrae, R.R., & Costa, P.T., Jr. (1990). *Personality in adulthood.* New York: Guilford.

McCrae, R.R., & Costa, P.T., Jr. (in press). Toward a new generation of personality theories: Theoretical contexts for the five-factor model. In J. S. Wiggins (Ed.), *The five-factor model of personality.* New York: Guilford.

Mischel, W. (1968). *Personality and assessment.* New York: Wiley

Mischel, W. (1973). Toward a cognitive social-learning reconceptualization of personality. *Psychological Review, 80,* 252–283.

Moos, R.H. (1973). Conceptualization of human environments. *American Psychologist, 28,* 652–665.

Moskowitz, D.S. (1990). Convergence of self-reports and independent observers: Dominance and friendliness. *Journal of Personality and Social Psychology, 58,* 1096–1106.

Murray, H.A. (1938). *Explorations in personality.* New York: Oxford University Press.

Nisbett, R.E., & Ross, L.D. (1980). *Human inference: Strategies and shortcomings of social judgments.* Englewood Cliffs, NJ: Prentice-Hall.

Ogilvie, D.M., & Ashmore, R.D. (1991). Self-with-other representation as units of analysis in self-concept research. In R.A. Curtis (Ed.), *The relational self: Theoretical convergences in psychoanalysis and social psychology* (pp. 282–314). New York: Guilford.

Ozer, D.J., & Reise, S.P. (1994). Personality assessment. In L.W. Porter & M.R. Rosenzweig (Eds.), *Annual review of psy-chology* (Vol. 45, pp. 357–388). Palo Alto, AD: Annual Reviews.

Pervin, L. (1994). A critical analysis of current trait theory. *Psychological Inquiry, 5,* 103–113.

Polkinghorne, D. (1988). *Narrative knowing and the human sciences.* Albany, NY: SUNY Press.

Revelle, W. (1995). Personality processes. In L.W. Porter & M.R. Rosenzweig (Eds.), *Annual review of psychology* (Vol. 46, pp. 295–328). Palo Alto, CA: Annual Reviews.

Rokeach, M. (1973). *The nature of human values.* New York: Free Press.

Rosenwald, G.C., & Ochberg, R.L. (Eds.). (1992). *Storied lives.* New Haven: Yale University Press.

Rosznafszky, J. (1981). The relationship of level of ego development to Q-sort personality ratings. *Journal of Personality and Social Psychology, 41,* 99–120.

Shweder, R.A. (1975). How relevant is an individual difference theory of personality? *Journal of Personality, 43,* 455–484.

Tellegen, A. (1982). *Brief manual for the Differential Personality Questionnaire.* Unpublished manuscript, University of Minnesota.

Thorne, A. (1989). Conditional patterns, transference, and the coherence of personality across time. In D.M. Buss & N. Cantor (Eds.), *Personality psy-chology: Recent trends and emerging directions* (pp. 149–159). New York: Springer.

Wiersma, J. (1988). The press release: Symbolic communication in life history interviewing. *Journal of Personality, 56,* 205–238.

Wiggins, J.S. (Ed.). (in press). *The five-factor model of personality.* New York: Guilford.

Winter, D.G. (1973). *The power motive.* New York: Free Press.

Wright, J.C., & Mischel, W. (1987). A conditional approach to dispositional constructs: The local predictability of social behavior. *Journal of Personality and Social Psychology, 53,* 1159–1177.

Concluding Comments

Reflecting on the McAdams' Piece

Four questions are helpful to evaluating a field-wide framework: (1) What is the central question about personality psychology the author is asking? Highly related to that: (2) Is the question, indeed, the central one (or, if not, a useful one) to ask about the field? More pragmatically, (3) What are the main organizational divisions of the field the author is proposing? and (4) Do the divisions neatly hold the various areas of research in the field?

McAdams' framework has become one of several influential frameworks. The most widespread framework remains the theoretical perspective-by-perspective approach. Another influential framework, the one employed in this readings book, is the systems framework for personality, which asks, "How does one study a system such as personality?"

McAdams' question is "What do we know when we know a person?" When you compare his question to the theory-by-theory approach and to the system framework's question—"How does one study a system such as personality?"— does one appeal to you more? Is there an advantage or drawback of one that stands out for you? Whether or not McAdams' framework is the best framework (or if there even is a best framework), his provides a thought-provoking introduction to the field, and to personality psychologists more generally.

Review Questions

1. What is a field-wide framework?
2. McAdams describes Lynn according to three levels of understanding: Levels I, II, and III. Can you describe the kinds of knowledge about a person that exist at each level? Which level provides the most intimate knowledge of a person?
3. McAdams spends considerable time talking about the pros and cons of trait descriptions of people, which he famously calls, "the psychology of strangers." What were some of the controversies that arose around the situationist critique of traits, and what are the advantages of traits, as now considered?
4. McAdams and his wife have strong emotional reactions to Lynn at first, and then later on. Generally speaking, can strong reactions influence how one person perceives another? Do you believe that they may have affected how they perceived Lynn?
5. McAdams makes the case that personality psychology should assist a person in analyzing someone else. How does a reliance on personality psychology help McAdams understand Lynn better than another party-goer might have understood her?

4

The Proper Use of Psychological Tests: An Expert Speaks

An Expert's Expert

A number of psychologists have earned reputations for their knowledge, balance, and wisdom in a particular area. With a few exceptions, these individuals have successfully balanced the conflicting demands of the field and have melded them seamlessly into workable, sensible, positions on a controversial topic or topics. Sometimes these special experts are asked to address the rest of a scientific or applied audience and share their views. For example, the *Journal of Personality* developed a series of articles (presently associated with winners of the Henry Murray award), that asks master psychologists to write on what they have learned from their work in the field, or that asks such eminent psychologists to examine an issue of current concern in the field. Other journals have similar programs.

These eminent psychologists can provide brief but effective teachings to those in the field regarding how to work more productively or accurately in an area of research or practice. Recent examples have included retrospective articles on inkblot techniques, on studying the personality of political leaders, and on finding the person in the data of the field (e.g., Holtzman, 2002; West, 2003; Winter, 2005).

These eminent psychologists are, for the most part, expected to write in a balanced but relatively informal approach. The scientist's good name renders it possible to put aside, at least for a moment, the copious references and marshaled evidence necessary in most journal articles. Rather, these articles are a form of informal tutorial—a chance to pull up a chair and comfortably listen to someone, a person who knows more than most, talk about how one can best work in a field.

Significance of the Reading

Few names are as familiar to psychologists interested in mental testing as that of Anne Anastasi (Hogan, 2003; Reznikoff & Procidano, 2001). She was known to generations of students as the author of *Psychological Testing*, which she edited until its seventh edition—and until she herself was 87 years old. She received numerous honors throughout her life, including the presidency of the American Psychological Association. When, at long last, she thought she was through winning honors, she received a telephone call from the White House, telling her she had received the National Medal for Science.

The following piece, "What Counselors Should Know about the Use and Interpretation of Psychological Tests," represents a distillation of how tests should be used (and how they might be misused). At the time she wrote this article, Anastasi was then professor emeritus of psychology at the Graduate School of Arts and Sciences, Fordham University, New York. The article appeared in the *Journal of Counseling and Development,* the flagship journal of the American Counseling Association. The American Counseling Association is an association for counselors of a wide variety of disciplinary backgrounds including those who have received masters' degrees in counseling in schools of education, social work, management, and psychology. Many members are entrusted with administering psychological tests and providing feedback to the individuals who take them.

The Watch List

Anastasi's considerable experience in writing textbooks assures, in this case, a comfortable and clear writing style. At the same time, she is writing for experienced professionals, and expects them to understand the general context of her remarks. At the outset, Anastasi mentions that counselors will be familiar with the relevant tests she is discussing, and, indeed, counselors would be well aware of those tests. Undergraduate psychology students, however, will be less familiar with them. In short, the number of commercially available psychological tests has increased steadily over the years, such that their listings and descriptions can now fill up a catalogue the size of a small yellow-pages phone book. Most counselors receive these catalogues from several companies throughout the year. Anastasi is referring to them in the aggregate, although later in the piece she will narrow her focus to tests of mental abilities.

Anastasi further remarks that most counselors will be familiar with "the basic requirements of proper test use." In that regard, she raises the issues of standard, "uniform administration and scoring procedures," which refers to the fact that a counselor should read instructions to test-takers in the same way for each person, and treat each person in as similar a fashion as possible (with some variations allowable as necessary for a person's individual needs). *Test norms,* which she also mentions, refer to the general level of scores people obtain on a test. An individual's scores are always referred to the norms to determine whether, for example, they have scored above or below average.

In the section, "Common Assessment Hazards," Anastasi leads off with the hazard of taking a single test score as a definite indicator of a person's ability or characteristic. She raises there the issue of the *standard error of measurement,* or *SEM.* The SEM is a statistic that allows the tester to know how likely it is that a person's true score falls within a given range of scores. On a good test, the SEM is small. For example, imagine that a person takes an intelligence test. A score of 119 on a good test may mean that the individual's real score has a 97% chance of falling between 114 and 122 (the range is not exactly symmetrical around the score). Less good tests often have larger SEMs. A less good test's SEM might indicate that the individual has a 97% chance of her true score falling between 108 and 128—a much broader and hence, less precise range. The point of the SEM is that the test administrator should remember that the score can never be interpreted as an absolute—rather it represents a range of possible performance. As human beings we have a tendency to prefer certainty and to forget these cautions at times.

The section following covers "Evolving Approaches to Test Validation." Test validation is the process of establishing that a test measures what it ought to. A test's validity refers to, in brief, that a test measures what it claims to, or ought to, measure. It means that a test of anxiety really measures a person's anxiety, or that a test of intelligence really measures an individual's intelligence.

The section, "Evolving Concepts of Intelligence," refers to Spearman's g and multiple facets of intelligence. Spearman's g is what is more commonly referred to as general intelligence—the idea that there exists a general form of intelligence that contributes to most or all more specific mental abilities.

Watch for these and other ideas as you read, and enjoy the article.

What Counselors Should Know about the Use and Interpretation of Psychological Tests

by Anne Anastasi

Source: Anastasi, A. (1992). What counselors should know about the use and interpretation of psychological tests. *Journal of Counseling and Development, 70,* pp. 610–616.

Counselors constitute a major group of test users. Moreover, because of the wide diversity of both counseling services and client populations served by different types of counselors, the tests used cover almost the entire range of available instruments. The relevant tests sample virtually the whole life span; they include measures of many aspects of both cognitive and affective behavior; and they represent all testing techniques, from projective and other clinical devices to self-administered inventories and computerized testing. I am starting with the assumption that most counselors already know about the basic requirements of proper test use, such as uniform administration and scoring procedures, appropriate use of norms, maintaining the security of test materials and observing copyright restrictions, and protecting the privacy of test takers and the confidentiality of the findings. Hence, I shall concentrate on a few key points that all too often receive inadequate attention from test users. Test misuses of this latter type are more subtle and less easily recognized than are the more obvious procedural errors, but they have potentially more serious consequences.

The Role of the Test User

The test user, as distinguished from the test author or publisher, is anyone who has the responsibility for choosing tests, for monitoring test administration and scoring (by persons or computers), and for interpreting test scores and using them as one source of information in making practical decisions. Any one test user may be responsible for one or more of these functions—and

often for all of them. If a test user as herein defined lacks adequate background for performing the required functions, he or she should have ready access to a properly qualified supervisor or consultant.

A conspicuous development in psychological testing during the 1980s and 1990s is the increasing recognition of the key role of the test user. Most popular criticisms of tests are clearly identifiable as criticisms of test use (or misuse), rather than criticisms of the tests themselves. Tests are essentially tools. Whether any tool is an instrument of good or harm depends on how the tool is used.

The growing concern with the test user is illustrated by the activities of broadly based national committees (see, e.g., Anastasi, in press; Eyde, Moreland, Robertson, Primoff, & Most, 1988, in press) and by the expanded coverage of test usage in the latest revision of the *Standards for Educational and Psychological Testing* (1985)[1]. In this edition of the *Standards,* 11 of the 16 chapters are devoted to the use of tests in different professional applications and with special populations, as well as to general standards for proper test administration, scoring, and reporting, and for protecting the rights of test takers.

Why are tests misused? One reason is the all too human desire for shortcuts, quick solutions, and clear-cut answers to our questions. This common human weakness has been capitalized by soothsayers over the centuries, from phrenologists to astrologers and other self-styled expert advisers. People seeking guidance are often attracted by the facile promises of charlatans, in contrast to the slower, deliberate considerations and the carefully qualified suggestions of the significantly trained professional. Similarly, if one or two short tests—whatever their technical limitations and defects—seem to offer a simple answer to questions about career choice, interpersonal difficulties, emotional problems, or learning deficiencies, many test takers will be temporarily satisfied.

At another level, some misuse of tests by a counselor or other test user may arise from time pressure or work overload, which renders shortcuts attractive. To some extent, too, there may be the tendency—deliberate or inadvertent—to shift decision-making responsibility to an impersonal agent such as a test. For the responsible professional, awareness of these common human reactions is the best protection against them.

A second major reason for the misuse of tests is inadequate or outdated knowledge about testing. This I believe to be the most frequent cause of test misuse, a conclusion that is supported by surveys conducted in the United States and elsewhere (Eyde et al., 1988, in press; Tyler & Miller, 1986). It is also the source of misuse that can be most directly affected by more and better training programs for test users. Accordingly, it is with this source of test misuse that the rest of my article is concerned.

What specialized knowledge do test users need? For the proper interpretation and application of test results, they need some basic understanding of (a) statistical techniques of psychometrics and (b) relevant facts and principles of behavioral science. The first has been called "psychometric literacy" (Lambert, 1989, August). It is essential, but it is not enough. We need to distinguish between the technical properties of a test and the substantive interpretation of a test score. The latter requires some knowledge about the behavior domain assessed by the test and the conditions that affect behavior development.

Statistical and Technical Knowledge about Tests

Nature of Individual Assessment

Counselors typically use tests as one source of information in individual assessment. The term *assessment* is being used increasingly to refer to the intensive study of an individual, leading to recommendations for action in solving a practical problem. The effectively functioning counselor engages in a continuing cycle of hypothesis formulation and hypothesis testing about the particular individual. Each item of information—whether it is an event recorded in the case history, a comment by the client, or a test score—suggests a hypothesis about the person, which will be either confirmed or refuted as other facts are gathered. Such hypotheses themselves indicate the direction of further lines of inquiry, such as choice of tests or follow-up questioning.

One should keep in mind that even highly reliable tests with well-established validity do not yield sufficiently precise results for individual assessment. Hence, counselors (as well as clinical psychologists) tend to be receptive to some instruments that, while psychometrically crude, may nevertheless provide a rich harvest of leads for further exploration. The ultimate responsibility for integrating the information and using it in individual assessment and decision-making rests with the counselor. Such responsibility, however, entails certain assessment hazards that the counselor must guard against.

Common Assessment Hazards

These hazards lead to frequent misuses of tests. The first is the *hazard of the single score* on any particular test. This test misuse arises from ignoring the chance variation in the score shown by the standard error of measurement (SEM). It involves using a single number to represent the individual's test performance, instead of computing a score band at a specified confidence level. This practice fails to allow for the random sampling fluctuations among sets of items and over short periods of time that are measured by traditional measures of test reliability. Such a misuse of test results may be compounded when evaluating a pattern of performance on a multi-score battery, unless all relevant statistical pitfalls are considered (see Anastasi, 1985a).

The second is the *hazard of the single time period.* Apart from the previously mentioned random errors, systematic and progressive changes occur over longer time periods. These are the changes that are likely to render old scores in a person's file untrustworthy. Such changes also argue against labeling an individual with a numerical score, rather than restricting the score to that person's performance on a specified test at a specified time. These improper practices assume trait stability regardless of intervening experiences. Periodic reevaluation is needed when a child is considered for educational placement, an employee for promotion or transfer, or a client for counseling or psychotherapy. There is evidence that, in such instances, it is the criterion performance itself, rather than just the test score, that is likely to change progressively over time (e.g., Henry & Hulin, 1987).

The third is the *hazard of the single indicator.* Failure to consider the moderate size of the correlations between different indicators of a behavioral construct may lead to undue reliance on scores from a single test, without corroborative and qualifying data from other tests or from other sources of information about the person. Examples of common constructs assessed in counseling include intelligence, scholastic aptitude, learning ability, attitude toward math, motivation for school learning, and interpersonal relations. It is well to ask what proportion of the variance of the behavioral construct under consideration is covered by any one test. Putting the question in this form highlights the limitations of a single indicator, while recognizing its demonstrated contribution to assessment. An easy way to estimate this proportion under ordinary conditions is to square the correlation between test score and criterion measure.

The fourth is the *hazard of illusory precision.* The availability of numerical scores from instruments designed chiefly as aids for the skilled practitioner (such as projective techniques) may create a misleading impression of quantification and objectivity. The interpretive pitfalls inherent in such instruments are not limited to misuse by inadequately qualified test users; they also occur in the rapidly proliferating computerized scoring systems that provide narrative interpretations of performance. These systems must demonstrate the reliability and validity of their score interpretations through the publication of adequate supporting data. Moreover, they can serve only as aids to the trained practitioner, not as a substitute for the practitioner. The special problems presented by commercially marketed computerized systems of narrative score interpretation have aroused widespread concern on the part of psychological practitioners, committees on testing, and national professional associations. Serious attention is being given to the formulation of workable guidelines for the effective use of such interpretive services (Butcher, 1987; Guidelines, 1986).

Evolving Approaches to Test Validation

Some recent developments in psychological testing reflect trends discernible in American psychology as a whole. Conspicuous among these trends is an increasing concern with theory and a movement away from the blind empiricism of earlier decades. This theoretical orientation is illustrated by the growing emphasis on constructs in the description of ability and personality, as well as the increasing use of construct validation in the development and evaluation of tests. The term *construct validity* was introduced into the psychometric vocabulary in the first edition of the testing *Standards (Technical Recommendations,* 1954). The discussions of construct validation that followed—and that continue with undiminished vigor—have served to make the implications of its procedures more explicit and to provide a systematic rationale for its use. In psychometric terminology, a construct is a theoretical concept closely akin to a trait. Constructs may be simple and narrowly defined, such as speed of walking or spelling ability, or they may be complex and broadly generalizable, such as mathematical reasoning, scholastic aptitude, neuroticism, or anxiety.

The overemphasis on purely empirical procedures during the early decades of the 20th century arose in part as a revolt against the armchair theorizing that all too often served as the basis for some so-called psychological writings of that period. But empiricism need not be blind, nor does theory need to be subjective speculation. Psychologists gradually realized that theory can be derived from an analysis of accumulated research findings, and it can in turn lead to the formulation of empirically testable hypotheses. Tests published since the 1970s show increasing concern with theoretical rationales throughout the test development process. A specific example of the integration of empirical and theoretical approaches is provided by the assignment of items to subtests on the basis of logical as well as statistical homogeneity. In other words, an item is retained in a scale if it had been written to meet the specifications of the construct definition of the particular scale and was also shown to belong in that scale by the results of statistical item analysis.

It is being recognized more and more that the development of a valid test requires multiple procedures, which are used sequentially, at different stages in test construction (Anastasi, 1986a; 1988, chap. 6; Jackson, 1970, 1973; Messick, 1980, 1988, 1989, 1991; *Standards,* 1985, pp. 9–18). Thus, validity is built into the test from the outset, rather than being apparently limited to the last stages of test development, as in the traditional reporting of criterion-related validation in test manuals. The validation process begins with the formulation of trait or construct definitions, which are derived from psychological theory, from prior research, or from systematic observation and analysis of real-life behavior domains, such as job analyses. Test items are then prepared to fit the construct definitions. Empirical item analyses follow, with the selection of the most valid items from the initial item pools. Other appropriate internal analyses may then be carried out, including factor analyses of item clusters or subtests. The final stage includes validation and cross-validation of various scores (and interpretive score patterns) through statistical analyses against real-life criteria.

The traditional concepts of content validity and criterion-related validity can be more accurately designated as content relevance and content representativeness for the first, and predictive and diagnostic utility for the second, as proposed by Messick (1980, 1988, 1989, 1991). In certain practical situations, data obtained by these traditional procedures may be needed to answer specific questions. Nevertheless, even in such cases, information about constructs enriches the understanding of the test findings. For one thing, constructs are more generalizable than are particular tested variables, and some generalizability beyond the immediate testing context is nearly always implied in the use of test results. As for criterion-related validity, ideally both tests and criteria should be described in terms of empirically established constructs, and the correspondence between the two sets of constructs investigated. Moreover, the constructs identified in the criteria (as in educational or work performance) could also be examined in relation to the goals explicitly set for such activities within specified value systems.[2]

Counselors are concerned with information on test validation, as reported in test manuals and related supplementary publications, for at least two reasons. First, such information should help in selecting appropriate tests and evaluating their potential effectiveness for specific uses. Second, the correct interpretation of test scores requires knowledge about what the particular test measures, as indicated by the validation data. Interpretation of test results in terms of constructs, rather than specific measured variables, is likely to be especially relevant for counselors. Most counseling situations call for a broad understanding of the individual's assets and liabilities, in contrast to those testing situations that require a matching of individual skills and qualifications to narrowly defined task performance.

Substantive Interpretation and Use of Test Results

What Test Results Do and Do Not Tell about a Person

In addition to basic knowledge about the statistical and technical properties of psychological tests illustrated in the preceding section, the counselor needs current knowledge about the behavior domain that the test is designed to assess. This requires familiarity with major substantive developments in the relevant areas of psychological science. A significant point for all test users to bear in mind is that test scores tell us *how well* individuals perform at the time of testing, not *why* they perform as they do. To find out why, we have to consider the test score within the person's *antecedent context.* We need to delve into the individual's reactional biography or learning history. In what environment did this person develop? What conditions and events were encountered, and how did the person respond to them?

From another angle, we need to examine the test score within the *anticipated context.* What is the setting—educational, occupational, societal—in which this person is expected to function, and for which he or she is being evaluated? What can we find out about the intellectual, emotional, and physical demands of that context? Several concepts encountered in the recent psychological literature, such as functional literacy and the assessment of competence, arise from this approach to test interpretation (Anastasi, 1988, pp. 424–428; Sticht, 1975; Sundberg, Snowden, & Reynolds, 1978). Can this person read at the level required for a job she is considering? Can this youth manage his own life in the community? Is this child ready to benefit from a particular educational program or some other planned intervention? Thus, we can see that the full understanding and proper interpretation of a test score has both a past and a future reference to specific real-life contexts.

It is now widely recognized in psychometrics that all cognitive tests measure *developed abilities*, which reflect the individual's learning history. This is equally true of tests traditionally labeled "aptitude tests" and those labeled "achievement tests." The two types of tests differ principally in the degree to which the requisite prior learning is specified and controlled (Anastasi, 1980; 1984; 1988, pp. 411–415).

The concept of developed abilities is also helpful in examining the widely debated question of *test bias*. The goal is for tests to be free from cultural bias against any group with which the tests are used. This does not mean that there can be no group differences in test scores. Such differences may correctly reflect differences in antecedent development of the skills and knowledge covered by the particular test, which may also be required for the criterion performance that the test is designed to assess—in a course of study, a job, or other real-life context. Essentially, a test is free from bias and is equally fair to two groups if its scores have the same validity for both groups and do not underpredict the performance of either group. In terms of the familiar regression model, this refers to the avoidance of slope bias and intercept bias (see Anastasi, 1988, pp. 193–201 for fuller discussion and references).

Integration of Cognitive and Affective Data

Another relevant idea contributed by psychological research concerns the interrelations of different behavior domains (for further discussion and references, see Anastasi, 1985b; 1988, pp. 368–370). We commonly think of different tests as assessing either abilities or personality—the latter covering such areas as motivation, emotion, interests, attitudes, values. There is increasing evidence of mutual influence between these two major

behavioral domains. Nor is this influence limited to immediate performance, as when a person tries harder or persists longer on a task that interests him or in an activity that ranks high in her value system. The influence is also evident in the development of traits over the life span. One way that motivation and other affective variables may contribute to the development of aptitudes is through the cumulative amount of time that the individual spends on a particular kind of activity relative to other, competing activities.

The effect of sheer time-on-task is enhanced by attention control. What one attends to, how deeply attention is focused, and how long attention is sustained contribute to one's cognitive growth. The selectivity of attention leads to selective learning—and this selection will differ among persons exposed to the same immediate situation. Such selective learning, in turn, may influence the relative development of different aptitudes and thereby contribute to the formation of different trait patterns. Essentially, the several aspects of attention control serve to intensify the effect of time devoted to relevant activities, and hence increase its influence on aptitude development. How much time and attention does the individual spend on a particular kind of activity, such as studying a certain subject or carrying out certain job-related functions? Does this student devote more time to studying for the math class or for the English lit. class? Does this employee devote more attention to cultivating favorable interpersonal relations with fellow workers and subordinates or to figuring out an improved method for performing the work?

The relation between personality and intellect is reciprocal. Not only do personality characteristics affect intellectual development, but intellectual level also affects personality development. The success an individual attains in the development and use of his or her aptitudes is bound to influence that person's emotional adjustment, interpersonal relations, and self-concept. In the self-concept, we can see most clearly the mutual influence of aptitudes and personality traits. The child's achievement in school, on the playground, and in other situations helps to shape her or his self-concept; and this concept at any given stage influences his or her subsequent performance. In this respect, the self-concept operates as a sort of private self-fulfilling prophecy. From the standpoint of test score interpretation, what all this means is that the prediction of a person's subsequent development can be substantially improved by combining information about motivation and interests with information about aptitudes.

Evolving Concepts of Intelligence

As a final example of the contributions of current psychological knowledge to effective test use, I have chosen the changing concepts of intelligence. This choice seems appropriate for two reasons: (a) the assessment of intelligence plays an important part in many types of counseling; and (b) among test users in general, there is still considerable misunderstanding about the nature of intelligence and what so-called intelligence tests measure. For several decades after the rise and popularization of intelligence tests, the term *intelligence* was burdened by excess meanings that accounted for common misinterpretations of test scores and misuses of tests. This situation led to the banning of intelligence tests in several school districts and to the elimination of the word *intelligence* from the titles of most recently developed or revised tests.

More recently, there has been a revival of interest in more sophisticated redefinitions of intelligence and a growing recognition of the contributions that appropriate measures of intelligence can make to the solution of practical problems. Intelligence is not a single, unitary ability, but rather a composite of several functions. The term denotes that combination of abilities required for survival and advancement within a particular culture. It follows that the specific abilities included in this composite, as well as their relative weights, vary with time and place. In different cultures and at different historical periods within the same culture, the qualifications for successful achievement differ. The changing composition of intelligence can also be seen within the life span of the individual, from infancy to late adulthood. One's relative ability tends to increase with age in those functions whose value is emphasized by one's experiential context; and it tends to decrease in those functions whose value is deemphasized.

Most well-known intelligence tests designed for school-age children or adults measure largely verbal abilities; to a lesser extent, they also cover abilities to deal with numerical and other abstract symbols. These are the abilities that predominate in school learning. Therefore, such intelligence tests can be regarded as measures of scholastic aptitude or school learning. Performance on these tests is both a reflection of prior educational achievement and a predictor of subsequent educational progress. Because the functions taught in school are of basic importance in modern, technologically advanced cultures, the score on a test of academic intelligence is also a partial predictor of performance in many occupations and other spheres of daily life. Much of our information about what intelligence tests measure comes from practical studies of the utility of tests in predicting educational and occupational achievement.

At a more theoretical level, basic research on the nature of intelligence has been proceeding apace. One approach is through the statistical procedures of factor analysis (Anastasi 1988, pp. 374–390). The controversy over Spearman's g versus the group factors or separate aptitudes proposed by Thurstone and others flourished in the 1920s and 1930s. Recently, this controversy has been revived and has received considerable attention in the popular media.

In trying to work our way through this tangle of conflicting claims, we should bear in mind at least two points. First, the general factor identified in any one battery has often been loosely described as Spearman's g, suggesting a comprehensive general ability that underlies all intellectual activity. Actually, it represents only a general factor common to the tests in that battery. To conclude from such an analysis that a given test is heavily loaded with Spearman's g is misleading. It would be more meaningful to say that the general factor identified in that battery is heavily loaded with what that test measures, and this can be specified by examining the content of that test (e.g., verbal comprehension, mechanical aptitude, or whatever). This is what is normally done in naming any factor identified in a factor analysis—one looks at the test or tests in which the factor is heavily loaded and names the factor accordingly. The same procedure should be followed in naming a factor common to the whole battery.

The second point pertains to *why* factor analysis is conducted. Factor analysis is no longer regarded as a means of searching for the primary, fixed, universal units of behavior, but rather as a method of organizing empirical data into useful categories through an analysis of behavioral consistencies. Like the test scores from which they were derived, factors are descriptive, not explanatory; they do *not* represent underlying causal entities. Interest has shifted to the conditions in the individual's learning history that lead to the formation of factors or traits. What brings about the particular behavioral relationships that lead to identifiable and differentiable ability constructs, such as verbal comprehension or numerical reasoning (Anastasi 1970, 1983, 1986b).

Once we recognize the descriptive nature of factors, we see that the description could occur at different levels. More and more, we are coming to think in terms of a hierarchical model of factors or abilities; at the top is a general factor; at the next level are broad group factors, similar to some of Thurstone's primary mental abilities; these major group factors subdivide into narrower group factors at one or more levels; the factors specific to each measure or indicator are at the bottom level. Different theories focus on one or another level of this comprehensive hierarchical model. No one level, however, need be regarded as of primary importance. Rather, each test constructor or test user should select the level most appropriate for her or his purpose.

Another approach for investigating the nature of human intelligence is that of cognitive psychology.[3] This is a more recent and rapidly spreading development in psychology as a whole. From the standpoint of testing, the principal contribution of cognitive psychology is its concern with what the individual does when performing an intellectual task. Cognitive research concentrates on the *processes* rather than the *products* of thinking. In contrast, test performance typically assesses the products, as reported in test scores. Although interest in processes is not new in the history of psychometrics, cognitive psychologists have carried the techniques of process analysis to new heights of refinement and sophistication. Knowledge about the processes an individual uses in solving problems or performing intellectual tasks is especially useful in diagnostic testing, because it can help to pinpoint the sources of an individual's difficulties. It is also highly relevant to the designing of training programs and other interventions to fit individual needs. Recognizing that what intelligence tests measure is not a fixed or unchanging entity within the individual, psychologists in several countries have been exploring training procedures for improving intelligence.[4]

Summary

In the proper and effective application of psychological tests, the counselor (among other test users) plays a prominent role. A major reason for the misuse of tests is inadequate or outdated knowledge about both the statistical aspects of testing technology and the psychological findings regarding the behavior assessed by the tests. Because advances in both kinds of knowledge are progressing rapidly, it is essential for test users to keep abreast of relevant developments in both areas. These needs of test users are receiving increasing attention through such channels as professional journals and other widely available publications, association meetings, refresher courses, and workshops. It is well to remember that many tests users may have completed their formal course training as much as a decade back, in courses taught by instructors whose own training may have been even further outdated. Just as old scores in the test taker's file need to be updated, so do old courses in the test user's educational history.

Notes

1. It is noteworthy that, in this edition, the last word in the title was changed from "tests" to "testing."
2. An unusually detailed and thoughtful analysis of validity from diverse angles can be found in Messick (1989).
3. See, e.g., Embretson (1983, 1986), Hunt (1985), Simon (1976), Sternberg (1981, 1984). For brief overview and additional references, see Anastasi (1988, pp. 159–161).
4. For brief overview and references, see Anastasi (1988, pp. 364–367).

References

Anastasi, A. (1970). On the formation of psychological traits. *American Psychologist, 25,* 899–910.

Anastasi, A. (1980). Abilities and the measurement of achievement. In W. B. Schrader (Ed.), *Measuring achievement: Progress over a decade* (pp. 1–10). San Francisco: Jossey-Bass.

Anastasi, A. (1983). Evolving trait concepts. *American Psychologist, 38,* 175–184.

Anastasi, A. (1984). Aptitude and achievement tests: The curious case of the Indestructible Strawperson. In B.S. Plake (Ed.), *Social and technical issues in testing: Implications for test construction and usage* (pp. 129–140). Hillsdale, NJ: Erlbaum.

Anastasi, A. (1985a). Interpreting scores from multiscore batteries. *Journal of Counseling and Development, 64,* 84–86.

Anastasi, A. (1985b). Reciprocal relations between cognitive and affective development: With implications for sex differences. In T.B. Sonderegger (Ed.), *Psychology and Gender* (Nebraska Symposium on Motivation. Vol. 32, pp. 1–35). Lincoln: University of Nebraska Press.

Anastasi, A. (1986a). Evolving concepts of test validation. *Annual Review of Psychology, 37,* 1–15.

Anastasi, A. (1986b). Experiential structuring of psychological traits. *Developmental Review, 6,* 181–202.

Anastasi, A. (1988). *Psychological testing* (6th ed.). New York: Macmillan.

Anastasi, A. (in press). The test user qualifications project: An evaluation. *American Psychologist.*

Butcher, J.N. (Ed.). (1987). *Computerized psychological assessment: A practitioner's guide.* New York Basic Books.

Embretson, S.E. (1983). Construct validity: Construct representation versus nomothetic span. *Psychological Bulletin, 93,* 179–197.

Embretson, S.E. (1986). Intelligence and its measurement: Extending contemporary theory to existing tests. In R. J. Sternberg (Ed.). *Advances in the psychology of human intelligence* (Vol. 3, pp. 355–368). Hillsdale, NJ: Erlbaum.

Eyde, L.D., Moreland, K.L., Robertson, G. J., Primoff, E.S., & Most, R.B. (1988). Test user qualifications: A data-based approach to promoting good test use. Issues in Scientific Psychology (Report of the Test User Qualifications Working Group of the Joint Committee on Testing Practices). Washington, DC: American Psychological Association.

Eyde, L.D., Moreland, K.L., Robertson, G. J., Primoff, E.S., & Most, R.B. (in press). Test user qualifications: Overview of a data-based project on promoting good test use. *American Psychologist.*

Guidelines for computer-based tests and interpretations. (1986). Washington, DC: American Psychological Association.

Henry, R.A., & Hulin, C.L. (1987). Stability of skilled performance across time: Some generalizations and limitations on utilities. *Journal of Applied Psychology, 72,* 457–462.

Hunt, E. (1985). Verbal ability. In R.J. Sternberg (Ed.), *Human abilities: An information-processing approach* (pp. 31–58). New York: Freeman.

Jackson, D.N. (1970). A sequential system for personality scale development. In C.D. Spielberger (Ed.), *Current topics in clinical and community psychology* (Vol. 2, pp. 61–96). Orlando, FL: Academic Press.

Jackson, D.N. (1973). Structured personality assessment. In B. B. Wolman (Ed.), *Handbook of general psychology* (pp. 775–792). Englewood Cliffs, NJ: Prentice-Hall.

Lambert, N.M. (1989, August). The crisis in measurement literacy in psychology and education. Invited address presented at the annual convention of the American Psychological Association, New Orleans, LA.

Messick, S. (1980). Test validity and the ethics of assessment. *American Psychologist, 35,* 1012–1027.

Messick, S. (1988). The once and future issues of validity: Assessing the meaning and consequences of measurement. In H. Wainer & H. Braun (Eds.), *Test validity* (pp. 35–45). Hillside, NJ: Erlbaum.

Messick, S. (1989). Validity. In R.L. Linn (Ed.), *Educational measurement* (3rd ed., pp. 13–103). New York: Macmillan.

Messick, S. (1991). Validity of test interpretation and use. In M.C. Alkin (Ed.), *Encyclopedia of education research* (6th ed.). New York: Macmillan.

Simon, H.A. (1976). Identifying basic abilities underlying intelligent performance of complex tasks. In L.B. Resnick (Ed.), *The Nature of Intelligence* (pp. 65–98). Hillsdale, NJ: Erlbaum.

Standards for educational and psychological testing. (1985). Washington, DC: American Psychological Association.

Sternberg, R.J. (1981). Testing and cognitive psychology. *American Psychologist, 36,* 1001–1011.

Sternberg, R.J. (1984). What cognitive psychology can (and cannot) do for test development. In B.S. Plake (Ed.), *Social and technical issues in testing: Implications for test construction and usage* (pp. 39–60). Hillsdale, NJ: Erlbaum.

Sticht, T.G. (Ed.). (1975). *Reading for working: A functional literacy anthology.* Alexandria, VA: Human Resources Research Organization.

Sundberg, N.D., Snowden, L.R., & Reynolds, W.M. (1978). Toward assessment of personal competence and incompetence in life situations. *Annual Review of Psychology, 29,* 179–221.

Technical recommendations for psychological tests and diagnostic techniques. (1954). Washington, DC: American Psychological Association.

Tyler, B., & Miller, K. (1986). The use of tests by psychologists: Report on a survey of BPS members. *Bulletin of the British Psychological Society, 39,* 405–410.

Concluding Comments

Do Anastasi's Comments Appear Reasonable?

Have you ever taken a psychological test from a counselor or psychotherapist? Did the individual follow the guidelines laid out by Anne Anastasi? If not, was the testing session better or worse than the one she described? Anastasi's suggestions are directed toward ensuring that the test user accurately communicates the way that test scores work. Again, assuming the test administrator did not do all that Professor Anastasi suggested, would some changes along the lines she suggested have improved the situation?

Review Questions

1. What is the nature of an expert's tutorial in the field? Is there something in particular that characterizes such articles?
2. What is the role of the test user, and why is it important?
3. What are some of the misuses of tests, and some of the hazards, that Anastasi identifies?
4. What is test validity?
5. How does Anastasi suggest that intelligence and personality interrelate?
6. What is the distinction between ability and achievement tests, and how has it changed over the years?

5

Exploring Parts of Personality with a Quasi-Experimental Design

Reading an Empirical Research Report

The most common type of peer-reviewed journal article in the sciences is the empirical research report. An empirical report is a written description of a study or studies that an author or authors have conducted. It is the workhorse of the scientific literature because it represents the point where knowledge is tested against the influences, actions, and other qualities of the real world.

Because these articles are so central and important to the field, it is worth reviewing how they come about. An empirical report typically begins when researchers decide they wish to find an answer to a question, such as, "What kinds of people like to study abroad?" The question may involve wanting to know more about the relationships among a set of (personality) variables, such as the traits of extroversion and friendliness, or it may involve testing a specific hypothesis about how certain variables of interest will behave under some conditions—for example, how an extrovert will behave on an airplane. To test their questions, called hypotheses, researchers design a study and then conduct it, collecting data, analyzing the data, and drawing conclusions about whether or not their hypothesis was correct. After the studies are carried out, the researcher(s) write up a report and submit it to a journal.

When a journal editor receives the manuscript, it is sent out to other scientists with expertise in the area who read the study and comment on it. Based on those comments, the editor makes a decision to accept or reject the study for the journal, or to invite a revised submission. The revision process helps the author add in necessary detail (and eliminate unnecessary detail), clarify points, weed out improper claims, and make sure the correct claims are being made. This is called the "peer-review process."

It is worth noting that empirical reports take on a variety of forms. They vary, for example, from the simple to the complex. At the simple end might be a study with a focused hypothesis, conducted by a single experimenter, who reports just a few statistical results. At the complex end might be a sophisticated or hard-to-examine hypothesis, examined by teams of researchers at multiple locations, involving multiple studies and experiments, and involving complex statistical tests.

The best journals can accept only a very few of the best research reports. Because the articles accepted in those journals often must please a number of hard-to-please reviewers, the best journals also tend to be somewhat conservative in what they will publish. For that reason, many other very good journals often publish equally important papers. There is a level of paper, however, that simply does not meet scientific standards, and will not be published by any reputable journal.

Empirical reports are divided into several parts. The "Introduction" sets out the problem and indicates how the research program will address it. The "Background" section fills in additional details about the research in the area and the procedures or measures encountered in it. The "Study" or "Experiment" section describes the methods employed to study the problem in some detail. The "Results" section reports statistical findings. Lastly, the "Discussion" section attempts to integrate the findings in the current literature.

One kind of empirical report is the quasi-experimental design. In a true experimental design, people are assigned randomly to groups, and each group gets a different treatment (e.g., people assigned to one group might take a course in psychology; those in the control group might take a different course). The experimenter then observes psychological differences between the two groups, and tries to characterize how the treatment (the course in psychology) changed one group.

In the quasi-experimental design, by contrast, there is no random assignment to groups; rather, the experimenter(s) identify already existing groups: e.g., college students who enrolled in a psychology course and those who didn't, and then, as before, differences between the groups on one or more psychological variables are examined. The quasi-experimental design is useful when the researcher wants to understand the difference between already-formed or naturally occurring groups. Its drawback, relative to a true experimental design, is that there may be a third variable that causes a difference between groups (e.g., socio-economic status) that is uncontrolled.

Significance of the Reading

The present article is an example of a research study—and, in particular, of a quasi-experimental study. The study examines the traits of need for achievement and sensation seeking, and whether students who study abroad, compared to students who do not, are different in those two traits. The need for achievement and sensation seeking represent two personality variables of interest. Studying abroad is the life criterion. The paper is reminiscent of the expression, "good things come in small packages," for it is very short, and yet gets the job done.

The Watch List

Because of its brevity, the authors have not used headings to mark off separate parts of the article. Nonetheless, a careful reader will be able to make out: (a) a combined Introduction and Background section, (b) a Methods section (which says, simply, that questionnaires containing the scales were administered to a sample of 378 participants, (c) a Results section, and then (d) the Discussion.

When you get to the Results section you will encounter some statistical abbreviations which represent standard APA style. If you have taken statistics, you will remember that "t" represents a test for the difference between two means. When the authors refer to ts, they are referring to several tests of the difference between two means. The number following the t in parentheses represents the degrees of freedom employed to conduct the statistical test. Finally, the t is assigned a value (after the = sign). Generally speaking, t values greater than 1.96, in this context, can be interpreted as representing a difference between the groups that would be unlikely to happen by chance ... i.e., a real difference. So, for example, "$t(152) = 2.78$" means that a statistical test called a t-test was conducted for the difference between two means, say, between study-abroad students and stay-at-home students on extraversion. The t was tested using 152 degrees of freedom (this is related to the sample size), and its value, 2.78, indicates that the difference in means was large enough that it was unlikely to have occurred by chance alone. The conclusion is that study-abroad students are different from other students.

Sensation Seeking and Need for Achievement among Study-Abroad Students

by Marvin L. Schroth and William A. McCormack

Source: Schroth, M.L. & McCormack, W.A. (2000). Sensation seeking and need for achievement among study-abroad students. *Journal of Social Psychology, 140,* 533–555.

Anderson (1995), in a major review of the literature, noted the lack of a comprehensive account for the process of cross-cultural adaptation. In the present study, we proposed that two personality dimensions, sensation seeking (Zuckerman, Eysenck, & Eysenck, 1978) and need for achievement (McClelland, Atkinson, Clark, & Cowell, 1953) may provide useful heuristics with which to interpret cross-cultural phenomena. Our focus was an examination of sensation-seeking and need-for-achievement personality traits among alumni from 14 countries in the California State University's International Program. Although most of the students spent an entire academic year abroad, some spent only one semester. The alumni had studied in Europe, Asia, Africa, Latin America, or the Middle East.

Sensation seeking is characterized by risk taking and a need for a variety of different sensations and experiences. The Sensation Seeking Scale, Form 5 (Zuckerman et al., 1978), consists of four subscales: Thrill and Adventure Seeking, which measures the desire to engage in sports and activities involving danger or speed; Experience Seeking, which measures the desire for unusual sensations or experiences associated with a nonconformist life style; Disinhibition, which measures the desire for social and sexual experiences as expressed in social drinking, partying, and a variety of sexual partners; and Boredom Susceptibility, which measures aversion to repetition, routine, and dull people. A total score is derived from the summation of the four subscale scores.

Need for achievement (McClelland et al., 1953) purports to measure intrinsic achievement motivation.

Helmreich and Spence's (1978) Work and Family Orientation Questionnaire measures three dimensions of achievement motivation by the following subscales: Work, which measures willingness to work hard; Mastery, which measures the preference for difficult tasks and the desire for excellence; Competitiveness, which measures the desire to compete against others.

In all, 378 participants (127 men, 251 women; mean age = 24.79 years, SD = 4.21) returned completed questionnaire forms. We set all statistical results for the present study at the .05 level of significance. Comparisons of the present study-abroad sample with a U.S. college sample in a previous study (Zuckerman, Kuhlman, Thornquest, & Kiers, 1991) on their scores on the Sensation Seeking Scale revealed the following results: The study-abroad men had significantly higher scores on the Experience Seeking subscale but lower scores on the Thrill and Adventure Seeking, Disinhibition, and Boredom Susceptibility subscales and on total scores, $ts(304)$ = 2.19-5.67. The study-abroad women had significantly higher scores on the Experience Seeking subscale than the U.S. college women, and the U.S. college women scored significantly higher on the Thrill and Adventure Seeking and Disinhibition subscales and on total scores, $ts(597)$ = 2.11–11.15. We found no significant differences between the female samples on the Boredom Susceptibility subscale, $t(597) > 1$.

On the Work, Mastery, and Competitiveness subscales, the study-abroad men had scores significantly higher than the norms for a comparable U.S. population in a previous study (Schroth & Andrew, 1987), $ts(279)$

Journal of Social Psychology, 140, 533–555, 2000. Reprinted with permission of the Helen Dwight Reid Educational Foundation. Published by Heldref Publications, 1319 Eighteenth St., NW, Washington, DC 20036-1802. Copyright © 2000.

= 6.45–27.40. The study-abroad women also had scores significantly higher than those of their U.S. college counterparts, $ts(391) = 9.54–27.28$

Motivational and demographic profiles emerge from the present data. In terms of sensation seeking, the present sample's low scores on Thrill and Adventure Seeking, Disinhibition, and Boredom Susceptibility subscales suggest they were serious young scholars who sought experiences not available at home. The finding does not fit the stereotype of sensation seekers in search of dangerous activities, parties, and so forth (Zuckerman, 1994). Instead, the study-abroad students' high scores on the Experience Seeking subscale suggest that their needs consist of seeking new experiences through the mind and senses by traveling abroad.

The selective nature of the International Program probably explains the higher scores on the Work, Mastery, and Competitiveness subscales of the alumni when compared with the U.S. norms. Self-selection may also have played a role, because for most students, a sojourn abroad entails considerable emotional and financial sacrifice. Given the foregoing caveats, it seems reasonable to speculate that the present results may generalize to other cross-cultural populations such as the Peace Corps and to professional groups such as anthropologists.

In her comprehensive review of the cross-cultural literature of adaptation, Anderson (1995) lamented the fact that research to solve the problems of cultural adaptation has superseded efforts to understand the process itself. She noted that investigators have limited themselves to particular subgroups—exchange students, Peace Corps volunteers, and others—with the result that different models have led to different findings and incomparability of results, which are isolated from the broad stream of psychological-adjustment literature.

The unique type of experience seeking that emerged in the present study, coupled with achievement motivation, may provide heuristics with which to interpret different kinds of cross-cultural data associated with tourism, volunteer work, study abroad, or all of the foregoing. The present data also provide inferences with which to speculate about the cognitive processes that may explain different ways that individuals respond to cross-cultural situations.

References

Anderson, L. (1995). A new look at an old construct: Cross-cultural adaptation. *International Journal of Intercultural Relations, 18*, 293–328.

Helmreich, R.L., & Spence, J.T. (1978). The Work and Family Orientation Questionnaire: An objective instrument to assess components of achievement motivation and attitudes toward family and careers. In *JASS catalog of selected documents in psychology*. Washington, DC: American Psychological Association.

McClelland, D.C., Atkinson, J.W., Clark, R.A., & Cowell, E.L. (1953). *The achievement motive*. New York: Appleton-Century-Crofts.

Schroth, M.L., & Andrew, D.F. (1987). Study of need-achievement motivation among Hawaiian college students. *Perceptual and Motor Skills, 64*, 1261–1262.

Zuckerman, M. (1994). Behavioral expressions and biosocial bases of sensation seeking. New York: Cambridge University Press.

Zuckerman, M., Eysenck, S., & Sysenck, H.J. (1978). Sensation seeking in England and America: Cross-cultural, age and sex comparisons. *Journal of Counseling and Clinical Psychology, 46*, 130–149.

Zuckerman, M., Kuhlman, D.M., Thornquest, M., & Kiers, H. (1991). Five (or three) robust questionnaire scale factors of personality without culture. *Personality and Individual Differences, 12*, 929–941.

Concluding Comments

The Article's Implications

Knowing this general finding, would it affect how you would talk to a study-abroad participant the next time you spoke to one? Would it suggest, for example, a particular kind of conversation you might want to have with such an individual or a question you might ask? Do you find it useful to modify how you talk to someone based on some knowledge of their possible psychological characteristics, or is that troublesome to you?

Review Questions

1. What are the major parts of a peer-reviewed article?
2. What is a *t*-test used for?
3. The article is concerned with the need for achievement. Why do you think the authors believed that would be related to study abroad?
4. The article also is concerned with sensation-seeking. Again, why do you think the authors believed that would be related to study abroad?
5. The authors studied a special group: alumni who had participated in the California State University's International Program. Do you think that is a good sample? An interesting one?
6. The authors' findings indicate that only some aspects of sensation-seeking are related to study abroad. What were those and what does it say about study abroad students?

6

Exploring Parts of Personality
with a Field Study

Reading about a Field Study

As noted in Chapter 5, the most common type of scientific journal article reports empirical findings. An empirical report is a written description of an investigation by a researcher or researchers that involves collecting data about the real world. Such articles are the workhorse of the scientific literature because they represent the point at which knowledge is tested against the influences, actions, and other qualities of the real world.

Because these empirical articles are so central and important to the field, it is worth understanding some of the varieties of empirical studies that exist. One such kind of study is the field study. A field study, which is sometimes called a field experiment, is one in which a relationship is studied in a natural environment such as a mall, a parking lot, or a nursing home (Cozby, 2001; Sommer & Sommer, 1997). In one such study, researchers proposed a personality dynamic by which people seek to bask in the reflected glory of an institution—such as a sports team of a university. The researchers sampled the number of times that students wore clothing that identified their school after their football team won, and after it lost. Students more frequently wore the school-identifying apparel after the team won. They also exhibited a tendency to refer to the team as "we" (as opposed to "they") after the team won (Cialdini et al., 1976). Employing a play on words regarding the field study idea, the subtitle of the article was, "Three (football) Field Studies."

Most designs in field studies are quasi-experimental. Recall that in the quasi-experimental design there is no random assignment to groups; rather, the experimenter(s) identify already existing groups such as college students who are on campus after the football team wins or loses. Then, the differences between groups on one or more psychological variables are examined. Sometimes such designs are called ex post facto, meaning after the fact. That is because the groups are formed not through random assignment, but after something has happened for the groups to form (Cozby, 2001).

To review another idea, empirical reports are divided into several parts. The Introduction sets out the problem and indicates how the research program will address it. The Background section fills in additional details about the nature of research in the area. The "Study" or "Experiment" section describes in some detail the methods and procedures employed to study the problem. The "Results" section reports statistical findings. The "Discussion" section attempts to integrate the findings in the current literature. An optional "Conclusion" section may follow.

Significance of the Reading

The article included here reports a field study concerning study habits and extraversion. This article, "Study Habits and Eysenck's Theory of Extraversion-Introversion," appeared in the *Journal of Research in Personality*, the official journal of the Association of Research in Personality, and one of the central journals in the field. About 200 studies investigate the relation between personality and study habits (there are more than 2,300 articles with "study habits" in the title, abstract, or listed as key word). As a consequence, any single contribution is a modest one. Modest though any single contribution is, a great deal of time and work is necessary for even a single study. A typical study such as the one featured here can require months of preparation, months to conduct, a year or more to write, a year or more to go through the peer-review process, and finally a year's wait to be published! It is not uncommon for an empirical piece to take about 4 years from beginning to end (where the end—one hopes—is being published).

To tie together the pre-existing research literature, the introduction and background sections of an article are intended to inform the reader about the existing scientific literature and how this specific study fits in. Campbell and Hawley's article, for example, provides a useful look at the nature of extraversion as described by Hans Eysenck, and its potential relations to studying. The authors are careful to indicate research publications related to extraversion and studying that were available at the time they conducted their research, as well as where research was lacking. Researchers undertaking follow-up studies would be likely to use Campbell and Hawley's work as one review when considering what kinds of studies were needed next.

The Watch List

The present article studies the trait of extraversion-introversion in relation to study habits in a library. The article is a field study in that the researchers did their data collection in a library. Two samples are collected and the paper also employs a combined sample (referred to also as sample 3).

The authors of this study employ analysis of variance, and an F-test to determine the psychological significance of differences between and among group means. Analysis of variance is a technique for testing the difference between two or more group means. It can also be used—and the authors use it—for testing the differences among two groups across different conditions. At one point in the results, for example, the authors say:

The first hypothesis was tested by performing separate 2 (Floors 1 and 3 vs. 2) x 2 (Sex) analyses of variance for each sample and for the two samples combined, with extraversion scores as the depen-dent variable.

In simplified statistical language, the authors are saying that they calculated average levels of extraversion for groups of people in varying conditions: the mean for male students on Floor 2 of the library, the mean for female students on Floor 2, the mean for male students on Floors 1 and 3 combined, and so forth. The analysis of variance technique compares these means.

Table 1 shows the similarities between the two samples on extraversion. Table 2 shows mean extraversion as a function of where a student likes to sit in the library. Students who have not yet had statistics can examine the mean extraversion scores to get a general understanding of what is going on. Those who have had statistics can make use of the statistical tests. Table 3 presents correlations (a measure of the strength of relationship between two variables) between various behaviors and preferences, and extraversion. The higher the correlation, the stronger the relationship. Correlations, often denoted as r in an article, of close to 1.0 or −1.0 represent very strong relationships. An $r = 1.0$ indicates that the two variables rise and fall together. An $r = -1.0$ indicates that as one variable rises, the other falls. An $r = 0.0$ indicates no relationship. The correlations here, between personality characteristics and preferred study conditions, are moderate and meaningful in strength.

Many of the numbers in the tables have superscripts associated with them. These superscripts indicate whether various results (e.g., the differences among the multiple groups in Table 2, or the level of correlation in Table 3) could be expected by chance alone, or whether it is more likely that they arose because of true differences in the psychological makeup of the students (i.e., are "statistically significant" in the mathematical lingo).

The article does an impressive job of indicating how even a simple personality variable can influence real life behavior.

Study Habits and Eysenck's Theory of Extraversion-Introversion

by John B. Campbell and Charles W. Hawley

Source: Campbell, J.B. & Hawley, C.W. (1982). Study habits and Eysenck's theory of extroversion-introversion. *Journal of Research in Personality, 16,* 139–146.

Sommer (1966) provided intriguing data on students' preferred study locations in college libraries. Students differed markedly in the architectural settings they preferred, and their self-reports indicated that the need to be with or away from other people, the amount of noise, and the presence or absence of distractions were major factors in determining study location. Although Sommer did not address the issue of personality characteristics which might covary with differential seating choice, he concluded that "the ideal library would contain a diversity of spaces that would meet the needs of introverts and extroverts" (1966, p. 246).

It is certainly logical to propose that extraversion-introversion is related to differential library study locations, particularly in the context of Eysenck's (1967) theory of personality. Eysenck discussed extraversion-introversion in terms of observed behavioral tendencies and presumed underlying neurological states. At the behavioral level, "the typical extravert is sociable...needs to have people to talk to, and does not like reading or studying by himself" (Eysenck & Eysenck, 1968, p. 6). Thus, the predicted relationship to study locations is explicit. A relationship between extraversion-introversion and study location can also be predicted at the level of the neurological theory. Eysenck (1967) proposed that introverts have a lower threshold of arousal of the reticular activating system than do extraverts. Thus, introverts experience greater arousal to lower intensity stimulation than do extraverts. However, introverts also experience transmarginal inhibition, a reduction in cortical arousal or excitation once stimulus intensity exceeds an optimal level, at lower levels of stimulus

intensity than do extraverts; thus, introverts are stimulus shy while extraverts are stimulus hungry. Indirect support for Eysenck's neurological theory is provided by work on sedation threshold (e.g., Claridge & Herrington, 1960; Shagass & Kerenyi, 1958; but see Brody (1972) and Claridge (1967) for important qualifiers), responsivity to increasing stimulus intensity (e.g., Hill, 1975; Ludvigh & Happ, 1974; Shigehisa & Symons, 1973; Stelmack & Campbell, 1974; Stelmack & Mandelzys, 1975), and habituation (Smith & Wigglesworth, 1978). Eysenck's neurological model suggests that introverts will prefer study locations which minimize external stimulation, while extraverts will prefer seating arrangements that provide stimulation. Morgenstern, Hodgson, and Law's (1974) finding that introverts functioned less efficiently in a learning task in the presence of distraction, while extraverts improved their performance in the presence of distraction, is consistent with this prediction.

Eysenck's conception of vigilance is also potentially of relevance to library study patterns. The basic prediction is that introverts will be superior to extraverts on laboratory tasks that entail noticing an atypical occurrence in a long and repetitive stimulus array (e.g., a moving clock hand that sporadically makes a double jump). There is considerable support for this prediction (e.g., Bakan, 1959; Claridge, 1967; Mackworth, 1961; again, see Brody (1972) regarding ambiguities in the prediction). Eysenck (1967) attributed this phenomenon to the accumulation during the task of reactive inhibition which eventually produces an involuntary rest pause (IRP). If the IRP coincides with the atypical stimulus, the subject will fail to notice and to respond to that stimulus. Since extraverts are considered more susceptible to inhibition, they should experience more IRPs and consequently exhibit poorer vigilance performance (see Eysenck (1964) regarding introvert-extravert differences in IRPs on a motor task). If Eysenck is correct, then the monotony of studying should prompt extraverts to experience more IRPs and consequently to take more "study breaks" than introverts; that is, the reactive inhibition which accumulates during studying should necessitate more frequent intermissions for extraverts. Activity during and duration of the study break may reflect the social milieu, but the origin and frequency of such study pauses should be attributable to neurological differences between introverts and extraverts. There is no direct support for this prediction in the literature; Estabrook and Sommer (1966) found that extraverts reported spending their study breaks with other people, but there was no reported difference between introverts and extraverts in frequency of study breaks.

In summary, given Eysenck's two-level theory, it follows that introverts should choose to study where the number of people and amount of external stimulation are minimized, while extraverts should prefer locations where socializing opportunities abound and the level of external stimulation is high. In addition, extraverts should take more frequent study breaks than introverts.

Everett Needham Case Library at Colgate University provides an excellent opportunity to test these predictions. The library has three floors, representing two distinct seating plans.[1] Floors 1 and 3 contain individual desk carrels and small tables interspersed among 8-ft stacks. As a consequence of the design, socializing opportunities are limited, and, the authors propose, so are noise and external stimulation in general. There are some structural differences between the two floors (e.g., windows on Floor 3 but not on Floor 1); consequently, the decision on whether to equate the two floors will be based on the similarity of occupants' ratings of their stimulation levels. Floor 2, by contrast, contains a single, large, L-shaped reading area connecting the refer-

ence and reserve desks; seating is on sofas and easy chairs or at large tables. There are no barriers to sight or sound; consequently, socializing is frequent, and the level of visual and auditory stimulation is high.

Combining information about the structure of the library with the predictions derived from Eysenck's theory, the following hypotheses were proposed. First, introverts will tend to study on Floors 1 and 3, while extraverts tend to study on Floor 2. Second, extraverts will take more frequent study breaks than introverts. Finally, in terms of subjects' self-reports of what factors influence their study location, there will be positive correlations between extraversion and preferred levels of noise, crowdedness, and socializing opportunities, as well as with rated importance of socializing opportunities in choosing a study site.

Method

Subjects

Two samples of undergraduates studying at the Case library were obtained, the first in late November of 1978 and the second in late November and early December of 1979.[2] The first sample contained 30 males and 27 females, while the second consisted of 29 males and 26 females. The number of subjects sampled from Floors 1, 2, and 3 of the library were 19, 19, and 19 for Sample 1 and 15, 24, and 16 for Sample 2. All subjects were between 18 and 22 years of age.

Procedure

The procedures followed for the two samples were identical. The data were collected between 8:00 and 10:00 PM on week nights by an equal number of male and female interviewers. Every tenth student on a given floor, beginning with the first person the experimenter saw and continuing around the floor in a predetermined sequence, was selected to participate. Potential subjects were told they had been randomly selected to answer a survey on study skills and were asked if they

---

[1] The three floors actually are labeled A-level, Main, and Second. In the interest of clarity, they will be referred to here as Floors 1, 2, and 3.

[2] The authors thank Christopher Gardner, Kathryn Krause, and Mary Loughlin for their assistance with the Sample 1 data, and Stephen Ketterer and Hilary Kopp for collecting the data in Sample 2.

would complete two brief questionnaires. The first questionnaire was Form A of the Eysenck Personality Inventory (EPI; Eysenck & Eysenck, 1968). Ten potential subjects were not included in the first sample and nine were not included in the second sample because their scores on the Lie scale of the EPI were 5 or higher. The second questionnaire focused on studying habits and preferences. Subjects were asked to indicate, on a scale from 0 to 10, the number of times per hour that they take "study breaks (e.g., talking to someone, looking around the room, walking around, etc.)" when studying in the library. On a 1-to-6 scale, subjects also indicated the extent to which they were using reserve and/or reference materials that night (since these materials are located on Floor 2); how noisy their study location was at the moment; what their preferred levels of noise, crowdedness, and socializing opportunity were in the library; and how important socializing opportunities were in choosing a study location. The two questionnaires were presented in counterbalanced order. All subjects indicated their campus address so that a debriefing letter could be sent to them when all data had been collected for that sample.

Table 1 Mean Noise Level Ratings

Floor	Sample 1	Sample 2
1	1.84[a]	1.79[b]
2	3.47	3.60
3	1.89[a]	2.12[b]

[a,b] Within samples, entries with identical superscripts do not differ significantly ($p < .05$), using Newman-Keuls a posteriori contrasts.

Results

The data for one subject (a male) from Sample 1 and five subjects (two males and three females) from Sample 2 were discarded prior to analysis because the subject had indicated that he/she was using reserve and/or reference materials exclusively (i.e., a response of 6 on the 6-point scale) on that visit to the library. These deletions were necessitated by the fact that the reserved and reference materials are located on Floor 2 of the library.

Mean extraversion scores did not differ for the two samples ($M1 = 13.80$, $M2 = 12.88$, $F (1.104) = 1.65$, $p = .20$). Both mean scores closely approximate the mean score of 13.1 reported for American college students in the EPI Manual (Eysenck & Eysenck, 1968). There were no significant differences between the two samples on any of the criterion variables.

A preliminary 3(Floors) x 2(Sex) analysis of variance was conducted for both samples, with perceived noise level of the studying location as the dependent variable. For both samples, neither the main effect for Sex nor the two-way interaction was significant. The main effects for Floors, however, were highly significant ($F(2,50) = 18.96$, $p < .001$ for Sample 1; $F (2,44) = 12.47$, $p < .001$ for Sample 2). As indicated in Table 1, the significance was attributable to the difference between the mean noise levels for Floor 2 and for Floors 1 and 3. These data support the appropriateness of treating Floors 1 and 3 of the library as equivalent, since it is assumed that it is the differing levels of stimulation (e.g., noise level) on the different floors that produce their differing attractiveness for introverts and extraverts.

The first hypothesis was tested by performing separate 2(Floors 1 and 3 vs 2) x 2(Sex) analyses of variance for each sample and for the two samples combined, with extraversion scores as the dependent variable. As indicated in Table 2, the hypothesis received consistent support; that is, individuals studying on Floor 2 of the library were, on the average, more extraverted than individuals studying on Floors 1 and 3. The interactions of Floor and Sex were not significant; however, there was a main effect for Sex in sample two ($F (1,46) = 5.86$, $p < .05$), such that the mean extraversion scores were 11.85 for males and 14.09 for females.

Table 2 Mean Extraversion Scores

Floor	Sample 1[a]	Sample 2[b]	Combined[c]
1, 3	13.13	12.00	12.63
2	15.10	14.20	14.64

[a] $F(1, 52) = 4.12$, $p < .05$.
[b] $F(1, 46) = 5.55$, $p < .05$.
[c] $F(1, 102) = 7.95$, $p < .01$.

The results relevant to the second and third hypotheses appear in Table 3. All correlations were positive, as predicted, and 13 of the 15 coefficients reached statistical significance. For two of the five criterion variables, however, there was a failure to replicate a significant correlation across samples. This problem was most flagrant, and most damaging theoretically, in the case of the Study Breaks variable. All correlations for the combined samples were statistically significant, but the lack of consistency was disconcerting. Thus, the data clearly and reliably support the predictions of relationships between extraversion and three of the four criterion variables involved in the third hypothesis (preferred noise level, importance of socializing opportunities, and preferred level of socializing opportunities), while the status of the relationship predicted in the second hypothesis between extraversion and the Study Breaks variable remains unclear.

Table 3 Correlations of Extraversion with Criteria

Criterion	Sample		
	1	2	Combined
Frequency of study breaks	.42**	.04	.24**
Preferred level of noise	.23*	.37**	.29**
Preferred level of crowdedness	.09	.34**	.20*
Importance of socializing opportunities	.43**	.41**	.41**
Preferred level of socializing opportunities	.40**	.28*	.31**
N	56	50	106

* p < .05, one-tailed

* p < .01, one-tailed

Discussion

Since none of the between-sample differences in levels of extraversion or any of the criterion variables were statistically significant, the inconsistencies in obtained patterns of correlations are not directly attributable to differences in the composition of the samples. It remains possible, however, that the fact that the second sample was obtained approximately 1 week closer to the end of the semester (which occurs after the second week in December) had an effect. That is, the nearness of paper deadlines and final exams may have encouraged students in Sample 2 to take or to report fewer study breaks. This is consistent with the trend ($F(1,104) = 1.30$, $p = .25$) for fewer study breaks in Sample 2 ($M1 = 3.79$, $M2 = 3.18$). Greater occupancy of the library might also increase the salience of levels of crowdedness for both extraverts and introverts in Sample 2, thereby strengthening the observed relationship of extraversion to crowdedness. This reasoning is ad hoc, however, and it does not mitigate the failure to find reliable relationships between extraversion and both number of study breaks and preferred levels of crowdedness.

These data provide mixed support for both levels of Eysenck's theory of extraversion. The predicted behavioral difference emerged in both samples, with extraverts occupying locations that provided greater stimulation. This effect appeared reliably, despite the fact that both samples were obtained at the end of an academic term, when increased difficulty of obtaining any seat in a library that seats approximately 25% of the student population might well force some students to occupy seats they would not normally prefer. This pressure, of course, worked against the prediction by encouraging randomized seating.

Although the behavioral effect is clear, the theoretical interpretation of the effect is ambiguous. Floors 1 and 3 of the library were distinguished from Floor 2 on the basis of rated noise levels or levels of stimulation. It is also possible, however, that the observed effect is attributable to increased socializing opportunities on Floor 2. This is an important issue. While the differential presence of extraverts and introverts on various floors clearly supports Eysenck's position, an explanation in terms of levels of noise or stimulation is consistent with the neurological theory, but an interpretation in terms of differential socializing opportunities is consistent with the behavioral level of the theory. Notice that the two levels of the theory are separable.

The pattern of correlations between extraversion and the five self-report criteria is of some assistance here. Both the Study Breaks and Preferred Noise Level variables were derived from the neurological model. The predicted correlation is observed consistently for the latter variable, but inconsistently for the former. As Monte (1980) points out, however, the concept of IRPs is more clearly related to Eysenck's (1957) early neurological model than to his current (Eysenck, 1967) model. In addition, it is possible that study breaks are sufficiently influenced by social distractions and pressures that they constitute a poor medium for testing predictions regarding IRPs.[3] The two Socializing Opportunities variables, which were derived from the behavioral model, consistently demonstrated the predicted positive correlation with extraversion. The Preferred Crowdedness Level variable, which could reflect either level of stimulation or socializing opportunities, correlated positively with extraversion in Sample 2 but not in Sample 1. Thus, the pattern of correlations is somewhat more supportive of the predictions derived from the behavioral level of the theory, but the difference certainly is not compelling.

In summary, the present data provide support for Eysenck's (1967) theory regarding behavioral differences between extraverts and introverts, and they are consistent with the existing literature; however, it is not clear whether the observed differences are attributable to differential preferences for levels of stimulation or to differential preferences for levels of socializing opportunities. Although Eysenck clearly proposes that the neurological differences manifest themselves in the behavioral differences, findings consistent with one level of the overall theory do not necessarily imply support for the other level. Despite their frequent confounding in naturally occurring situations, further attempts to determine the relationship between and relative contribution of the two levels of Eysenck's theory are needed.

References

Bakan, P. (1959) Extraversion-introversion and improvement in an auditory vigilance task. *British Journal of Psychology, 50*, 325-332.

Brody, N. (1972). *Personality: Research and theory.* New York: Academic Press.

Claridge, G.S. (1967). *Personality and arousal.* Oxford: Pergamon.

Claridge,G.S., & Herrington, R.N. Sedation (1960). Threshold, personality and the theory of neurosis. *Journal of Mental Science, 106*, 1568-1583.

Estabrook, M., & Sommer, R. (1966). Study habits and introversion-extroversion. *Psychological Reports, 19,* 750.

Eysenck, H.J. (1957). *The dynamics of anxiety and hysteria.* London: Routledge & Kegan Paul.

Eysenck, H.J. (1964). Involuntary rest pauses in tapping as a function of drive and personality. *Perceptual and Motor Skills, 18*, 173-174.

Eysenck, H.J. (1967). *The biological basis of personality.* Springfield, Ill.: Thomas.

Eysenck, H.J., & Eysenck, S.B.G. (1968). *Manual to the Eysenck Personality Inventory.* San Diego: Educational and Industrial Testing Service.

Hill, A.B. (1975). Extraversion and variety seeking in a monotonous task. *British Hournal of Psychology, 66*, 9-13.

Ludvigh, E.J, & Happ, D. (1974). Extraversion and preferred level of sensory stimulation. *British Journal of Psychology, 65, 359-365.*

Mackworth, H.N. (1961). Researches on the measurement of human performance. In H. W. Sinaiko (Ed.) , *Selected papers on human factors in the design and use of control systems.* New York: Dover.

Monte, C.F. (1980). *Beneath the mask* (2nd ed.). New York: Holt, Rinehart & Winston, 1980.

Morgenstern, F.S., Hodgson,R.J., & Law, J. (1974). Work efficiency and personality: A comparison of introverted and extraverted subjects exposed to conditions of distraction and distortion of stimulus in a learning task. *Ergonomics, 17,* 211-220.

Shagass, C., & Kerenyi, A.B. (1958). Neurophysiologic studies of personality. *Journal of Nervous and Mental Disease, 126,* 141-147.

Shigehisa, T., & Symons, J. (1973). Effects of intensity of visual stimulation on auditory sensitivity in relation to personality. *British Journal of Psychology, 64,* 205-213.

Smith, B.D., & Wigglesworth, M.J. (1978). Extraversion and neuroticism in orienting reflex dishabituation. *Journal of Research in Personality, 12,* 384-296.

Sommer, R. (1966). The ecology of privacy. *Library Quarterly, 36,* 234-248.

Stelmack, R.M., & Campbell, K.B. (1974). Extraversion and auditory sensitivity to high and low frequency. *Perceptual and Motor Skills, 38,* 875-879.

Stelmack, R.M., & Mandelzys, N. (1975). Extraversion and pupillary response to affective and taboo words. *Psychophysiology, 12,* 536-540.

---

[3] Thanks are due to the Editor for suggesting this point.

Concluding Comments

Some Observations

The preceding article indicates how even a difference in one personality trait can determine something as commonplace and frequent as a choice of seating. If one trait can help forecast such behavior, then, to be sure, studying many traits together could lead to greater insight into how and why people behave as they do.

Review Questions

1. Can you describe what a field study is and how it differs from other empirical approaches?
2. The introduction connects this article to past empirical studies. Name one or two functions that such an introduction serves.
3. The article argues that extraversion-introversion may be important for choice of a study location in the library. What are some of the reasons given? Are there locations aside from libraries where this might be an issue?
4. Three tables of results are provided. Which of them was the most interesting to you, and why?
5. Are the results of this study believable to you? If so, why or why not?

7

Reading Programmatic Research: Studies about the Self

Reading Programmatic Research

The term *programmatic research* refers to the idea that research should follow an organized plan of investigation and discovery. For example, a scientist interested in studying perfectionism might begin by reviewing various measures of perfectionism and then, if necessary, develop his or her own, improved measure of perfectionism. Next, using such a measure, the scientist might compare perfectionistic tendencies with other personality characteristics. While doing so, the scientist might branch out and examine the influence that perfectionism has on other aspects of the individual's life: For example, how does perfectionism help or hinder performance at certain jobs? How does it play out in a marriage? Programmatic research can be contrasted with research in which the scientist jumps from topic to topic with less of a coherent plan for how to draw the research areas and findings together.

Engaging in programmatic research has a number of advantages for a scientist. The scientist builds laboratory skills as he or she masters the procedures, methods, and statistics necessary to study a particular phenomenon. In addition, the full understanding of a phenomenon typically requires many related research studies; by conducting many such studies the scientist obtains a richer understanding of the empirical findings. The multiple replications (and lack of replications) also teach the researcher which claims in the area can be made with confidence. Programmatic research fosters better scientific writing as well. When a researcher writes a series of related scientific reports, he or she gains the experience necessary to communicate findings in the clearest and most interesting way. As the researcher grows more experienced and more knowledgeable he or she becomes recognized as an authority in the area.

From the reader's standpoint, reports of programmatic research can be distinguished from individual research reports. Reports of programmatic research summarize the many related studies conducted by the scientist, along with related studies conducted by others. Reports of programmatic research differ from a single empirical report. Programmatic research reports are reviews of empirical reports that stem primarily from one research laboratory and that are enriched by the studies of authors working in the same or related areas.

Most commonly, reports of programmatic research appear as book chapters in edited volumes on a larger topic. For example, a chapter reporting the results of a research program studying perfectionism might appear with other chapters focused on such topics as procrastination, naïve optimism, and, self-consciousness, in an edited volume on personality traits. In addition, however, there exist journals that specialize in publishing the best among such programmatic reports. These journals include the highly prestigious *Psychological Review* (if they are very theoretical), *Psychological Bulletin* (if the ideas organize empirical psychological literature), or the *American Psychologist* (if the programmatic research is of general interest to a broad spectrum of psychologists).

Significance of the Reading

Markus and Nurius' "Possible Selves" is a report of programmatic research. In particular, it is a report of a theoretically driven empirical research program. The theory involved concerns the idea that people carry within themselves images of who they could be—possible selves. Psychologists and educators often speak of self-images—the image of oneself as one actually is, or of who one would like to be. Markus and Nurius' article recognized a general class of such selves—possible selves—into which could be placed specific examples such as one's actual and ideal self. Moreover, the article paints a picture of these selves in terms that make them recognizable and come alive. At the same time the article is successful in integrating considerable research on the self.

The present article is a classic by many measures. For example, it appeared in the highly prestigious and selective *American Psychologist.* One mathematical index of the impact of an article is referred to as the article's citation count. A citation (in this sense) occurs when a new publication refers to the original article or book in question (American Psychological Association, 2001). For example, I just cited the *Publication Manual of the American Psychological Association,* and a full reference to the publication is listed within the references section at the end of this book.

When an article is particularly useful to the field, it is cited frequently by many different authors. For that reason, citations are generally considered good measures of the importance of an article (Over, 1982; Endler, Rushton, & Roediger, 1978). Most articles, sad to say, are never cited in later publications at all. This is reflected in the fact that the average citation across all psychology articles (when last checked) was .9 (White & White, 1973). A few very popular articles may be cited 50 times or 70 times. By its 15th anniversary, "Possible Selves" had been cited by other authors in psychology about 300 times. (The most frequently cited books and articles concern frequently employed statistical techniques; Sternberg, 1992.) So, for an article dealing with a general research area, this article is highly influential by a citation count.

The Watch List

The lead sentence of the article is followed by six citations to earlier works in the field. Later portions of the article continue to cite long lists of earlier publications. The large number of earlier publications cited reflects the authors' attempt to cover the most important work in a large, diverse field in which there had already been a great amount of work. To those knowledgeable in the field, these lists of citations also can be useful in clarifying the kinds of evidence that the authors have based their work on. To those intending to pursue research in the field, such citations can help direct them to earlier work of importance. Those who are encountering the field for the first time, however, may wish to skip over such lists, stopping, perhaps, to check on a familiar name such as Freud—and that can make sense at the start.

After defining possible selves in the second section of the article, the third major section concerns the authors' cognitive approach to possible selves. The authors are using the term *cognitive* broadly here to include many internal motivational, emotional, and cognitive processes that involve the processing of information. At the time they were writing, cognitive psychology was a dominant approach to the field and included much more than mere memory, judgment, and decision-making. By labeling their approach cognitive, the authors clarified that they were interested in internal mental processes as opposed to, for example, social behavioral outcomes, or biopsychological topics, and also signaled that their language would be the general language of mental processes rather than, say, employing the more specific terms of psychodynamic theory.

Moving to the section entitled, "Exploring the Possible Self," be prepared to encounter some statistical tables and results. In particular, the authors report a series of correlations, denoted by the letter "r" as well as reports of the number of participants in a given study, denoted by the letter "N." Those unfamiliar with statistics should remember that correlations range from -1 to 1, where an $r = 1.0$ represents a perfect positive relationship between two variables—that is, as one goes up so does the other and as one goes down so does the other; $r = -1.0$ represents a perfect negative relationship (e.g., as one goes up the other goes down), and $r = 0.0$ indicates no relationship between the two variables.

The section "Possible Selves as Incentives" makes mention of the Thematic Apperception Test, or TAT. The Thematic Apperception Test is a projective test in which the examiner shows a series of pictures to the test-taker and the test-taker responds by telling a story in response to each one. In these TAT research studies, the stories are evaluated according to the motives that the test-taker has expressed. Scores are often generated for certain specific motives such as the need for achievement, or affiliation (that is, friendship), or power.

The section "Possible Selves as Context for the Now Self" ties this work in with important, but more technical, cognitive findings. If you find yourself having some difficulty with this section, don't despair, as the argument returns to a more accessible level when the next section begins on Self-Concept Theory.

Possible Selves

by Hazel Markus and Paula Nurius

Source: Markus, H. & Nurius, P. (1986). Possible selves. *American Psychologist, 41*, 954–969.

Self-concept research has revealed the great diversity and complexity of self-knowledge and its importance in regulating behavior (cf. Carver & Scheier, 1982; Gergen, 1971; Greenwald & Pratkanis, 1984; Higgins, 1983; Kihlstrom & Cantor, 1984; McGuire & McGuire, 1982). But there is one critical domain of self-knowledge that remains unexplored. It is the domain of *possible selves*. This type of self-knowledge pertains to how individuals think about their potential and about their future. Possible selves are the ideal selves that we would very much like to become. They are also the selves we could become, and the selves we are afraid of becoming. The possible selves that are hoped for might include the successful self, the creative self, the rich self, the thin self, or the loved and admired self, whereas the dreaded possible selves could be the alone self, the depressed self, the incompetent self, the alcoholic self, the unemployed self, or the bag lady self.

An individual's repertoire of possible selves can be viewed as the cognitive manifestation of enduring goals, aspirations, motives, fears, and threats. Possible selves provide the specific self-relevant form, meaning, organization, and direction to these dynamics. As such, they provide the essential link between the self-concept and motivation.

The assistant professor who fears he or she will not become an associate professor carries with him or her much more than a shadowy, undifferentiated fear of not getting tenure. Instead the fear is personalized, and the professor is likely to have a well-elaborated possible self that represents this fear—the self as having failed, as looking for another job, as bitter, as a writer who can't get a novel published. Similarly, the person who hopes to lose 20 pounds does not harbor this hope in vague abstraction, but rather holds a vivid possible self—the self as thinner, more attractive, happier, with an altogether more pleasant life.

In this article we examine the theoretical features of possible selves and illustrate some of the important ways in which they mediate personal functioning. In particular, possible selves are linked to the dynamic properties of the self-concept—to motivation, to distortion, and to change, both momentary and enduring. A discussion of the nature and function of possible selves is followed by an exploration of the role of possible selves in a comprehensive theory of the self-concept.

Possible Selves: A Definition

Antecedents of Possible Selves

Possible selves derive from representations of the self in the past and they include representations of the self in the future. They are different and separable from the current or now selves, yet are intimately connected to them. Possible future selves, for example, are not just *any* set of imagined roles or states of being. Instead they represent specific, individually significant hopes, fears, and fantasies. I am *now* a psychologist, but I *could* be a restaurant owner, a marathon runner, a journalist, or the parent of a handicapped child. These possible selves are individualized or personalized, but they are also distinctly social. Many of these possible selves are the direct result of previous social comparisons in which the individual's own thoughts, feelings, characteristics, and behaviors have been contrasted to those of salient others. What others are now, I could become.

An individual is free to create any variety of possible selves, yet the pool of possible selves derives from the categories made salient by the individual's particular socio-cultural and historical context and from the models, images, and symbols provided by the media and by the individual's immediate social experiences. Possible selves thus have the potential to reveal the inventive and constructive nature of the self but they also reflect the extent to which the self is socially determined and constrained (cf. Elder, 1980; Meyer, 1985; Stryker, 1984). The 1984 Olympic games probably created powerful possible selves for some young runners. Many no doubt absorbed the performance of Carl Lewis within the realm of their own possible selves, just as Carl Lewis claimed to have used the early track victories of Jesse Owens to create a possible self and to give a specific cognitive form to his desire to become the world's fastest runner. Similarly Geraldine Ferraro fostered the creation of a new possible self, that of a political self, a leader self, for many American women. And James Fixx, the expert on running who died of a heart attack while jogging, was the source of a compelling negative possible self for many runners.

Past selves, to the extent that they may define an individual again in the future, can also be possible selves. An adult, for example, will never be an eight-year-old child again. Some critical aspects of the child self, however, may remain within the self-concept as a possible self (see Block, 1981; Brim & Kagan, 1980). And under some circumstances, this self-view may be activated and become influential in directing behavior, such as in a visit home over the holidays. The selves of the past that remain and that are carried within the self-concept as possible selves are representative of the individual's enduring concerns and the actions that gave rise to these concerns. Thus, the successful possible self may include the fact that "I once got the best grades in my class." The socially anxious possible self is linked with the memory that "I used to be afraid of people." And the unwanted possible self is tied to the painful image of always being "the last one chosen for the softball team." Development can be seen as a process of acquiring and then achieving or resisting certain possible selves. Through the selection and construction of possi-

ble selves individuals can be viewed as active producers of their own development (e.g., Kendall, Lerner, & Craighead, 1984; Lerner, 1982).

Consequences of Possible Selves: A Cognitive Approach

A focus on the self-knowledge that accompanies an individual's goals, fears, and threats is a natural extension of a cognitive approach to the study of the self-concept. In this approach the self-concept is viewed as a system of affective-cognitive structures (also called theories or schemas) about the self that lends structure and coherence to the individual's self-relevant experiences. (For a full discussion of these and related ideas, see Epstein, 1973; Greenwald & Pratkanis, 1984; Kihlstrom & Cantor, 1984; Markus & Sentis, 1982; Markus & Wurf, in press; Rogers, 1981.)

Self-schemas are constructed creatively and selectively from an individual's past experiences in a particular domain. They reflect personal concerns of enduring salience and investment, and they have been shown to have a systematic and pervasive influence on how information about the self is processed. In particular domains, these well-elaborated structures of the self shape the perceiver's expectations. More-over, they determine which stimuli are selected for attention, which stimuli are remembered, and what type of inferences are drawn (e.g., Greenwald & Pratkanis, 1984; Kihlstrom & Cantor, 1984; Markus, 1983; Markus & Sentis, 1982). In this way, the self-concept becomes a significant regulator of the individual's behavior. The recent empirical work from this cognitive perspective lends strong support to many ideas of the early self theorists (e.g., Allport, 1943; Kelly, 1955; Krech & Crutchfield, 1948; Snygg & Combs, 1949) who argued that the self-structure is the most important in the psychological field and is the one that organizes the individual's interpretations of the world.

Studies on the functions of self-knowledge have focused nearly exclusively on how well-substantiated or factual self-conceptions constrain information processing. But individuals also have ideas about themselves that are not as well anchored in social reality. They have ideas, beliefs, and images about their potential and about their goals, hopes, fears. This is particularly so in those domains that are important for self-definition. To be sure, this self-knowledge is of a different type than the self-knowledge of one's gender, or race, or the self-knowledge of one's preferences or habits. Most obviously, as representations of the self in future states, possible selves are the views of the self that often have not been verified or confirmed by social experience (cf. Epstein, 1973; Snyder, Tanke, & Berscheid, 1977; Swann, 1983). Yet self-knowledge of this type should not be dismissed, for it is entirely possible that this variety of self-knowledge also exerts a significant influence on individual functioning, and it is the purpose of this article to explore the nature of this influence. We suggest first that possible selves are important because they function as incentives for future behavior (i.e., they are selves to be approached or avoided), and second, because they provide an evaluative and interpretive context for the current view of self.

With respect to the first function, self-knowledge not only provides a set of interpretive frameworks for making sense of past behavior, it also provides the means-ends patterns for new behavior. Individuals' self-knowledge of what is possible for them to achieve is motivation as it is particularized and individualized; it serves to frame behavior, and to guide its course. In this role possible selves function as the personalized carriers (representations) of general aspirations, motives, and threats and of the associated affective states. They serve to select among future behaviors (i.e., they are selves to be approached or to be avoided).

The second important function of possible selves derives from their role in providing a context of additional meaning for the individual's current behavior. Attributes, abilities, and actions of the self are not evaluated in isolation. Their interpretation depends on the surrounding context of possibility. Thus, the student with a physician possible self will attach a different interpretation to a grade of A in organic chemistry than will someone without this possible self. Similarly, the person with the alone or lonely possible self is likely to imbue a broken lunch date with much greater negative significance than someone without this negative possible self. Possible selves furnish criteria against which outcomes are evaluated.

Further, because possible selves are not well-anchored in social experience, they comprise the self-knowledge that is the most vulnerable and responsive to changes in the environment. They are the first elements of the self-concept to absorb and reveal such change. As representations of potential, possible selves will thus be particularly sensitive to those situations that communicate new or inconsistent information about the self. A poor grade on an exam will not permanently challenge an individual's enduring sense of self as "intelligent" or "hardworking," but it will give temporary substance to a possible self as "drop-out" or "academic failure." And the activation of these possible selves will influence the individual's current self-evaluation of intelligence.

Related Approaches

The notion of self-concept extending both backward and forward through time appears in the literature in diverse forms. James (1910) used the term "potential social Me" and distinguished it from the "immediate present Me" and the "Me of the past." Freud (1925) wrote about the "ego ideal," which referred to the child's conception of what the parents consider morally good. For Horney (1950), neurosis occurred when the idealized self became the focus of the individual's thoughts, feelings, and actions. The concept of the "ideal self," the individual's view of "how I should be," was important in the work of Rogers (1951) and he claimed that the individual's self-regard depended on the discrepancy between the actual self and the ideal self. The notion of potential selves also intrigued Gergen (1972), and he has argued that their range and complexity have been ignored in the focus on the "central tendencies" of the self (p. 64). Similarly, Gordon (1968) analyzed the retrospective, current, and prospective elements of the self, and Schutz (1964) has discussed tenses of self, noting the difference between the Present Tense (acts in progress) and the Future Present Tense, which includes anticipated or imagined acts.

More recently, Levinson (1978) has described "the Dream" and has been concerned with the imagined possibilities of the self as motivating forces. The Dream is a personal construction that contains the "imagined self" associated with a variety of goals, aspirations, and values, both conscious and unconscious. With maturation, the Dream becomes cognitively refined and more motivationally powerful. Levinson, however, has focused on dreams; he has not analyzed nightmares or negative possibilities. Similarly, Cummings (1979) wrote of a personally salient "lost dream or hope" that when reinstated can serve as a powerful therapeutic procedure to overcome problems such as addiction, negativism, and lack of caring.

Recent reviews of the empirical literature on the self-concept from both the psychological and sociological perspective (e.g., Epstein, 1984; Gecas, 1982; Greenwald & Pratkanis, 1984; Suls, 1982; Zurcher, 1977), reveal that except for some limited attention to the "ideal self," the content of conceptions of the self, other than those of the current self, have not been emphasized. There have been a variety of efforts to empirically explore individuals' understanding of the future (e.g., Davids & Sidman, 1962; De Volder & Lens, 1982; Wallace, 1956), but this work has rarely been concerned with how the future is represented in the self-concept.

The link between the future and the self-concept is implicit in the writings of the symbolic interactionists who argue that the self as an organizer of behavior is always anticipating, always oriented to the future (Lindesmith & Strauss, 1956; Stryker, 1980). To Mead (1934), having a self implies the ability to rehearse possible courses of action depending on a reading of the other person's reactions and then being able to calibrate one's subsequent actions accordingly. Whenever individuals engage in this type of role taking, they are in the process of creating potential selves, and there can be as many of these selves as there are times when the self is the object of definition, expectation, or evaluation. Other sociological theorists extended Mead's idea and tackled directly the relation between the self (or identity) and motivation. Foote (1951), for example, believed that all motivation was a consequence of the individual's set of identities. The individual acts so as to express his or her identity: "Its products are ever-evolving self-conceptions" (p. 17), and "When doubt of identity creeps in, action is paralyzed" (p. 18). When action does manage to proceed with an uncertain identity, it is completely robbed of its meaning. More recently Stryker (1968, 1984) contended that identities continually seek validation and that the most important behavior is in the service of confirming particular identities. And the more important the identity, the more it is in need of validation.

Similarly, psychologists Gollwitzer and Wicklund (1985) have linked the self-concept to motivation through the concept of self-definitions. Self-definitions are construed primarily as goals or ideals and are described as conceptions of the self as having a readiness to engage in certain classes of behavior. And there are a number of recent theories of motivation that also can be interpreted as efforts to relate the self or the ego to specific actions. These theories conceptualize goals as a vital part of the self-concept, just as Erikson (1946, 1950) viewed the psychosocial crises as critical tasks of identity formation (see also Adler, 1929). Thus Greenwald (1982) referred to ego tasks, Little (1983) to personal objects, Cantor to life tasks (Cantor, Markus, Niedenthal, & Nurius, 1986), and Markus (1983) to self-schemas. Instead of focusing on how individuals expect to perform on a certain task (e.g., Atkinson, 1958; Lewin, Dembo, Festinger, & Sears, 1944), on the type of proximal goals they set (e.g., Bandura & Schunk, 1981; Manderlink & Harackiewicz, 1984), or on the cognitive representation of the goal object (e.g., Mischel & Baker, 1975), these theorists have focused more globally on what individuals hope to accomplish with their lives and what kind of people they would like to become as the significant elements of motivation.

The few empirical findings on what people believe is possible for them suggest that individuals do have access to this type of self-knowledge and are willing to report it, although these studies have focused almost exclusively on positive possibility. In a study of 12-year-old children, McGuire and Padawer-Singer (1976) asked the question "Tell us about yourself" and found that 12% of the sample mentioned "hopes and desires" and 18% mentioned career aspirations. Singer (1975) found that daydreams are often completely dominated by self-relevant images of the future. Rosenberg (1979) has investigated the "desired adult self" and asked questions such as "What personality would you like to have when you grow up?" Older children put great emphasis on interpersonal traits in describing their hoped for personality, whereas the younger children rely on social identities (groups, roles, statuses, or social categories). There have been only a few attempts to relate people's performance to what they believe is possible for them. Turner (1978; see also Willerman, Turner, & Peterson, 1976) noted that having respondents report what they are maximally capable of doing in a relevant situation rather than what they typically do or what they expect to do increases the size of the correlations between self-reports and subsequent behavior. And Gregory, Cialdini, and Carpenter (1982) found that many more people who imagined themselves with cable television subscribed to it than did those who simply listened to a persuasive message about its virtues.

The Working Self-Concept

In most theoretical statements, the self-concept is characterized as a complex dynamic phenomenon (e.g., Cantor & Kihlstrom, 1983; Epstein, 1973; Gergen, 1967; Greenwald, 1980; Kelly, 1955; McGuire, 1984; Mead, 1934; Rosenberg, 1979; Tesser & Campbell, 1984). Turner (1968), for example, discussed "the passing images of self arising and changing in every relationship the individual enters" (p. 94). Yet the empirical work, with a notable recent exception (see Higgins, 1983) lags far behind these very rich conceptualizations. The traditional view features the self-concept as a fairly uniform, monolithic structure, consistent over time, comprising some number of physical features or psychological structures that abstract the essential traits from the individual's past behavior.

Most self-concept inventories ask, in effect, who you are *now*, but they do not inquire who you want to be, or who you are afraid of becoming. The self-concept is a more expansive phenomenon than is reflected by the typical descriptions of it. It extends its reach deeper in time. The self-concept reflects the potential for growth and change, and all the values that are attached to these possible future states.

The value of considering the nature and function of possible selves is most apparent if we examine not *the* self-concept, which is typically regarded as a single, generalized view of the self, but rather the current or *working* self-concept. Not all self-knowledge is available for thinking about the self at any one time. The working self-concept derives from the set of self-conceptions that are presently active in thought and memory. It can be viewed as a continually active, shifting array of available self-knowledge. The array changes as individuals experience variation in internal states and social circum-

stances. The content of the working self-concept depends on what self-conceptions have been active just before, on what has been elicited or made dominant by the particular social environment, and on what has been more purposefully invoked by the individual in response to a given experience, event, or situation.

In a similar formulation, Burke (1980) found that like the self-concept, the sociologist's concept of identity cannot be used as a basis for competent performance because it is much too stable and removed from the demands and constraints of the moment-to-moment situation. Instead he proposed that it is self-images which can be viewed as current working copies of the basic identities that guide performance.

The individual's collection of self-conceptions and self-images can include the good selves (the ones we remember fondly), the bad selves (the ones we would just as soon forget), the hoped-for selves, the feared selves, the not-me selves, the ideal selves, the ought selves. They can vary dramatically in their degree of affective, cognitive, and behavioral elaboration. They also vary in valence. Some self-conceptions are regarded as positive and others as negative. A third dimension of variation, already implicit in the examples given here, is what Schutz (1964) called the "tense" of self, and more recently, what Nuttin and Lens (1984) referred to as "temporal sign" of the self. That is, where in time is the particular self-conception located? Many of an individual's self-conceptions are images of the *now* or current selves; they describe the self as it presently is perceived by the individual: other self-conceptions, however, are possible selves. These may be past selves that no longer characterize the self, but under some circumstances could be relevant again, or they may be future selves, images of the self that have not yet been realized but that are hoped for or feared.

Some conceptions of the self, because of their importance in identifying or defining the self, are likely to be chronically accessible, and these views can be considered as "core" self. These may include what Gordon (1968) referred to as factual self-conceptions; those of maximum perceived "actuality" (e.g., ascribed characteristics, major roles, and memberships), as well as self-conceptions that are especially significant, conceptions that have been called self-schemas (e.g., Markus, 1977) or salient identities (Stryker, 1984). Other self-conceptions vary in their accessibility depending on the individual's affective or motivational state or on prevailing social conditions.

Under some circumstances, perhaps following a defeat, a loss, or a lapse in willpower, the working self-concept will be dominated by conceptions of negative possibility. The working self-concept of the dieting individual who succumbs to a third slice of pizza will include not only some actual representations of self, but also a variety of self-conceptions of negative possibility. Some of these are quite likely to be realized (e.g., tomorrow's self in too-tight pants), whereas others may be quite improbable and relatively impoverished in their specific cognitive elaboration (e.g., the obese self, the out-of-control self).

In other instances, the working self-concept may contain largely positive possibilities. Thus, when a sophomore is rewarded for giving the right answer to the professor's question, the student's working self-concept is likely to contain core conceptions of the self as competent and a good student, as well as a number of self-conceptions representing positive possibility, both those that are quite probable (getting a good grade on the next exam) and those that are much more remote (the *summa cum laude* self). This description of the working self-concept draws on recent descriptions of memory priming (cf. Higgins & King, 1981; Wyer & Srull, 1984) in which activating a particular self-conception is assumed to activate other closely related conceptions and also to increase the likelihood that it will be activated again.

A focus on possible selves is broadly construed as an effort to tie self-cognition to motivation, but as a consequence it also relates self-cognitions to self-feelings or affect. Affect is generated in one of several ways. First, each identity or self-conception has a particular affect attached to it. Thus, when a negative possible self is activated, for example, it brings with it the associated negative affect, which, in turn, can have a marked impact on the form and content of subsequent behavior (cf. Bower, 1981; Clark & Isen, 1982; Salovey & Rodin, 1985). From this perspective, self-esteem is not a stable overall estimation of one's worth as an individual, but rather a variable value that is a function of the valences of the self-conceptions comprising the working self-concept at a given time. Heise (1977), in what he termed affect control theory, argued that identities are accompanied by particular feelings that serve as guide-lines for interpreting and creating events. An individual's behavior is determined by efforts to confirm these fundamental self-feelings. Thus, the identity of mother carries with it a large number of positive sentiments, and the individual behaves so as to maintain these positive feelings. If these self-feelings cannot be maintained, a new identity must be selected.

Second, affect derives from conflicts or discrepancies within the self-concept. To the extent that individuals can or cannot achieve particular self-conceptions or identities they will feel either positively or negatively about themselves. This view is consistent with the early self theorists who suggested that affective and motivational states can be systematically related to shifts or conflicts within the self-concept (e.g., Cooley, 1902; Freud, 1925; James, 1890; Sullivan, 1953), as well as with a variety of recent theoretical approaches that relate goals and outcomes to emotions (e.g., Abelson, 1981; de Rivera, 1982; Higgins, 1983; Higgins, Klein, & Strauman, 1985; Janis & Mann, 1977; Lynch, 1981; Roseman, 1982; Toda, 1982). Thus in Higgins's (1983) self-concept discrepancy theory, he relates disappointment, for example, to a discrepancy between the actual self and the ideal self, and anxiety to a discrepancy between the actual self and the ought self (an image of self held by another).

Exploring the Possible Self

We assume that all individuals have possible selves and that they can easily reflect upon them. The nature of these possible selves, their importance to the individual, their degree of cognitive and affective elaboration, and their link to specific plans and behavioral strategies will, of course, vary depending on the individual's position in the life span. In an initial study, we asked 210 male and female college students about the role of possibility within the self-concept. Based on the responses to an earlier study in which we asked another group of students to "tell us about what is possible for you," we developed a questionnaire that listed 150 possibilities for the self. These items derived from six categories: (a) general descriptors or adjectives typically found in self-concept inventories, for example, creative, selfish, intelligent; (b) physical descriptors, for example, good-looking, blind, wrinkled, or athletic; (c) life-style possibilities, such as having an active social life, being health conscious, a cancer victim, or alcohol dependent; (d) general abilities, for example, able to fix things, able to cook well, able to influence people, or knowledgeable about art or music; (e) possibilities reflecting various occupational alternatives, such as business executive, supreme court justice, artist, taxi driver, or police officer; and finally (f) possibilities directly tied to the opinions of others, such as being appreciated, loved, feared, or unpopular.

In each of the six domains, a third of the possibilities had been judged as positive, a third as negative, and a third as neutral. For each item, we asked respondents whether it described them now.

We then assessed possible selves by asking (a) whether the item had described them in the past, (b) whether the item was ever considered as a possible self, (c) how probable the possible self was for them, and (d) how much they would like the item to be true for them.

In general, the frequency of endorsements indicated that most of the items were meaningful to a majority of the respondents. Table 1 shows a representative subset of endorsements for positive and negative items in each domain. Virtually all respondents thought it was possible for them to be rich, admired, successful, secure, important, a good parent, in good shape, and to travel the world. In contrast, almost none of our respondents thought it was possible that they could be a welfare recipient, a spouse or child abuser, a janitor, or a prison guard. On the average, 80 (with a range from 32 to 147) of the total 150 items were endorsed as selves that had been considered possible. For now selves, the average number of endorsed was 51 (range from 28 to 93), and for past selves, the average was also 51 (range from 28 to 93). A third of the subjects indicated that they thought about how they were in the past a great deal of the time, or all the time, whereas 65% reported that they thought about themselves in the future a great deal of the time, or all the time.

A consistent positive bias was also noted in the endorsements. The overall ratio of positive to negative selves ever considered was almost four to one (although this ratio varied considerably by domain), with 44% of the subjects reporting having considered *all* of the positive items as possible. In contrast, only 3% of the respondents had considered *all* the negative items, and half of our respondents report never having considered

Table 1 Percentage of Respondents Endorsing Selected Self Items

Item	Does this describe you now?	Have you ever considered this a possible self?
Personality		
Happy	88.0	100.0
Confident	83.8	100.0
Depressed	40.2	49.6
Lazy	36.2	48.3
Life Style		
Travel widely	43.6	94.0
Have lots of friends	74.6	91.2
Be destitute	4.5	19.6
Have nervous breakdown	11.1	42.7
Physical		
Sexy	51.7	73.5
In good shape	66.7	96.5
Wrinkled	12.0	41.0
Paralyzed	2.6	44.8
General abilities		
Speak well publicly	59.0	80.3
Make own decisions	93.2	99.1
Manipulate people	53.5	56.6
Cheat on taxes	9.4	17.9
Others' feelings toward you		
Powerful	33.3	75.2
Trusted	95.7	99.1
Unimportant	12.8	24.8
Offensive	24.8	32.5
Occupation		
Media personality	2.2	56.1
Owner of a business	1.4	80.3
Janitor	2.6	6.8
Prison guard	0.0	4.3

more than 25% of the negative items as possible selves. In addition, the positive selves were also *thought* about more than the negative and were predicted as being much more probable.

These data suggest that individuals can reflect on their possible selves and that these selves are not identical with descriptions of their current or now selves. These students imagine an extremely heterogeneous set of possibilities for themselves, and these possibilities do not appear to be particularly constrained by their current or now selves, even in domains such as personality, others' feelings toward them, and physical characteristics. On the contrary, they seem to believe that they are quite likely to change, often quite dramatically. Thus, although we found a strong positive correlation between the items endorsed in the past and the items endorsed as currently descriptive ($r = .68$), the relationship between the items ever considered and the items currently descriptive was significantly lower ($r = .21$). In fact, it is only the negative past selves that had a substantial relation with the selves imagined as possible ($r = .55$). Thus, to the extent that individuals admit to something negative as a past self, they seem to believe that such a characteristic might also describe them in the future.

A central assumption of this expanded view of the self-concept is that dimensions of self other than the now self should make meaningful contributions to the explanation of variance in an individual's current affective and motivational states. We attempted to gain some general idea about these states by requiring respondents to complete the Affect Balance Scale (Derogatis, 1975), the Rotter Locus of Control Scale (Rotter, 1966), the Rosenberg Self-Esteem Scale (Rosenberg, 1965), and a Hopelessness Scale (Beck, Weissman, Lester, & Trexler, 1974) designed to assess general expectations and feelings about the future. These scales were completed before the possible selves questionnaire. We regressed criterion variables such as positive and negative affect, hopelessness, esteem, and locus of control on the various self components (past selves, now selves, ever-considered selves, and the probably selves) in separate models and found that each of the components significantly contributed to several of the dependent measures. Each of the self components was a significant predictor for esteem, and for global predictions about the future; and probable selves contributed significantly to the explanation of positive affect, and personal control (Table 2).

Table 2 Multiple Correlation Coefficients between Measures of Affect, Control, Esteem, and Self-Concept Components

Criterion variable	Does this describe you in the past	Does this describe you now	Have you ever considered this as a possible self	How probable is this positive self
Positive affect[a]	.31***	.26*	.21	.32***
Negative affect[a]	.30***	.39****	.13	.21
Locus of Control[b]	.14	.24*	.31***	.27**
Esteem[c]	.43****	.59****	.44****	.42****
How positive is future?	.31***	.41****	.41****	.51****

[a]Based on Derogatis's (1975) Affect Balance Scale. Positive affect reflects responses to Joy, Contentment, Affection, and Vigor subscales. Negative affect reflects responses to Depression, Anxiety, Guilt, and Hostility.

[b]Based on Rotter's (1966) Locus of Control Measure; high scores reflect greater internal locus of control.

[c]Based on Rosenberg's (1965) Self-Esteem Scale.

*$p < .01$, **$p < .05$, ***$p < .01$, ****$p < .001$

In a separate study (N = 136), to evaluate the relative contribution of possible selves to these measures of the individual's current affective and motivational state, a more stringent method of analysis was used. Using stepwise regressions, *now* selves were first entered, followed by *ever considered* selves in one model, *probable* selves in a second model, and *like-to-be* selves in a third model. We sought to evaluate whether in explaining current affective or motivational states, possible selves would provide additional explanatory power beyond that which the now self conceptions could offer. This method tests for the significance of that portion of the individual's affective state, motivational state, self-esteem, and perceived control that is separately and independently attributable to the possible self components (e.g., ever-considered, probable, and like-to-be selves).

Figure 1 shows these results. It illustrates the relationship between positive now selves and negative affect, hopelessness, and esteem, as well as these relationships when positive ever-considered selves are added to now selves, when positive probable selves are added to now selves, and when positive like-to-be selves are added to now selves. Also indicated is the significance of

the unique contribution of these components when the contribution of the now self is accounted for. Thus, for example, knowing an individual's estimates of the probability of certain possible selves considerably augments our ability to explain current negative affect.

All of these possible self components were found to contribute significant additional variance to the explanation of all the dependent measures. The probable and like-to-be self components reflected very strong and consistent unique contributions. These findings indicate that there are indeed independent dimensions within the self-concept that may be importantly related to the individual's current affective state (cf. Higgins, 1983). It is reasonable therefore to assume that the nature of an individual's working self-concept states could vary systematically with that individual's affective and motivational state, and vice versa.

Possible Selves as Incentives

The inclusion of a sense of what is possible within the self-concept allows it to become dynamic. Some possible selves stand as symbols of hope, whereas others are

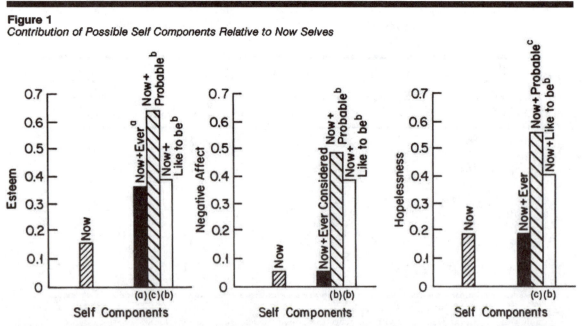

Figure 1
Contribution of Possible Self Components Relative to Now Selves

Note. Letters in parentheses denote significance of the unique, *additional* variance explained in the dependent variable by ever-considered, probable, or like-to-be selves after now selves have been accounted for.
[a]p = .05. [b]p = .01. [c]p = .001.

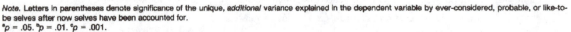

reminders of bleak, sad, or tragic futures that are to be avoided. Yet all of these ideas about what is possible for us to be, to think, to feel, or to experience provide a direction and impetus for action, change, and development. Possible selves give specific cognitive form to our desires for mastery, power, or affiliation, and to our diffuse fears of failure and incompetence. Some motives, such as hunger or thirst, appear to work directly to energize or activate behavior. Other motives (the need for achievement, for example) do not appear to instigate behavior directly. Instead, they are mediated by what the individual believes to be possible and by the importance assigned to these possibilities.

Recent theories of motivation (e.g., Atkinson & Birch, 1978; de Rivera, 1982; Raynor, 1974; Weiner, 1974) view motives as "dispositions" within an individual to strive to approach a particular class of positive incentives (*goals*) or to avoid a particular class of negative incentives (*threats*). Possible selves represent these motives by giving specific *cognitive* form to the end states (goals and threats), to the associated plans or pathways for achieving them, and to the values and affect associated with them. Thus, two individuals may feel an equally strong need for achievement, yet the dynamics of action that follow as a result of these needs depend on the particular possible selves that currently encode these strivings.

The importance of motives, goals, and values as major components of personality has been obvious to many theorists (James, 1910; Lewin, 1935; McClelland, 1951; Tolman, 1932). Some have focused on the mental representations of motives (Kagan, 1972; Kuhl, 1984; Nuttin, 1972, 1982; Schank & Abelson, 1977), whereas others have pursued the relationship between the self and motivation (Lewin et al., 1944). Most recently Nuttin (1984) has criticized psychology's preoccupation with the impersonal, the instinctual, or the unconscious nature of human motivation. He argued for the need to personalize motivation and for the value of studying how motivation is transformed into the activity of goal setting and into the concrete intentions and plans of which we are more or less aware.

Theories of motivation have not been specific about the elements of self-knowledge that give shape to the relations between the self and motivations. Several critical questions remain unanswered. How are the motives, goals, and values cognitively represented and communicated within the self-system? What structures carry them? In what ways do they function? The contribution of the notion of possible selves to these traditional frameworks is to suggest that some of the dynamic elements of personality may be carried in specific cognitive representations of the self in future states. For example, goals can rarely be cognized in total abstraction. It is not the abstract "getting a BA" or "my having a BA." In Lewin's (1935) language, there is a piece of self in that goal space.

Possible selves are represented in the same way as the here-and-now self (imaginal, semantic) and can be viewed as cognitive bridges between the present and future, specifying how individuals may change from how they are now to what they will become. When certain current self-conceptions are challenged or supported, it is often the nature of the activated possible selves that determines how the individual feels and what course the subsequent action will take.

The concept of possible selves allows us to make a more direct connection between motives and specific actions. For example, in the early studies of need for affiliation by Shipley and Veroff (1958), individuals were asked to stand while others in the group rated their acceptability as a potential friend. On a subsequent Thematic Apperception Test (TAT) measure, the individuals who came under scrutiny by their peers produced more imagery indicating a desire for affiliation than those who were not led to question their social acceptance. This relationship between the concern over social acceptance and affiliation imagery, documented in numerous studies of affiliation motivation, may well have been mediated and guided by the possible selves that were currently active in the working self-concept because of the recent peer evaluation experience. Specifically, the experimental manipulation may have primed a variety of specific negative possible selves (e.g., the unwanted self, the alone self, the unpopular self), or perhaps, for some, positive possible selves (e.g., good friend, popular, and admired). The subsequent focus on affiliation displayed in the TAT stories may then have derived from imaging how to avoid the negative possible selves being realized or how to approach the positive possible selves. In contrast, these types of affiliation-related possible selves were probably not salient in the working self-concepts of those who did not experience the scrutiny of their peers.

More recently, Taylor (1983) has described the need for people to gain a sense of mastery as they adjust to life-threatening events like cancer. Gaining a feeling of control over the event appears vital to successful coping. But how is the need for mastery represented within the self-system? We suggest here that this need will only be effective in motivating behavior to the extent that it has been elaborated into a specific possible self. The desire to gain control or to display competence is probably not sufficient. To be effective this desire must be translated into a vision of the self as healthy, active, and strong and must be accompanied by specific plans and strategies for becoming these possible selves. These possible selves are cognitive representations of the incentives for mastery, and without them there should be little instrumental behavior in the direction of mastery.

Similarly, in discussing the role of self-knowledge in motivating behavior, Bandura (1982) demonstrated the importance of individuals' beliefs about their efficacy. An efficacy expectation is the individual's belief that he or she is competent to perform a required behavior. Here we would speculate that general beliefs about efficacy can be particularly influential to the extent they are linked to specific, clearly envisioned possible selves. For example, Bandura described a study by Dowrick (1977) in which children with severe deficiencies in their social and psychomotor skills were helped to perform a task with all of their mistakes and the external aids cropped out of the tape. After viewing their successful performance on the tape, the performance of the handicapped children was enhanced relative to baseline levels on other filmed but not observed activities. The videotape created and fortified specific positive possible selves for the children that functioned as powerful incentives and standards for future successful task performance.

In general, the phenomenon of agency, whether it is characterized as effectance motivation (Harter, 1978; White, 1959), personal causation (deCharms, 1968), intrinsic motivation (Deci, 1975), self-control (Mischel & Mischel, 1977), or will could be interpreted in terms of the individual's ability to develop and maintain distinct possible selves. Similarly, the lack of these agentic qualities may be related to the existence of well-elaborated negative possible selves that give vivid, cognitive

form to an individual's fears and insecurities, but that do not contain strategies or self-scripts for how to escape them.

In an effort to explore how possible selves might function as incentives, Porter, Markus, and Nurius (1984) examined the possible selves of individuals who had recently experienced a life crisis. The responses of 30 victims of a life crisis (loss of a long-standing relationship, death of a loved one) where compared with the response of 30 individuals who had not experienced a life crisis.

Prior to completing the possible selves questionnaire and affect measures described earlier, these participants were asked to describe their life crisis and then to evaluate the degree to which they felt they had recovered from the crisis. The crisis subjects were divided into those who indicated that they had recovered from a crisis and those who indicated they had not. Subjects who claimed they had not yet recovered in comparison to the noncrisis controls were significantly more likely to endorse the following as now selves: not in control, weak, likely to die young, not able to fit in, poor, fearful, resentful, underachiever, depressed, and stupid. Respondents who felt they had recovered from the crisis did not appear to be any better off, at least with respect to descriptions of the now self. Thus, good recovery subjects in comparison to noncrisis controls were significantly more likely to endorse lonely, underachiever, unemployed, poor, weak, and resentful as now selves, and they did not differ from the poor recovery subjects on these items. In comparison to the crisis subjects, the noncrisis subjects were significantly more likely to describe themselves as optimistic, secure, respected, successful, adjusted, interesting, loved, happy, and confident.

Had we only inquired about the now or current self (i.e., how do you describe yourself?), it would have appeared that the poor and good recovery individuals were not different from each other; individuals in both groups would have appeared to be in grave distress. Yet when we compared the possible selves of these groups, the picture was very different. In comparison to the crisis subjects, noncrisis controls were significantly more likely to endorse the following possible future selves: optimist, long-lived, helpful, lots of friends, happy, satisfied, confident, and secure. The two crisis groups are quite different from each other, however. The poor recovery respondents thought that it was possible for them to be unpopular, nonaggressive, unimportant, weak, unable to fit in, or a failure, to die young, have a heart attack, become depressed, or experience a breakdown. These individuals had negative now selves and even more negative possible selves. In contrast, those who said they were recovered from their crises, even though they were not doing well at the time of the survey, thought it was possible for them to be motivated, independent, rich, creative, trusted, active, powerful, intelligent, and attractive and to win high honors. Most important, they found these possible selves to be significantly *more likely* than did the noncrisis controls.

There are several intriguing interpretations of these findings. It may be that these very positive possible selves of the good recovery group are a result of the positive affect that accompanies a feeling that one is recovered from a life crisis. Or alternatively, it may be that the presence of these possible selves, or the ability to construct them, may have actually facilitated recovery. That is, these possible selves may be the carriers or cognitive representations of feelings of mastery. The fact that the high recovery subjects endorsed many positive possible selves, and evaluated them to be quite likely, suggests that these selves were available in the working self-concepts of these respondents and were functioning as incentives.

It may be, of course, that individuals who claimed to have recovered from their crisis had generally higher feelings of self-efficacy or effectance, yet it would still be useful for therapy situations to know the precise cognitive representation given to these feelings and how these feelings manifest themselves in the working self-concept.

Possible Selves as Context for the Now Self

Beyond their role as incentives, possible selves function to provide an evaluative and interpretive context for the now self. The meaning given to a particular self-relevant event depends on the context of possibility that surrounds it. Thus, an individual's failure to secure a desired job will be much more than a single stroke of bad luck if the event activates an "unsuccessful professional" possible self. The failure may be temporarily devastating if this possible self comes complete with thoughts of not

deserving the job because of underlying incompetence, images of being pitied by associates, or fears of never getting a job at all or of working somewhere quietly and bitterly as an insignificant clerk. Given this context of negative possibility, the individual is likely to experience at least momentary feelings of low self-esteem. For a period of time some behavioral outcomes will seem more probable (e.g., not getting another job), whereas other outcomes and the behavioral paths leading to them will seem less likely and perhaps impossible to pursue. For instance, actions that require a self-presentation as competent or confident are difficult to negotiate when behavior is mediated by a working self-concept that features the "unsuccessful professional" possible self as a focal point.

In contrast, achieving a desired goal, perhaps completing an important qualifying exam, is likely to activate positive possibilities such as the "successful professional" possible self. In this context, finishing the exam takes on a very distinctive set of meanings. For some period of time, the self is not just a self that has passed qualifying exams, but a self that could earn a Ph.D., administer a research program, and take a trip to the south of France on sabbatical leave. The individual's feelings and immediate actions are likely to be markedly influenced by the nature of this context of possibility.

Kahneman and Tversky (1982) have suggested that in making decisions about the future people run mental simulations by constructing scenarios. The ease with which a particular event can be simulated is used to evaluate the propensity of the system to produce that state. They argued that we are biased in favor of events for which plausible or "easy" scenarios can be found and correspondingly biased against bizarre events or strange coincidences. Many possible selves are achieved through mental simulations, yet this type of self-knowledge does not always exert its influence on the individual in direct proportion to the ease with which it can be formulated or the likelihood of being realized.

Thus, for many, being rich, famous, enviably productive, completely happy, or thin are not "easy" scenarios because they are fairly remote possibilities and they would involve surprising changes in behavior. Yet should circumstances come to pass that lead to the certain prognosis that we have absolutely no chance of becoming famous, thin, or rich, many of us would become quite distressed. In much the same way, the possible selves of being destitute or terminally ill are not "easy" scenarios, yet they are also not easily removed from the self-concept. The probabilities attached to these events are low, yet they are greater than zero and as such can have a powerful influence on the individual through the context of meaning they provide for the now self.

The self-conception "I am 10 pounds overweight" is a different self-conception when linked with the possible self of "I could be quite thin" than when linked with the possible self "I will always be fat." Similarly, the meaning of the self-conception "I am poorly paid" derives its meaning from the surrounding context of possibility. It is not the same when considered with the destitute possible self and when considered with the fabulously rich possible self (cf. Crosby, 1982). What matters is not the ease with which these possibilities can be simulated, or their actual potential for being realized. What is important is that they exist as enduring elements that can be activated as part of a working self-concept and that can function as referents or standards by which the now self is evaluated and interpreted.

Possible Selves: Consequences for Self-Concept Theory

Every theory of the self-concept must confront a number of controversial issues. These include whether the self is a distorter, whether the self-concept is stable or malleable, whether there is one true self or many selves, and what the nature of the relationship is between the self-concept and behavior. Current theory and data provide a variety of contradictory answers to these questions. However, if possible selves are included within the boundaries of the self-concept, many of these conflicting results can be reconciled.

The Self as a Distorter

The now self is subject to a variety of social reality constraints that are often difficult to ignore (at least for long). It must be a fairly faithful rendering of the individual's experience. But the individual alone is the final arbiter for the possible self. The contents of an individ-

ual's possible selves are frequently hidden and protected from scrutiny of others, if not from their influence and they represent the creative, productive efforts of the self-system. A possible self, like the Messiah prophecy, cannot be disproven. Only the individual himself or herself can determine what is possible, and only the individual can decide what is challenging, confirming, or diagnostic of this possibility. For this reason, positive possible selves can be exceedingly liberating because they foster hope that the present self is not immutable. At the same time, negative possible selves can be powerfully imprisoning because their associated affect and expectations may stifle attempts to change or develop. Positive and negative possible selves are alike, however, in that they often make it difficult for an observer to fully understand another person's behavior.

Both recent and classic literature of the self highlight the individual's apparent tendency to distort information or events so as to verify or sustain the prevailing view of self (e.g., Greenwald, 1980). When people seem to be particularly sensitive to their successes and positive outcomes while at the same time forgetting or failing to attend to their failures, they are seen as distorting or as conveniently revising social reality. Similarly, individuals who view themselves as stupid and incompetent in the face of notable intellectual achievements are accused of irrational thinking. Yet charges of distortion and irrationality can only be made to the extent that we know the nature of the self-conceptions that are mediating relevant behavior. When a possible self is active in the working self-concept, we may often appear to be behaving in ways that are inconsistent, crazy, or seriously at odds with what others perceive to be our "true" selves.

Consider the person who experiences a failure and who subsequently appears through self-relevant statements and behavior to be ignoring it or rejecting it. To an observer, this appears quite reasonably as some type of distortion. Yet the impact of the self-conceptions of failure that accompany this experience can be significantly minimized if the individual challenges them by recruiting conceptions of past successes and future positive possibilities into the working self-concept. Although the now self may be challenged by the failure, the elaborated network of positive possibilities remains intact. These possibilities can remain as possibilities (although not indefinitely), and thereby serve as internal resources for the individual allowing him or her to ward off, at least temporarily, threats to self-esteem.

For similar reasons it may be difficult to convince an individual with a negative view of self of the irrationality of his or her thinking (e.g., "you have completed three years of college with high grades, how can you be stupid?"). Such confrontations may be largely ineffective if this individual's working self-concept is elaborated by a number of vivid negative possible selves (a failure, a drop-out, incompetent, worthless). Beck (1976) claimed that such self-conceptions are particularly likely when an individual has experienced death or loss at an early age and that such conceptions can form the basis of a stable, depressive schema. As conceptions of the "possible," these cognitions are unlikely to be changed in response to arguments about their irrationality. These possibilities are representations of fears and they remain possibilities.

The importance of possible selves in self-definition is thus critical in explaining the frequent lack of agreement between individuals' self-perceptions and how they are viewed by others. After reviewing over 50 studies, Shrauger and Schoeneman (1979) concluded that "there is no clear indication that self-evaluations are influenced by the feedback received from others in naturally occurring situations" (p. 549). Most often this disparity is explained in terms of the active distorting nature of the self-concept (cf. Gecas, 1982; Rosenberg, 1981). Yet an alternative explanation is that others' perceptions of an individual are unlikely to reflect or to take into account possible selves. In fact, one of the dramatic differences between self-perception and the perception of others can be found in the simple fact that when we perceive ourselves, we see not only our present capacities and states but also our potential: what we hope to become, what we plan to do, what we are worried will happen, and so on. When we perceive another person, or another perceives us, this aspect of perception, under most conditions, is simply not evident and typically there is little concern with it.

The power of possible selves may also explain other types of bias such as the perseverance of attributions. For example, Ross, Lepper, and Hubbard (1975) arranged an experimental situation so that the subjects either succeeded or failed. The task involved judging suicide notes for their authenticity. Later in the experi-

ment these subjects were told that the success or failure feedback was a hoax and had been manipulated by the experimenter. Yet success subjects persevered in the belief that they had high abilities to make accurate judgments. These findings need not imply distortion on the part of these subjects. They may well have recruited the sensitive or the perceptive possible selves into their working self-concepts. The presence of these possible selves would then have facilitated higher judgments of ability relative to those who did not have an opportunity to activate these possible selves.

Self-Concept Change

The question of whether the self-concept is stable or malleable is a continually controversial one (Block, 1981; Costa & McCrae, 1980; Shrauger & Schoeneman, 1979; Wylie, 1979). Studies over the life course seem to demonstrate an impressive continuity and stability of the self-concept. Similarly, recent empirical work on processes in the service of the self-concept suggests that individuals will go to great lengths to avoid changing the self-concept and to maintain or verify their self-conceptions (Greenwald, 1980; Swann, 1983; Swann & Hill, 1982). Other self-concept researchers claim, however, that the self-concept is highly, perhaps infinitely, malleable (e.g., Gergen, 1972; Tedeschi & Lindskold, 1976), and in turn they have gathered empirical evidence to support these ideas. Certainly, most research on behavioral and attitudinal consistency would imply that stability is really the exception. Moreover, at an intuitive level, it seems that our self-conceptions can change quite dramatically, depending on the nature of the social situation.

Expanding the scope of the self-concept to include possible selves allows us to account for both its situational and temporal malleability and for its overall stability. The now self, the self that is very much a part of the public domain may indeed remain basically stable. This stability may be a result of invariances in social feedback, in the targets of social comparison provided by the environment, or a result of individuals' needs to present themselves in a consistent fashion. However, because possible selves are less tied to behavioral evidence and less bounded by social reality constraints, they may be quite responsive to change in the environment and may in fact be the elements of the self-concept that reflect such change.

When a self-conception is challenged, there is likely to be a sudden and powerful flood of bad feeling. The negative affect that wells up at such times, whether shame, embarrassment, fear, or anger, may be a direct consequence of the activation of a variety of negative possible selves and their associated fears and anxieties. It is, however, unlikely that such a change in the working self-concept would be revealed by a standard self-concept inventory because these instruments typically ask about generalized or average views of self. Yet it would be misleading to suggest that the self-conception has remained the same or has ignored the challenge (for related empirical work, see Fazio, Effrein, & Falender, 1981; Jones, Rhodewalt, Berglas, & Skelton, 1981; Markus & Kunda, in press; Morse & Gergen, 1970). The challenge is likely to be very clearly reflected in the set of possible selves that becomes available and that provides the interpretive and evaluative context for the now self. Such variation in the content of an individual's working self-concept can have powerful consequences for mood, for temporary self-esteem, for immediately occurring thoughts and actions, and perhaps for more gradual long term changes in self.

Virtually all empirical studies documenting the resistance of the self-concept to change report only that individuals show resistance to challenging feedback, or do not accept it (e.g., Greenwald, 1980; Greenwald & Pratkanis, 1984; Markus, 1977, 1983; Swann & Hill, 1982; Tesser & Campbell, 1984). These studies have not explored what actually happens to the individual's self-relevant thoughts, feelings, and actions in the course of this resistance. Thus Swann and Hill (1982) found, for example, that when individuals who believed themselves to be dominant were rated by others as submissive, they sought out people who could affirm their self-conceptions of dominance. Are we to conclude from these efforts toward self-verification that no change occurred in the self-concept? Surely, the working self-concept must vary as a result of a serious challenge to a prevailing self-conception. From the cognitive literature, for example, we know that merely thinking about an event makes it seem more probable (Carroll, 1978). Entertaining possibilities of one's self as submissive is likely to have an impact on one's current state and on

future self-relevant thinking even if one's global self-evaluation on a dominance/submissive scale does not change.

Possible selves then may be the instruments of the intense temporary changes in self-evaluation that seem critical in everyday functioning. They may also be the mechanisms of the more long-term enduring changes in self-concept that seem intuitively inevitable, but are not evident in studies of self-conception over the life course. Thus, an individual's view of himself or herself as independent, successful, or competent may be remarkably stable over periods as long as 35 years (e.g., Baltes, Reese, & Lipsitt, 1980; Block, 1981; Lerner, 1984). Yet the context of possibility that surrounds and embeds these self-views may have undergone substantial changes during this period. As the repertoire of possible selves is elaborated or depleted, the meaning of particular core self-descriptors may change markedly. Thus "competent" for a 17-year-old may be tied to the desire to live on his or her own and a dream of becoming president. At 40, the same label of "competent" may be linked with the hope of being a good parent and the possibility of acquiring stock options. There is some stability to be sure, but there has also been a tremendous growth, change, and development of the self that would not be adequately mirrored by a statement that the self-concept remains stable.

One True Self versus Many Selves

A third question related to the previous two concerns whether there is a single underlying authentic self that is the essence of the person, or whether the self is a collection of masks each tied to a particular set of social circumstances (cf. Gergen, 1972). If we consider possible selves as systematic components of the self-concept, we can conceive of a self-concept that is diverse and multifaceted without being fake, wishy-washy, or incoherent. Possible selves provide for a complex and variable self-concept but are authentic in the sense that they represent the individual's persistent hopes and fears and indicate what could be realized given appropriate social conditions.

To suggest that there is a single self to which one "can be true" or an authentic self that one can know is to deny the rich network of potential that surrounds individuals and that is important in identifying and descriptive of them. Possible selves contribute to the fluidity or malleability of the self because they are differentially activated by the social situation and determine the nature of the working self-concept. At the same time, the individual's hopes and fears, goals and threats, and the cognitive structures that carry them are defining features of the self-concept; these features provide some of the most compelling evidence of continuity of identity across time.

The Relationship of the Self-Concept to Behavior

The goal of nearly all research on the self-concept is to relate the self-concept to ongoing behavior. The general notion is that if we want to change behavior, for instance, academic performance, we need to change the academic self-concept. Similarly many therapies, particularly cognitive therapies, are based on the premise that an individual's maladaptive behavior is directly related to dysfunctional thoughts about the self. Although most theorists assume that self-knowledge is one of the most important regulators of behavior, only a few, most notably Carver and Scheier (1982), have worked to establish these links. For the most part, the problems of the self-concept and self-regulation have been pursued in two largely non-overlapping literatures.

The difficulty in forging this link is that although an individual's behavior is often extremely variable, the self-concept is typically assumed to be a fairly stable, generalized, or average view of the self. How is this type of structure to mediate a diversity of behavior? In most discussions of self or ego therapy, the mediating role of the self has been accorded considerable importance (e.g., Blankenstein & Polivy, 1982; Karoly & Kanfer, 1982; Kendall, 1983; Wachtel, 1977). What is lacking, however, is an explication of the precise nature of the self-concept and how it may actually work to perform its assumed regulation of behavior.

Recently, various cognitive therapies have begun to invoke specific self-relevant thoughts as significant behavioral mediators (Mahoney & Arnkoff, 1978; Meichenbaum, 1977; see Cantor & Kihlstrom, 1982; Karoly & Kanfer, 1982; Kendall, 1983; McMullin & Giles, 1985 for reviews). There are, however, several

problems with therapies that concentrate on specific self-cognitions. Given the view of the working self-concept proposed here, the set of self-cognitions available to an individual for thinking about the self at one point may be quite different from the set available in the next hour. In the proper supportive environment, as during the therapy session, the individual may be able to maintain a particular working set of positive thoughts about herself or himself, but in a different context it may be difficult to hold these same thoughts in working memory.

Furthermore, if possible selves are assumed to function as incentives for behavior, it is necessary to work with individuals so that they generate self-conceptions of possibility to support the positive self-statements developed in therapy. Positive thoughts about the self may be ineffective if they are accompanied by well-elaborated conceptions of negative possibility. For example, in a study of the possible selves of delinquent youths, Oysterman and Markus (1986) studied 100 adolescents aged 14 to 16 years of age who were non-delinquent or delinquent and residing in a group home or confined to a state training school. Using an open-ended format to elicit possible selves, the respondents were asked for their expected, hoped for, and feared selves. We found that delinquent youths were quite likely to have high self-esteem but that they had a relatively constricted sense of possibility, both hoped for and feared possibility. For those in the state training school, 35% to 40% of their feared possible selves could be categorized as criminal (e.g., criminal, murderer, pusher, junkie, physical abuser of spouse or child). In contrast, the feared possible selves of the nondelinquent youth were a much more diverse and somewhat less negative set. They included what we termed poor selves (e.g., on ADC, no job, poor housing, cannot pay bills) and selves reflecting negative mental states (e.g., depressed, paranoid). For individuals like these delinquent youths, developing a system of positive self-relevant thoughts that can regulate behavior may well depend on helping them create for themselves a broader context of specific positive possibility in the domain of concern. In short, specifying the role of the self-concept in behavioral regulation depends on a thorough analysis of the nature and valence of possible selves.

Conclusions

Conceptions of possibility may be significant in analyzing a broad range of phenomena that implicate the self. Thus, difficulties in an interpersonal relationship may reflect the fact that one person's behavior is being guided by a possible self that the other person has no access to, or is unwilling to acknowledge. Decision making is also an arena where possible selves can have an influence. Many important decisions involve a process of imaging the self under various alternative outcomes. Yet in some decisions, such as the decision to purchase a particular car or a certain cologne, a possible self, rather than the current self will be envisioned and guide the process.

The nature and complexity of an individual's repertoire of possible selves may also be a significant source of individual differences. An optimist is a person who extrapolates possible selves on the basis of positive current experiences, whereas a pessimist extrapolates possible selves on the basis of negative current experiences. Simone de Beauvoir (1952) believed that it was the lot of women in particular to dwell on their possibilities and to agonize over them. She wrote "for women condemned to passivity, the inscrutable future is haunted by phantoms...; being unable to act, she worries...in her imagination all possibilities have equal reality" (p. 673). Further, developmental variation in the ability to construct and maintain possible selves is likely to be associated both with the child's ability to engage in self-control and self-regulation and with the adult's approach to aging. Probably everyone over 30 has experienced the anguish of realizing that a cherished possible self is not to be realized, even though this possible self remains as vivid and compelling as the day it was constructed.

We have argued here for a more extensive study of self-knowledge, one that takes seriously the individual's conception of possibility. The goal was to underline the interdependence between the self-concept and motivation and to suggest the value of examining motivation not as a generalized disposition or a set of task-specific goals, but as an individualized set of possible selves. In our analysis we have linked possible selves to motivation and to change, both the momentary changes associated with variation in the content of the working self-concept, and more enduring changes. Possible selves can then be seen as personalized cognitive carriers of some of the dynamic aspects of personality. Exactly how these possible selves operate within the self-system remains to be demonstrated in future empirical work. For example, do individuals seek to reduce discrepancy between now selves and their positive possible selves or do they strive to maintain a discrepancy between their now selves and certain negative possible selves? As psychology returns again to an emphasis on motives and goals, the study of possible selves can provide an effective bridge between motivation and cognition.

References

Abelson, R.P. (1981). Psychological status of the script concept. *American Psychologist, 36,* 715–729.

Adler, A. (1929). *The science of living.* New York: Greenberg.

Allport, G.W. (1943). *Becoming: Basic considerations for a psychology of personality.* New Haven, CT: Yale University Press.

Atkinson, J. (Ed.). (1958). *Motives in fantasy, action & society.* New York: Van Nostrand.

Atkinson, J.W., & Birch, D. (1978). *An introduction to motivation* (rev. ed.). New York: Van Nostrand.

Baltes, P.B., Reese, H.W., & Lipsitt, L.P. (1980). Life-span developmental psychology. *Annual Review of Psychology, 31,* 65–110.

Bandura, A. (1982). The self and mechanisms of agency. In J. Suls (Ed.), *Psychological perspectives on the self* (Vol. 1, pp. 3–40). Hillsdale, NJ: Erlbaum.

Bandura, A., & Schunk, D.H. (1981). Cultivating competence, self-efficacy and intrinsic interest through proximal self-motivation. *Journal of Personality and Social Psychology, 41,* 586–598.

Beck, A.T. (1976). *Cognitive therapy and the emotional disorders.* New York: International University Press.

Beck, A.T., Weissman, H.W., Lester, D., & Trexler, L. (1974). The assessment of pessimism: The Hopelessness Scale. *Journal of Consulting and Clinical Psychology, 42,* 861–865.

Blankenstein, K.R., & Polivy, J. (Eds.). (1982). *Self-control and self-modification of emotional behavior.* New York: Plenum Press.

Block, J. (1981). Some enduring and consequential structures of personality. In A.I. Rubin, J. Arnoff, A.M. Barclay, & R.A. Zucker (Eds.). *Further explorations in personality* (pp. 27–43). New York: Wiley.

Bower, G.H. (1981). Mood and memory. *American Psychologist, 36,* 129–148.

Brim, O.G., & Kagan, J.K. (1980). *Constancy and change in human development.* Cambridge, MA: Harvard University Press.

Burke, P.J. (1980). The self: Measurement requirements from an interactionist perspective. *Social Psychology Quarterly, 43,* 18–29.

Cantor, N., & Kihlstrom, J.F. (1982). Cognitive and social processes in personality. In G.T. Wilson & C. Franks (Eds.), *Contemporary behavior therapy* (pp. 142–201). New York: Guilford Press.

Cantor, N., & Kihlstrom, J.F. (1983). *Social intelligence: The cognitive basis of personality* (Tech. Rep. No 60). Ann Arbor: University of Michigan.

Cantor, N., Markus, H., Niedenthal, P., & Nurius, P. (1986). On motivation and the self-concept. In R.M. Sorrentino & E.T. Higgins (Eds.), *Motivation and cognition: Foundations of social behavior* (pp. 96–127). New York: Guilford Press.

Carroll, J.S. (1978). The effect of imagining an event on expectations for the event: An interpretation in terms of the availability heuristic. *Journal of Experimental Social Psychology, 14,* 88–96.

Carver, C.S., & Scheier, M. (1982). Control theory: A useful conceptual framework for personality social, clinical, and health psychology. *Psychological Bulletin, 92,* 111–135.

Clark, M.S., & Isen, A.M. (1982). Toward understanding the relationship between feeling states and social behavior. In A. Hastorf & A.M. Isen (Eds.). *Cognitive social psychology* (pp. 73–108). New York: Elsevier.

Cooley, C.H. (1902). *Human nature and the social order.* New York: Charles Scribner's Sons.

Costa, B.T., & McCrae, R.R. (1980). Still stable after all these years: Personality as a key to some issues in adulthood and old age. In P.B. Baltes & O.G. Brim (Eds.), *Life span development and behavior* (Vol. 3, pp. 5–102). New York: Academic Press.

Crosby, F. (1982). *Relative deprivation & working women.* New York: Oxford University Press.

Cummings, N.A. (1979). Turning bread into stones: Our modern antimiracle. *American Psychologist, 34,* 1119–1129.

Davids, A., & Sidman, J. (1962). A pilot study—impulsivity, time orientation and delayed gratification in future scientists and in underachieving high school students. *Exceptional Children, 29,* 1970–1974.

de Beauvoir, S. (1952). *The Second Sex* (H.M. Parshley, Trans.). New York: Random House.

deCharms, R. (1968). *Personal causation.* New York: Academic Press.

Deci, E.L. (1975). *Intrinsic motivation.* New York: Plenum Press.

de Rivera, T. (1982). *A structural theory of emotions.* New York: International University Press.

Derogatis, L.R. (1975). *The affect balance scale.* Baltimore: Clinical Psychometric Research.

De Volder, M., & Lens, W. (1982). Academic achievement and future time perspective as a cognitive-motivational concept. *Journal of Personality and Social Psychology, 42,* 566–571.

Dowrick, P.W. (1977). *Videotype replay as observational learning from oneself.* Unpublished manuscript, University of Auckland.

Elder, G.H., Jr. (1980). Adolescence in historical perspective. In J. Adelson (Ed.), *Handbook of adolescent psychology* (pp. 3–46). New York: Wiley.

Epstein, S. (1973). The self-concept revisited, or a theory of a theory. *American Psychologist, 28,* 404–416.

Epstein, S. (1984). The self-concept: A review and the proposal of an integrated theory of personality. In E. Staub (Ed.). *Personality: Basic issues and current research* (pp. 81–132). Englewood Cliffs, NJ: Prentice-Hall.

Erikson, E. (1946). Ego development and historical change. *The Psychoanalytic Study of the Child, 2,* 359–396.

Erikson, E. (1950). Identification as the basis for theory of motivation. *American Psychological Review, 26,* 14–21.

Fazio, R.H., Effrein, E.A., & Falender, V.J. (1981). Self-perceptions following social interaction. *Journal of Personality and Social Psychology, 41,* 232–242.

Foote, N.N. (1951). Identification as the basis for a theory of motivation. *American Sociological Review, 16,* 14–21.

Freud, S. (1925). *Collected papers.* London: Hogarth Press.

Gecas, V. (1982). The self-concept. *Annual Review of Sociology, 8,* 1–33.

Gergen, K.J. (1967). *To be or not to be a single self: Existential-perspectives on the self.* Gainesville: University of Florida Press.

Gergen, K.J. (1972). Multiple identity: The healthy, happy human being wears many masks. *Psychology Today, 5,* 31–35, 64–66.

Goldrich, T. (1967). A study in time orientation: The relationship between memory for past experiences and orientation to the future. *Journal of Personality and Social Psychology, 6,* 216–221.

Gollwitzer, P.M., & Wicklund, R.A. (1985). The pursuit of self-defining goals. In J. Kuhl & J. Beckman (Eds.). *Action control: From cognition to behavior* (pp. 61–85). New York: Springer-Verlag.

Gordon, C. (1968). Self-conceptions: Configurations of content. In C. Gordon & K. Gergen, (Eds.), *The self in social interaction* (pp. 115–132). New York: Wiley.

Greenwald, A.G. (1980). The totalitarian ego: Fabrication and revision of personal history. *American Psychologist, 35,* 603–618.

Greenwald, A.G. (1982). Ego task analysis: An integration of research on ego involvement and self-awareness. In A.H.

Hastorf & A.M. Isen (Eds.), *Cognitive and social psychology* (pp. 109–147). New York: Elsevier/ North Holland.

Greenwald, A.G., & Pratkanis, A.R. (1984). The self. In R.S. Wyer & T.K. Srull (Eds.), *Handbook of social cognition* (pp. 129–178). Hillsdale, NJ: Erlbaum.

Gregory, W.L., Cialdini, R.B., & Carpenter, K.M. (1982). Self-relevant scenarios as mediators of likelihood estimates and compliance: Does imagining make it so? *Journal of Personality and Social Psychology, 43,* 89–99.

Harter, S. (1978). Effectance motivation reconsidered: Toward a developmental model. *Human Development, 21,* 34–64.

Heise, D. (1977). Social action as the control of affect. *Behavioral Science, 22,* 163–177.

Higgins, E.T. (1983). Manuscript in preparation, New York University.

Higgins, E.T., & King, G. (1981). Accessibility of social constructs: Information-processing consequences of individual and contextual variability. In N. Cantor & J.F. Kihlstrom (Eds.), *Personality, cognition, and social interaction* (pp. 69–121). Hillsdale, NJ: Erlbaum.

Higgins, E.T., Klein, R., & Strauman, T. (1985). Self-concept discrepancy theory: A psychological model for distinguishing among different aspects of depression and anxiety. *Social Cognition, 3,* 51–76.

Horney. (1950). *Neurosis and human growth.* New York: Norton.

James, W. (1890). *The principles of psychology.* New York: Holt.

James, W. (19l0). *Psychology: The briefer course.* New York: Holt.

Janis, I.L., & Mann, L. (1977). *Decision making.* New York: Free Press.

Jones, E.E., Rhodewalt, F., Berglas, S., & Skelton, J.A. (1981). Effects of strategic self-presentation on subsequent self-esteem. *Journal of Personality and Social Psychology, 41,* 407–421.

Kagan, J. (1972). Motives and development. *Journal of Personality and Social Psychology, 22,* 51–66.

Kahneman, D., & Tversky, A. (1982). The simulation heuristic. In D. Kahneman & A. Tversky (Eds.), *Judgment under uncertainty: Heuristics and biases* (pp. 201–208). Cambridge, England: Cambridge University Press.

Karoly, P., & Kanfer, F.H. (Eds.). (1982). *Self-management and behavior change: From theory to practice.* New York: Pergamon Press.

Kelly, G.A. (1955). *The psychology of personal constructs* (Vols. 1 & 2). New York: Norton.

Kendall, P.C. (Ed.). (1983). *Advances in cognitive-behavioral research and therapy* (Vol. 2). New York: Academic Press.

Kendall, P.C., Lerner, R.M., & Craighead, W.E. (1984). Human development and intervention in childhood psychotherapy. *Child Development, 55,* 71–82.

Kihlstrom, J.F., & Cantor, N. (1984). Mental representations of the self. In L. Berkowitz (Ed.), *Advances in experimental and social psychology* (Vol. 15, pp. 1–47). New York: Academic Press.

Krech, D., & Crutchfield, R. (1948). *Theory and problems of social psychology.* New York: McGraw-Hill.

Kuhl, J. (1984). Volitional aspects of achievement motivation and learned helplessness: Toward a comprhensive theory of action control. *Personality Research, 13,* 99–171.

Lerner, R.M. (1982). Children and adolescents as producers of their own development. *Developmental Review, 2,* 342–370.

Lerner, R.M. (1984). *On the nature of human plasticity.* New York: Cambridge University Press.

Lessing, E.E. (1968). Demographic, developmental, personality correlates of length of future time perspective. *Journal of Personality, 36,* 183–201.

Levinson, D.J. (1978). *The seasons of a man's life.* New York: Ballantine Books.

Lewin, K. (1935). *A dynamic theory of personality.* New York: McGraw-Hill.

Lewin, K., Dembo, T., Festinger, L., & Sears, P.S. (1944). Level of aspiration. In J. McV. Hunt (Ed.), *Personality and the behavior disorders* (pp. 333–378). New York: Ronald Press.

Little, B. (1983). Personal projects: A rationale and method for investigation. *Environment and Behavior, 15,* (3) 273–305.

Lindesmith, A.R., & Strauss, A.L. (1956). *Social psychology.* New York: Holt, Rinehart & Winston.

Lynch, M.D. (1981). Self-concept development in childhood. In N.D. Lynch, A.A. Morem-Hebeisen, & K.J. Gergen (Eds.), *Self-concept: Advances in theory and research* (pp. 119–132). Cambridge, MA: Ballinger.

Mahony, M.J., & Arnkoff, D. (1978). Cognitive and self-control therapies. In S.L. Garfield & A.E. Bergin (Eds.), *Handbook of psychotherapy and behavior change* (2nd ed., pp. 689–722). New York: Wiley.

Manderlink, G., & Harackiewicz, J.M. (1984). Proximal versus distal goal setting and intrinsic motivation. *Journal of Personality and Social Psychology, 47,* 918–928.

Markus, H. (1977). Self-schemata and processing information about the self. *Journal of Personality and Social Psychology, 35* (2), 63–78.

Markus, H. (1983). Self-knowledge: An expanded view. *Journal of Personality, 51* (3), 543–565.

Markus, H., & Kunda, Z. (in press). Stability and malleability of the self-concept. *Journal of Personality and Social Psychology.*

Markus, H., & Sentis, K. (1982). The self in social information processing. In J. Suls (Ed.), *Psychological perspectives of the self* (pp. 41–70). Hillsdale, NJ: Erlbaum.

Markus, H., & Wurf, E. (in press). The dynamic self-concept: A social-psychological perspective. In M.R. Rosenzweig & L.W. Porter (Eds.), *Annual review of psychology* (Vol. 38). Palo Alto, CA: Annual Reviews.

McClelland, D.C. (1951). *Personality.* New York: Dryden Press.

McGuire, W.J. (1984) Search for the self: Going beyond self-esteem and the reactive self. In R.A. Zurcher, J. Arnoff, & A.I. Rabin (Eds.), *Personality and the prediction of behavior*. New York: Academic Press.

McGuire, W.J., & McGuire, C.V. (1982). Significant others in self space: Sex differences and developmental trends in social self. In J. Suls (Ed.), *Psychological perspectives on the self* (pp. 71–96). Hillsdale, NJ: Erlbaum.

McGuire, W.J., & Padawer-Singer, A. (1976). Trait salience in the spontaneous self-concept. *Journal of Personality and Social Psychology, 33*, 743–754.

McMullin, R.E., & Giles, T.R. (1985). *A cognitive-behavior therapy: A restructuring approach*. New York: Plenum Press.

Mead, G.H. (1934). *Mind, self and society*. Chicago: University of Chicago Press.

Meichenbaum, D. (1977). *Cognitive-behavioral modification: An integrative approach*. New York: Plenum Press.

Meyer, J. (1985, October). *Societal and historical constraints on the self*. Paper presented at the Social Science Research Council Conference on Selfhood through the Life Course, Sanford, CA.

Mischel, W., & Baker, N. (1975). Cognitive appraisals and transformations in delay behavior. *Journal of Personality and Social Psychology, 31*, 254–261.

Morse, S., & Gergen, K.J. (1970). Social comparison, self-consistency, and the concept of the self. *Journal of Personality and Social Psychology, 16*, 148–156.

Nuttin, J.R. (1972). The outcome of a behavioral act: Its reinforcement and information functions in human learning and perception. In *Abstract Guide of the XXth International Congress of Psychology*. Tokyo, Japan: International Congress of Psychology.

Nuttin, J.R. (1982). *A conceptual model of motivation and the cognitive processing of needs*. Lecture presented at Notre Dame University, South Bend, Indiana.

Nuttin, J.R. (1984). *Motivation, planning, and action: A relational theory of behavior dynamics*. Hillsdale, NJ: Erlbaum.

Oyserman, D., & Markus, H. (1986). *Possible selves, motivation, and delinquency*. Unpublished manuscript, University of Michigan.

Porter, C., Markus, H. & Nurius, P.S. (1984). *Conceptions of possibility among people in crisis*. Unpublished manuscript, University of Michigan.

Raynor, J.O. (1974). Future orientation in the study of achievement motivation. In J.W. Atkinson & J.O. Raynor (Eds.), *Motivation and achievement* (pp. 121–154). Washington, DC: Winston.

Rogers, C. (1951). *Client-centered therapy: Its current practice, implications, and theory*. Boston: Houghton-Mifflin.

Rogers, T.B. (1981). A model of the self as an aspect of the human information-processing system. In N. Cantor & J.F. Kihlstrom (Eds.), *Personality, cognition and social interaction* (pp. 193–214). Hillsdale, NJ: Erlbaum.

Roseman, I.J. (1982, May). *Cognitive determinants of emotions*. Paper presented at the Emotion Research Conference, New School for Social Research.

Rosenberg, M. (1965). *Society and the adolescent self-image*. Princeton, NJ: Princeton University Press.

Rosenberg, M. (1979). *Conceiving the self*. New York: Basic Books.

Rosenberg, M. (1981). The self-concept: Social product and social force. In M. Rosenberg & R.H. Turner (Eds.), *Social psychology: Sociological perspectives* (pp. 593–624). New York: Basic Books.

Ross, L., Lepper, M., & Hubbard, M. (1975). Perseverance is self-perception and social perception: Biased attributional processes in the debriefing paradigm. *Journal of Personality and Social Psychology, 32*, 880–892.

Rotter, J.B. (1966). Generalized expectancies for internal versus external control of reinforcement. *Psychological Monographs, 80*.

Salovey, P., & Rodin, J. (1985). Cognitions about the self: Connecting feeling states and social behavior. In L. Wheeler (Ed.), *Review of personality and social psychology* (Vol. 6, pp. 143–167). Beverly Hills, CA: Sage.

Schank, R.C., & Abelson, R.P. (1977). *Scripts, plans, goals, and understanding*. Hillsdale, NJ: Erlbaum.

Schutz, A. (1964). On multiple realities. In M. Natanson (Ed.), *Collected papers of Alfred Schutz* (Vol. 1, pp. 207–259). The Hague: Martinus Nijhoff.

Shipley, T.E., & Veroff, J. (1958). A projective measure of need for affiliation. In J. Atkinson (Ed.), *Motives in fantasy, action, and society* (pp. 83–94). New York: Van Nostrand.

Shrauger, J.S., & Schoeneman, T.J. (1979). Symbolic interactionist view of self-concept: Through the looking glass darkly. *Psychological Bulletin, 86*, 549–573.

Singer, J.L. (1975). Navigating the stream of consciousness. Research in daydreaming and related inner experience. *American Psychologist, 30*, 727–738.

Snyder, M., Tanke, E.D., & Berscheid, E. (1977). Social perception and personal behavior: On the self-fulfilling nature of social stereotypes. *Journal of Personality and Social Psychology, 35*, 656–666.

Snygg, D., & Combs, A.W. (1949). *Individual behavior: A new frame of reference for psychology*. New York: Harper & Row.

Stryker, S. (1968). Identity salience and role performance: The relevance of symbolic interaction theory for family research. *Journal of Marriage and the Family, 30*, 558–564.

Stryker, S. (1980). *Symbolic interactionism*. Menlo Park, CA: Benjamin/Cummings.

Stryker, S. (1984). Identity theory: Developments and extensions. In (Chair), *Self and social structure, conference on self and identity*. Symposium conducted at the meeting of the British Psychological Society, University College, Cardiff, Wales.

Sullivan, H.S. (1953). *The interpersonal theory of psychiatry.* New York: Norton.

Suls, J. (Ed.) (1982). *Psychological perspectives on the self* (Vol. 1). Hillsdale, NJ: Erlbaum.

Swann, W.B., Jr. (1983). Self-verification: Bringing social reality into harmony with the self. In J. Suls & A.G. Greenwald (Eds.), *Social psychological perspectives on the self* (Vol. 2, pp. 33–66). Hillsdale, NJ: Erlbaum.

Swann, W.B., Jr., & Hill, C.A. (1982). When our identities are mistaken: Reaffirming self-conceptions through social interraction. *Journal of Personality and Social Psychology, 43,* 59–66.

Taylor, S.E. (1983). Adjustment to threatening events: A theory of cognitive adaptation. *American Psychologist, 38,* 1161–1173.

Teahan, J.E. (1958). Future in time perspective, optimism and academic achievement. *Journal of Abnormal and Social Psychology, 57,* 379–380.

Tedeschi, J.T., & Lindskold, S. (1976). *Social psychology.* New York: Wiley.

Tesser, A., & Campbell, J. (1984). Self-definition and self-evaluation maintenance. In J. Suls & A. Greenwald (Eds.), *Social psychological perspectives on the self* (Vol. 2, pp. 1–32). Hillsdale, NJ: Erlbaum.

Toda, M. (1982). *Man, robot, and society: Models and speculations.* Boston: Martinus Nijhoff.

Tolman, E.C. (1932). *Purposive behavior in animals and men.* New York: Appleton-Century.

Turner, R.B. (1978). Consistency, self-consciousness, and the predictive validity of typical and maximal personality measures. *Journal of Research in Personality, 12,* 117–132.

Turner, R.H. (1968). The self-conception in social interaction. In C. Gordon & K.J. Gergen (Eds.), The self in social interaction (pp. 93–106). New York: Wiley.

Wachtel, P. (1977). *Psychoanalysis and behavior therapy: Toward an integration.* New York: Basic Books.

Wallace, M. (1956). Future time perspective in schizophrenia. *Journal of Abnormal and Social Psychology, 52,* 240–245.

Weiner, B. (1974). Achievement motivation as conceptualized by an attribution therapist. In B. Weiner (Ed.), *Achievement motivation and attribution theory.* Morristown, NJ: General Learning Press.

White, R.W. (1959). Motivation reconsidered: The concept of competence. *Psychological Review, 66,* 297–333.

Willerman, L., Turner, R.G., & Peterson, M. (1976). A comparison of the predictive validity of typical and maximal personality measures. *Journal of Research in Personality, 10,* 482–492.

Wyer, R.S., & Srull, T.K. (1984). *Handbook of social cognition.* Hillsdale, NJ: Erlbaum.

Wylie, R.C. (1979). *The self-concept* (Vols. 1 & 2, rev. ed.). Lincoln: University of Nebraska Press.

Zurcher, L.A. (1977). *The mutable self: A self-concept for social change.* Beverly Hills: Sage.

Concluding Comments

An Appreciation

With the conclusion of possible selves, Markus and Nurius succeeded in synthesizing a diverse set of concepts about the self, from Freud's ego-ideal to contemporary research on the now self. Their concept of "possible selves" provided a new category of mental models central to the functioning of personality. Moreover, they showed how contemporary research can illuminate many of the implications of these possible selves. That is, they showed how possible selves matter for the individual and influence how the individual conducts his or her life.

Review Questions

1. What is programmatic research and what are its advantages?
2. What is an article's citation rate and how is it informative?
3. Markus and Nurius include a variety of selves amidst possible selves, including the "now" self and Freud's idea of an ego-ideal or ideal self. What other kinds of selves do they include in the possible self category?
4. College students were the participants in some of the first studies on possible selves. Markus describes the possible selves of college students in some detail. What are they like? Would you say college students have a realistic picture of their own possible selves?
5. Markus relates two studies that examined both self-esteem or well-being, and possible selves. The first dealt with recent widows, and the second with adolescents who were delinquent or otherwise wards of the state. What did self-esteem and well-being predict? What did positive and negative selves predict?
6. Markus describes some very specific possible selves, such as the homeless self and the thin self. What other specific examples of such selves does she describe?
7. This was a peer-reviewed article in the *American Psychologist*. Articles are chosen for that journal because they are of general interest to psychologists. What sorts of psychologists would be interested in this article and why?

8

How Good Is the Measure
of the Parts?

Reading a Test Review

One cannot conduct personality research, or understand the personality system itself, without good measures of the central parts of personality. Good measures of personality's parts are one key basis of the discipline's activities. Over the 20th century, psychologists developed a wide range of methods for measuring aspects of personality. Over time, hundreds of measures of personality parts were developed. The myriad measures often mean there exists more than one alternative test or scale to assess a given part of personality. Some of these tests are better than others.

You may recall from your courses that psychological tests are evaluated according to several criteria. Of these, probably the two most important are reliability and validity. Reliability concerns the degree to which a test measures an attribute with consistency. Validity concerns the degree to which the test measures what it ought to measure or what it claims to measure. The best psychological tests undergo a rigorous series of empirical studies before they are released. These studies help guide the tests' development. After their release, the tests' evaluations continue as they are employed in ever more settings.

For example, during the development process, a test will be administered to a sample; its best items will be identified, and its less good items dropped. More items may be added or revised so as to further improve the instrument. During its development phase, a large sample, called the standardization sample, will be collected. This standardization sample will be used to provide norms for subsequent test users. Norms include statistics such as what the average person scores on the test. This is important to know so that new test-takers can be evaluated according to those averages. The test developers hope that the final product will be reliable and possess some forms of validity before its release.

Once the test is released, however, its performance will be judged by independent researchers in a number of new settings and information from those additional studies will contribute to the overall evaluation of the measurement instrument.

With some of the above in mind, let's turn to the predicament of the psychologist who wants to measure a part of personality. First he or she must identify the test or tests that measure the given part of personality. Having done so, the psychologist needs to figure out which tests would be best to use. One way to do this is to read through the test manual and independently evaluate the studies that led up to the test's release, and then go on to examine all the published subsequent studies using the test, so as to draw an independent conclusion as to how good the test is. When searching for a key test, a research-oriented psychologist might well choose to do this. It is, however, a highly time-consuming process; moreover, only some psychologists have sufficient specialized knowledge of tests to fully evaluate what they read.

An alternative approach is to identify an authoritative review of the test. Psychologists interested in a given test can look up a review of it in any of several sources. Test reviews appear in measurement textbooks and in the scientific journal literature more generally. Certain books may review particular groups of tests. For example, the book *Measures of Personality and Social Psychological Attitudes* (Robinson, Shaver, & Wrightsman, 1991) includes a review of a limited number of generally available measures relevant to personality and social psychologists. Beyond that, there exist more general reviews of measurement instruments. The *Sixteenth Mental Measurements Yearbook* (Spies & Plake, 2005), published every two years, and *Tests in Print VII* (Murphy et al., 2006), published every three years, are two series of volumes devoted to the review of psychological tests.

The Review in Context

Braden's review of the widely used Wechsler Intelligence Scale for Children (3rd edition) appeared in the *Mental Measurements Yearbook,* a volume that provides a comprehensive set of reviews for numerous psychological tests and measures. The review covers the Wechsler Intelligence Scale for Children, which is one of the most central and widely employed intelligence tests in the field. New versions of the WISC scale are introduced at regular intervals. Familiarizing yourself with the 3rd edition of the test can help provide some background on what the test is like (a new edition was recently released). The WISC is an important measure of childhood intelligence, and the greater a test's importance, often the longer and more extensive the reviews of the test will be. The editors of the Buros Institute's *Mental Measurements Yearbook,* where this review appeared, recognized the importance of the Wechsler test by publishing several reviews of the test back-to-back so the reader could benefit from multiple opinions. This reading focuses in depth on one of those reviews.

The Watch List

Dr. Braden, the author, assumes that psychologists and others reading his review are experienced with the subject matter, and, in this case, with earlier versions of the WISC itself. The article's Introduction therefore, quickly touches on a number of technical issues. Later, he will explain these in greater detail. For example, the author refers to psychological scales as possessing "better floors and ceilings." A "floor" in this context, is the lowest score a person can possibly get; a "ceiling" is the highest score a person can get. Floors and ceilings limit the range of a test. The author hopes that most test-takers will experience a few questions that are too easy for them (so they don't score at the bottom—the floor), and a few that are too hard (so they don't score at the top—the ceiling). "Factor structure" refers to the correlations among the test subscales, and what that says about how many intelligences are being measured.

In the next section, "Description," the reader is reminded that the WISC tests employ a hierarchical model of intelligence, with general (Full-Scale) IQ at the top. General Intelligence, in turn, is divided into Verbal and Performance Intelligences. Verbal IQ concerns the ability to understand language, and to reason about propositions; Performance IQ concerns the ability to perform various nonverbal reasoning tasks, such as putting together a puzzle. The test is further divided into four subsidiary IQ's: Verbal Comprehension (VC), Perceptual Organization (PO), Freedom from Distractibility (FFD), and Processing Speed (PS). Note that these four subsidiary factors will be referred to by their abbreviations later in the article.

Each factor of intelligence, in turn, is generated from a composite of a particular group of the 12 subtests. A given WISC-III subtest is simply a collection of items with similar content. For example, the Vocabulary subtest consists of questions about vocabulary. The Picture Completion subtest consists of pictures, each of which is missing a part that needs to be identified, and so on. You do not need to know what each subtest on the WISC is in order to understand the article.

In "Norms and Reliability," the term *internal consistency* arises—this is simply a specific kind of reliability coefficient. Note that smaller portions of a test (e.g., one subtest) will generally have lower reliabilities; the full test reliability is what counts here.

In the section "Factorial Validity," be prepared to read the abbreviations for those four factors (see above: VC, PO, etc.). The term factor validity itself refers to whether the major areas of the test are composed of subscales that are more closely related to one another correlationally than to subscales in other areas. For example, to take Verbal Comprehension (VC) for a moment: subtests that make it up should be more correlated with one another than, say, with subtests that make up a different area such as Freedom from Distractibility (FFD).

Note the reference, also, to the test's Index scores. These are a form of IQ scale based on the WISC's factor-based scales (that is, the scales constructed based on sets of items that cluster numerically together).

"Convergent/Divergent Validity" refers to the idea that the specific IQ's should converge (i.e., correlate highly) with other measures of the same sort of IQ, e.g., one verbal IQ score with a verbal IQ score on another test. Divergent validity means that one kind of IQ (e.g., verbal) should be distinct from other kinds of IQ in the sense that it will possess a relatively low correlation with those other kinds, for example, verbal IQ should correlate only modestly with perceptual-organizational IQ.

The section on "Theory-Expected Group Differences" discusses the performance of different groups on the test. In the case of people with different ethnic makeup, items are carefully selected so as to avoid any bias. In some cases, the test may "overcorrect" or "overpredict," in effect becoming biased toward rather than against minorities. The aim is to be as exactly fair as possible.

Review of the Wechsler Intelligence Scale for Children, Third Edition

by Jeffery P. Braden

Source: Braden, J.P. (1995). Review of the Wechsler Intelligence Scale for Children, Third Edition. In J. C. Conoley & J. C. Impara (Eds.), *The Twelfth Mental Measurements Yearbook* (pp. 1098–1103). Lincoln, NE: Buros Institute of Mental Measurement.

Note: This WISC-III review from the Mental Measurements Yearbook (MMY) series is reproduced with the permission of the Buros Institute of Mental Measurements. Editor's note: The Mental Measurements Yearbook and the WISC tests are constantly being updated both in concept and format. This selection is intended to introduce students to the issues in reading a test review, and does not reflect either changes in the MMY (or WISC) since their respective publication dates. For example, current MMY reviews are separated into five general categories: test description, test development, technical, commentary, and summary.

The WISC-III is the third generation of the Wechsler Intelligence Scale for Children. Its predecessor, the WISC-R, is simply the most popular and widely researched test of children's intelligence in history (see reviews listed in the test description). The WISC-III promises to improve the WISC-R through contemporary and representative norms, better floors and ceilings for subtests, new artwork and items sensitive to multicultural and gender concerns, and improved clarity of factor structure—all while maintaining "the basic structure and content of the WISC-R" (manual, p. 11). This review will address the degree to which the WISC-III fulfills its dual promises to improve the WISC-R without radically altering it; or, to put it into advertising language, the degree to which the WISC-III reflects a "new and improved original recipe" for intellectual assessment.

Description

The WISC-III is a collection of 13 distinct subtests (see description) divided into two scales—a Verbal Scale and a Performance Scale. The six Verbal Scale tests use language-based items, whereas the seven Performance Scale tests use visual-motor items that are less dependent on language. The overlap between the WISC-R and WISC-III is substantial in all common subtests (approximately 72% of WISC-R items appear unchanged in WISC-III subtest versions), and many subtests now include colorful, gender- and minority-sensitive artwork. New items were added to subtests that had insufficient floors (i.e., not enough easy items) or ceilings (i.e., not enough difficult items). A new subtest (Symbol Search) was added to the Performance Scale. Practitioners familiar with the WISC-R will appreciate the cogent description of key subtest changes on pages 14–18, and the summary of administration rules (manual, Table 3.3, pp. 44–45).

Five of the subtests in each scale produce scale-specific IQs (i.e., Verbal IQ and Performance IQ), and the 10 subtest scores produce a Full Scale IQ (FSIQ). The Verbal/Performance distinction is popular for many reasons, including: (*a*) its consistency with preschool and adult versions of the Wechsler tests (providing a "womb-to-tomb" test sequence with the WPPSI-R, WISC-III, WAIS-R/WAIS-III), (*b*) the ability to estimate intelligence independently in language-loaded versus language-reduced tasks, and (*c*) the varied subtest format holds the interest of the client over the test session.

Most of these features are unchanged from the WISC-R. However, the recommended order of subtest administration is different (i.e., the WISC-III begins with Picture Completion), and the WISC-III now provides for direct calculation of Index scores. The last change is significant; WISC-R users often reorganized subtests into factor scores for Verbal Comprehension (VC), Perceptual Organization (PO), and Freedom from Distractibility (FFD) (e.g., Kaufman, 1979; Sattler, 1992). The new Symbol Search subtest (along with Coding) creates a fourth factor, named Processing Speed (PS). Norms and procedures for organizing 12 WISC-III subtests into four index scores (VC, PO, FFD, and PS) are described in the WISC-III manual. The Mazes subtest contributes only to the calculation of IQs as an alternate test; none of the four factors include it.

Norms and Reliability

The normative sample is large (*N* = 2,200) and remarkably representative of 1988 U.S. Census data. Subtest reliabilities (expressed as internal consistencies for all but the speeded subtests of Symbol Search and Coding) are moderate to excellent (.61 to .92). The consistency of IQs and Indexes is very good to excellent (.80 to .97). Subtest stability coefficients, based on 353 children subdivided into three age groups, are adequate but slightly lower than WISC-R subtest stabilities (.56 to .89). IQ and Index stability is mostly good to excellent (.74 to .95; only one coefficient is below .80). The manual provides a wealth of technical data that consistently attest to the adequacy of the instrument. Interrater reliabilities for selected Verbal Scale subtests are excellent (all greater than .92). The contemporary norms yield IQs that are 2–7 points lower than those obtained on the WISC-R. A "drop" in IQ is expected because of population drift (see Flynn, 1984, 1987). Subtest specificities and guidelines for subtest interpretation are also available from independent sources (Bracken, McCallum, & Crain, 1993; Kamphaus & Platt, 1992).

Validity

Although the WISC-III has been available for only 4 years at the time of this review, it already boasts a substantial body of research addressing its validity. If I included the literature addressing the WISC-R (much of which applies to the WISC-III), I would be writing well into the next century. Therefore, I will (*a*) limit my review only to studies of the WISC-III, and (*b*) I will organize the validity literature into five categories. These categories are factorial validity, convergent/divergent validity, theory-expected group differences, differential validity/bias, and clinical validity.

Factorial Validity

The WISC-III factor structure is largely congruent with a four-factor hierarchical model (i.e., Full Scale IQs estimate broad intelligence, with VC, PO, FFD, and PS subfactors). Although the addition of index scores (and confirmatory factor analyses to support them) is a major improvement in the WISC-III over the WISC-R, these improvements are unlikely to resolve the question of "How many factors are in the Wechsler?" Factor analyses using orthogonal rotation or confirmatory procedures from the normative sample (manual, pp. 187–196) and other samples (e.g., Hishinuma & Yamakawa, 1993; Roid, Prifitera, & Weiss, 1993) generally support the four-factor "Index" model. However, hierarchical factor analyses cast doubt on the composition, stability, and uniqueness of indexes (Carroll, 1993). Even the confirmatory factor analyses presented in the manual and elsewhere (e.g., Kamphaus, Benson, Hutchinson, & Platt, 1994) are not entirely consistent in yielding a four-factor solution. The available data suggest the "Index" model in the WISC-III better approximates reality than the traditional Verbal/Performance/Full Scale approach in the WISC-R, but the number, reliability, composition, and interpretation of subfactors are not, and may never be, fully resolved.

Convergent/Divergent Validity

The manual reports strong correlations between WISC-III metrics and comparable metrics from the WPPSI-R, WISC-R, WAIS-R, Otis-Lennon School Ability Test, and Differential Ability Scales (*r*s between WISC-III IQs and comparable composites range from .59 to .92). Item analyses (Sattler & Atkinson, 1993) show appropriate gradations of difficulty from the WPPSI-R to the WISC-III. Additionally, independent studies report correlations between WISC-III IQs/Indexes and comparable metrics from other batteries are well within acceptable limits (see Bracken, 1993; Carvajal, Hayes, Lackey et al., 1993). These results imply good convergent validity for the WISC-III. Likewise, studies reported in the manual and elsewhere describe lower correlations among noncomparable metrics (e.g, the WISC-III PS and the Peabody Picture Vocabulary Test—Revised; Carvajal, Hayes, Miller, Wiebe, & Weaver, 1993). Taken together, these data attest to the convergent and divergent validity of the WISC-III.

Predictive Validity

Studies presented in the manual and subsequent publications support the ability of the WISC-III to predict relevant outcomes. The most important of these is academic achievement in children. The WISC-III manual reports appropriate correlations with achievement (pp. 204–209), and studies published since test publication also report appropriate IQ-achievement correlations in children representing normal (Weiss, Prifitera, & Roid, 1993), referred (Wessel & Potter, 1994), learning disabled (LD) (Slate, Jones, Graham, & Bower, 1994), severely emotionally disturbed (SED) (Teeter & Smith, 1993), language/speech impaired (L/S) (Doll & Boren, 1993), and hearing-impaired/deaf (Maller & Braden, 1993) clinical categories.

Theory-Expected Group Differences

The manual also summarizes studies evaluating the degree to which gifted, mentally deficient, SED, LD, epileptic, attention-deficit-disordered (ADD), hearing-impaired/deaf, and L/S children show atypical WISC-III scores or patterns. Although the numbers of subjects in these groups are limited, the results are consistent with expected values. Published studies (some of which are elaborations of studies summarized in the manual) corroborate theory-expected patterns of performance in children in the following clinical categories: gifted (e.g.,

Levinson & Folino, 1994), referred for assessment (Prewett & Matavich, 1994; Wessel & Potter, 1994), SED (Teeter & Smith, 1993), at-risk (Hishinuma & Yamakawa, 1993), LD (Dumont & Faro, 1993; Prifitera & Dersh, 1993; Roid et al., 1993; Slate et al., 1994; Smith, Buckley, & Pingatore, 1992), dyslexic (Newby, Recht, Caldwell, & Schaefer, 1993), generic special education (Post, 1992), ADD (Anastopoulos, Spisto, & Maher, 1994; Prifitera & Dersh, 1993; Schwean, Saklofske, Yackulic, & Quinn, 1993), L/S children (Doll & Boren, 1993; Phelps, Leguori, Nisewaner, & Parker, 1993), and hearing-impaired/deaf (Maller & Braden, 1993). There are two exceptions of theory-expected differences. First, although L/S children have lower Verbal than Performance IQs, their Performance IQs (and PO Indexes) are significantly lower than average (Doll & Boren, 1993; Phelps et al., 1993). Second, the Processing Speed Index was not lower than other Index scores in LD children (Smith et al., 1992).

Differential Validity/Bias

A thorough WISC-III bias study was conducted in conjunction with the standardization of the Wechsler Individual Achievement Tests (WIAT; T4:2938). Unfortunately, the results of this study are not in the WISC-III manual. Instead, the results are presented in Weiss et al. (1993). Although there was little evidence that the WISC-R was biased for gender or minority groups, the WISC-III renorming took many steps to eliminate bias, including (*a*) review of items by experts, (*b*) item analyses to revise or eliminate items with differential functioning, and (*c*) predictive validity contrasts (using WISC-III scores to predict achievement scores and classroom grades). The procedures employed in these efforts are consistent with contemporary practices. The WISC-III exhibits little predictive bias when used with males, females, whites, blacks, and Hispanics (Weiss et al., 1993). Marginal findings of intercept bias suggest that the WISC-III may overpredict achievement in blacks, and underpredict English grades for females. Additional studies of Tohono O'Odham Native-American children (Tanner-Halverson, Burden, & Sabers, 1993) also support the validity of the Verbal/Performance distinction for assessing minority children. The magnitude and direction of these findings suggest the

WISC-III is equally valid for native English-speaking children regardless of gender or ethnicity.

Clinical Validity

Although all of the preceding types of validity contribute to the WISC-III's clinical use and interpretation, to what degree can the WISC-III be used to identify exceptionality? It is tempting to infer good clinical validity from strong theory-expected group differences, but it is wrong to do so. To say that a group of children (e.g., ADD) show WISC-III mean scores concordant with theoretical expectations is different from saying the WISC-III is sensitive to diagnosing ADD. Concluding diagnostic sensitivity from theory-expected observations would be analogous to the following reasoning: squirrels eat nuts (confirmed theoretical prediction); my mother eats nuts (clinical observation); therefore, my mother is a squirrel (clinical diagnosis). Instead, tests must provide evidence of differential diagnosis (i.e., theory-expected differences occur in clinical groups, but not in normal groups).

The WISC-III goes well beyond its predecessor in providing support for clinical diagnosis. First, it lists the reliability of differences between IQs and indexes at commonly accepted clinical levels. Second, it lists the frequency of occurrence for comparisons between scores. The availability of both approaches to detecting intra-individual differences is a major improvement over the WISC-R (which only provided reliability data).

However, the evidence to date suggests that the WISC-III is not terribly sensitive to abnormal clinical conditions. For example, few ADD children exhibit popular WISC-III subtest profiles, IQs, and Index rules (e.g., low scores on the Arithmetic, Coding, Information, and Digit Span, or ACID profile) (Anastopoulos, Spisto, & Maher, 1994; Prifitera & Dersh, 1993). Strict application of diagnostic rules yields few false positives (i.e., few "normals" are identified as "abnormal"), but they also yield false negatives (i.e., most "abnormals" are identified as "normal"). This means that practitioners can be reasonably confident that children with "abnormal" profiles are likely to be abnormal, but many abnormal children will not show abnormal profiles. Relaxing WISC-III diagnostic rules decreases false negatives, but

also increases false positives (Prifitera & Dersh, 1993). Naglieri (1993) provides tables that can help practitioners correct for multiple WISC-III comparisons within an individual (i.e., if practitioners treat each score contrast as an independent comparison, they will artificially inflate the number of abnormal contrasts), and Kramer (1993) provides errors of estimate for subtest score comparisons.

Much like its predecessor and its companion batteries, the WISC-III does not provide "response validity" data. I define "response validity" evidence showing that test-defined typologies respond differently to treatments or interventions. The practice of (a) inferring psychological deficits based on test scores and (b) suggesting psychoeducational programs on the basis of these classifications is widespread. Malpractice is also aided and abetted by "guides" to the Wechsler Scales, some of which fail to provide data to support their occasionally sensational recommendations and claims (e.g., Jones & James, 1993). This is unfortunate, because scholarly approaches to WISC-III diagnosis (e.g., Kaufman, 1994a; Sattler, 1992) are often brushed with the same broad strokes applied to less-than-scholarly works. The only reliable connection between test scores and differential responses to treatment is the tendency for high-IQ children to learn more, and learn faster, than average- or low-IQ children. However, those who demand a link between intra-individual conditions and differential treatment outcomes will be dissatisfied with the WISC-III (e.g., Little, 1992; Shaw, Swerdlik, & Laurent, 1993).

Evaluation of the WISC-III

The popularity of the WISC-R insures that the WISC-III will be among the most widely studied, criticized, and used tests. As of this writing, I found 11 reviews of the WISC-III in the professional literature (Carroll, 1993; Edwards & Edwards, 1993; Little, 1992; Kaufman, 1992, 1994a, 1994b; Post & Mitchell, 1993; Roid, 1990; Sattler, 1992; Shaw, Swerdlik, & Laurent, 1993; Sternberg, 1993). These reviews, and my own analysis, largely concur in identifying many strengths and weaknesses in the WISC-III. They also extend some key disagreements surrounding the use and interpretation of cognitive tests.

Strengths

There are many improvements in the WISC-III that will make it more attractive and easier to administer and score. Subtest materials are contemporary, generally well made, and free from overt bias and dated material. The examiner's record form is designed well and contains all the materials needed to derive IQs and three of four Indexes. The WISC-III manual cover allows examiners to stand it up when testing, and all criteria for scoring children's verbal responses are located in the administration section. Confidence intervals for IQs and Indexes are tabled, and adjust for regression to the mean (but see Sattler, 1992, pp. 1037–1041 for the desirability of this practice).

The WISC-III is also strong from a scientific perspective. WISC-III norms are excellent, and its psychometric adequacy continues to set a standard for other tests. The manual provides a thorough and lucid presentation of reliability and validity data, which strongly support the adequacy of the WISC-III (with few exceptions). Modifications improved the reliability and validity of the WISC-III over its predecessors (and many rivals), including the four-factor model, improved scoring criteria for verbal tests, reduced "floor" and "ceiling" effects, reliability- and frequency-of differences tables, and direct examination of ethnic and gender bias. One rarely mentioned advantage is the availability of a conformed achievement battery (the WIAT). This allows practitioners to identify discrepancies between aptitude and achievement while correcting for regression effects using conformed tests (as recommended by Braden, 1987; Reynolds et al., 1984; Shepard, 1980). The WIAT manual provides the information needed to determine discrepancies between FSIQ and WIAT subtests and composites. Flanagan and Alfonso (1993a, 1993b) provide the information needed to determine discrepancies between VIQ, PIQ, and WIAT subtests and composites.

Weaknesses

Although the WISC-III is undoubtedly one of the best intelligence tests available today, it is not perfect. Administration and scoring concerns include the rela-

tive flimsiness of the Coding answer template, the need to buy additional forms to administer Symbol Search (needed to derive the PS factor), possible confusion regarding Object Assembly pieces (some look the same on both sides), and questions about the actual amount of time needed to administer the test (the manual claims 50–70 minutes, but 80–90 minutes is a more reasonable estimate). These concerns fall in the "minor complaints" category, but they suggest room for improvement.

Other concerns are more critical. Despite improvements in WISC-III subtests, subtest stability is no better (and may be worse) than WISC-R stability. Some subtests added bonus points for speed, which may depress scores in bright children who are reflective or otherwise slow to respond. Item content changes may render the test more acceptable to contemporary sensitivities, but removal of items relating to violence and vice may also inhibit its clinical value (Kaufman, 1994b). The meaning and interpretation of the FFD and PS factors are largely unknown. Although the WISC-R and WISC-III factor structures are extremely similar (Parker & Atkinson, 1994), the PS factor is new and awaits research to document its clinical value and meaning. Available research (e.g., theory-expected differences) is largely supportive of the PS Index, but some research (e.g., Anastopoulos et al., 1994; Smith et al., 1993) fails to provide evidence of diagnostic utility.

Unresolved Disputes

Critics have voiced other concerns regarding the WISC-III. Among the most popular is the failure to radically restructure the WISC-III (e.g., Carroll, 1993; Little, 1992; Shaw, Swerdlik, & Laurent, 1993; Sternberg, 1993). However, critics vary widely regarding *how* to restructure the WISC-III. For example, Sternberg (1993) argues for a test reflecting multiple intelligences (e.g., Gardner, 1983), whereas Carroll (1993) wants the test to reflect a singular, hierarchical cognitive model. Little (1992) questions the value of latent constructs (e.g., intelligence); but even reviewers who embrace intelligence nonetheless characterize the WISC-III as "a new and improved dinosaur" (e.g., Shaw et al., 1993, p. 159).

The dynamic tension between researchers and clinicians spawns these criticisms. Researchers (who write most reviews) adopt strong views about what intelligence should be, and then criticize the WISC-III for failing to fulfill that vision. Clinicians are less likely to assume what intelligence "should be," and are more concerned about practical methods for estimating cognitive abilities. The WISC-III clearly reaches out to clinicians. Given the diversity of opinion regarding the value and nature of intelligence, the pragmatic approach has a strong non-nonsense appeal. I agree with Kaufman's (1994b) conclusion that "the WISC-III is excellent" (p. 354).

Summary

The WISC-III handily achieves the goals that drove revision of the test (i.e., updated norms, improved subtest characteristics and content, and enhanced factor structure—all within the historical WISC-R structure). The changes are nearly all for the better from the perspectives of the practitioner and the psychometrician. Although the manual does not provide data in a few areas (most notably related to diagnostic utility and outcome validity), it provides substantially more information than any other in the Wechsler series—and most other tests as well. The WISC-III is likely to remain the test of choice among practitioners and clinical researchers for assessing children's intelligence, although the Differential Ability Scales (T4:800), Stanford Binet: Fourth Edition (T4:2553), and the Woodcock-Johnson Psycho-Educational Battery—Revised (415) are worthy (and more economical) contenders to the preschool through young adult testing throne. The WISC-III offers evolutionary, not revolutionary, progress towards better assessment of cognitive abilities. Those who want a revolution will be disappointed with the WISC-III, but those who value moderate advances in clinical practice will value the WISC-III.

Reviewer's References

Anastopoulos, A. D., Spisto, M. A., & Maher, M. C. (1994). The WISC-III Freedom from Distractibility factor: Its utility in identifying children with Attention Deficit Hyperactivity Disorder. *Psychological Assessment, 54*(1), 174-186.

Bracken, B. A. (Ed.). (1993). *Monograph series advances in psychoeducational assessment: Wechsler Intelligence Scale for Children: Third Edition; Journal of Psychoeducational Assessment.* Brandon, VT: Clinical Psychology Publishing Co., Inc.

Bracken, B. A., McCallum, R. S., & Crain, R. M. (1993). WISC-III subtest composite and reliabilities specificities: Interpretive aids. In B. A. Bracken (Ed.), *Monograph series advances in psychoeducational assessment: Wechsler Intelligence Scale for Children: Third Edition; Journal of Psychoeducational Assessment* (pp. 22–34). Brandon, VT: Clinical Psychology Publishing Co., Inc.

Braden, J. P. (1987). A comparison of regression and standard score discrepancy methods for learning disabilities identification: Effects on racial representation. *Journal of School Psychology, 25,* 23–29.

Carroll, J. B. (1993). What abilities are measured by the WISC-III? In B. A. Bracken (Ed.), *Monograph series advances in psychoeducational assessment: Wechsler Intelligence Scale for Children: Third Edition; Journal of Psychoeducational Assessment* (pp. 134–143). Brandon, VT: Clinical Psychology Publishing Co., Inc.

Carvajal, H. H., Hayes, J. E., Lackey, K. L., Rathke, M. L., Wiebe, D. A., & Weaver, K. A. (1993). Correlations between scores on the Wechsler Intelligence Scale for Children-III and the General Purpose Abbreviated Battery of the Stanford-Binet IV. *Psychological Reports, 72*(3), 1167–1170.

Carvajal, H., Hayes, J. E., Miller, H. R., Wiebe, D. A., & Weaver, K. A. (1993). Comparisons of the vocabulary scores and IQs on the Wechsler Intelligence Scale for Children-III and the Peabody Picture Vocabulary Test—Revised. *Perceptual and Motor Skills, 76*(1), 28–30.

Doll, B., & Boren, R. (1993). Performance of severely language-impaired students on the WISC-III, language scales, and academic achievement measures. In B. A. Bracken (Ed.), *Monograph series advances in psychoeducational assessment: Wechsler Intelligence Scale for Children: Third Edition; Journal of Psychoeducational Assessment* (pp. 77–86). Brandon, VT: Clinical Psychology Publishing Co., Inc.

Dumont, R., & Faro, C. (1993). A WISC-III short form for learning-disabled students. *Psychology in the Schools, 30*(3), 212–219.

Edwards, R., & Edwards, J. L. (1993). The WISC-III: A practitioner perspective. In B.A. Bracken (Ed.), *Monograph series advances in psychoeducational assessment: Wechsler Intelligence Scale for Children: Third Edition; Journal of Psychoeducational Assessment* (pp. 144–150). Brandon, VT: Clinical Psychology Publishing Co., Inc.

Flanagan, D. P., & Alfonso, V. C. (1993a). Differences required for significance between Wechsler Verbal and Performance IQs and WIAT subtests and composites: The predicted-achievement method. *Psychology in the Schools, 30,* 125–132.

Flanagan, D. P., & Alfonso, V. C. (1993b). WIAT subtest and composite predicted-achievement values based on WISC-

III Verbal and Performance IQ. *Psychology in the Schools, 30*(4), 310–320.

Flynn, J. R. (1987). Massive IQ gains in 14 nations: What IQ tests really measure. *Psychological Bulletin, 101,* 171–191.

Flynn, J. R. (1984). The mean IQ of Americans: Massive gains 1932 to 1978. *Psychological Bulletin, 95,* 29–51.

Gardner, H. (1983). *Frames of mind: The theory of multiple intelligences.* New York: Basic Books.

Hishinuma, E. S., & Yamakawa, R. (1993). Construct and criterion-related validity of the WISC-III for exceptional students and those who are "at risk." In B. A. Bracken (Ed.), *Monograph series advances in psychoeducational assessment: Wechsler Intelligence Scale for Children: Third Edition* (pp. 94–104). Brandon, VT: Clinical Psychology Publishing Co., Inc.

Jones, D. R., & James, S. (1993). Best uses of the WISC-III. In B. Vance (Ed.), *Best practices in assessment for school and clinical settings* (pp. 231–269). Brandon, VT: Clinical Psychology Publishing Co., Inc.

Kamphaus, R. W., & Platt, L. O. (1992). Subtest specificities for the WISC-III. *Psychological Reports, 70*(3), 899–902.

Kamphaus, R. W., Benson, J., Hutchinson, S., & Platt, L. O. (1994). Identification of factor models for the WISC-II. *Educational and Psychological Measurement, 54*(1), 174–186.

Kaufman, A. S. (1992). Evaluation of the WISC-III and WPPSI-R for gifted children. *Roeper Review, 14*(3), 154–158.

Kaufman, A. S. (1979). *Intelligent testing with the WISC-R.* New York: John Wiley & Sons.

Kaufman, A. S. (1994a). *Intelligent testing with the WISC-III.* New York: Willey.

Kaufman, A. S. (1994b). King WISC the third assumes the throne. *Journal of School Psychology, 31,* 345–354.

Kramer, J. H. (1993). Interpretation of individual subtest scores on the WISC-III. *Psychological Assessment, 5*(2), 193–196.

Levinson, E. M., & Folino, L. (1994). Correlations of scores on the Gifted Evaluation Scale with those on the WISC-III and Kaufman Brief Intelligence Test for students referred for gifted evaluation. *Psychological Reports, 74*(2), 419–424.

Little, S. G. (1992). The WISC-III: Everything old is new again. *School Psychology Quarterly, 7*(2), 148–154.

Maller, S. J., & Braden, J. P. (1993). The construct and criterion-related validity of the WISC-III with deaf adolescents. In B. A. Bracken (Ed.), *Monograph series advances in psychoeducational assessment: Wechsler Intelligence Scale for Children: Third Edition; Journal of Psychoeducational Assessment* (pp. 105–113). Brandon, VT: Clinical Psychological Publishing Co., Inc.

Naglieri, J. (1993). Pairwise and ipsalve comparisons of WISC-III IQ and Index scores. *Psychological Assessment, 5*(1), 113–116.

Newby, R. F., Recht, D. R., Caldwell, J., & Schaefer, J. (1993). Comparison of WISC-III and WISC-R IQ changes over a 2-year time span in a sample of children with dyslexia. In B. A. Bracken (Ed.), *Monograph series advances in psychoeducational assessment: Wechsler Intelligence Scale for Children: Third Edition; Journal of Psychoeducational Assessment* (pp. 87–93). Brandon, VT: Clinical Psychology Publishing Co., Inc.

Parker, K. C. H., & Atkinbson, L. (1994). Factor space of the Wechsler Intelligence Scale for Children—Third Edition: Critical thoughts and recommendations. *Psychological Assessment, 6*(3), 201–208.

Phelps, L., Leguori, S., Nisewaner, K., & Parker, M. (1993). Practical interpretations of the WISC-III with language-disordered children. In B. A. Bracken (Ed.), *Monograph series advances in psychoeducational assessment: Wechsler Intelligence Scale for Children: Third Edition; Journal of Psychoeducational Assessment* (pp. 71–85). Brandon, VT: Clinical Psychology Publishing Co., Inc.

Post, K. R. (1992). *A comparison of WISC-R and WISC-III scores on urban special education students.* Unpublished educational specialist thesis, James Madison University, Harrisonburg, VA.

Post, K. R., & Mitchell, H. R. (1993). The WISC-III: A reality check. *Journal of School Psychology, 31*(4), 541–545.

Prewett, P. N., & Matavich, M. A. (1994). A comparison of referred students' performance on the WISC-III and the Stanford-Binet Intelligence Scale: Fourth Edition. *Journal of Psychoeducational Assessment, 12*(11), 42–48.

Prifitera, A., & Dersh, J. (1993). Base rates of WISC-III diagnostic subtest patterns among normal, learning-disabled, and ADHD samples. In B. A. Bracken (Ed.), *Monograph series advances in psychoeducational assessment: Wechsler Intelligence Scale for Children: Third Edition; Journal of Psychoeducational Assessment* (pp. 43–55). Brandon, VT: Clinical Psychology Publishing Co., Inc.

Reynolds, C. R. (1984). Critical measurement issues in learning disabilities. *Journal of Special Education, 18,* 451–476.

Roid, G. H. (1990, August). *Historical continuity in intelligence assessment: Goals of the WISC-III standardization.* Paper presented at the annual meeting of the American Psychological Association, Boston.

Roid, G. H., Prifitera, A., & Weiss, L. G. (1993). Replication of the WISC-III factor structure in an independent sample. In B. A. Bracken (Ed.), *Monograph series advances in psychoeducational assessment: Wechsler Intelligence Scale for Children: Third Edition; Journal of Psychoeducational Assessment* (pp. 6–21). Brandon, VT: Clinical Psychology Publishing Co., Inc.

Sattler, J. M. (1992). *Assessment of children* (updated & revised 3rd ed.). San Diego: Jerome M. Sattler.

Sattler, J. M., & Atkinson, L. (1993). Item equivalence across scales: The WPPSI-R and WISC-III. *Psychological Assessment, 5*(2), 203–206.

Schwean, V. L., Saklofske, D. H., Yackulic, R. A., & Quinn, D. (1993). WISC-III performance of ADHD children. In B. A. Bracken (Ed.), *Monograph series advances in psychoeducational assessment: Wechsler Intelligence Scale for Children: Third Edition; Journal of Psychoeducational Assessment* (pp. 56–70). Brandon, VT: Clinical Psychology Publishing Co., Inc.

Shaw, S. R., Swerdlik, S. E., & Laurent, J. (1993). [Review of the WISC-III.] In B. A. Bracken (Ed.), *Monograph series advances in psychoeducational assessment: Wechsler Intelligence Scale for Children: Third Edition; Journal of Psychoeducational Assessment* (pp. 151–159). Brandon, VT: Clinical Psychology Publishing Co., Inc.

Shepard, L. (1980). An evaluation of the regression discrepancy method for identifying children with learning disabilities. *Journal of Special Education, 14,* 79–91.

Slate, J. R., Jones, C. H., Graham, L. S., & Bower, J. (1994). Correlations of WISC-III, WRAT-R, KM-R, and PPVT-R scores in students with specific learning disabilities. *Learning Disabilities Research and Practice, 9*(2), 104–107.

Smith, D. K., Buckley, S., & Pingatore, M. (1992, August). *WSC-III/KBIT relationships in students with learning disabilities.* Paper presented at the annual meeting of the American Psychological Association, Washington, DC.

Sternberg, R. J. (1993). Rocky's back again: A review of the WISC-III. In B. A. Bracken (Ed.), *Monograph series advances in psychoeducational assessment: Wechsler Intelligence Scale for Children: Third Edition; Journal of Psychoeducational Assessment* (pp. 161–164). Brandon, VT: Clinical Psychology Publishing Co., Inc.

Tanner-Halverson, P., Burden, T., & Sabers, D. (1993). WISC-III normative data for Tohono O'Odham Native-American Children. In B. A. Bracken (Ed.), *Monograph series advances in psychoeducational assessment: Wechsler Intelligence Scale for Children: Third Edition; Journal of Psychoeducational Assessment* (pp. 125–133). Brandon, VT: Clinical Psychology Publishing Co., Inc.

Teeter, P. A., & Smith, P. L. (1993). WISC-III and WJ-R: Predictive and discriminant validity for students with severe emotional disturbance. In B. A. Bracken (Ed.), *Monograph series advances in psychoeducational assessment: Wechsler Intelligence Scale for Children: Third Edition; Journal of Psychoeducational Assessment* (pp. 114–124). Brandon, VT: Clinical Psychology Publishing Co., Inc.

Weiss, L. G., Prifitera, A., & Roid, G. (1993). The WISC-III and the fairness of predicting achievement across ethnic and gender groups. In B. A. Bracken (Ed.), *Monograph series advances in psychoeducational assessment: Wechsler Intelligence Scale for Children: Third Edition; Journal of Psychoeducational Assessment* (pp. 35–42). Brandon, VT: Clinical Psychology Publishing Co., Inc.

Wessel, J., & Potter, A. (1994). *Analysis of WISC-III data from an urban population of referred children.* Paper presented at the annual meeting of the National Association of School Psychologists Association, Seattle, WA. (Eric Document Reproduction No. ED371051)

Witworth, J. R. & Sutton, D. L. (1993). *WISC-III compilation.* Novato, CA: Academic Therapy Publications.

Concluding Comments

The Status of the WISC-III

The author does an admirable job of describing the reactions to an important test such as the WISC-III, particularly:

> Critics have voiced.... concerns regarding the WISC-III.... The dynamic tension between researchers and clinicians spawns these criticisms. Researchers (who write most reviews) adopt strong views about what intelligence should be, and then criticize the WISC-III for failing to fulfill that vision.

This is particularly true in the contentious area of intelligence research, where a number of very smart—and equally opinionated individuals—operate.

> Clinicians, are less likely to assume what intelligence "should be," and are more concerned about practical methods for estimating cognitive abilities. The WISC-III clearly reaches out to clinicians... [and] ... is excellent.

That is, the pragmatic need of the clinician is met by the test. On the other hand, theoreticians and researchers will continue to search for better ways to think about intelligence, as well as to develop future measures of it.

Review Questions

1. What role do psychological tests play in personality research?
2. What are some major sources of test reviews?
3. Why would a psychologist want to read a test review?
4. What is the overall reliability of the WISC-III?
5. What are the major factors measured by the WISC-III?
6. What are some group differences that the WISC-III predicts?
7. Does the reviewer believe the WISC-III is a good test? Why?

9

Some Funny Stuff

On Professional Humor

Are psychologists ever entertaining? Humorous writing emerges in, well, the most serious of circumstances.

Sigmund Freud was quite interested in humor, and wrote a lengthy treatise on jokes and the unconscious. In it, Freud (1905/1961) recounted many jokes, witticisms, puns, and other forms of comedy, among them, "Human life falls into two halves. In the first half we wish the second one would come; and in the second we wish the first one were back" (Freud, 1923/1961, p. 66). Freud, moreover, often put his sense of humor to use.

In, "A Seventeenth-Century Demonological Neurosis," he examines the case of a painter who believed he had become possessed by the Devil. Freud argues it was not the Devil who possessed the painter, but rather the painter who possessed a severe neurosis. Synthesizing the documents of the case, Freud concludes that the afflicted painter had become depressed by the death of his own father. Shortly thereafter, the painter had imagined signing a contract with the Devil. Freud comments about the terms of the agreement, gently substituting a psychiatric for a religious interpretation:

> His father, then, had died and he had in consequence fallen into a state of melancholia; whereupon the Devil had approached him and asked him why he was so downcast and sad, and had promised "to help him in every way and to give him support."
>
> Here was a person, therefore, who signed a bond with the Devil in order to be freed from a state of depression. Undoubtedly an excellent motive, as anyone will agree who can have an understanding sense of the torments of such a state and who knows as well how little medicine can do to alleviate this ailment. (Freud, 1923/1961, p. 81)

Freud's remark is both sympathetic to the (then mostly) untreatable condition of severe depression, and with that sympathy, makes light of the painter's perception that he had committed a grievous sin.

Although behavioral scientists were often serious, others borrowed their techniques and imbued them with lightness and fun. Early animal trainers freely employed behavioral techniques so as to manage the actions of the animals they guided. In the

104

United States, vaudeville entertainers included behaviorally oriented animal trainers who paraded cleverly behaving kittens and ducks in front of audiences. This failed to garner much interest on the part of the audience, however.

Stage hypnotists took their turn with the audiences. The hypnotists offered to put audience members into a trance so as to make them act like kittens and ducks. For reasons that defy logic, audience members who were not entertained by clever kittens and ducks, were far more fond of behaving like ducks—in front of large groups of strangers, and even their friends. Stage hypnotism became a staple of American entertainment.

To return to animal training, the most remarkable trainer was the eminent behaviorist B. F. Skinner himself. Although (to the best of my knowledge) he never appeared on stage as an animal trainer, much of his life's work of course concerned the control of prediction of animal behavior.

"This is a history of a crackpot idea," began Skinner's account of the history of one such project. It involved the harnessing of an array of pigeons to guide a missile toward its target. (This was the 1940s, during World War II, and a time in which the use of pigeons on the battlefield would have been viewed as a necessary wartime sacrifice; it was also, of course, before electronic devices could do what they can today.)

The pigeons sat in small harnesses, within cylinders that were stacked rather like coffee cans on their sides. The pigeons watched the image of the target that was projected onto a screen, through a lens at the front of the missile. As they pecked, electronic equipment integrated their responses into messages to the missile's guidance system.

After years of arguing that the system might work, Skinner and his colleagues were finally granted the opportunity to display a working model of it to a panel of scientists. Skinner and his colleagues had arranged to display a version of the missile itself, and illustrate how it could guide itself (on wheels) across a room toward a target. The scientists observing the demonstration, however, requested that the lid be taken off the missile so they could see what occurred inside. The sight of the pigeons pecking away toward the target was certainly remarkable!

As Skinner recounted, "… the spectacle of a living pigeon carrying out its assignment, no matter how beautifully, simply reminded the committee of how utterly fantastical our proposal was. I will not say that the meeting was marked by unrestrained merriment, for the merriment was restrained. But it was there, and it was obvious that our case was lost." As the door to the committee room closed, a colleague advised Skinner, "Why don't you go out and get drunk!" (Skinner, 1960, p. 34).

Humor arose in clinical work as well. The famed 20th century diagnostician, Paul E. Meehl, was a witty—and sometimes outspoken—critic of the field. The opening of one of his articles contained this joke on the empirical tendencies of those trained at the University of Minnesota at the time:

Once upon a time there was a young fellow who, as we say, was "vocationally maladjusted." He wasn't sure what the trouble was, but he knew that he wasn't happy in his work… He went to the counseling bureau of a large midwestern university... and there he was interviewed by a world-famous vocational psychologist. When the psychologist explained that it would first be necessary to take a fourteen-hour battery of tests, the young man hesitated a little; after all, he was still employed at his job and fourteen hours seemed like quite a lot of time. "Oh, well," said the great psychologist reassuringly, "don't worry about that. If you're too busy, you can arrange to have my assistant take these tests for you. I don't care who takes them, just so long as they come out in quantitative form." (Meehl, 1973, p. 228)

Meehl was not always happy with the intellectual level of other psychologists, and he was blunt enough to aim some "destructive criticism"—as he openly referred to it—at his colleagues. The article, "Why I No Longer Attend Case Conferences," was an explanation of why he could no longer stand to listen to practicing psychologists discussing the patients they were trying to help. Near the introduction, he notes that:

Somehow the group situation brings out the worst in many people, and results in an intellectual functioning that is at the lowest common denominator, which in clinical psychology and psychiatry is likely to be pretty low. (Meehl, 1973, p. 228)

And elsewhere:

The tradition of exaggerated tenderness in psychiatry and psychology reflects our "therapeutic attitude" and contrasts with that of scholars in fields like philosophy or law, where a dumb argument is called a dumb argument, and he who makes a dumb argument can expect to be slapped down by his peers.... [back to psychology:] the most inane remark is received with joy and open arms as part of the groupthink process. (Meehl, 1973, p. 228)

The article continues to detail the many statistical and logical fallacies that those attempting to help a patient might engage in. Among them was "Uncle George's pancakes fallacy"—a technique whereby members of a case management team could argue that the patient wasn't really disordered (Meehl, 1973, p. 239). The "pancakes" fallacy works this way:

. . . you call to mind a friend or relative who has exhibited a sign or symptom similar to that of the patient. For example, a patient does not like to throw away leftover pancakes and he stores them in the attic. A mitigating clinician says, "Why, there is nothing so terrible about that—I remember good ole Uncle George from my childhood, he used to store uneaten pancakes in the attic." The proper conclusion from such a personal recollection is, of course, not that the patient is mentally well but the good ole Uncle

George—whatever may have been his other delightful qualities—was mentally aberrated. (Meehl, 1973, p. 239)

Bringing us up to more recent history, Greenwald's (1980) "The Totalitarian Ego" was a treatise on the problems of egotism and the difficulty people sometimes faced when trying to take responsibility for anything negative. The footnote to that article noted that the acknowledgments would appear in the back of the article rather than its more customary placement on the front page. The curious reader who turned to the back found these lines:

> The reader of this article should appreciate that the author is prepared to take full responsibility only for the good ideas that are to be found in it. I'm nonetheless grateful to the following people, who commented on earlier drafts… [a long list of names followed]. If this disguise of gratitude is itself seen as inept, then the reader should know that it was at the suggestion of Robert B. Zajonc, modified with the help of Robert Trivers. (Greenwald, 1980)

All the examples thus far appeared in otherwise serious journals and books. There also have been, however, publications devoted to psychological humor. It is from such publications that the readings for this chapter are drawn.

Significance of the Articles

These next two articles, "The Minnesota Multiphasic Personality Inventory (MMPI) Updated: 1998 Edition" and "A Brief Report on Clinical Aspects of Procrastination: Better Late Than Never" are drawn from the *Journal of Polymorphous Perversity*.

"Polymorphous Perversity" was Freud's term for the fact that the infant could derive pleasure—sexual pleasure, he supposed—from any of a variety of bodily sensations. Some people take (or took) Freud's theory extremely seriously, whereas others found it, well, amusing. The *Journal of Polymorphous Perversity* has published humorous articles about psychology for more than two decades. The articles reprinted here have virtually no significance whatsoever—except perhaps to indicate that psychologists sometimes possess, and occasionally express, a sense of humor.

The Watch List

The present articles are unrelated to the rest of these readings, and except for having appeared in the *Journal of Polymorphous Perversity*, to each other.

The Minnesota Multiphasic Personality Inventory (MMPI) Updated: 1988 Edition refers to a revision of the widely-used true-false test of psychopathology. The author, Albert Rosen, was professor of psychology at Galludet College in Washington, DC, and published a number of serious articles on the MMPI and its revisions, as well as on projective and other tests.

Karen Alberding, David Antonuccio, and Blake H. Tearnan, were the authors responsible for *A Brief Report on Clinical Aspects of Procrastination*. The authors' affiliation was with the Veteran's Administration Medical Center at Reno, NV. Procrastination is, of course, the putting off until tomorrow of what you could do today. There is a considerable body of serious research on the topic. The present selection is certainly among the more interesting and delightful (and brief) discussions of the topic.

As you read, note that, to determine issues of priority (e.g., which scientist came up with an idea first—and when), most journals report when a manuscript was received and then revised. Note the journal's dates for this article. Both selections, recall, were originally articles in the *Journal of Polymorphous Perversity*, although reprinted versions are reproduced here.

The Minnesota Multiphasic Personality Inventory (MMPI) Updated: 1988 Edition

by Albert Rosen, Ph.D.

Source: Rosen, A. (1989). The Minnesota Multiphasic Personality Inventory (MMPI) Updated: 1988 Edition. In G. C. Ellenbogen (Ed.). *The Primal Whimper* (pp. 69–70). New York: Ballantine Books.

The Minnesota Multiphasic Personality Inventory (MMPI), with 566 true-or-false items, first appeared 45 years ago but is now sadly outdated. Based upon the weight of his vast clinical intuition, not to mention quite a bit of clinical experience as well, the author presents here revised items which he feels will greatly enhance the reliability and validity of this powerful personality measure.

Answer each item T(rue) or F(alse).

I am easily awakened by the firing of cannons.
I believe I am following others.
I was not very strict with my parents.
Most of the time I don't like to read newspaper articles about nuclear accidents nearby.
My sex life is satisfactory, except when I am with another person.
I am troubled by attacks of optimism.
I get nervous when I handle $100,000 bills.
It takes a lot of argument to convince most people that they are lying.

Sometimes I feel that things are real.
When I grow up I want to be a child.
I try to steal people's thoughts and ideas when they are not looking.
I believe that my home life is as miserable as that of most people I know.
I am afraid when I look down from the ground floor of a building.
I have many enemies who secretly love me.
There was too much love and companionship in my family.
I am sexually attracted to beings from outer space.
As a youngster, I was usually suspended from school for attending.
I frequently notice that I am not trembling.
I have nightmares every day.
I am liked by most people, unless they know me.
I get happy easily and then can get over it soon.
I think I would like the work of a robot.

A Brief Report on Clinical Aspects of Procrastination: Better Late Than Never

by Kathy Alberding, M.S.W., David Antonuccio, Ph.D., Blake H. Tearnan, Ph.D.

Source: Alberding, K., Antonuccio, D., Tearnan, B. H. (1989). A brief report on clinical aspects of procrastination: Better late than never. In G. C. Ellenbogen (Ed.). *Oral sadism and the vegetarian personality* (p. 122). New York: Bruner/Mazel.

This is a brief report of a full-length article the authors are planning to write on the topic of procrastination as a mature psychological defense. The authors have not, however, had the time to do a thorough literature review, or any, for that matter, but all have experience with the topic and fully intend to do such a review in the near future.

There are several advantages of procrastination, not the least of which is that it allows an individual the opportunity to think a task through (D'Lay, in press). When the authors actually get around to writing the article, they expect to give it the thorough, detailed treatment this topic deserves.

References

D'Lay, I. (1925). *Don't rush into anything.* Peoria: Turtle Publications, in press.

Acknowledgments: The authors would like to extend their appreciation to those who expressed interest in contributing to this report but who never found sufficient time to do so: Patricia Chatham, Ph.D., Stephanie Dillon, Ph.D., William Danton, Ph.D., Norman Kerbel, M.A., Kathryn McFadden, M.S., David Hutchison, M.D., Carol Vasso, and Julie Anderson.

(Received: December 3, 1975. Revised: September 12, 1986.

Concluding Comments

There is humor to be found in psychological writing, whether it is the witticism or dramatic scene hidden in the midst of serious articles, or an explicit piece of satire in a journal such as the *Journal of Polymorphous Perversity*. As few and far between as such passages may be, they are welcome and keep us smiling, chuckling, and on a few occasions, laughing out loud, within an otherwise serious field.

Review Questions

1. What are some examples of studies of humor conducted by psychologists?
2. Is humor an important individual differences variable?
3. Has there ever been a journal that published only satirical articles about psychology?

10

Reading Freud on Psychodynamics

Reading Freud and the Early Twentieth-Century Grand Theorists

A number of thinkers have attempted to understand human beings and their societies through the application of a few simple, powerful principles. Jean-Jacques Rousseau described a social contract that bound individuals and society. Adam Smith outlined the power of capitalism and free markets. Less successfully, perhaps, Karl Marx and Fredrick Engels tried to understand all of history through the lens of class conflict. Charles Darwin's theory of evolution—his explanation for the origin of diverse biological species—has provided a basis for modern biology.

A parallel group of figures emerged within the field of personality psychology. These figures possessed grand visions and simple, clear, ideas for explaining the basis of human personality. They are often referred to as "Grand Theorists," in reference to the grand sweep of their ideas. Among this group are individuals of varying familiarity, including Sigmund Freud, Alfred Adler, Carl Jung, George Kelly, Abraham Maslow, Carl Rogers, Gordon Allport, and others. For example, Abraham Maslow and Carl Rogers viewed human beings as on a voyage toward self-discovery. Gordon Allport emphasized the power of traits—biopsychosocial consistencies of behavior—in explaining a person's actions. And George Kelly saw the individual as a personal scientist trying to predict and control his or her environment.

Perhaps no figure among them has been as influential and important to the history of psychology as has Sigmund Freud (Westen, 1998). Freud developed the central ideas of psychodynamic theory in the late 1800s with his colleague, Joseph Breuer. Those ideas included that there existed within an individual's mind unconscious intentions and motives that directed him or her, and of which the individual was unaware. Freud came to these ideas by examining cases of clients suffering from various psychological ailments in his clinical practice. The grandness of the theory began to emerge as Freud began to apply his ideas to an understanding of more and more aspects of the individual's psyche. He applied the theory, in turn, to dreams, to everyday errors of behavior, to jokes, to artwork, and even to the structure of society itself.

This also promoted interest in the theory. After all, few people would have the opportunity to witness the remarkable cases he observed in the clinic office. But anyone could observe, along with Freud, such mental events as slips of the tongue and nightmares. Freud wrote *The Psychopathology of Everyday Life,* to use his psychodynamic theory to examine phenomena such as slips of the tongue, pen, and behavior. Its remarkably simple point is that people suffer from conflicting intentions and motives at all stages of their behavior, and that they are unaware of such processes. Nonetheless, to a careful observer, these unconscious motives can be revealed through the study of "parapraxes"— errors in speech and behavior. Freud's book was later condensed and used as the opening of the lectures of his broader *Introductory Lectures on Psychoanalysis*—the reading included here.

The Present Reading

At the time he produced the *Introductory Lectures in Psychoanalysis*, "Freud had been acting as his own best popularizer for nearly two decades," wrote his biographer, Peter Gay (1988, p. 368). The *Introductory Lectures* were first delivered at the University of Vienna in the winter terms of 1915–1916, and 1916–1917. The series of lectures were delivered to a growing audience of physicians and the generally interested public. One audience member at the time was Freud's daughter, Anna, destined to become a psychoanalyst and Grand Theorist in her own right (Gay, 1988, p. 368). When the *Introductory Lectures* were published, they were widely read and translated. They sold perhaps 500,000 copies in the original German and were translated into 15 languages, including English, Chinese, Japanese, Serbo-Croatian, and Hebrew (Gay, 1988, p. 369).

The *Introductory Lectures in Psychoanalysis* is divided into three parts. The first part, "Parapraxes," concerned everyday slips of the tongue and errors of behavior. It served the purpose of allowing the casual listener to move from everyday observations into a deeper, more subtle theory of psychoanalysis. The *Introductory Lectures'* second section, "Dreams" examined one of the most mysterious realms of psychological events from a psychoanalytic perspective: why people have the dreams they do. The *Lectures'* third section presented Freud's "General Theory of Neuroses"—his general theory of how the mind worked, and how abnormal symptoms arose within it.

The public persona of a scientist at the turn of the last century was rather different than it is today. Today we may imagine scientists as team players, working with colleagues in a university or laboratory setting. The scientist of the turn of the last century was a different, perhaps more romantic, figure. He or she was a loner who worked apart from the crowd: a hero and a detective who spoke to the opinion-makers through public lectures. At the opening of these lectures, we "hear" Sigmund Freud's lectures, and imagine him in this romantic role as a scientist, a detective, and psychoanalyst all rolled into one.

The Watch List

Lecture I of the *Introductory Lectures* (not included here) provides an overview of Freud's plan for the lectures he will be giving, and an explanation of their form. Lectures II through IV, which make up this reading, collectively introduce Freud's detailed study of errors in behavior—the most accessible portion of his theory and a good choice for the opening of the work.

The three lectures (II, III, and IV) are all under the name "Parapraxes"—Freud's term for errors of behavior including slips of tongue, errors of the pen, and certain errors of behavior as well.

As you begin Lecture II, be alert to the fact that the lectures were originally delivered in German, and many of the slips of the tongue must be translated into English, which means that for an English-speaking reader, some effort must be exerted in understanding some of the speech errors discussed. Be sure to read the footnotes, which often provide additional insight about the slips of the tongue.

Also in Lecture II, Freud refers to a *Weltanschauung,* which is a world view, and to psychoanalysis, which was Freud's name for his theory. Note Freud's strictly deterministic attitude toward slips: that is, there must be an identifiable cause for any slip of the tongue. Toward the middle of the selection, Freud refers to "Two writers… (a philologist and a psychiatrist)." A philologist is a linguist.

Lecture III continues the discussion of parapraxes. By now you will be more used to Freud's approach and language. Do note, however, toward the very end of this lecture, Freud's remark that not all the intentions behind a slip will come true. Freud here is foreshadowing a later point within the *Introductory Lectures*: that through psychoanalysis a person may make conscious formerly unconscious intentions, analyze them, and in some cases move beyond them.

Lecture IV concludes the discussion of parapraxes. Early on, Freud raises the issue of the "perseveration" of disturbing thoughts and motives. In this context, perseveration refers to the persistence of an idea or a train of thought. With this idea, Freud begins to reveal his general point: there can be mental ideas and intentions that are pushed away from consciousness but that continue to exert an influence on the individual. This idea—of unconscious intentions that exert continuous pressure on the mind—is a key to understanding his idea of the dynamic unconscious.

Introductory Lectures on Psychoanalysis

by Sigmund Freud

Source: Freud, S. (1966). Introductory lectures on psychoanalysis. J. Strachey (Trans. and Ed.). [Selections: Lecture II: Parapraxes, pp. 25–39; Lecture III: Parapraxes (Cont.), pp. 40–42, 46–47, 49–51, 57–59; Lecture IV: Parapraxes (Concluded): 61–67.] New York: W. W. Norton. [Original work published 1917].

Lecture II: Parapraxes

LADIES AND GENTLEMEN—We will not start with postulates but with an investigation. Let us choose as its subject certain phenomena which are very common and very familiar but which have been very little examined, and which, since they can be observed in any healthy person, have nothing to do with illnesses. They are what are known as 'parapraxes,'[1] to which everyone is liable. It may happen, for instance, that a person who intends to say something may use another word instead (a *slip of the tongue [Versprechen]*), or he may hear wrongly something that has been said to him (a *mishearing [Verhören]*)—on the assumption, of course, that there is no organic disturbance of his powers of hearing....

The following selections were lightly edited and abridged so as to emphasize key parts of the argument. From here forward in this selection, each omission is marked with an ellipsis ("…").

---

[1] ['*Fehlleistungen,*' literally 'faulty acts' or 'faulty functions.' The general concept did not exist before Freud, and an English term was invented for its translation. The whole of *The Psychopathology of Everyday Life* (1901b) (Norton, 1965), is devoted to a discussion of them. Freud often used them in his didactic writings (as he does here) as the most suitable material for an introduction to his theories. They were, indeed, among the earliest subjects of his own psychological investigations. Some account of the history of his interest in them will be found in the Editor's Introduction to the sixth volume of the *Standard Edition.* Since there will be a large number of references to that work in the present lectures, the abbreviation 'P.E.L.' will be used here in order to economize space. The page references in all such cases will be to the *Standard Ed.* and the Norton edition.]

But you will protest with some annoyance: There are so many vast problems in the wide universe, as well as within the narrower confines of our minds…that it does really seem gratuitous to waste labour and interest on such trivialities. …I should reply: Patience, Ladies and Gentlemen!

…Are there not very important things which can only reveal themselves, under certain conditions and at certain times, by quite feeble indications? I should find no difficulty in giving you several examples of such situations. If you are a young man, for instance, will it not be from small pointers that you will conclude that you have won a girl's favour? Would you wait for an express declaration of love or a passionate embrace? Or would not a glance, scarcely noticed by other people, be enough? A slight movement, the lengthening by a second of the pressure of a hand? And if you were a detective engaged in tracing a murder, would you expect to find that the murderer had left his photograph behind at the place of the crime, with his address attached? Or would you not necessarily have to be satisfied with comparatively slight and obscure traces of the person you were in search of? So do not let us under-estimate small indications; by their help we may succeed in getting on the track of something bigger. Furthermore, I think like you that the great problems of the universe and of science have the first claim on our interest. But it is as a rule of very little use to form an express intention of devoting oneself to research into this or that great problem. One is then often at a loss to know the first step to take. It is more promising in scientific work to attack whatever is immediately before one and offers an opportunity for research. If one does so really thoroughly and without prejudice or preconception, and if one has luck, then, since everything is related to everything, including small things to great, one may gain access even from such unpretentious work to study of the great problems. That is what I should say in order to retain your interest, when we deal with such apparent trivialities as the parapraxes of healthy people.

Let us now call in someone who knows nothing of psychoanalysis, and ask him how he explains such occurrences. His first reply will certainly be: 'Oh! That's not worth explaining: they're just small chance events.' What does the fellow mean by this? Is he maintaining that there are occurrences, however small, which drop out of the universal concatenation of events—occurrences which might just as well not happen as happen? If anyone makes a breach of this kind in the determinism of natural events at a single point, it means that he has thrown overboard the whole *Weltanschauung* of science. Even the *Weltanschauung* of religion, we may remind him, behaves much more consistently, since it gives an explicit assurance that no sparrow falls from the roof without God's special will. I think our friend will hesitate to draw the logical conclusion from his first reply; he will change his mind and say that after all when he comes to study these things he can find explanations of them. What is in question are small failures of functioning, imperfections in mental activity, whose determinants can be assigned. A man who can usually speak correctly may make a slip of the tongue (1) if he is slightly indisposed and tired, (2) if he is excited and (3) if he is too much occupied with other things. It is easy to confirm these statements. Slips of the tongue do really occur with particular frequency when one is tired, has a headache or is threatened with migraine. In the same circumstances proper names are easily forgotten. Some people are accustomed to recognize the approach of an attack of migraine when proper names escape them in this way.[2] When we are excited, too, we often make mistakes over words—and over *things* as well, and a 'bungled action' follows. Intentions are forgotten and a quantity of other undesigned actions become noticeable if we are absent-minded—that is, properly speaking, if we are concentrated on something else. A familiar example of this absent-mindedness is the Professor in

Fliegende Blätter[3] who leaves his umbrella behind and takes the wrong hat because he is thinking about the problems he is going to deal with in his next book. All of us can recall from our own experience instances of how we can forget intentions we have formed and promises we have made because in the meantime we have had some absorbing experience.

This sounds quite reasonable and seems safe from contradiction, though it may not be very interesting, perhaps, and not what we expected. Let us look at these explanations of parapraxes more closely.

The alleged preconditions for occurrence of these phenomena are not all of the same kind. Being ill and disturbances of the circulation provide a physiological reason for the impairment of normal function; excitement, fatigue and distraction are factors of another sort, which might be described as psychophysiological... what we find does not tally entirely with this attention theory of parapraxes, or at least does not follow from it naturally. We discover that parapraxes of this kind and forgetting of this kind occur in people who are *not* fatigued or absent-minded...

There are a large number of procedures that one carries out purely automatically, with very little attention, but nevertheless performs with complete security. A walker, who scarcely knows where he is going, keeps to the right path for all that, and stops at his destination without having *gone astray [vergangen]*. Or at all events this is so as a rule. An expert pianist strikes the right keys without thinking. He may, of course, make an occasional mistake; but if automatic playing increased the danger of bungling, that danger would be at its greatest for a virtuoso, whose playing, as a result of prolonged practice, has become *entirely* automatic. We know, on the contrary, that many procedures are carried out with quite particular certainty if they are not the object of a specially high degree of attention,[4] and that the mishap of a parapraxis is liable to occur precisely if special importance is attached to correct functioning and there has therefore certainly been no distraction of the necessary attention. It could be argued that this is

---

[2] [This was a personal experience of Freud's. P.E.L., 21.]

[3] [The comic weekly.]

[4] [Freud has often suggested elsewhere that functions may be performed more accurately in the absence of conscious attention. See P.E.L., 132.]

the result of 'excitement,' but it is difficult to see why the excitement should not on the contrary *increase* the attention directed to what is so earnestly intended. If by a slip of the tongue someone says the opposite of what he intends in an important speech or oral communication, it can scarcely be explained by the psycho-physiological or attention theory.

There are, moreover, a number of small subsidiary phenomena in the case of parapraxes, which we do not understand and on which the explanations so far given shed no light. For instance, if we have temporarily forgotten a name, we are annoyed about it, do all we can to remember it and cannot leave the business alone. Why in such cases do we so extremely seldom succeed in directing our attention, as we are after all anxious to do, to the word which (as we say) is 'on the tip of our tongue' and which we recognize at once when we are told it? Or again: there are cases in which the parapraxes multiply, form chains, and replace one another. On a first occasion one has missed an appointment. On the next occasion, when one has firmly decided not to forget *this* time, it turns out that one has made a note of the wrong hour. Or one tries to arrive at a forgotten word by roundabout ways and thereupon a second name escapes one which might have helped one to find the first. If one searches for this second name, a third disappears, and so on. As is well known, the same thing can happen with misprints, which are to be regarded as the parapraxes of the compositor. An obstinate misprint of this kind, so it is said, once slipped into a social-democrat newspaper. Its report of some ceremonial included the words: 'Among those present was to be noticed His Highness the *Kornprinz.*' Next day an attempt was made at a correction. The paper apologized and said: 'We should of course have said "the *Knor-prinz.*"[5] People speak in such cases of a 'demon of misprints' or a 'type-setting fiend'—terms which at least go beyond any psycho-physiological theory of misprints.[6]

Perhaps you are familiar, too, with the fact that it is possible to *provoke* slips of the tongue, to produce them, as it were, by suggestion. An anecdote illustrates this. A stage neophyte had been cast for the important

part in [Schiller's] *Die Jungfrau von Orleans* of the messenger who announces to the King that 'der Connétable schickt sein Schwert zurück [the Constable sends back his sword].' A leading actor amused himself during the rehearsal by repeatedly inducing the nervous young man to say, instead of the words of the text: 'der Komfortabel schickt sein Pferd zurück [the cab-driver sends back his horse].[7] He achieved his aim: the wretched beginner actually made his début at the performance with the corrupt version, in spite of having been warned against it, or perhaps *because* he had been warned.

No light is thrown on these small features of parapraxes by the theory of withdrawal of attention. The theory need not on that account be wrong, however; it may merely lack something, some addition, before it is entirely satisfying. But some of the parapraxes, too, can themselves be looked at from another point of view.

Let us take *slips of the tongue* as the most suitable sort of parapraxis for our purpose—though we might equally well have chosen slips of the pen or misreading.[8] We must bear in mind that so far we have only asked when—under what conditions—people make slips of the tongue, and it is only to that question that we have had an answer. But we might direct our interest elsewhere and enquire why it is that the slip occurred in this particular way and no other; and we might take into account what it is that emerges in the slip itself. You will observe that, so long as this question is unanswered and no light thrown on the product of the slip, the phenomenon remains a chance event from the psychological point of view, even though it may have been given a physiological explanation. If I make a slip of the tongue, I might obviously do so in an infinite number of ways,

---

[5] [What was intended was the 'Kronprinz (Crown Prince).' 'Korn' means 'corn' and 'Knorr' means 'protuberance.']
[6] [Cf. P.E.L., 130–1.]

[7] [There seems to be some confusion here. Actually (in Act I, Scene 2 of the play) it is the King himself who announces the Constable's defection.]
[8] [It is most unfortunate from the point of view of the translator that Freud chose slips of the tongue as his most frequent examples of parapraxes in all three of these lectures, since they are from their very nature, peculiarly resistant to translation. We have, however, followed our invariable practice in the *Standard Edition* and kept Freud's instances, with footnote and square bracket explanations, rather than replace them by extraneous English ones. Plenty of the latter will be found elsewhere, especially in papers by A. A. Brill (1912) and Ernest Jones (1911).]

the right word might be replaced by any of a thousand others, it might be distorted in countless different directions. Is there something, then, that compels me in the particular case to make the slip in one special way, or does it remain a matter of chance, of arbitrary choice, and is the question perhaps one to which no sensible answer at all can be given?

Two writers, Meringer and Mayer (a philologist and a psychiatrist), in fact made an attempt in 1895 to attack the problem of parapraxes from this angle. They collected examples and began by treating them in a purely descriptive way. This, of course, provides no explanation as yet, though it might pave the way to one. They distinguish the various kinds of distortions imposed by the slip on the intended speech as 'transpositions,' 'presonances [anticipation],' 'post-sonances [perseverations],' 'fusions (contaminations)' and 'replacements (substitutions).' I will give you some examples of these main groups proposed by the authors. An instance of transposition would be to say *the Milo of Venus* instead of 'the Venus of Milo' (a transposition of the order of the words); an instance of a pre-sonance [anticipation] would be: 'es war mir *auf der Schwest*...auf der Brust so schwer';[9] and a post-sonance [perseveration] would be exemplified by the well-known toast that went wrong: 'Ich fordere Sie *auf, auf* das Wohl unseres Chefs *auf*zustossen' [instead of *an*zustossen].[10] These three forms of slip of the tongue are not exactly common. You will come on much more numerous examples in which the slip results from contraction or fusion. Thus, for instance, a gentleman addressed a lady in the street in the following words: 'If you will permit me, madam, I should like to *begleit-digen* you.' The composite word,[11] in addition to the '*begleiten* [to accompany],' evidently has concealed in it '*beleidigen* [to insult].' (Incidentally, the young man was not likely to have much success with the lady.) As an example of a substitution Meringer and

Mayer give the case of someone saying: 'Ich gebe die Präparate in den *Brief*kasten' instead of '*Brüt*kasten.'[12]

The attempted explanation which these authors base on their collection of instances is quite peculiarly inadequate. They believe that the sounds and syllables of a word have a particular 'valency' and that the innervation of an element of high valency may have a disturbing influence on one that is less valent. Here they are clearly basing themselves on the far from common cases of pre-sonance and post-sonance; these preferences of some sounds over others (if they in fact exist) can have no bearing at all on other effects of slips of the tongue. After all, the commonest slips of the tongue are when, instead of saying one word, we say another very much like it; and this similarity is for many people a sufficient explanation of such slips. For instance, a Professor declared in his inaugural lecture: 'I am not '*geneigt* [inclined]' instead of '*geeignet* [qualified]' to appreciate the services of my highly esteemed predecessor.' Or another Professor remarked: 'In the case of the female genitals, in spite of many *Versuchungen* [temptations]— I beg your pardon, *Versuche* [experiments]....'[13]

The most usual, and at the same time the most striking kind of slips of the tongue, however, are those in which one says the precise opposite of what one intended to say. Here, of course, we are very remote from relations between sounds and the effects of similarity; and instead we can appeal to the fact that contraries have a strong conceptual kinship with each other and stand in a particularly close psychological association with each other.[14] There are historical examples of such occurrences. A President of the Lower House of our Parliament once opened the sitting with the words: 'Gentlemen, I take notice that a full quorum of members is present and herewith declare the sitting *closed*.'[15]

Any other familiar association can act in the same insidious fashion as a contrary one, and can emerge in

---

[9] [The phrase intended was: 'it lay on my breast so heavily.' The meaningless '*Schwest*' was a distortion of "*Brust* (breast)' owing to an anticipation of the '*schw*' of '*schwer* (heavily)" This and the preceding example are also in P.E.L., 53–4.]

[10] ['I call on you to *hiccough* to (instead of 'drink to') the health of our Chief.' This, too, occurs in P.E.L., 54, where, however, the translation is slightly different.].

[11] [A meaningless one.]

[12] ['I put the preparation into the letter-box' instead of 'incubator,' literally, 'hatching-box.' These last two examples occur in P.E.L., 68 and 54.]

[13] [P.E.L., 69 and 78-9.]

[14] [Cf. below, p. 178 ff.]

[15] [P.E.L., 59. The example was also used by Freud in one of his very last writings, the unfinished 'Some Elementary Lessons in Psychoanalysis' (1940b[1938]).]

quite unsuitable circumstances. Thus, on the occasion of a celebration in honour of the marriage of a child of Hermann von Helmholtz to a child of Werner von Siemens, the well-known inventor and industrialist, it is said that the duty of proposing the young couple's health fell to the famous physiologist Du Bois-Reymond. No doubt he made a brilliant speech, but he ended with the words: 'So, long life to the new firm of Siemens and Halske!' That was, of course, the name of the *old* firm. The juxtaposition of the two names must have been as familiar to a Berliner as Fortnum and Mason would be to a Londoner.[16]

We must therefore include among the causes of parapraxes not only relations between sounds and verbal similarity, but the influence of word-associations as well. But that is not all. In a number of cases it seems impossible to explain a slip of the tongue unless we take into account something that had been said, or even merely thought, in an earlier sentence. Once again, then, we have here a case of perseveration, like those insisted upon by Meringer, but of more distant origin.—I must confess that I feel on the whole as though after all this we were further than ever from understanding slips of the tongue.

Nevertheless, I hope I am not mistaken in saying that during this last enquiry we have all of us formed a fresh impression of these instances of slips of the tongue, and that it may be worth while to consider that impression further. We examined the conditions under which in general slips of the tongue occur, and afterwards the influences which determine the kind of distortion which the slip produces. But we have so far paid no attention whatever to the *product* of the slip considered by itself, without reference to its origin. If we decide to do so, we are bound in the end to find the courage to say that in a few examples what results from the slip of the tongue has a sense of its own. What do we mean by 'has a sense'? That the product of the slip of the tongue may perhaps itself have a right to be regarded as a completely valid psychical act, pursuing an aim of its own, as a statement with a content and sig-

nificance. So far we have always spoken of 'parapraxes [faulty acts],' but it seems now as though sometimes the faulty act was itself quite a *normal* act, which merely took the place of the other act which was the one expected or intended.

The fact of the parapraxis having a sense of its own seems in certain cases evident and unmistakable. When the President of the Lower House with his first words *closed* the sitting instead of opening it, we feel inclined, in view of our knowledge of the circumstances in which the slip of the tongue occurred, to recognize that the parapraxis had a sense. The President expected nothing good of the sitting and would have been glad if he could have brought it to an immediate end. We have no difficulty in pointing to the sense of this slip of the tongue, or, in other words, in interpreting it. Or, let us suppose that one lady says to another in tones of apparent admiration: 'That smart new hat—I suppose you *aufgepatzt* [a non-existent word instead of *aufgeputzt* (trimmed)] it yourself?' Then no amount of scientific propriety will succeed in preventing our seeing behind this slip of the tongue the words: 'This hat is a *Patzerei* [botched-up affair].' Or, once more, we are told that a lady who was well-known for her energy remarked on one occasion: 'My husband asked his doctor what diet he ought to follow; but the doctor told him he had no need to diet: he could eat and drink what I want.' Here again the slip of the tongue has an unmistakable other side to it: it was giving expression to a consistently planned programme.[17]

If it turned out, Ladies and Gentlemen, that not only a *few* instances of slips of the tongue and of parapraxes in general have a sense, but a considerable number of them, the *sense* of parapraxes, of which we have so far heard nothing, would inevitably become their most interesting feature and would push every other consideration into the background. We should then be able to leave all physiological or psycho-physiological factors on one side and devote ourselves to purely psychological investigations into the sense—that is, the meaning or purpose—of parapraxes. We shall therefore make it our business to test this expectation on a considerable number of observations.

[16] [In the original: 'as Riedel and Beutel would be to a Viennese.' This last was a well-known outfitter's shop in Vienna. Siemens and Halske were, of course, the great electrical engineers.]

[17] [These two last examples appear in P.E.L., 87 and 70.]

But before carrying out this intention I should like to invite you to follow me along another track. It has repeatedly happened that a creative writer has made use of a slip of the tongue or some other parapraxis as an instrument for producing an imaginative effect. This fact alone must prove to us that he regards the parapraxis—the slip of the tongue, for instance—as having a sense, since he has produced it deliberately....

A[n]... impressive example has been discovered by Otto Rank [1910a] in Shakespeare. It is from *The Merchant of Venice,* in the famous scene in which the fortunate lover chooses between the three caskets, and perhaps I cannot do better than read you Rank's short account of it:

'A slip of the tongue occurs in Shakespeare's *Merchant of Venice* (Act III, Scene 2), which is from the dramatic point of view extremely subtly motivated and which is put to brilliant technical use. Like the slip in *Wallenstein* to which Freud has drawn attention, it shows that dramatists have a clear understanding of the mechanism and meaning of this kind of parapraxis and assume that the same is true of their audience. Portia, who by her father's will has been bound to the choice of a husband by lot, has so far escaped all her unwelcome suitors by a fortunate chance. Having at last found in Bassanio the suitor who is to her liking, she has cause to fear that he too will choose the wrong casket. She would very much like to tell him that even so he could rest assured of her love; but she is prevented by her vow. In this internal conflict the poet makes her say to the suitor she favours:

I pray you tarry; pause a day or two
Before you hazard: for, in choosing wrong,
I lose your company; therefore forbear a while:
There's something tells me (*but it is not love*)
I would not lose you....
                    ...I could teach you
How to choose right, but then I am forsworn;
So will I never be; so may you miss me;
But if you do you'll make me wish a sin,
That I have been forsworn. Beshrew your eyes,
They have o'erlooked me, and divided me;
One half of me is yours, the other half yours,—
Mine own, I would say; But, if mine, then yours,
And so all yours.

The thing of which she wanted to give him only a very subtle hint, because she should have concealed it from him altogether, namely, that even before he made his choice she was *wholly* his and loved him—it is precisely this that the poet, with a wonderful psychological sensitivity, causes to break through openly in her slip of the tongue; and by this artistic device he succeeds in relieving both the lover's unbearable uncertainty and the suspense of the sympathetic audience over the outcome of his choice.'

Observe, too, how skillfully Portia in the end reconciles the two statements contained in her slip of the tongue, how she solves the contradiction between them and yet finally shows that it was the slip that was in the right:

'But, if mine, then yours, And so all yours.'

It has occasionally happened that a thinker whose field lies outside medicine has, by something he says, revealed the sense of a parapraxis and anticipated our efforts at explaining them. You all know of the witty satirist Lichtenberg (1742–1799), of whom Goethe said: 'Where he makes a jest a problem lies concealed.' Sometimes the jest brings the *solution* of the problem to light as well. In Lichtenberg's *Witzige and Satirische Einfälle* [Witty and Satirical Thoughts, 1853] we find this: 'He had read so much Homer that he always read *"Agamemnon"* instead of *"angenommen* [supposed]".' Here we have the whole theory of misreading.[18]

We must see next time whether we can go along with these writers in their view of parapraxes.

Lecture III: Parapraxes (Continued)

LADIES AND GENTLEMEN,—We arrived last time at the idea of considering parapraxes not in relation to the intended function which they disturbed but on their own account; and we formed an impression that in particular cases they seemed to be betraying a sense of their own. We then reflected that if confirmation

[18] [Lichtenberg was a favourite author of Freud's and many of his epigrams are discussed in *Jokes and Their Relation to the Unconscious* (1905c), (Norton, 1960). The Agamemnon remark is further considered below, p. 70. It is quoted in the book on jokes (p. 93) as well as in P.E.L., 112, where Goethe's comment also appears. (P.E.L., 218).]

could be obtained on a wider scale that parapraxes have a sense, their sense would soon become more interesting than the investigation of the circumstances in which they come about.

Let us once more reach an agreement upon what is to be understood by the 'sense' of a psychical process. We mean nothing other by it than the intention it serves and its position in a psychical continuity. In most of our researches we can replace 'sense' by 'intention' or 'purpose.'[19] Was it, then, merely a deceptive illusion or a poetic exaltation of parapraxes when we thought we recognized an intention in them?

We will continue to take slips of the tongue as our examples. If we now look through a considerable number of observations of that kind, we shall find whole categories of cases in which the intention, the sense, of the slip is plainly visible. Above all there are those in which what was intended is replaced by its contrary. The President of the Lower House [pp. 34] said in his opening speech: 'I declare the sitting closed.' That is quite unambiguous. The sense and intention of his slip was that he wanted to close the sitting. 'Er sagt es ja selbst'[20] we are tempted to quote: we need only take him at his word. Do not interrupt me at this point by objecting that that is impossible, that we know that he did not want to close the sitting but to open it, and that he himself, whom we have just recognized as the supreme court of appeal, could confirm the fact that he wanted to open it. You are forgetting that we have come to an agreement that we will begin by regarding parapraxes on their own account; their relation to the intention which they have disturbed is not to be discussed till later. Otherwise you will be guilty of a logical error by simply evading the problem that is under discussion—by what is called in English 'begging the question.'

In other cases, where the slip does not express the precise contrary, an opposite sense can nevertheless be brought out by it. 'I am not *geneigt* [inclined] to appreciate the services of my predecessor' [p. 33]. *Geneigt* is not the contrary of *geeignet* [qualified], but it expresses openly something which contrasts sharply with the situation in which the speech was to be made.

In yet other cases the slip of the tongue merely adds a second sense to the one intended. The sentence then sounds like a contraction, abbreviation or condensation of several sentences. Thus, when the energetic lady said: 'He can eat and drink what I want' [p. 35], it was just as though she had said: 'He can eat and drink what he wants; but what has *he* to do with wanting? *I* will want instead of him.' A slip of the tongue often gives the impression of being an abbreviation of this sort. For instance, a Professor of Anatomy at the end of a lecture on the nasal cavities asked whether his audience had understood what he said, and, after general assent, went on; 'I can hardly believe that, since even in a city with millions of inhabitants, those who understand the nasal cavities can be counted *on one finger*.... I beg your pardon, on the fingers of one hand.' The abbreviated phrase has a sense too—namely, that there is only one person who understands them.[21]

In contrast to these groups of cases, in which the parapraxis itself brings its sense to light, there are others in which the parapraxis produces nothing that has any sense of its own, and which therefore sharply contradict our expectations. If someone twists a proper name about by a slip of the tongue or puts an abnormal series of sounds together, these very common events alone seem to give a negative reply to our question whether all parapraxes have some sort of sense. Closer examination of such instances, however, shows that these distortions are easily understood and that there is by no means so great a distinction between these more obscure cases and the earlier straight-forward ones.

A man who was asked about the health of his horse replied; 'Well, it *draut* [a meaningless word]... it *dauert* [will last] another month perhaps.' When he was asked what he had really meant to say, he explained that he had thought it was a '*traurige* [sad]' story. The combination of '*dauert*' and '*traurig*' had produced '*draut*.[22]

Another man, speaking of some occurrences he disapproved of, went on: 'But then facts came to

---

[19] [It has been thought best to translate the German word 'Tendenz' by 'purpose' throughout these lectures. The meanings of the two words do not, however, coincide, and in a few passages some such rendering as 'trend' would be preferable. 'Tendenz' is almost never equivalent to 'tendency,' though the adjective 'tendenziös' has become naturalized in the English form of 'tendentious,' as applied, for instance, to a play 'with a purpose.']

[20] ['He says so himself.' This is a line from the standard German translation of a phrase in *Figaro* which occurs repeatedly in the sextet in Act III.]

[21] [Repeated from P.E.L., 78.]

[22] Meringer and Mayer [P.E.L., 58].

Vorschwein [a non-existent word, instead of *Vorschein* (light)]....' In reply to enquiries he confirmed that the fact that he had thought these occurrences '*Schweinereien*' ['disgusting,' literally 'piggish']. '*Vorschein*' and '*Schweinereien*' combined to produce the strange word '*Vorschwein*.[23]

You will recall the case of the young man who asked the unknown lady if he might '*begleitdigen*' her [p. 33]. We ventured to divide up this verbal form into '*begleiten* [accompany]' and '*beleidigen* [insult],' and we felt certain enough of this interpretation not to need any confirmation of it. You will see from these examples that even these obscurer cases of slips of the tongue can be explained by a convergence, a mutual '*interference*,' between two different intended speeches; the differences between these cases of slips arise merely from the fact that on some occasions one intention takes the place of the other completely (becomes a substitute for it), as in slips of the tongue that express the contrary, whereas on other occasions the one intention has to be satisfied with distorting or modifying the other, so that composite structures are produced, which make sense, to a greater or lesser degree, on their own account.

We seem now to have grasped the secret of a large number of slips of the tongue...

I am particularly interested, however, in your next question: how does one discover the two mutually interfering purposes? ...One of the two, the purpose that is disturbed, is of course unmistakable; the person who makes the slip of the tongue knows it and admits to it. It is only the other, the disturbing purpose, that can give rise to doubt and hesitation...

Do you not feel inclined to object?...You proceed ' . . . Now let us take another example—the one in which a speaker proposing the toast of honour on a ceremonial occasion called on his audience to hiccough [*aufzustossen*] to the health of the Chief. You say that the disturbing intention in this case was an insulting one: that was what was opposing the speaker's expression of respect. But this is pure interpretation on your part, based upon observations apart from the slip of the tongue. If in this instance you were to question the person responsible for the slip, he would not confirm your idea that he intended an insult; on the contrary, he

would energetically repudiate it. Why, in view of this clear denial, do you not abandon your unprovable interpretation?'

Yes. You have lighted on a powerful argument this time. I can imagine the unknown proposer of the toast. He is probably a subordinate to the Chief of the Department who is being honoured—perhaps he himself is already an Assistant Lecturer, a young man with excellent prospects in life. I try to force him to admit that he may nevertheless have had a feeling that there was something in him opposing his toast in honour of the Chief. But this lands me in a nice mess. He gets impatient and suddenly breaks out: 'Just you stop trying to cross-question me or I shall turn nasty. You're going to ruin my whole career with your suspicions. I simply said "*aufstossen* [hiccough to]" instead of "*antossen* [drink to]" because I'd said "auf" twice before in the same sentence. That's what Meringer calls a perseveration and there's nothing more to be interpreted about it. D'you understand? *Basta*!'—H'm! That was a surprising reaction, a truly energetic denial....

When someone charged with an offense confesses his deed to the judge, the judge believes his confession; but if he denies it, the judge does not believe him. If it were otherwise, there would be no administration of justice, and in spite of occasional errors we must allow that the system works...

In the law courts it may be necessary for practical purposes to find a defendant guilty on circumstantial evidence... neither are we obliged to disregard the circumstantial evidence... But if the subject does not himself give us the explanation of the sense of a parapraxis, where are we to find the starting-points for our interpretation—the circumstantial evidence? In various directions...

I have already given you an example of a combination of a forgetting with an error, the case of someone forgetting an appointment and on a second occasion, having firmly decided not to forget *this* time, turning up at the wrong hour. An exactly similar case was reported to me from his own experience by a friend with literary as well as scientific interests. 'Some years ago,' he told me, 'I allowed myself to be elected to the committee of a certain literary society, as I thought that the organization might one day be able to help me to have my play produced; and I took a regular part, though without

---

[23] Meringer and Mayer [P.E.L., 57]

being much interested, in the meetings which were held every Friday. Then, a few months ago, I was given the promise of a production at the theatre at F.; and since then I have regularly *forgotten* the meetings of the society. When I read your book on the subject I felt ashamed of my forgetfulness. I reproached myself with the thought that it was shabby behaviour on my part to stay away now that I no longer needed these people, and resolved on no account to forget the next Friday. I kept on reminding myself of this resolution until I carried it into effect and stood at the door of the room where the meetings were held. To my astonishment it was locked; the meeting was over. I had in fact made a mistake over the day; it was now Saturday!'

It would be agreeable to add further, similar examples. But I must proceed, and give you a glimpse of the cases in which our interpretation has to wait for the future for confirmation. The governing condition of these cases, it will be realized, is that the present psychical situation is unknown to us or inaccessible to our enquiries. Our interpretation is consequently no more than a suspicion to which we ourselves do not attach too much importance. Later, however, something happens which shows us how well-justified our interpretation had been. I was once the guest of a young married couple and heard the young woman laughingly describe her latest experience. The day after her return from the honeymoon she had called for her unmarried sister to go shopping with her as she used to do, while her husband went to his business. Suddenly she noticed a gentleman on the other side of the street, and nudging her sister had cried: 'Look, there goes Herr L.' She had forgotten that this gentleman had been her husband for some weeks. I shuddered as I heard the story, but I did not dare to draw the inference. The little incident only occurred to my mind some years later when the marriage had come to a most unhappy end.[24]

Maeder tells of a lady who, on the eve of her wedding had forgotten to try on her wedding-dress and, to her dressmaker's despair, only remembered late in the evening. He connects this forgetfulness with the fact that she was soon divorced from her husband. I know a lady now divorced from her husband, who in managing

her money affairs frequently signed documents in her maiden name, many years before she in fact resumed it—I know of other women who have lost their wedding-rings during the honeymoon, and I know too that the history of their marriages has given a sense to the accident.—And now here is one more glaring example, but with a happier ending. The story is told of a famous German chemist that his marriage did not take place, because he forgot the hour of his wedding and went to the laboratory instead of to the church. He was wise enough to be satisfied with a single attempt and died at a great age unmarried.

The idea may possibly have occurred to you that in these examples parapraxes have taken the place of the omens or auguries of the ancients. And indeed some omens were nothing else than parapraxes, as, for instance, when someone stumbled or fell down. Others of them, it is true, had the character of objective happenings and not of subjective acts. But you would hardly believe how difficult it sometimes is to decide whether a particular event belongs to the one group or to the other. An act so often understands how to disguise itself as a passive experience.

All those of us who can look back on a comparatively long experience of life will probably admit that we should have spared ourselves many disappointments and painful surprises if we had found the courage and determination to interpret small parapraxes experienced in our human contacts as auguries and to make use of them as indications of intentions that were still concealed. As a rule we dare not do so; it would make us feel as though, after a detour through science, we were becoming superstitious again. Nor do all auguries come true, and you will understand from our theories that they do not all need to come true.

Lecture IV: Parapraxes (Concluded)

…The most interesting questions which we have raised about parapraxes and not yet answered are perhaps these. We have said that parapraxes are the product of mutual interference between two different intentions, of which one may be called the disturbed intention and the other the disturbing one. The disturbed intentions give no occasion for further questions, but concerning the latter we should like to know, first, what sort of

---

[24] [This example and the two next will be found P.E.L., 203–4.]

intentions emerge as a disturbance to others, and secondly what is the relation of the disturbing intentions to the disturbed ones?

If you will allow me, I will once more take slips of the tongue as representatives of the whole class and I will reply to the second question before the first.

In a slip of the tongue the disturbing intention may be related in its content to the disturbed one, in which case it will contradict it or correct it or supplement it. Or—the more obscure and more interesting case—the content of the disturbing intention may have nothing to do with that of the disturbed one.

We shall have no difficulty in finding evidence of the former relation in instances we already know and in similar ones. In almost every case in which a slip of the tongue reverses the sense, the disturbing intention expresses the contrary to the disturbed one and the parapraxis represents a conflict between two incompatible inclinations. 'I declare the sitting opened, but I should prefer it to be already closed' is the sense of the President's slip of the tongue [p. 34]. A political periodical which had been accused of corruption defended itself in an article the climax of which should have been: 'Our readers will bear witness to the fact that we have always acted in the most *unself-seeking* manner.' But the editor entrusted with the preparation of the article wrote 'in the most *self-seeking* manner.' That is to say, he was thinking: 'This is what I am obliged to write; but I have different ideas.' A [German] member of parliament who was insisting that the truth should be told to the Emperor '*rückhaltlos* [unreservedly]' evidently heard an inner voice that was shocked at his boldness and, by a slip of the tongue, changed the word into '*rückgratlos* [spinelessly].'[25]

In the instances already familiar to you which give an impression of being contractions or abbreviations, what we have before us are corrections, additions or continuations, by means of which a second purpose makes itself felt alongside of the first. 'Facts came to

Vorschein [light]-better to say it straight out—they were *Schweinereien* [disgusting]; well then, facts came to *Vorschwein* [p. 42].' 'Those who understand this can be counted *on the fingers of one hand*—no, there's really only *one* person who understands it, so: can be counted *on one finger* [p. 41].' Or: 'My husband can eat and drink what he wants. But, as you know, *I* don't put up with his wanting anything at all, so: he can eat and drink what *I* want [p. 35].' In all these cases, then, the slip of the tongue arises from the content of the disturbed intention itself or is connected with it.

The other sort of relation between the two mutually interfering intentions seems puzzling. If the disturbing intention has nothing to do with the disturbed one, where can it have come from and why is it that it makes itself noticeable as a disturbance at this particular point? The observation which can alone give us the answer to this shows that the disturbance arises from a train of thought which has occupied the person concerned a short time before and, whether it has already been expressed in speech or not, produces this subsequent effect. It must in fact, therefore, be described as a perseveration, though not necessarily as the perseveration of spoken words. In this case too an associative link between the disturbing and the disturbed intentions is present; but it does not lie in their content but is artificially constructed, often along extremely forced associative paths.

Here is a simple example of this, derived from my own observation. I once met two Viennese ladies in the lovely Dolomites, who were dressed in walking clothes. I accompanied them part of the way, and we discussed the pleasures and also the trials of spending a holiday in that way. One of the ladies admitted that spending the day like that entailed a good deal of discomfort. 'It is certainly not at all pleasant,' she said, 'if one has been tramping all day in the sun and has perspired right through one's blouse and chemise.' In this sentence she had to overcome a slight hesitation at one point. Then she continued: 'But then when one gets "nach *Hose*" and can change....' This slip of the tongue was not analysed but I expect you can understand it easily. The lady's intention had obviously been to give a more complete

---

[25] This was in the German Reichstag in November 1908. [A fuller account of this appears P.E.L., 95–6. The preceding slip will be found P.E.L., 120–1.]

list of her clothes: blouse, chemise and *Hose* [drawers]. Reasons of propriety led her to omit any mention of the '*Hose*.' But in the next sentence, with its quite independent content, the unspoken word emerged as a distortion of the similar-sounding 'nach *Hause* [home].'[26]

We can now turn, however, to the main question, which we have long postponed, of what sort of intentions these are, which find expression in this unusual fashion as disturbers of other intentions. Well, they are obviously of very different sorts, among which we must look for the common factor. If we examine a number of examples with this in view, they will soon fall into three groups. The first group contains those cases in which the disturbing purpose is known to the speaker and moreover had been noticed by him before he made the slip of the tongue. Thus, in the '*Vorschwein*' slip [p. 42] the speaker admitted not only that he had formed the judgement '*Schweinereien*' about the events in question, but also that he had had the intention, from which he afterwards drew back, of expressing his judgement in words. A second group is made up of other cases in which the disturbing purpose is equally recognized as his by the speaker, but in which he was unaware that it was active in him just before he made the slip. Thus, he accepts our interpretation of his slip, but nevertheless remains to some extent surprised at it. Instances of this kind of attitude can perhaps be found in other sorts of parapraxes more easily than in slips of the tongue. In a third group the interpretation of the disturbing intention is vigorously rejected by the speaker; he not only denies that it was active in him before he made the slip, but seeks to maintain that it is entirely foreign to him. You will recall the example of the 'hiccough' [p. 49] and the positively rude denial, which I brought on myself from the speaker by uncovering his disturbing intention. As you know, we have not yet come to any agreement in our views on these cases. *I* should pay no attention to the denial put forward by the proposer of the toast and should persist in my interpretation unruf-

fled, while *you*, I suppose, are still affected by his protest and raise the question of whether we ought not to give up interpreting parapraxes of this kind and regard them as purely physiological acts in the pre-analytic sense. I can well imagine what it is that deters you. My interpretation carries with it the hypothesis that intentions can find expression in a speaker of which he himself knows nothing but which I am able to infer from circumstantial evidence. You are brought up short in the face of such a novel and momentous hypothesis. I can understand that, and I see your point so far as that goes. But one thing is certain. If you want to apply consistently the view of parapraxes, which has been confirmed by so many examples, you will have to make up your mind to accept the strange hypothesis I have mentioned. If you cannot do that, you will have once more to abandon the understanding of parapraxes which you have only just achieved.

Let us consider for a moment what it is that unites the three groups, what it is that the three mechanisms of slips of the tongue have in common. It is fortunately unmistakable. In the first two groups the disturbing purpose is recognized by the speaker; furthermore, in the first group that purpose announces itself immediately before the slip. But in both cases *it is forced back. The speaker decides not to put it into words, and after that the slip of the tongue occurs: after that, that is to say, the purpose which has been forced back is put into words against the speaker's will, either by altering the expression of the intention which he has permitted, or by mingling with it, or by actually taking its place.* This, then, is the mechanism of a slip of the tongue.

On my view, I can bring what happens in the *third* group into complete harmony with the mechanism I have described. I have only to assume that what distinguishes these three groups from one another is the differing extent to which the intention is forced back. In the first group the intention is there and makes itself noticed before the speaker's remark; only then is it rejected; and it takes its revenge in the slip of the tongue. In the second group the rejection goes further: the intention has already ceased to be noticeable before the remark is made. Strangely enough, this does not in the

---

[26] [Freud later included this anecdote in the 1917 edition of P.E.L., 64–5.]

least prevent it from playing its part in causing the slip. But this behaviour makes it easier for us to explain what happens in the third group. I shall venture to assume that a purpose can also find expression in a parapraxis when it has been forced back and not noticed for a considerable time, for a very long time perhaps, and can for that reason be denied straight out by the speaker. But even if you leave the problem of the third group on one side, you are bound to conclude from the observations we have made in the other cases that *the suppression of the speaker's intention to say something is the indispensable condition for the occurrence of a slip of the tongue.*

We may now claim to have made further advances in our understanding of parapraxes. We know not only that they are mental acts, in which we can detect sense and intention, not only that they come about through mutual interference between two different intentions, but beyond this we know that one of these intentions must have been in some way forced back from being put into effect before it can manifest itself as a disturbance of the other intention…But parapraxes are the outcome of a compromise: they constitute a half-success and a half-failure for each of the two intentions; the intention which is being challenged is neither completely suppressed nor, apart from special cases, carried through quite unscathed…

But there is one point more to which I would draw your attention. I would ask you to bear in mind as a model the manner in which we have treated these phenomena… We seek not merely to describe and to clarify phenomena, but to understand them as signs of an interplay of forces in the mind, as a manifestation of purposeful intentions working concurrently or in mutual opposition. We are concerned with a *dynamic view* of mental phenomena….

Concluding Comments

How Does Freud Conclude the Lectures on Parapraxes?

With the conclusion of Lecture IV, Freud completes his logical program: to make clear that there exist mental ideas and intentions that are "forced back"—either consciously or unconsciously—and that continue to influence the individual's verbal behavior and expressions of actions more generally. Lecture IV continues to cover a variety of related topics. Freud concludes by noting one further mystery... that once explained, the meaning of slips of the tongue are fairly clear. So why, he wonders, haven't people realized it before? He says he will answer the question later... thus artfully foreshadowing his discussion of psychological defense mechanisms. With that, Lecture IV concludes.

Review Questions

1. The introduction to the article refers to "grand theorists" of personality psychology. What is meant by the phrase, "grand theorist"?
2. The introduction to the article speaks of differences in the style and nature of scientists at the turn of 20th century and now. What are some of those differences?
3. Freud introduces the idea of slips of the tongue and other sorts of slips. What other kinds of slips does he discuss?
4. In developing his theory of slips of the tongue (and slips of behavior), Freud makes use of a considerable amount of empirical evidence. What kind of empirical evidence is he using? What are some of the benefits and drawbacks of that kind of evidence?
5. Freud notes that there already existed a number of explanations for slips of the tongue at the time he wrote. What were some of the explanations that he reviews?
6. Freud goes on to suggest that most or all slips of the tongue concern a conflict between intentions. One of these intentions is expressed by what the person is trying to say. The other intention disturbs it. Freud discusses three sorts of awareness of the interfering intention. What are those three levels of awareness? Why are they important to introducing Freud's dynamic theory of the mind?
7. Freud delivered these lectures on slips or errors of behavior at the University of Vienna as part of a larger series of lectures. What were the lectures called and what was their purpose?

11

Personality Dynamics in a Clinical Case Study

Reading a Case Study

A clinical case study can clarify a principle, or establish an example of good practice, or describe a mysterious incident that requires further study. With the advent of modern psychology, much psychological detective work was pursued by case study: Sigmund Freud, Gordon Allport, and Carl Rogers, among others, all employed it as a method of exposition, clarification, and (to differing degrees) research (e.g., Allport, 1965; Freud, 1963; Rogers, 1951). During the mid-20th century, however, the case study fell into a state of disrepute. Psychologists became concerned that many such individual studies were atypical, unrepresentative, and potentially biased. That attitude coincided with the rise of statistical methods in the field, and the advent of the large sample study. In the large sample study, far more limited data was obtained from far more people. Whereas a psychologist might get to know the target individual in a case study—and to be able to describe him or her in some detail—the individuals in large statistical samples were assessed on a smaller number of variables; often, the researcher and individual research participant would barely know of each other.

For a long while, case studies were relegated to the backseat of psychological literature. To be sure, they still served the purpose of illustrating psychological principles and exhibiting good practices. Case studies, however, were rarely published in peer-reviewed journals. Other parts of the psychological literature, however, made fairly widespread use of case studies. Some journals of clinical and counseling psychology continued to report case studies—notably psychoanalytic journals. Test manuals made good use of case studies to illustrate the use and interpretation of tests. Often textbooks on personality psychology and psychological testing employed cases more generally to illustrate various principles. Few mainstream journals, however, published many case studies of psychological assessments.

Perhaps the pendulum swung too far in the direction of the statistical. More recently, a few journals, at least, have indicated their increased willingness to consider publishing case studies. This increased interest has been expressed both in editorial statements, as well as in the publication of some exemplary instances of the genre (e.g., McAdams & West, 1997). A good case study can provide a balanced example of how psychological processes operate, as well as indicating the real world implications around it. Such is the case with the article here.

Significance of the Article

The present case study concerns a young man accused of an acquaintance rape, who is counseled to confess, and who, indeed, confesses to the crime. And yet, others around him wondered if he actually carried out what he had confessed to.

Usually, of course, people make false statements to make themselves look good or to exploit others. Is there a sense in which a false confession can satisfy personal needs? Unfortunately, many confessions have later been documented as false. This surprising idea is examined in this case. There are other reasons the case is significant. First, the case involves a legal determination of whether the suspect made a false confession. Legal standards differ from scientific standards; in either case, however, the truth can be hard to ascertain. Second, the case involves the application of psychological tests to inform the psychologists, courts, and readers of the individual's personality. That data is used to understand his possible motives or, perhaps, tendencies to falsely confess. Finally, courtroom dramas, even if largely behind the scenes as in this case, tend to be intrinsically captivating.

The article is set in the military justice system. The crime and aftermath took place somewhere in California. The author, a psychologist in the Navy Medical Service Corps, had been asked to assess the defendant. The accused had been referred to the author by his defense attorney, after the attorney became unusually concerned that his client had falsely confessed to a crime. Nothing specific is said as to what raised those concerns. The psychologist noted that he had usually assisted the prosecution in such cases.

The Watch List

The article, although a case study, is divided into the standard format of a brief empirical article; that is, with Introduction, Methods, and Results sections.

The Introduction of the article is concerned with sensitizing the reader to the potential possibility of false confession, and is a relatively accessible passage.

The Methods section is concerned with quickly enumerating the several clinical tests that were employed.

Two of the tests were general-purpose measures of psychopathology. The Millon Clinical Multiaxial Inventory-III is a broad measure of personality disorders (e.g., narcissistic personality disorder, psychopathic personality disorder, schizotypal personality disorder). The MMPI-2 is a measure of psychopathology more generally, that includes, among many scales, measures of schizophrenia, obsessive-compulsive tendencies, somatization, and the like.

The remaining three tests were more focused on personality issues theoretically related to making confessions, and false confessions in particular. Self-monitoring scales measure the degree to which a person modifies his or her behavior to suit the situation. The Gudjonsson Suggestibility Scale, as the name suggests, is a measure of *interrogative suggestibility*, the degree to which a person in a closed situation (e.g., an interrogation) will be influenced by a version of events provided by someone else. The Gudjonsson Compliance Scale is a measure of the degree to which a person agrees to say or do something in order to obtain immediate gain.

The article's Results section then goes through the defendant's scores on a number of the tests. Central among these scores was the "19 out of 20" the defendant obtained on the Gudjonsson Compliance Scale. It is worth noting that the mean score for men on the scale is about an 8, with a standard deviation of about 3.0 (and is very similar for women; Gudjonsson & Sigurdsson, 2003). A score of "19 out of 20" means the young man was well into the 99% percentile in compliance.

Military Court-Martial: A Case Study

by Stephen A. Talmadge

Source: Talmadge, S. A. (2001). Possible false confession in a military court-martial: A case study. *Military Psychology,*

13, 235–241.

It has long been known and well documented that people make false confessions (Gudjonsson, 1999). For example, 200 people confessed to kidnapping Charles Lindbergh's child. In writing about the psychology of confession evidence and possible reasons for people confessing to crimes they did not commit, Kassin (1997) pointed out that confessions play a vital role in law enforcement and are also a source of recurring controversy. For instance, research has shown that people find it difficult to believe that anyone would confess to a crime that he or she did not commit (Kassin & Wrightsman, 1981). Unlike the first part of the 20th century, American police tactics now rely almost entirely on psychological methods to obtain confessions. One of the most widely used police interrogation training manuals (Inbau, Reid, & Buckley, 1986) teaches investigators techniques (maximization-minimization, communicating promises and threats by implication, interrogation room design, etc.) to exert pressure on suspects to maximize stress and the likelihood of obtaining a confession. This manual pays little attention to the phenomena of false confessions. Inbau et al. (1986) wrote that "although recent Supreme Court opinions have contained derogatory statements about 'trickery' and 'deceit' as interrogation devices, no case has prohibited their usage" (p. 320). Confession evidence issues are complex and are faced by judges and juries routinely.

This article documents one such case in which a military attorney requested assistance in preparation for a general court-martial. He had concerns that his client might have confessed to an acquaintance rape but in fact might not be guilty of this act. Acquaintance rapes occur more often than stranger rapes (Koss & Harvey, 1991), and I have been involved in a number of acquaintance rape cases in the military justice system. I usually work for the prosecution, so I was surprised when a defense attorney contacted me. I explained that my role as a forensic psychologist had been to dispel the many rape myths for members and triers of fact and that I had never testified about false confessions. I also told the attorney that I was skeptical that I would be of benefit to the defendant. Notwithstanding these reservations, the attorney decided to have me officially appointed to the side of the defense for consultation and potential testimony. The attorney was aware that military courts had previously admitted false confession expert testimony (Agar, 1999).

Method

Assessment of the defendant, who was a service member, began after explaining to him that his evaluation would be confidential unless I was called to testify.

The evaluation included a clinical interview and administration and interpretation of psychological scales and tests. These instruments and interpretations included the Millon Clinical Multiaxial Inventory-III (MCM-III) test (Millon, Davis, & Millon, 1997), the Minnesota Multiphasic Personality Inventory-2 (MMPI-2) test (Butcher, 1992), the Gudjonsson Suggestibility Scale (Gudjonsson, 1984) and Compliance Scale (Gudjonsson, 1989), and the Self-Monitoring Scale (Snyder, 1974). These measures were decided on a priori and provided convergent sources of information. Both the MMPI-2 and the MCMI-III have been extensively researched and are general personality measures not specifically designed for forensic purposes (McCann & Dyer, 1996; Pope, Butcher, & Seelen, 1996). The MCMI-III is not without its critics when used for forensic purposes (Rogers, Salekin, & Sewell, 1999). The MMPI-2, the MCMI-III, and the Self-Monitoring measures, although not directly related to the legal issue of false confession, were included to serve as sources of data about psychological constructs relevant to the forensic issue under consideration (Heilbrun, 1992). The Self-Monitoring Scale is a measure of self-observation and self-control, guided by situational cues to social appropriateness. It has not been widely used in legal contexts but seemed relevant as validity and reliability for the scale have been shown (Snyder, 1974). The Gudjonsson Suggestibility Scale measures the extent to which individuals yield to suggestive questions and the extent to which individuals can be made to shift their replies once interpersonal pressure has been applied. The Gudjonsson Compliance Scale measures acceptance and compliance with requests and a person's tendency to obey negative instructions for immediate instrumental gain. Both Gudjonsson scales are applicable to interrogative situations involving retracted confession statements, and both were validated and used in the legal system (Gudjonsson, 1990). However, neither was developed in the United States legal system.

The defendant's medical and service records were reviewed, as were the Department of Defense Form 458 charge sheets, his rights waivers, polygraph examination sheets, the investigating agency's reports, and the defendant's statements.

Results

The defendant's medical history and psychiatric history were noncontributory. His psychosocial history was significant for the absence of antisocial behaviors or conduct disorder, and the fact that he joined the military because "my brother-in-law talked me into it, and it was something I always wanted to do." His military history was also unremarkable except for two things: his supervisor's testimony that he was a cooperative person and that he had a previous nonjudicial punish-

ment for assault. The accused explained the nonjudicial punishment for assault by saying that he was surprised when he walked into a "blanket party" for a new member of the squad, but participated anyway. He denied having had any knowledge of this assault beforehand.[1]

The defendant produced a valid MCMI-III profile (Disclosure base rate [BR] = 52, Desirability BR = 74, Debasement BR = 42). His highest clinical scale, and the only one that was elevated significantly (BR = 83), was the Dependent personality pattern. Individuals scoring highly on this scale have a cooperative personality style.

The defendant's MMPI-2 was also a valid profile (L scale T = 56, F scale T = 42, K scale T = 54). The only scale that was elevated was the Social Introversion scale (T = 65). This profile suggested an individual that is probably easily frightened and sees himself as very shy, bashful, introverted, and easily embarrassed.

On the Gudjonsson Suggestibility Scale, the defendant's yield score was 2, his shift score was 0, and his total score was 2. This instrument did not suggest that the defendant was suggestible; the mean yield score on the Gudjonsson Suggestibility Scale in the normative sample for men was 5.2, and the mean shift score for men was 2.8, giving the total suggestibility mean score for males of 7.0

The defendant endorsed 19 out of 20 questions in the direction of being compliant on the Gudjonsson Compliance Scale.

The defendant's score was 14 on the Self-Monitoring Scale. A score of 15 is considered indicative of high self-monitoring (75th percentile), and a score of less than 9 is considered indicative of low self-monitoring (25th percentile) in the normative sample. The defendant's score suggests that, out of a concern for social appropriateness, he is particularly sensitive to the expression and self-presentation of others in social situations and uses these cues as guidelines for monitoring and managing his own self-presentation and expressive behavior.

---

[1] *A blanket party* is a colloquial term that usually means a simple assault in which a blanket is thrown over the assailant so that he is unaware of the identity of the group that is hitting him.

Accused's Account of the Interviews

The defendant gave a statement to an investigator in which he denied accusations of rape and communicating a threat. This statement was signed about 2 hr after he signed his rights waiver when the interview began, which was given in the investigator's office and not in an interrogation room

Three weeks later, the defendant was given a polygraph test and was questioned in a small room set up for interrogations. He denied the allegation (lack of consent) during the polygraph test but was told afterward that he had failed it. He was told that he would not get into trouble for lying. The investigator put his hands on the defendant's shoulder and his knees, and told him that they would be on a first-name basis. The defendant was repeatedly asked similar questions about engaging in sex without consent, and after he replied that he could not remember doing so, the investigator told him to think harder and try to remember. The accused was told more than once to think of the impact that his forgetfulness might have when his commanding officer reviewed the investigation. Approximately 5 hr after the interrogation began, the defendant signed an admission statement.

Four days after this second interview, he was again given a polygraph test and interrogated. He again denied the allegation of communicating threats and was told that he failed this polygraph too. The defendant was repeatedly asked about making threats, and his denials resulted in expressions of disbelief on the part of the interrogator, who reminded him again of the impact that his forgetfulness might have on his commanding officer. The defendant signed a confession that he communicated a threat to the alleged victim after about 4 hr of questioning.

Four days later the accused was given another polygraph and interrogated by a third investigator. After about 30 min the defendant signed an admission that he had forced the victim to engage in intercourse. The defendant said that this statement was made quickly because of his experiences during the previous interrogations.[2]

---

[2] I do not know whether the defendant failed the polygraphs.

Discussion

The defendant was in a situation that was not as coercive as some situations that are clearly unacceptable. (He was given sufficient food and bathroom breaks, was not questioned in a sleep-deprived condition, and was not tortured.) However, investigators admitted on the witness stand that they had used certain techniques to obtain a confession. These included some of the techniques from the Inbau and Reid police-training manual (Inbau et al., 1986), such as the interrogation room design, befriending the suspect, and not accepting denials. In addition, the defendant may have thought that there existed infallible scientific evidence that he was lying, that his lack of memory of the incident would be viewed negatively by his commanding officer, and that as soon as he remembered things the way the interrogator wished, he would be allowed to terminate the interview.

I presented the psychological testing and scale data visually to the court members and testified that the accused was the type of person that attempts to please others, to look desirable, has a cooperative personality style, and is a follower rather than a leader. In the presentation I explained that the discrepancy between the low score on a measure of interrogative suggestibility and the high score on a measure of interrogative compliance might mean that the defendant may not be willing to personally accept a proposition or request but may make a conscious decision to carry out the request or proposition even though he does not agree privately.

I was not allowed to use the words *polygraph* or *lie detector* in court. The results of polygraphs are inadmissible evidence in military courts since the U.S. Supreme Court decision in *United States v. Scheffer* (Goldzband, 1999). Furthermore, judges are sensitive to anything that prejudices the jury and invades their province of determining truth and finding fact.

Conclusions

I could not validate with independent evidence whether the defendant made a false confession. Even if a judge would allow this testimony—and it was clear in this case he would not—it is inappropriate to proffer expert testimony as to whether a confession is false without corroborating, independent evidence. The decision of whether a confession is true or false falls only within the province of the judge and the trier of fact and not to the expert witness. However, the psychologist who is asked to assist in the military judicial system can nonetheless be valuable to the defense and the prosecution.

In this case, the defendant was acquitted because the prosecution did not have a strong case other than the defendant's confession. Although the confession was admitted into evidence, the jury members apparently gave his confession little weight. In addition, the lack of audiotaping or videotaping of police interrogations makes it difficult for court members to properly assess the evidence. In fact, a more complete audiovisual record would help the jury members to evaluate the level at which the defendant volunteered information and how truthful the overall statement was. Although false confessions have been elicited in the laboratory (Kassin & Kiechel, 1996; Kassin & McNall, 1991), more research is needed to strengthen empirical knowledge and broaden the base of scientific knowledge to satisfy the decision rendered in *Daubert v. Merrell Dow Pharmaceuticals, Inc.* (1993).

Acknowledgments

Views expressed in this article are the author's and do not necessarily reflect the official policy of the Department of Defense or other departments of the United States Government.

References

Agar, J.R. (1999). The admissibility of false confession expert testimony. *The Army Lawyer, 26,* 26–43.

Butcher, J.N. (1992). *Essentials of MMPI-2 and MMPI-A interpretation.* Minneapolis: University of Minnesota Press.

Daubert v. Merrell Dow Pharmaceuticals, Inc., 113 S. Ct 2786 (1993).

Goldzband, M.G. (1999). Polygraphy revisited: U.S. v. Schef-fer. *Journal of the American Academy of Psychiatry and the Law, 27,* 133–142.

Gudjonsson, G.H. (1984). A new scale of interrogative suggestibility. *Personality and Individual Differences, 5,* 303–314.

Gudjonsson, G.H. (1989). Compliance in an interrogative situation: A new scale. *Personality and Individual Differences, 10,* 535–540.

Gudjonsson, G.H. (1990). One hundred alleged false confession cases: Some normative data. *British Journal of Clinical Psychology, 29,* 249–250.

Gudjonsson, G.H. (1999). The making of a serial false confessor: The confessions of Henry Lee Lucas. *Journal of Forensic Psychiatry, 10,* 416–426.

Heilbrun, K. (1992). The role of psychological testing in forensic assessment. *Law and Human Behavior, L16,* 257–272.

Inbau, F.E., Reid, J.E., & Buckley, J.P. (1986). *Criminal interrogation and confessions* (3rd ed.). Baltimore: Williams & Wilkins.

Kassin, S.M. (1997). The psychology of confession evidence. *American Psychologist, 52,* 221–233.

Kassin, S.M., & Kiechel, K.L. (1996). The social psychology of false confessions: Compliance, internalization, and confabulation. *Psychological Science, 7,* 125–128.

Kassin, S., & McNall, K. (1991). Police interrogations and confessions: Communicating promises and threats by pragmatic implication. *Law and Human Behavior, 15,* 233–251.

Kassin, S.M., & Wrightsman, L.S. (1981). Coerced confessions, judicial instructions, and mock juror verdicts. *Journal of Applied Social Psychology, 11,* 489–506.

Koss, M.P., & Harvey, M.R. (1991). *The rape victim: Clinical and community interventions* (2nd ed.). Newbury Park, CA: Sage.

McCann, J.T., & Dyer, F.J. (1996). *Forensic assessment with the Millon Inventories.* New York: Guilford.

Millon, T., Davis, R.D., & Millon, C. (1997). *MCMI-III manual* (2nd ed.). Minneapolis: National Computer Systems.

Pope, K.S., Butcher, J.N., & Seelen, J. (1996). *The MMPI, MMPI-2, and MMPI-A in court.* Washington, DC: American Psychological Association.

Rogers, R., Salekin, R.T., & Sewell, K.W. (1999). Validation of the Millon Multiaxial Inventory for Axis II disorders: Does it meet the Daubert standard? *Law and Human Behavior, 23,* 425–443.

Snyder, M. (1974). Self-monitoring of expressive behavior. *Journal of Personality and Social Psychology, 30,* 526–537.

Concluding Comments

Is He Innocent?

As the author makes clear, we cannot know for sure what happened in this alleged case of acquaintance rape. The author does do a good a job of raising doubts about the confession—or at least convincing us that the defendant would be exactly the sort of individual who would be willing to falsely confess. The court appeared to agree. Its final determination, one of law and evidence, was to acquit the defendant. Thus, personality became a clue in this legal drama, and psychological tests assessed the defendant's personality, providing further evidence for the court. Although personality cannot be considered a decisive factor in most cases, it can raise issues and concerns, as it does here.

Review Questions

1. What has been the view of the importance of case studies over the history of modern psychology?
2. What are some of the advantages of case studies?
3. This article presents an empirical study of a case of possible false confession. What sort of research design is used in this article and what kinds of scientific evidence are presented?
4. A variety of psychological tests were used in this study. Why were the tests employed and what advantage, if any, do you think they brought to the study?
5. What do the Gudjonsson scales measure and why were they employed in this study?
6. The author employed other psychological scales as well. One of these was the Minnesota Multiphasic Personality Inventory. What is that test and what does it measure?

12

Dynamics of Self-Control

Studying Personality Processes (Quasi-) Experimentally

Our personality—the sum total of our psychological processes—is constantly processing information: about motives and emotions, models of the self and world, and the possibilities of social action. Studying such processes opens a window to our interior self and its activities. Some personality processes are accessible to consciousness. These include everything from tricks of emotional self-control to rules for mental calculation. An example of mental self-control is, if you become angry, to count to 10 before you say anything to the person who made you angry.

Personality processes can be studied experimentally or quasi-experimentally. Quasi-experimental research divides people into two or more groups depending on the psychological process the individual uses. For example, in relation to the "count to 10" rule for maintaining self-control after getting angry: there are those who know and use the rule, and those who don't. A researcher could divide children into two groups: those who say they use the "count to 10" rule, and those who don't, and then determine whether the "count to 10" group actually can control their anger better than others. A quasi-experimental design involves sorting people according to the mental processes they already employ. It omits true randomization

Such personality processes also can be manipulated according to random assignment, and therefore studied with true experimental designs. For example, one group of people can be asked to count to 10 when angry, before saying anything; a second group could be asked to simply say something, without the pause.

Either way, mental processes—especially those that begin in consciousness—are particularly of interest in relation to self-control, because a person can consciously modify the way he or she thinks about a situation (or, with greater difficulty, feels about a situation) by learning new outlooks.

The Specific Article

Each of us is taught—and uses—a variety of techniques of mental control, such as counting to 10 when angry, so as to calm ourselves a bit before deciding to say or do something we might later regret. The use of a specific mental technique can be represented as a psychological variable, in the sense that some people use it, and some people don't. Similarly, employing an optimistic viewpoint, or blocking out certain thoughts, also represent forms of mental self-control and can be thought of as additional psychological variables.

Experimental research is particularly useful for teasing out the influences of different, but related, variables. Two variables examined by Norem in this article involve genuine optimism on the one hand, and defensive optimism on the other. Here the use of a particular mental outlook is employed to group people together. As it turns out, both optimists and defensive optimists appear optimistic to others, but only one group is openly optimistic. Defensive optimists, by contrast, appear to actively shut out negative but relevant information. Each kind of optimism can be viewed as an approach to self-control. Is one better than the other?

Examining people's naturally occurring mental strategies can shed some light on what does and doesn't work in terms of conscious information processing. It may turn out, for example, that some mental styles lead to greater psychological health than do others. By knowing more about those styles, people can be better advised about how to enhance their own psychological health and well-being.

The Watch List

The Introduction to the article introduces the distinction between people who are optimists and those who are defensive optimists, defines them, and asks whether they are equally well adapted psychologically.

In the Methods section, Norem refers to a longitudinal study—one that studied participants over time—and the waves of data that were collected. Waves, in this context, refer to the intervals during which data was collected. Typically data is collected on participants at periodic intervals rather than continuously. So, one group might be followed at five-year intervals for 20 years: at the outset of year one, year 5, 10, 15, and 20. Those five periods of data collection can also be referred to as five waves of data. Norem also mentions *attrition*, which in this context, refers to the number of people who dropped out or who the experimenters lost contact with, over time.

In the measures section of Wave 1, a reference is made to *Cronbach's a*. This statistic, otherwise known as *coefficient alpha*, is simply a measure of test reliability.

The results commence with a discussion of the Life Orientation Test, a measure of optimism. The author comments that the distribution optimism scores exhibited negative skewness—that is, there was a tendency for individuals to fall above the mean and to be balanced by more extreme low scores. This meant that two out of three individuals were classified as optimists. Norem used a second scale, The Balanced Inventory of Desirable Responding (BIDR), to measure defensiveness. Among the two thirds of the optimists, those who scored highly on the BIDR were considered defensive. By doing this, Norem established the two quasi-experimental groups she hoped to compare.

Defensive Self-Deception and Social Adaptation among Optimists

by Julie K. Norem

Source: Norem, J. (1999). Defensive self-deception and social adaptation among optimists. *Journal of Research in Personality*, 33, 549–555.

1. Introduction

Optimism and self-deception (specifically self-enhancement) are often positively correlated, and the latter may help to maintain the former. Both are also often related to positive adjustment, especially in self-report data and of affect measures. In their influential paper, Taylor and Brown (1988) argued that the illusory optimism and self-enhancement processes ("positive illusions") were fundamental to mental health, a position that forms one of the pillars of the burgeoning positive psychology movement.

Somewhat surprisingly, however, there have been few efforts to disentangle the roles played by optimism and illusion in determining adjustment-related outcomes. In one exception, researchers found that unrealistic optimism and dispositional optimism were correlated, and the interaction between them predicted negative health-related outcomes: that is, people who were high on both did particularly badly (Davidson & Prkachin, 1997).

Though it is somewhat circular, researchers have argued that the illusions of the well-adjusted are sufficiently "mild" and flexible enough to prevent potential negative consequences, and there is some evidence that optimism can lead to positive consequences, such as careful consideration of negative information, even if it is threatening to the self (e.g., Aspinwall & Brunhart, 1996; Taylor, Collins, Skokan, & Aspinwall, 1989). Others have argued, however, that there are likely to be important limits on the flexibility of those who deceive themselves (Norem, 1998). Particularly when optimistic beliefs are maintained through self-deception, their adaptive value may be limited. The purpose of this paper is to examine more closely some of the ill-defined margins of the relations among optimism, self-enhancing self-deception, and social adaptation.

The motivational and affective benefits of optimism and self-enhancement are clear: both tend to relate to approach motivation and feeling in control, which are related to effort and personal achievement, creating a virtuous cycle. Optimism also plays a relatively clear role in interpersonal relations. It is related to extraversion and the disposition to experience positive affect; people who are upbeat and happy make a better first impression, and are often more fun to be around than more pessimistic or negative people.

The role of self-deceptive self-enhancement in personal relationships is less clearly positive. Defensive self-enhancement can be interpersonally aversive, as theorists of narcissism and related constructs have long argued (Bushman & Baumeister, 1998; John & Robins, 1994). Overall, previous research suggests that self-enhancing beliefs have both costs and benefits (Paulhus, 1998; Robins & Beer, 2001).

Using a person-centered approach, I will compare the social outcomes over time of college women who are equivalently optimistic, but who differ in self-deception. Based on previous work, I predict that self-deceptive optimists will form less supportive and less intimate personal relationships than non-defensive optimists.

2. Method

2.1 Participants and Procedure

The data reported below are from a longitudinal study of adaptation and goal pursuit among college women. The sample is comprised of 90 women who entered

Wellesley College (an elite, all-female liberal arts college) in 1993. They ranged in age from 18 to 20; 54 classified themselves as Caucasian American, 27 as Asian or Asian American, 3 as African or African American, 2 as Latina, and 4 as other. All participated for monetary compensation or coupons to campus eateries. Only data from Waves 1, 4, and 5 that are directly relevant to the above hypothesis will be described. Ninety women participated in Wave 1, 70 participated in Waves 1 and 4, and 48 participated in Waves 1, 4, and 5. Attrition analyses revealed no systematic personality differences at Wave 1 between those who remained in the study and those who did not.

Wave 1 participants were recruited for the study during one of their first-year orientation meetings. Volunteers took home a large packet of questionnaires, which were returned via campus mail. Wave 4 participants were contacted by telephone during the spring of their senior year. They were asked to fill out a questionnaire, and to have two "close friends who know them well" fill out the short acquaintance rating form described below. Wave 5 participants were contacted by telephone one year after they had graduated and asked to fill out the final questionnaire.

2.2 Measures

2.2.1. Wave 1

Life orientation test (LOT; Scheier & Carver, 1985). This 12-item questionnaire is designed to measure dispositional optimism. Chronbach's a for this sample was .78.

Balanced inventory of desirable responding (BIDR; Paulhus & Reid, 1991). The first 20 items, which form the self-deception (SD) scale, are designed to measure "honest" (i.e., consciously held) but inflated beliefs that are self-enhancing. It is scored so that only those who give exaggeratedly desirable responses will generate high scores. Cronbach's a for this sample was .79.

Actual selves. Participants were asked to list eight attributes that described themselves "as they actually are." Two raters then rated each characteristic according to how positive they thought it was. The correlation between the raters was $r = .73$. The ratings were averaged across raters and then summed for each self-listing to obtain an overall objective positivity rating.

Self-attributes questionnaire (SAQ, Pelham & Swann, 1989). The SAQ measures self-esteem, and other aspects of self-concept structure across 10 life domains. The mean of the 10 SAQ ratings was used to form a positive self-evaluation scale.

2.2.2. Wave 4

Acquaintance ratings. Participants asked two close friends to rate them on various characteristics, and on their relationship with the participant. This report will focus on the likeability, emotional closeness, and modesty ratings provided by the acquaintances. The average correlation between the raters across all the ratings was $r = 47$.

Social support network ratings (Reifman, Biernat, & Lang, 1991). Participants were asked to list their 10 closest friends on campus, and then to indicate how much of various kinds of social support they received from those friends. Ratings were summed across network members and standardized across types of support to create indices of emotional support, material support, and companionship.

2.2.3. Wave 5

Contact with Wellesley social network. Participants indicated the number of times they had in-person, phone, email, or mail contact with each member of the social network they described in Wave 4. These responses were standardized and summed to create a "total contact" index.

3. Results

The LOT scores showed negative skewness, so participants in the upper two-thirds of the distribution were classified as optimists. Those below the median on the SD subscale of the BIDR were classified as non-defensive and those above the median were classified as defensive. Crossing these two categories resulted in 33 non-defensive optimists and 45 defensive optimists. Although the LOT was correlated with the SD (r [90] = .32, $p = .002$), non-defensive and defensive optimists did not differ in their levels of optimism (non-defensive $M = 2.71$, defensive $M = 2.63$, t (76) = .65, $p = .51$, two-tailed). As would be expected, they did differ in average

SD scores (non-defensive *M* = 5.03, defensive *M* = 6.47; *t* (76) = -1.44, *p* = .032, one-tailed).

To explore the validity of this classification, I ran a two-way (defensive vs. non-defensive; optimism vs. pessimism) repeated measures ANOVA, with the standardized SAQ scores (self-evaluation) and positivity ratings (evaluations by raters of the actual selves characteristics listed by the participants) as repeated measures. There was no main effect of defensiveness or optimism on either self-evaluation (*F* [1, 75] = .003, *p* = .95) or evaluation by others (*F* [1,75] = .213, *p* = .64). There was, however, a significant interaction effect (*F* [1,75] = 128.039, *p* = .0001). Non-defensive optimists evaluated themselves less positively than the average for the sample (*M* = -.39, *SD* = .81), whereas others evaluated them more positively than the average (*M* = .43, *SD* = .77). In contrast, defensive optimists evaluated themselves more positively than the average participant (*M* = .41, *SD* = 1), whereas observers evaluated them less positively than the average participant (*M* = -.35, *SD* = 1). The defen-

sive optimists thus show inflated self-evaluations both as measured in self-report on the BIDR, and as indicated by the discrepancy between their self-evaluations and others' evaluations of them, which is a typical measure of self-enhancement. This pattern also appears in the acquaintance ratings. These ratings are from people selected as "close friends" by the participants themselves. Their friends reported that the defensive optimists were significantly less modest, significantly less emotionally close to them, and marginally less likable than the non-defensive optimists (see Table 1).

The defensive optimists also seem to perceive their relationships less positively than the non-defensive optimists do. Their social support ratings indicate that they get as much material support from their friends as the non-defensive optimists do, but they receive significantly less companionship and emotional support from those friends (see Table 1). After graduating, they also maintain less contact with their college friends than non-defensive optimists (see Table 1).

Table 1 Relationship Differences between Defensive Optimists and Non-Defensive Optimists

	Mean		SD		*t*	*p*
	Def.	Non-def	Def.	Non-def		
Friends' report						
Likeability	-.15	.30	1.14	.71	1.47	.070
Closeness	-.51	.37	.97	.83	3.04	.002
Modesty	-.35	.46	.97	.86	2.79	.004
n	21	19				
Social support						
Material	-.06	-.01	.94	1.05	.20	.420
Emotional	-.24	.18	.89	1.02	1.69	.049
Companionship	-.25	.19	1.03	.79	1.82	.037
n	32	29				
W#5 contact						
	-.25	.29	1.12	1.12	1.871	.035
n	21	22				

Note. All *p*-values are one-tailed; scores are standardized.

4. Discussion

The findings reviewed here converge with previous research on defensiveness and narcissism. They offer some additional support for the contentions that there are costs to self-enhancement when it comes to relationships with others, and that the presence of optimism does not necessarily offset those costs.

There are obvious limitations to the extent to which we can generalize from these data. The sample is limited in size and representativeness. The defensiveness classification was inexact, and motivated primarily by a low power situation that made more sophisticated statistical analyses of interactions unfeasible. Moreover, the processes underlying these findings are not tested, and clearly require more investigation.

Nevertheless, these data are illustrative and instructive because they focus not on individual achievement, but on social relationships. Thorough understanding of the implications of self-enhancement and optimism requires careful consideration of outcomes across life domains, over time, and in both interpersonal and intrapsychic contexts. Cultural variations in particular may significantly influence the response of the environment to individuals' self-enhancement (Norem & Change, 2001). It may be that self-enhancement motivates individual agency and achievement, but impedes the development of emotional intimacy, interpersonal sensitivity, and communal effort. Given the current popularity and public policy aims of the positive psychology movement, it is particularly important to have a nuanced and sophisticated understanding of both the costs and the benefits of different psychological processes, and to be sensitive to different individual and communal goals that may influence the relative weight of those costs and benefits.

References

Aspinwall, L.G., & Brunhart, S.M. (1996). Distinguishing optimism from denial: Optimistic beliefs predict attention to health threats. *Personality and Social Psychology Bulletin, 22* (10), 993–1003.

Bushman, B.J., & Baumeister, R.F. (1988). Threatened egotism, narcissism, self-esteem, and direct and displaced aggression: Does self-love or self-hate lead to violence? *Journal of Personality and Social Psychology, 75* (l), 219–229.

Davidson, K., & Prkachin, K. (1997). Optimism and unrealistic optimism have an interacting impact on health-promoting behavior and knowledge changes. *Personality and Social Psychology Bulletin, 23* (6), 617–625.

John, O.P., & Robins, R.W. (1994). Accuracy and bias in self-perception: Individual differences in self-enhancement and the role of narcissism. *Journal of Personality and Social Psychology, 66* (l), 206–219.

Norem, J.K., & Chang, E.C. (2001). A very full glass: Adding complexity to our thinking about the implications and applications of optimism and pessimism research. In E.C. Chang (Ed.), *Optimism and pessimism: Implications for theory, research, and practice* (pp. 347–367). Washington, DC: American Psychological Association.

Paulhus, D.L. (1998). Interpersonal and intrapsychic adaptiveness of trait self-enhancement: A mixed blessing? *Journal of Personality and Social Psychology, 74,* 1197–1208.

Paulhus, D.L., & Reid, D.B. (199l). Enhancement and denial in socially desirable responding. *Journal of Personality and Social Psychology, 60* (2), 307–317.

Pelham, B.W., & Swann, W.B. (1989). From self-conceptions to self-worth: On the sources and structure of global self-esteem. *Journal of Personality and Social Psychology, 57* (4), 672–680.

Reifman, A., Biernat, M., & Lang, E.L. (199l). Stress, social support, and health in married professional women with small children. *Psychology of Women Quarterly, 15,* 431–445.

Robins, R.W., & Beer, J.S. (2001). Positive illusions about the self: Short-term benefits and long-term costs. *Journal of Personality and Social Psychology, 80,* 340–352.

Scheier, M.F., & Carver, C.S. (1985). Optimism, coping, and health: Assessment and implications of generalized outcome expectancies. *Health Psychology, 4* (3), 219–247.

Taylor, S.E., & Brown, J.D. (1988). Illusion and well-being: A social psychological perspective on mental health. *Psychological Bulletin, 103* (2), 193–210.

Taylor, S.E., Collins, R.L., Skokan, L.A., & Aspinwall, L.G. (1989). Maintaining positive illusions in the face of negative information: Getting the facts without letting them get to you. *Journal of Social and Clinical Psychology, 8* (2), 114–129.

Concluding Comments

Optimism Isn't Everything

The quasi-experimental research represented in this article, despite the limitations pointed out by the author, raises the important idea that not all optimism is alike. Even two people with the same apparent levels of optimism may derive different gains from the attribute, depending upon whether or not their optimism is a result of their genuine and open experience or of defensive self-enhancement. Genuine optimism trumps self-enhanced optimism in this regard.

Review Questions

1. What is quasi-experimental research and how does it differ from correlational research?
2. What is a personality process; can you provide an example?
3. Can you describe one of the personality scales used in this study?
4. What is the difference between genuine optimism and self-enhanced optimism? Might there be another kind of optimism that also could be studied?
5. What were the advantages of being a genuine optimist versus a self-enhanced optimist?

13

Changing Personality

Reading a Summary of Studies

The development of techniques for improving personality and psychological health is one of the missions of personality psychology. There are many such techniques, but one of the most surprising concerns the health benefit of writing about troubling life experiences. Might that improve the individual's mental health? This review of the literature gathered the positive evidence for such an effect of self-disclosure in writing, and exposed readers to a fascinating pattern of results.

True, someone wishing personally to conduct research in the area might wish to seek out a more careful analysis: one that might delineate the findings in greater detail than is done here. Such reviews often attempt to determine the exact conditions under which a given effect can be found or not found. The author, Jamie Pennebaker, does briefly and helpfully summarize some of these conditions in the article under "Procedural Differences That Affect the Disclosure Effects," but mostly refers the reader to a more detailed report—a (then) submitted manuscript, which has since been published (Smyth, 1998). Reviews such as Smyth's are considered "critical reviews," or "methodological reviews."

The purpose here was different: Simply, to argue on the basis of the evidence for the existence of a particular experimental effect.

Significance of the Article

When Jamie Pennebaker first announced that writing about suppressed emotional experiences improved the functioning of a person's immune system, his work was greeted with surprise and skepticism. How could writing about troubling experiences for a little while reduce, for example, the number of visits that college students made to their health center over the following year? Now that the work has been solidly replicated, the reaction has been, well, that it all makes a lot of sense.

After all, since Sigmund Freud first outlined the limits of personal consciousness, and argued that it required strengthening, psychologists have understood that the conscious examination of one's own mind may foster mental health in some instances. Freud urged people to, "make the unconscious conscious." Since Freud's time, there has been a growing recognition that encouraging people to bring their suppressed or unconscious thoughts into awareness, and to then examine them, can, in some instances, improve mental health. Actually, even re-examining ostensibly logical, conscious thoughts can change mental health. Considered more generally, the degree to which one can bring clarity to one's own emotional concerns is an important type of personality dynamic.

Professor Pennebaker has promoted the importance of recording and examining suppressed, painful, never-before-shared thoughts. He believes that such dynamic change can improve an individual's mental health. This article examines the research program he began and others have joined him in.

The Watch List

This article accomplishes a lot in a very brief time. It begins with an Introduction concerned with describing the experimental procedure of writing about one's emotional secrets, goes on to discuss the effect of such writing, then examines the limits of such findings, and concludes with a brief comment on the significance of the effect.

In the section, "Parameters of Writing and Talking Associated with Health Improvements," Pennebaker refers to the technique he will discuss as a *disclosure paradigm*. Disclosure refers to acknowledgement (anonymously) of a secret source of concern. Paradigm, in this context, refers to a general set of experimental procedures used to study a phenomenon of interest (here: emotional disclosure).

In the "Effects of Disclosure" section, readers may be frustrated that Table 1 doesn't contain more detail about the meaning of the individual effects that researchers have obtained for the disclosure procedure. In fact, Table 1 doesn't specify the direction of effects, though the text makes it reasonably clear that all the observed effects are in a desirable direction; that is, that the effects represent improvements in all instances. The review appeared in a journal which prefers relatively brief articles, and to summarize all the work quickly required some important compromises.

At the outset of the section on "Procedural Differences That Affect the Disclosure Effects," the term *boundary conditions* is employed. Boundary conditions refer to the specification of the conditions under which scientific principles apply—the procedures and methods that can be used to obtain the effect, and the variations on them which, importantly, do not obtain the effect. If a scientist can help place boundaries on effects, it helps other researchers replicate and extend findings.

Virtually all forms of psychotherapy—from psychoanalysis to behavioral and cognitive therapies—have been shown to reduce distress and to promote physical and mental well-being (Mumford, Schlesinger, & Glass, 1983; Smith, Glass, & Miller, 1980). A process common to most therapies is labeling the problem and discussing its causes and consequences. Further, participating in therapy presupposes that the individual acknowledges the existence of a problem and openly discusses it with another person. As discussed in this article, the mere act of disclosure is a powerful therapeutic agent that may account for a substantial percentage of the variance in the healing process.

Writing about Emotional Experiences as a Therapeutic Process

by James W. Pennebaker

Source: Pennebaker, J. W. (1997). Writing about emotional experiences as a therapeutic process. *Psychological Science, 8,* 162–166.

Virtually all forms of psychotherapy—from psycho-analysis to behavioral and cognitive therapies—have been shown to reduce distress and to promote physical and mental well-being (Mumford, Schlesinger, & Glass, 1983; Smith, Glass, & Miller, 1980). A process common to most therapies is labeling the problem and discussing its causes and consequences. Further, participating in therapy presupposes that the individual acknowledges the existence of a problem and openly discusses it with another person. As discussed in this article, the mere act of disclosure is a powerful therapeutic agent that may account for a substantial percentage of the variance in the healing process.

Parameters of Writing and Talking Associated with Health Improvements

Over the past decade, several laboratories have been exploring the value of writing or talking about emotional experiences. Confronting deeply personal issues has been found to promote physical health, subjective well-being, and selected adaptive behaviors. In this section, the general findings of the disclosure paradigm are discussed. Whereas individuals have been asked to disclose personal experiences through talking in a few studies, most studies involve writing.

The Basic Writing Paradigm

The standard laboratory writing technique has involved randomly assigning each participant to one of two or more groups. All writing groups are asked to write about assigned topics for 3 to 5 consecutive days, 15 to 30 min each day. Writing is generally done in the laboratory with no feedback given. Participants assigned to the control conditions are typically asked to write about superficial topics, such as how they use their time. The standard instructions for those assigned to the experimental group are a variation on the following:

> For the next 3 days, I would like for you to write about your very deepest thoughts and feeling about an extremely important emotional issue that has affected you and your life. In your writing I'd like you to really let go and explore your very deepest emotions and thoughts. You might tie your topic to your relationships with others, including parents, lovers, friends, or relatives, to your past, your present, or your future, or to who you have been, who you would like to be, or who you are now. You may write about the same general issues or experiences on all days of writing or on different topics each day. All of your writing will be completely confidential. Don't worry about spelling, sentence structure, or grammar. The only rule is that once you begin writing, continue to do so until your time is up.

The writing paradigm is exceptionally powerful. Participants—from children to the elderly, from honor students to maximum security prisoners—disclose a remarkable range and depth of traumatic experiences: Lost loves, deaths, incidents of sexual and physical

Pennebaker, J. W. (1997). Writing about emotional experiences as a therapeutic process. *Psychological Science, 8,* 162–166.

abuse, and tragic failures are common themes in all of the studies. If nothing else, the paradigm demonstrates that when individuals are given the opportunity to disclose deeply personal aspects of their lives, they readily do so. Even though a large number of participants report crying or being deeply upset by the experience, the overwhelming majority report that the writing experience was valuable and meaningful in their lives.

Effects of Disclosure on Outcome Measures

Researchers have relied on a variety of physical and mental health measures to evaluate the effect of writing. As depicted in Table 1, writing or talking about emotional experiences, relative to writing about superficial topics, has been found to be associated with significant drops in physician visits from before to after writing among relatively healthy samples. Writing or talking about emotional topics has also been found to have beneficial influences on immune function, including t-helper cell growth (using a blastogenesis procedure with the mitogen phytohemagglutinin), antibody response to Epstein-Barr virus, and antibody response to hepatitis B vaccinations. Disclosure also has produced short-term changes in autonomic activity (e.g., lowered heart rate and electrodermal activity) and muscular activity (i.e., reduced phasic corrugator activity).

Self-reports also suggest that writing about upsetting experiences, although painful in the days of writing, produces long-term improvements in mood and indicators of well-being compared with writing about control topics. Although a number of studies have failed to find consistent effects on mood or self-reported distress, Smyth's (1996) recent meta-analysis on written-disclosure studies indicates that, in general, writing about emotional topics is associated with significant reductions in distress.

Behavioral changes have also been found. Students who write about emotional topics show improvements in grades in the months following the study. Senior professionals who have been laid off from their jobs get new jobs more quickly after writing. Consistent with the direct health measures, university staff members who write about emotional topics are subsequently absent from their work at lower rates than control participants. Interestingly, relatively few reliable changes emerge using self-reports of health-related behaviors. That is, after writing, experimental participants do not exercise more or smoke less. The one exception is that the study with laid-off professionals found that writing reduced self-reported alcohol intake.

Procedural Differences That Affect the Disclosure Effects

Writing about emotional experiences clearly influences measures of *physical* and *mental health*. In recent years, several investigators have attempted to define the boundary conditions of the disclosure effects. Some of the most important findings are as follows:

Writing versus talking about traumas. Most studies comparing writing versus talking either into a tape recorder (Esterling, Antoni, Fletcher, Margulies, & Schneiderman, 1994) or to a therapist (Donnelly & Murray, 1991; Murray, Lamnin, & Carver, 1989) find comparable biological, mood, and cognitive effects. Talking and writing about emotional experiences are both superior to writing about superficial topics.

Topic of disclosure. Whereas two studies have found that health effects occur only among individuals who write about particularly traumatic experiences (Greenberg & Stone, 1992; Lutgendorf, Antoni, Kumar, & Schneiderman, 1994), most studies have found that disclosure is more broadly beneficial. Choice of topic, however, may selectively influence the outcome. For beginning college students, for example, writing about emotional issues related to coming to college influences grades more than writing about traumatic experiences (Pennebaker & Beall, 1986; Pennebaker, Colder, & Sharp, 1990).

Length or days of writing. Different experiments have variously asked participants to write for 1 to 5 days, ranging from consecutive days to sessions separated by a week, writing sessions have ranged from 15 to 30 min in length. In Smyth's (1996) meta-analysis, he found a promising trend suggesting that the more days over which the experiment lapses, the stronger the effects. Although this was a weak trend, it suggests that writing once each week over a month may be more effective

Table 1 Effects of Disclosure on Various Outcome Parameters

Outcome	Studies
Physician Visits (comparison of number before and after writing)	
Reductions lasting 2 months after writing	Cameron and Nicholls (1996), Greenberg and Stone (1992), Greenberg, Wortman, and Stone (1996), Krantz and Pennebaker (1996), Pennebaker and Francis (1996), Pennebaker, Kiecolt-Glaser, and Glaser (1988), Richards, Pennebaker, and Beal (1995)
Reductions lasting 6 months after writing	Francis and Pennebaker (1992), Pennebaker and Beall (1986), Pennebaker, Colder, and Sharp (1990)
Reductions lasting 1.4 years after writing	Pennebaker, Barger, and Tiebout (1989)
Physiological Markers	
Long-term immune and other serum measures	
Blastogenesis (t-helper cell response to phytohemagglutimin)	Pennebaker et al. (1988)
Epstein-Barr virus antibody titers	Esterling, Antoni, Fletcher, Margulies, and Schneiderman (1994), Lutgendorf, Antoni, Kumar, and Schneiderman (1994)
Hepatitis B antibody levels	Petrie, Booth, Pennebaker, Davison, and Thomas (1995)
Natural killer cell activity	Christensen et al. (1996)
CD-4 (t-lymphocyte) levels	Booth, Petrie, and Pennebaker (in press)
Liver enzyme levels (SGOT)	Francis and Pennebaker (1992)
Immediate changes in autonomic and muscular activity	
Skin conductance, heart rate	Dominguez et al. (1995), Hughes, Uhlemann, and Pennebaker (1994), Pennebaker, Hughes, and O'Heeron (1987), Petrie et al. (1995)
Corrugator activity	Pennebaker et al. (1987)
Behavioral Markers	
Grade Point Average	Cameron and Nicholls (1996), Krantz and Pennebaker (1996)
Reemployment following job loss	Spera, Buhfeind, and Pennebaker (1994)
Absenteeism from work	Francis and Pennebaker (1992)
Self-Reports	
Physical symptoms	Greenberg and Stone (1992), Pennebaker and Beall (1985), Richards et al. (1995), Failure to find effects, Pennebaker et al. (1988, 1990), Petrie et al. (1995)
Distress, negative affect, depression	Greenberg and Stone (1992), Greenberg et al., (1996), Murray and Segal (1994), Rimé (1995), Spera et al. (1994), Failure to find effects Pennebaker and Beall (1986), Pennebaker et al. (1988), Pennebaker and Francis (1996), Petrie et al. (1995)

Note: Only studies published or submitted for publication are included. Several studies found effects that were qualified by a second variable (e.g., stressfulness of topic). See also Smyth (1996) for a detailed account.

than writing four times within a single week. Self-reports of the value of writing do not distinguish shorter from longer writing sessions.

Actual or implied social feedback. Unlike psychotherapy, the writing paradigm does not employ feedback to the participant. Rather, after individuals write about their own experiences, they are asked to place their essays into an anonymous-looking box with the promise that their writing will not be linked to their names. In one study comparing the effects of having students either write one paper that would be handed in to the experimenter or write on a "magic pad" (on which the writing disappears when the person lifts the plastic writing cover), no autonomic or self-report differences were found (Czajka, 1987).

Individual differences. No consistent personality or individual difference measures have distinguished who does versus who does not benefit from writing. The most commonly examined variables that have not been found to relate to outcomes include sex, age, anxiety (or negative affectivity), and inhibition or constraint. The one study that preselected participants on hostility found that those high in hostility benefited more from writing than those low in hostility (Christensen, et al., 1996).

Educational, linguistic, or cultural effects. Within the United States, the disclosure paradigm has benefited senior professionals with advanced degrees at rates comparable to those for maximum security prisoners with sixth-grade educations (Richards, Pennebaker, & Beal, 1995; Spera, Buhrfeund, & Pennebaker, 1994). Among college students, no differences have been found as a function of the students' ethnicity or native language. The disclosure paradigm has produced consistently positive results among French-speaking Belgians (Rime, 1995), Spanish-speaking residents of Mexico City (Dominguez, et al., 1995), and English-speaking New Zealanders (Petrie, Booth, Pennebaker, Davison, & Thomas, 1995).

Summary

When individuals write or talk about personally upsetting experiences in the laboratory, consistent and significant health improvements are found. The effects are found in both subjective and objective markers of health and well-being. The disclosure phenomenon appears to generalize across settings, most individual differences, and many Western cultures, and is independent of social feedback.

Why Does Writing Work?

Most of the research on disclosure has been devoted to demonstrating its effectiveness rather than on identifying the underlying mechanisms. Two very broad models that have been proposed to explain the value of disclosure invoke inhibitory processes and cognitive processes.

Inhibition and Disclosure

The original theory that motivated the first studies on writing was based on the assumption that not talking about important psychological phenomena is a form of inhibition. Drawing on the animal and psychophysiological literatures, we posited that active inhibition is a form of psychological work. This inhibitory work, which is reflected in autonomic and central nervous system activity, could be viewed as a long-term, low-level stressor (cf. Selye, 1976). Such stress, then, could cause or exacerbate psychosomatic processes, thereby increasing the risk of illness and other stress-related disturbances. Just as constraining thoughts, feelings, or behaviors linked to an emotional upheaval is stressful, letting go and talking about these experiences should, in theory, reduce the stress of inhibition (for a full discussion of this theory, see Pennebaker, 1989).

Findings to support the inhibition model of psychosomatics are accumulating. Individuals who conceal their gay status (Cole, Kemeny, Taylor, & Visscher, 1996), conceal traumatic experiences in their past (Pennebaker, 1993a), or are considered inhibited or shy by other people (e.g., Kagan, Reznick, & Snidman, 1988) exhibit more health problems than those who are less inhibited. Whereas inhibition appears to contribute to long-term health problems, the evidence that disclosure reduces inhibition and thereby improves health has not materialized. For example, Greenberg and Stone (1992) found that individuals benefited as much from writing about traumas about which they had told others as from writing about traumas about which they had kept secret. Self-reports of inhibition before and after writing have not consistently related to health changes. At this point, then, the precise role of inhibition in promoting health within the writing paradigm is not proven.

Cognitive Changes Associated with Writing

In the past decade, several studies have persuasively demonstrated that writing about a trauma does more than allow for the reduction of inhibitory processes. For example, in a recent study, students were randomly assigned either to express a traumatic experience using bodily movement, to express a traumatic experience first through movement and then in written form, or to exercise in a prescribed manner for 3 days, 10 min. per day (Krantz & Pennebaker, 1996). Whereas participants in the two movement-expression groups reported that they felt happier and mentally healthier in the months after the study, only the movement-plus-writing group showed significant improvements in physical health and grade point average. The mere expression of a trauma is not sufficient. Health gains appear to require translating experiences into language.

In recent years, we have begun analyzing the language that individuals use in writing about emotional topics. Our first strategy was to have independent raters evaluate the essays' overall contents to see if it was possible to predict who would benefit most from writing. Interestingly, judges noted that essays of people who benefited from writing appeared to be "smarter," "more thoughtful," and "more emotional" (Pennebaker, 1993b). However, the relatively poor interjudge reliability led us to develop a computerized text-analysis system.

In 1991, we created a computer program called LIWC (Linguistic Inquiry and Word Count) that analyzed essays in text format. LIWC was developed by having groups of judges evaluate the degree to which 2000 words or word stems were related to each of several dozen categories (for a full description, see Pennebaker & Francis, 1996). The categories included negative emotion words (*sad, angry*), positive emotion words (*happy, laugh*), causal words (*because, reason*), and insight words (*understand, realize*). For each essay that a person wrote, we were able to quickly compute the percentage of total words that represented these and other linguistic categories.

Analyzing the experimental subjects' data from six writing studies, we found three linguistic factors reliably predicted improved physical health. First, the more that individuals used positive emotion words, the better their subsequent health. Second, a moderate number of negative emotion words predicted health. Both very high and very low levels of negative emotion words correlated with poorer health. Third, and most important, an increase in both causal and insight words over the course of writing was strongly associated with improved health (Pennebaker, Mayne, & Francis, in press). Indeed, this increase in cognitive words covaried with judges' evaluations of the construction of the narratives. That is, people who benefited from writing began with poorly organized descriptions and progressed to coherent stories by the last day of writing.

The language analyses are particularly promising in that they suggest that certain features of essays predict long-term physical health. Further, these features are congruent with psychologists' current views on narratives. The next issue which is currently being addressed, is the degree to which cohesive stories or narratives predict changes in real-world cognitive processes. Further, does a coherent story about a trauma produce improvements in health by reducing ruminations or flashbacks? Does a story ultimately result in the assimilation of an unexplained experience, thereby allowing the person to get on with life? These are the theoretical questions that psychologists must address.

Implications for Treatment

Almost by definition, psychotherapy requires a certain degree of self-disclosure. Over the past 100 years, the nature of the disclosure has changed depending on the prevailing therapeutic winds. Whether the therapy is directive or evocative, insight-oriented or behavioral, the patient and therapist have worked together to derive a coherent story that explains the problem and, directly or indirectly, the cure. As the research summarized here suggests, the mere disclosing of the person's problem may have tremendous therapeutic value in and of itself.

The writing paradigm points to one of several possible active ingredients associated with psychotherapy. Most studies that have been conducted using this technique have not examined individuals with major emotional or physical health problems or substance abuse problems. One obvious question is the degree to which writing can serve as a supplement to—or even a substitute for—some medical and psychological treatments. Translating important psychological events into words is uniquely human. Therapists and religious leaders have known this intuitively for generations. Psychologists specializing in language, cognition, social processes, and psychotherapy can work together in better understanding the basic mechanisms of this phenomenon.

Acknowledgments: Preparation of this article was aided by grants from the National Science Foundation (SBR-9411674) and the National Institutes of Health (MH52391).

References

Booth, R.J., Petrie, K.J., & Pennebaker, J.W. (in press). Changes in circulating lymphocyte numbers following emotional disclosure. Evidence of buffering. *Stress Medicine.*

Cameron, L.D., & Nicholls, G. (1996). *Expression of stressful experiences through writing: A self-regulation approach.* Manuscript submitted for publication.

Christensen, A.J., Edwards, D.L., Wiebe, J.S., Benotsch, E.G., McKelvey, L., Andrews, M., & Lubaroff, D.M. (1996). Effect of verbal self-disclosure on natural killer cell activity. Moderation influence on cynical hostility. *Psychosomatic Medicine, 58,* 150–155.

Cole, S.W., Kemeny, M.W., Taylor, S.E., & Visscher, B.R. (1996). Elevated health risk among gay men who conceal their homosexual identity. *Health Psychology, 15,* 243–251.

Czajka, J.A. (1987) *Behavioral inhibition and short term physiological responses.* Unpublished master's thesis. Southern Methodist University, Dallas, TX.

Dominguez, B., Valerrama, P., Meza, M.A., Perez, S.L., Silva, A., Martinez, G., Mendez, V.M., & Olvera, Y. (1995). The roles of emotional reversal and disclosure in clinical practice. In J.W. Pennebaker (Ed.), *Emotion disclosure and health* (pp. 255–270). Washington, D.C., American Psychological Association.

Donnelly, D.A., & Murray, E.J. (1991). Cognitive and emotional changes in written essays and therapy interviews. *Journal of Social and Clinical Psychology, 10,* 334–350.

Esterling, B.A., Antoni, M.H., Fletcher, M.A., Margulies, S., & Schneiderman, N. (1994). Emotional disclosure through writing or speaking modulates latent Epstein-Barr virus antibody titers. *Journal of Consulting and Clinical Psychology, 62,* 130–140.

Francis, M.E., & Pennebaker, J.W. (1992). Putting stress into words. Writing about personal upheavals and health. *American Journal of Health Promotion, 6,* 280–287.

Greenberg, M.A., & Stone, A.A. (1992). Writing about disclosed versus undisclosed traumas. Immediate and long term effects on mood and health. *Journal of Personality and Social Psychology, 63,* 75–84.

Greenberg, M.A., Wortman, C.B., & Stone, A.A. (1996). Emotional expression and physical health. Revising traumatic memories or fostering self regulation. *Journal of Personality and Social Psychology, 71,* 588–602.

Hughes, C.F., Uhlmann, C. & Pennebaker, J.W. (1994). The body's response to psychological defense. *Journal of Personality, 62,* 565–585.

Kagan, J., Reznick, J.S., & Snidman, N. (1988). Biological bases of childhood shyness. *Science, 240,* 167–171.

Lutgendorf, S.K., Antonu, M.H., Kumar, M. & Schneiderman, N. (1994). Changes in cognitive coping strategies predict EBV antibody titre change following a stressor disclosure induction. *Journal of Psychosomatic Research, 38,* 63–78.

Mumford, E., Schlesinger, H.J., & Glass, G.V., (1983). Reducing medical costs through mental health treatment. Research problems and recommendations. In A. Broskowski, E. Marks, & S.H. Budman (Eds.), *Linking health and mental health* (pp. 257–273). Beverly Hills, CA, Sage.

Murray, E.J., Lammon, A.D., & Carver, C.S. (1989). Emotional expression in written essays and psychotherapy. *Journal of Social and Clinical Psychology, 8,* 414–429.

Murray, E.J., & Segal, D.L. (1994). Emotional processing in vocal and written expression of feelings about traumatic experiences. *Journal of Traumatic Stress, 7,* 391–405.

Pennebaker, J.W. (1989). Confession inhibition, and disease. In L. Berkowitz (Ed.), *Advances in experimental and social psychology* (Vol. 22, pp. 211–244). New York, Academic Press.

Pennebaker, J.W. (1993a). Mechanisms of social constraint. In D.M. Wegner & J.W. Pennebaker (Eds.), *Handbook of mental control* (pp. 200–219). Englewood Cliffs, NJ, Prentice Hall.

Pennebaker, J.W. (1993b). Putting stress into words. Health, linguistic, and therapeutic implications. *Behaviour Research and Therapy, 31,* 539–548.

Pennebaker, J.W., Barger, S.D., & Tiebout, J. (1989). Disclosure of traumas and health among Holocaust survivors. *Psychosomatic Medicine, 51,* 577–589.

Pennebaker, J.W., & Beall, S.K. (1986). Confronting a traumatic event. Toward an understanding of inhibition and disease. *Journal of Abnormal Psychology, 95,* 274–281.

Pennebaker, J.W., Colder, M., & Sharp, L.K. (1990). Accelerating the coping process. *Journal of Personality and Social Psychology, 58,* 528–537.

Pennebaker, J.W., & Francis, M.E. (1996). Cognitive emotional and language processes in disclosure. *Cognition and Emotion, 10,* 601–626.

Pennebaker, J.W., Hughes, C.F., & O Heeron, R.C. (1987). The psychophysiology of confession. Linking inhibitory and psychosomatic processes. *Journal of Personality and Social Psychology, 52,* 781–793.

Pennebaker, J.W., Kiecolt-Glaser, J., & Glaser, R. (1988). Disclosure of traumas and immune function. Health implications for psychotherapy. *Journal of Consulting and Clinical Psychology, 56,* 239–245.

Pennebaker, J.W., Mayne, T.J., & Francis, M.E. (in press). Linguistic predictors of adaptive bereavement. *Journal of Personality and Social Psychology.*

Petrie, K.J., Booth, R.J., Pennebaker, J.W., Davison, K.P., & Thomas, M.G. (1995). Disclosure of trauma and immune response to a hepatitis B vaccination program. *Journal of Consulting and Clinical Psychology, 63,* 787–792.

Richards, J.M, Pennebaker, J.W., & Beal, W.E. (1995, May). *The effects of criminal offense and disclosure of trauma on anxiety and illness in prison inmates.* Paper presented at the annual meeting of the Midwest Psychological Association, Chicago.

Rime, B. (1995). Mental rumination, social sharing, and the recovery from emotional exposure. In J.W. Pennebaker (Ed.), *Emotion, disclosure and health* (pp. 271–292). Washington, D.C., American Psychological Association.

Selye, H. (1976). *The stress of life.* New York, McGraw-Hill.

Smith, M.L., Glass, G.V., & Miller, R.L. (1980). *The benefits of psychotherapy.* Baltimore, Johns Hopkins University Press.

Smyth, J.M. (1996). *Written emotional expression. Effect sizes, outcome types and moderating variables.* Manuscript submitted for publication.

Spera, S.P., Buhrfeund, E.D., & Pennebaker, J.W. (1994). Expressive writing and coping with job loss. *Academy of Management Journal, 37,* 722–733.

Concluding Comments

Writing as Therapy

Whether or not you find these studies on disclosure surprising, they are certainly important. They provide clear experimental demonstrations of how, when a person reveals his or her personal experiences, and thinks about them, and feels them, it brings about healthful benefits. As Pennebaker remarks, such self-disclosure is part of the process of most psychotherapies, and may account in part for their generally positive impacts on people who undergo them. His innovation was to create a well-controlled laboratory demonstration of such an effect. Finding more definite answers to important questions, in this way, is a central part of the scientific process.

Review Questions

1. Pennebaker begins by describing the Emotional Expression Paradigm. What are some of its distinguishing characteristics? What does paradigm mean in this context?
2. Pennebaker goes on to describe some of the major influences that expressing oneself in writing can bring about. He reviews findings in several areas. Can you identify the areas and give an example of an outcome for each?
3. This article is Pennebaker's review of research that occurred in his own and others' laboratories on an emotional expression paradigm. The introduction that discusses Pennebaker's article makes a distinction between reviews of research and "critical" or "methodological" reviews. How is this review different from those other sorts of reviews?
4. Pennebaker originally believed that keeping secrets required inhibitions, and that inhibition would disrupt health because it required effort. Later research, however, has suggested that even expressing emotionally sensitive events that have been shared with others in the past still causes gains in health. How does Pennebaker now view the causes of greater health?
5. Pennebaker describes new software for understanding people's emotional stories. How does it work and what has it revealed about who benefits from emotional expression?

14

Studying Personality across Time

Reading Longitudinal Research

Empirical studies of personality development can be divided into two broad types according to the research design they employ. The first type of study employs a cross-sectional approach, in which two or more different groups of individuals of different ages are compared. The second group of studies employs longitudinal research studies, for which one group of individuals is studied over time.

Cross-sectional designs are more frequently employed because they are more economical and easier to carry out. They are also quite useful. For example, say one is comparing one group of 10-year-olds to a (different) group of 20-year-olds. Such a research design can permit the identification of many areas in which the 20-year-olds have attained greater maturity and functioning, relative to the 10-year-olds. At the same time, though, the cross-sectional design has its limits. It is difficult to tell, for example, whether groups are different solely due to age, or whether other differences between the two groups (when they grew up, etc.), might account for some results. In addition, using two groups of different people, there will be random differences—and hence, random error—in the different personalities included in each group.

By contrast, longitudinal studies study the same individuals over time. Perhaps the most crucial advantage of longitudinal studies is that one can see developmental processes unfold in the same individuals as they mature. In longitudinal studies, each individual serves as his or her own comparison person over time. In such a longitudinal study, a 10-year-old will be paired with his or her late 20-year-old self. That means that processes unique to that individual can be charted over time. Moreover, for the group as a whole, each 10-year-old serves as his or her own control, and any changes that are observed at age 20 can be ascribed more clearly to developmental processes (as opposed to random differences between unrelated individuals in the cross-sectional design). That has the consequence of reducing any random differences across groups, making it easier to see how qualities at 10 years of age predict qualities at 20. In longitudinal studies, in other words, time becomes the crucial focal variable in a way that it simply cannot be in cross-sectional designs. It is for such reasons that the longitudinal study is frequently regarded as the gold standard of developmental research.

The Present Article

Only a limited number of longitudinal studies exist in personality psychology that cover a substantial number of years. That makes each such study an invaluable resource. The present article presents some results from the Project Competence longitudinal study of 205 children. The focus of the Project Competence study is on three areas of life outcomes, all having to do with the development of competence: academic achievement, rule-abiding versus rule-breaking conduct, and social competence. The participants in the study have been examined thus far through age 20. Such studies require huge degrees of organization, as 20 years spans the central professional life span of many study directors, who themselves obtain their first positions around age 30 and may not be collecting the second wave of such data until they have reached the age of 50. For reasons explained above, each such date of data collection provides a precious opportunity for important new findings. In this study, a number of personality attributes at age 10 are used to predict a person's competence at age 20.

The Watch List

The opening of the article poses a question that may seem a little odd from the context of contemporary personality psychology. That is: "Are personality traits real?" Most people would assume that personality traits are real—and indeed, every indication is that they are quite real and of importance. In the mid-1970's, however, a debate broke out over whether such perceived differences in traits were overemphasized, and, in fact, largely (though not entirely) a matter of stereotyped perception on the part of people, including personality psychologists. More information about this debate can be found in your textbook in sections on traits, or on the *person-situation* debate or elsewhere. At any rate, the debate was mostly decided in favor of the fact that traits really exist and are of significance for the individual. The authors use this as an organizing question for their study, perhaps because the study does show how powerful an influence traits can have.

In the section "Childhood Competence Predicts Adaptation," the authors note that the assessment of the child's competence proceeded qualitatively through a combination of data sources. This is common in such studies, as the kinds of data collected are substantial and may change over time. That is, a child's competence is typically assessed by having a professional who is associated with the study make a global assessment of the individual on the basis of all the information on file.

Note the study investigator's definition of *mastery orientation* as a composite motive or style that maps onto the need for achievement, in part. Consider how mastery orientation might be the same or different from achievement motivation.

Note that Auke Tellegen's Multidimensional Personality Questionnaire (MPQ) is a scale that overlaps considerably with measures of the Big Five personality traits (a somewhat more widely used assessment approach). The MPQ is notable, however, for its theoretical attention to the measurement of positive and negative emotionality. The theory behind the MPQ considers such emotionality as central to personality description, development, and outcomes. Positive emotionality is highly related to such other personality traits as (high) extraversion. Negative emotionality is highly related to such traits as neuroticism and disagreeableness.

Transactional Links between Personality and Adaptation from Childhood through Adulthood

by Rebecca L. Shiner and Ann S. Masten

Source: Shiner, R. & Masten, A. (2002). Transactional links between personality and adaptation from childhood through adulthood. *Journal of Research in Personality*, *36*, 580–588.

1. Introduction

Are personality traits real? Following many years of heated debate among psychologists about the answer to this question, Tellegen (1991) put forth a "strong trait position": "We can begin by defining a trait as an inferred relatively enduring organismic (psychological, psychobiological) structure underlying an extended family of behavioral dispositions. In the case of personality traits it is expected that the manifestations of these dispositions can substantially affect a person's life" (p. 13). Over the last couple decades, some of the most compelling evidence for this "strong trait position" has come from research tracking individuals over the course of their lives to determine whether their earlier personality differences have predicted their later life outcomes. A number of longitudinal studies have documented that, indeed, personality predicts a variety of life outcomes, across developmental periods marked by significant changes in environmental contexts (Shiner & Caspi, in press).

We present here a synopsis of recent findings obtained from one study in particular—the Project Competence longitudinal study, which has followed a group of 205 individuals, recruited from a normative school population, from approximately age 10 to age 20, and again to age 30 (Garmezy & Tellegen, 1984; Masten et al., 1995, 1999). We have found evidence that the participants' personalities at age 10 predicted their adaptation at age 20 during the transition from late adolescence to "emerging adulthood" (Arnett, 2000), and still predicted adaptation at age 30 during early adulthood. Childhood personality differences also predicted changes in adaptation over those same time periods. Surprisingly, the converse has also been observed: In some cases, personality at age 20 was predictable from childhood adaptation and childhood adaptation predicted changes in personality from age 10 to 20. The picture emerging from this longitudinal study is one of bidirectional connections between personality and external adaptation: It appears that personality "can substantially affect a person's life," but it is also likely that life experiences and adaptation can substantially affect a person's personality.

Table 1   Correlations between Childhood Personality Traits and Concurrent Age-20 and Age-30 Adaptation 10 and 20 Years Later

Competent adaptation	Childhood personality traits (age 10)			
	Mastery Motivation	Academic Conscientiousness	Surgency	Agreeableness
Academic achievement				
Concurrent	.42***	.19**	.54***	.07
Age 20	.33***	.41***	.13	.26***
Age 30	.26***	.27***	.22**	.21**
Work competence				
Age 20	.22**	.26***	.23**	.31***
Age 30	.20**	.15*	.19**	.14
Rule-abiding conduct vs. antisocial behavior				
Concurrent	.25**	.37***	-.08	.46***
Age 20	.27***	.33***	-.01	.43***
Age 30	.20**	.26***	.14	.26***
Peer or friend relationships				
Concurrent	.22**	.32***	.35***	.19**
Age 20	.32***	.02	.37***	.21**
Age 30	.14	-.07	.19**	.17*
Romantic relationships				
Age 20	.13	-.07	.18*	.06
Age 30	.11	-.02	.24***	.07

Note. *p < .05. **p < .01. ***p < .001. N = 190 for analyses involving competence at age 10 and age 20. N = 178 for analyses involving competence at age 30. Correlations between childhood personality and concurrent and age-20 adaptation were published in "Linking childhood personality with adaptation: Evidence for continuity and change across time into late adolescence," by R. L. Shiner, 2000, *Journal of Personality and Social Psychology, 78.* Table 4, p. 316. Copyright 2000 by the American Psychological Association. Adapted with permission. Correlations between childhood personality and age 30 adaptation will appear in Shiner et al. (in press).

2. Childhood Personality Predicts Adaptation 10 and 20 Years Later

Life outcomes can be defined in a variety of ways (Shiner & Caspi, in press). Outcome criteria in Project Competence have been defined in terms of competence in "developmental tasks," the benchmarks by which adaptation in development is judged to be going well or not, in sociocultural and historical context (Masten et al., 1995, 1999). In the United States at this time, the salient developmental tasks of the school years involve effectiveness in three domains: *academic achievement; rule-abiding versus rule-breaking conduct* in the context of home, school, and community; and peer *social competence,* in relation to getting along with other children and developing friendships. As youth move throughout adolescence and enter adulthood, the nature of these three tasks changes: secondary and higher education require increasingly complex knowledge and skills; conduct standards increasingly encompass law-abiding behavior; and peer social competence increasingly focuses on self-selected friendships and close, reciprocal bonds. During adolescence, important new domains of adaptation emerge as youth begin to engage the tasks of work and romantic relationships; these tasks become salient markers of competence in adulthood.

In the Project Competence longitudinal study, we have examined whether the participants' childhood personalities related to their concurrent competent adaptation and whether their childhood personalities fore-shadowed their relative success or failure at mastering developmental tasks at age 20 and age 30 (Shiner, 2000; Shiner, Masten, & Roberts, in press). The participants' childhood personalities were assessed by combining the reports of their parents, their teachers, and clinical interviewers who met with the children themselves (Shiner, 2000). Competence in developmental task domains was assessed by multiple methods and informants (see Masten et al., 1995, 1999; Roisman, Masten, Coatsworth, & Tellegen, 2002). Table 1 shows the correlations between the participants' personality differences at age 10 and their adaptation at ages 10, 20, and 30. Results for the childhood traits serve to illustrate the overall conclusion that childhood personality meaningfully predicted adaptation across long stretches of time.

Children high on Agreeableness were characterized as high on prosocial traits (e.g., kind, generous, considerate, and cooperative) and low on hostile-disagreeable traits (e.g., selfish, egotistical, aggressive, and hurtful). This childhood trait did not predict academic achievement concurrently but did emerge as a modest predictor of academic success at ages 20 and 30. Not surprisingly, childhood Agreeableness also predicted lower levels of antisocial conduct and better relationships with friends across all the time periods. The results for Surgency and Agreeableness suggest that both extraversion and prosocial tendencies may contribute in important ways to the development of positive relationships with friends.

In carrying out the preceding analyses, we recognized the possibility that the apparent relationship between childhood personality and later adaptation could have been obtained merely because of the stability of the participants' adaptive functioning over time. For example, it was possible that childhood Agreeableness only predicted later rule-abiding conduct because rule-abiding conduct was itself so strongly stable over

time (Masten et al., 1995). We were interested in whether childhood personality *added* to the prediction of adaptation over time, even after taking into account childhood adaptation in the same domains; we conducted a series of analyses to address this question (Shiner, 2000; Shiner et al., in press). We found that, in many cases, childhood personality added to the prediction of later competence, even when controlling for gender, age, IQ, and childhood performance in the same domain of competence. Another way of looking at these results is that childhood personality predicted *changes* in competent adaptation across time. For example, childhood Academic Conscientiousness predicted increasingly high levels of academic achievement from age 10 to age 20, and also from age 10 to age 30. These analyses thus provided more compelling evidence that childhood personality contributes to youths' emerging success or failure at mastering developmental tasks. Overall, the findings from Project Competence fit with those obtained in other longitudinal projects: Childhood personality does meaningfully predict a variety of important life outcomes, even over long periods of time (Shiner & Caspi, in press) and even when taking earlier adaptation into account.

3. Childhood Adaptation at Age 10 Predicts Age 20 Personality

After finding that childhood personality was a robust predictor of later adaptation, we became interested in the converse possibility that childhood adaptation shapes personality functioning across time. In recent years, an increasingly large number of studies have documented that adult personality is concurrently associated with life adaptation (Shiner & Caspi, in press); we were interested in determining whether adult personality traits were predictable from childhood histories of adaptive functioning and, particularly, whether children's adaptive functioning predicted changes in personality across time. Success or failure at crucial age-salient adaptive tasks may have implications for personality development (Masten & Coatsworth, 1995; Sroufe & Rutter, 1984). For example, children who have difficulty making friends could potentially become more chronically reactive to stress and hostile over time. Children who excel academically could become increasingly self-controlled because they devote more and more of their time into tasks requiring focused attention; their self-control could then be reinforced through habitual practice and through positive reinforcement from adults.

To determine the links between early adult personality and previous adaptation, we first obtained the correlations between self-reported personality at age 20 and (1) concurrent adaptation, and (2) adaptation 10 years previously (Shiner, Masten, & Tellegen, 2002); these correlations are presented in Table 2. Self-reported personality was obtained using the Multi-dimensional Personality Questionnaire (MPQ; Tellegen, 1985; Tellegen & Waller, 1992), a reliable omnibus personality measure that yields scores on three higher-order scales: Positive Emotionality, Negative Emotionality, and Constraint. Individuals high on Positive Emotionality are predisposed to be positively and actively engaged with their social and work environments and to experience activated-positive emotions such as enthusiasm, zest, and well-being; this trait overlaps to some degree with Extraversion. Positive Emotionality at age 20 was not predictable from childhood adaptation, although it was associated with concurrent positive friend and romantic relationships (similar to the findings obtained for the childhood trait of Surgency). Individuals endorsing high levels of Constraint tend to be cautious, planful, harm-avoidant, and more traditional and conventional; those low on Constraint tend to acknowledge higher levels of impulsiveness and sensation-seeking and to reject conventional values. Constraint overlaps to some degree with Conscientiousness. Constraint at age 20 was associated with rule-abiding versus antisocial conduct, both in childhood and concurrently (similar to the findings obtained for the childhood trait of Academic Conscientiousness).

The most striking findings were obtained for Negative Emotionality, which taps an individual's tendency to experience negative emotions such as anxiety, resentment, and anger in a wide variety of situations and to have negatively charged relationships. This age 20 trait was correlated with nearly across-the-board poor adaptation concurrently and 10 years previously. We also found that, after controlling for gender, age, and the set of childhood personality traits, poor aca-

demic achievement and higher antisocial conduct in childhood predicted higher levels of NEM over time, consistent with the possibility that successes or failures in these salient developmental tasks contribute to changes in personality over time. In contrast, childhood adaptation did not predict Positive Emotionality or Constraint from age 10 to age 20 once earlier personality differences were controlled. Thus, young adults who are high on Negative Emotionality are more likely to have a history of adaptive failure, and such adaptive failure may actually contribute to personality change. Children with a track record of poor academic achievement and more antisocial conduct appear to become increasingly high strung, alienated, and hostile over time. Future analyses of data from this study will examine whether the history of adaptive success or failure continues to forecast changes in personality across the early adult years.

4. Transactions between Personality and Adaptation over Time

To return to the question with which we began this paper: Are personality traits real? Tellegen (1991) suggested that one way of establishing the reality of personality traits was to examine them longitudinally: "Important longitudinal studies completed or underway…permit or will permit evaluation of the stability and change of personality traits, and their contributions to personal environments and life outcomes" (p. 30). Findings from the longitudinal Project Competence study provide evidence for the validity of personality traits: Personality differences appear to play a role in how youth meet environmental demands and new developmental challenges. More enthusiastic, high-aspiring children and more conscientious, controlled children are more likely to attain higher academic achievement and better work competence. More extraverted, expressive children are more likely to have positive friendships and romantic relationships. More kind, considerate children are less likely to evidence antisocial behavior as young adults. Importantly, childhood personality differences also predict changes in adaptation over time. But, the relationship between personality and adaptation is more complex: Some aspects

Table 2 Correlations of Age 20 Personality Traits with Adaptation 10 Years Earlier and Concurrent Adaptation

Competent adaptation	Age 20 personality traits		
	Positive Emotionally	Negative Emotionally	Constraint
Academic achievement			
Age 10	.14	–.34***	–.11
Concurrent	.04	–.29***	.11
Work competence			
Concurrent	.06	–.36***	–.16
Rule-abiding conduct vs. antisocial behavior			
Age 10	–.07	–.21**	.23**
Concurrent	–.09	–.28***	.28***
Peer or friend relationships			
Age 10	.15	–.22**	.08
Concurrent	.41***	–.28***	–.12
Romantic relationships			
Concurrent	.24**	.16	–.08

Note. *p < .05. **p < .01. ***p < .001. Adult personality traits were measured using the Multidimensional Personality Questionnaire (MPQ). N = 187. Data in this table were published in "A developmental perspective on personality in emerging adulthood: Childhood antecedents and concurrent adaptation," by R. L. Shiner, A. S. Masten, and A. Tellegen, 2002. *Journal of Personality and Social Psychology, 83.* Table 4, p. 1171. Copyright 2002 by the American Psychological Association. Adapted with permission.

of adult personality are predicted by childhood adaptation, and in some cases childhood adaptation predicts the course of personality development across time. These findings suggest that there are likely to be transactions between personality and adaptation, with mutual influences occurring over time.

Future work should examine the pathways linking personality and adaptation. First, we need to understand more about mediating processes. How exactly do specific personality traits shape day-to-day functioning, and how does developmental success or failure shape consistent patterns of behavior, emotion, and thought in individuals? Second, the research suggesting links between personality and adaptation points to the fact that some personality differences put youth at risk for negative life outcomes; yet, many youth with "challenging" personalities still manage to thrive. It will be important to understand the processes that allow such youths to deal adaptively with their personalities. Third, although there is moderate continuity in temperament and personality differences by the preschool years (Roberts & DelVecchio, 2000), findings from Project Competence and other longitudinal studies suggest that personality can and does change (Caspi & Roberts, 2001). To understand personality development in childhood and adolescence, it will be necessary to learn more about the circumstances in which temperament and personality change. Understanding the processes that shape personality and competence in childhood, adolescence, and adulthood will require not only longitudinal designs but also more dynamic developmental models of personality that reflect the complex transactions of living and developing systems.

Acknowledgments

This work was supported in part by a grant from the Colgate Research Council. The results were based on data collected as part of the Project Competence longitudinal study, which has been supported through grants to Ann Masten, Auke Tellegen, and Norman Garmezy from the National Institute of Mental Health (MH33222), the William T. Grant Foundation, the National Science Foundation (SBR-9729111), and the University of Minnesota.

References

Arnett, J. J. (2000). Emerging adulthood: A theory of development from the late teens through the twenties. *American Psychologist, 55,* 469–480.

Caspi, A., & Roberts, B. W. (2001). Personality development across the life course: The argument for change and continuity. *Psychological Inquiry, 12,* 49–66.

Garmezy, N., & Tellegen, A. (1984). Studies of stress-resistant children: Methods, variables, and preliminary findings. In F. Morrison, C. Lord, & D. Keating (Eds.), *Advances in applied developmental psychology* (Vol. 1, pp. 231–387). New York: Academic Press.

Masten, A. S., & Coatsworth, J. D. (1995). Competence, resilience, & psychopathology. In D. Cicchetti & D. Cohen (Eds.), *Developmental psychopathology: Vol. 2 Risk, disorder, and adaptation* (pp. 715–752). New York: Wiley.

Masten, A. S., & Coatsworth, J. D., Neemann, J., Gest, S. D.,

Tellegen, A., & Garmezy, N. (1995). The structure and coherence of competence from childhood through adolescence. *Child Development, 66,* 1635–1659.

Masten, A. S., Hubbard, J. J., Gest, S. D., Tellegen, A., Garmezy, N., & Ramirez, M. L. (1999). Competence in the context of adversity: Pathways to resilience and maladaptation from childhood to late adolescence. *Development and Psychopathology, 11,* 143–169.

Roberts, B. W., & DelVecchio, W. F. (2000). The rank-order consistency of personality traits from childhood to old age: A quantitative review of longitudinal studies. *Psychological Bulletin, 126,* 3–25.

Roisman, G. I., Masten, A. S., Coatsworth, J. D., & Tellegen, A. (2002). *Salient and emerging developmental tasks in the transition to adulthood.* Unpublished manuscript, University of Minnesota, Twin Cities Campus.

Shiner, R. L. (2000). Linking childhood personality with adaptation: Evidence for continuity and change across time into late adolescence. *Journal of Personality and Social Psychology, 78,* 310–325.

Shiner, R. L., & Caspi, A. (in press). Personality differences in childhood and adolescence: Measurement, development, and consequences. *Journal of Child Psychology and Psychiatry and Allied Disciplines.*

Shiner, R. L., Masten, A. S., & Roberts, J. M. (in press). Childhood personality foreshadows adult personality and life outcomes two decades later. *Journal of Personality* (special issue on personality development).

Shiner, R. L., Masten, A. S., & Tellegen, A. (2002). A developmental perspective on personality in emerging adulthood: Childhood antecedents and concurrent adaptation. *Journal of Personality and Social Psychology, 83,* 1165–1177.

Sroufe, L. A., & Rutter, M. (1984). The domain of developmental psychopathology. *Child Development, 55,* 17–29.

Tellegen, A. (1985). Structure of mood and personality and their relevance to assessing anxiety, with an emphasis on self-report. In A. H. Tuma & J. D. Maser (Eds.), *Anxiety and the anxiety disorders* (pp. 681–706). Hillsdale, NJ: Erlbaum.

Tellegen, A. (1991). Personality traits: Issues of definition, evidence, and assessment. In W. M. Grove & D. Cicchetti (Eds.), *Thinking clearly about psychology, Vol. 2. Personality and psychopathology* (pp. 10–35). Minneapolis, MN: University of Minnesota Press.

Tellegen, A., & Wallter, N. G. (1992). *Exploring personality through test construction: Development of the Multi-dimensional Personality Questionnaire (MPQ).* Minneapolis: Unpublished manuscript, University of Minnesota

Concluding Comments

This article paints a picture of 10-year-old, mastery-oriented, conscientious children growing into high-achieving and well-adjusted 20-year-old young adults. The authors caution that, for other children, a string of failures of competence can lead to negative affectivity and hostility in the young person and put him or her at risk in regard to a later good adjustment. Quite independently from all that, 10-year-olds require some positive affect (surgency and extraversion), as well as some agreeableness, to make friends with others.

Review Questions

1. What is a longitudinal design and why is it important to the study of developmental psychology and personality in particular?
2. How do the authors define mastery motivation? How is that the same or different from achievement motivation?
3. Looking at the correlations in Table 1, can you describe what qualities predict better academic attainment in 20-years-olds?
4. Looking at the correlations in Table 2, can you describe what predicts positive relationships in 20-year-olds?
5. What evidence do the authors present for whether traits exist?

15

Reviewing a Book on Personality Development

Using Book Reviews

In a given year, dozens of books are written in psychology in addition to the hundreds of articles that are published. A given book's scientific status can vary widely. On the one hand, books often are not peer-reviewed in the same way as journal articles (see Chapter 4). On the other hand, the added length of books means that they can often provide more background on a topic and address it in greater depth than can a journal article. Moreover, there are many types of books in the field.

From a reader's standpoint, it is useful to distinguish between two categories of books: those by a single author or author team and those that are edited. Authored volumes are books by one or more authors presenting a topic or topics in some detail. The reader of these books will experience a continuity of style across the volume, as a single voice representing one or more authors discusses the book's topics. Edited volumes are books of papers by different authors all on related topics. Here, the reader will experience a diversity of viewpoints on a particular topic. Because editors often take a hands-off approach to such books, the chapters may vary considerably from one another, even as to the degree the topic in question is addressed.

It would be impossible to read all of the books that are published in psychology, and so one is dependent to a great extent, on one's own knowledge of the author, interest in the topic, and book reviews, to guide one through the field. Certain journals, such as the *Journal of Personality Assessment* and *Intelligence* often set aside pages for book reviews. Reviews of psychological books also appear in more general publications such as the *New York Review of Books*, and the like.

The central location for book reviews in the discipline of psychology, however, is PsychCRITIQUES, a searchable database of up-to-date reviews of recently released books. PsychCRITIQUES recently replaced *Contemporary Psychology: The APA Review of Books*. That glossy newsprint-style publication was the forerunner of PsychCRITIQUES, and for most of the latter 20th century, that publication included dozens of reviews of books relevant to the field of psychology as a whole. Even so, PsychCRITIQUES and its forerunner publication cannot review all of the books in the field. The editors must choose the books within the discipline that they feel are most significant. Then, they must find a psychologist willing to review the book. This provides a first "gate-keeping" function that generally directs attention toward the more important books that are published.

A well-written book review of a professional psychological book is not much different than a book review of a general sort. For that reason, most students will find these reviews familiar in style and scope. It is useful to keep the two missions of the review separate: the description of the work, and the evaluation of the work. Regarding the contents, if the review is a good one, you should be able to figure out what the book is intended to do and what its coverage actually consists of. You can decide whether that interests you, apart from the reviewer's evaluation. The second part of the review is the reviewer's evaluation of the book. A good reviewer will tell you in so many words what philosophical, scientific, or political perspective he or she is employing, to help you decide whether you might evaluate the book from the same or from a different perspective. You can then decide whether you might agree with the reviewer's evaluation of the book or not.

Significance of the Reading

Most books receive only one review, of course, and so represent only one reviewer's opinion—albeit an informed one. Books that are regarded as very important, however, sometimes will receive multiple reviews. Such a book was Judith Rich Harris' (1998) *The Nurture Assumption: Why Children Turn Out the Way They Do*. The book argued the controversial hypothesis that parents matter far less in the upbringing of a child than is commonly believed. Moreover, the author and book attracted considerable media attention.

To give the book its due, the editors solicited two reviews of the book rather than one, and both from eminent developmental psychologists. Both reviews are reprinted here. As the reviewers note, the book makes a strong argument about the reasons children grow up the way they do.

The Watch List

Williams' review, "*Peering into the Nature-Nurture Debate*," is the first and it is remarkably accessible to a reader. She does, however, refer to two then-current events that are now no longer quite as current. She refers to a "media frenzy second only to Monicagate"— the reference was to President Clinton's affair with Monica Lewinski. She also refers to students' violence in the schools. Her review appears shortly after the Jonesboro slayings, which involved a 12- and 14-year-old who entered their school in Jonesboro, AK, with high-powered rifles and killed four of their classmates as well as a revered teacher in March of 1998.

Plomin's review, "Parents and Personality," is a bit more technical in nature. In the opening section, Plomin refers to *accounting for the variance*. Accounting for the variance refers to the ability to use psychological variables to explain the degree to which a target person varies from average. The better a variable is at predicting whether a person will be above or below average on a given attribute, the more variance is explained. Plomin employs percentages to describe the amount of variance explained (accounted for). At one point, he refers to the environment accounting for "more than half the variance" of an outcome—a substantial amount—in the section on "Nonshared Environment." To better understand these expressions, it is best to consult a statistics book directly.

The section "Genetic Mediation" discusses the concept of mediation. Mediation has a specific meaning in certain statistical techniques. You can think of it conceptually as the idea that genetics not only directly causes an outcome, but can also regulate (mediate) other relationships. For example, genetics governs how a person's eyes develop and see. As such, genes also mediate the fact that a person responds to paintings. That is, without the genetic regulation that constructs eyes for human beings, there would be little of interest in regard to an artist's paintings. This is, again, a rather sophisticated concept handled in a quick fashion in the review.

Under the "Peers" section, the phrase "primate and hominid parenting" refers to parenting by primates, such as monkeys and great apes, and by human beings, respectively.

In the "Do Parents Matter?" section of Plomin's review, he says that "Parenting is not a main effect nor is environment a main effect." Here, he is referring again to a type of statistical outcome involving analysis of variance. A first approximation to such statements is that "parenting has no simple, direct influence on child personality, and the same is true for the environment."

Peering into the Nature-Nurture Debate

by Wendy M. Williams

Source: Williams, W. M. (1999). Peering into the nature-nurture debate. *Contemporary Psychology: The APA Review of Books, 44,* 267–269.

The battle cry of mothers everywhere—"If your friend Norbert jumped off the Brooklyn Bridge, would you jump off, too?"—can finally be answered with a triumphant, "Yes!" That is, according to Judith Rich Harris, whose book *The Nurture Assumption: Why Children Turn Out the Way They Do* has caused a media frenzy second only to Monicagate. Unless you've been doing fieldwork in Antarctica, you have undoubtedly read at least a few of the media reports on Harris and her thesis that one's peers matter more than previously thought and parents matter less. From the cover of *Newsweek* to a BBC documentary, Harris has seized the popular press unlike any psychologist since the publication in 1995 of *The Bell Curve* by Herrnstein and Murray.

Harris's well-written and intriguing book challenges the "nurture-assumption" which presumes that children are the products of their (mostly parental) environments. Her perspective is that it is the environment more broadly construed—peers, friends, schools—as well as the contribution of genes that shapes children's behavior, rather than parental influence per se. Harris attacks the popular and widely accepted notion that children turn out the way they do because of how their parents treat them. She argues through the use of multiple examples spanning a broad range of disciplines that parents' role as shapers of their children's development has been greatly exaggerated, concluding that parents' main contribution consists of the genes they transmit to their offspring.

As evidence, Harris cites the fact that children of immigrants adopt the language and ways of the dominant culture external to their homes and notes that children, like Cinderella in the classic fairy tale, often behave one way at home with their parents but entirely differently in the world at large. Harris points out, for example, that birth order effects are evident in the home, where the eldest child bosses the others around, but disappear when the children are out in the world in other environments. And dishonesty in the home is a poor predictor of dishonesty outside the home. Referring to people who delay childbearing because they believe it requires a huge commitment, in an article by Gladwell (1998), Harris is quoted in *The New Yorker* as saying: "If they knew that it was O.K. to have a child and let it be reared by a nanny or put in a daycare center, or even to send it to a boarding school, maybe they'd believe that it would be O.K. to have a kid" (p. 63).

Harris's book makes wonderful reading because she is a consummate storyteller. In anecdotes and lively descriptions she reminds us how we sought desperately in childhood and adolescence to emulate our peers and often do the exact opposite of our parents' wishes. Harris explains that evolutionary principles dictate that children identify with and affiliate with their peers if they wish to survive in the dominant culture their peers create. Children are depicted, correctly, as possessing innately different temperaments. Harris relates the story of her own children, one biological and one adopted, who responded in opposite fashion to an overzealous dog: One child was timid and fearful, whereas the other was fearless. Thus, Harris argues that the fact that a parent encourages all of her children to be receptive to dogs, for example, does not mean that all of the children will act this way. Much of parents' influence on their children is attributed to shared genes, and Harris notes that parents are credited or blamed unfairly when tractable children are parented in a positive way and turn out well, or when difficult children are parented in an authoritarian fashion and turn out to be rebellious.

Readers with a background in developmental or child psychology will be struck repeatedly by how much of these arguments they have heard before, albeit in different guises. Consider one example. In an ongoing dialogue in the nature-nurture debate focusing on the influence of parental style on children's intellectual development, Scarr (1985) has argued that

> the implications...for improving children's intellectual functioning by intervention in mothers' control and discipline techniques are dismal. Even if we could dramatically improve a mother's positive behaviors toward her child, her improved behavior would have little payoff in the child's IQ score. (p. 505)

Scarr's position has been that mothers with higher IQs tend to have children with higher IQs, and that these mothers also tend to have more effective parental styles. On this view, the findings showing a link between parental style and children's cognitive competence are actually due to the effect of shared genetically transmitted intelligence between mother and child. Like Harris, Scarr believes that parents' behaviors are correlated with their children's because of shared genes, and that what we observe in the world of parenting and child development is explicable even if parents have no effects on their children, or vice versa. Harris distills the findings of this and other empirical research, churning the argument by adding the "all-peer-all-the-time" focus.

In fact, Harris has mixed an amalgam of the work of many researchers, each of whom focused on a portion of the puzzle of parent-child influences. The resulting product is an artful commingling of findings from diverse disciplines: psychology, sociology, anthropology, behavior genetics, evolutionary biology, and literature. One problem with her approach, though, is that the reader is often not given a fair rendering of the other side of each issue. For example, despite the inherent difficulties of studying parental influences on children, there are studies documenting cause and effect relationships. One study of Dutch mothers' interactions with nine-month olds examined parental responsiveness to infants and the role of parental stimulation of infants in

the infants' development (Riksen-Walraven, 1978). Mothers were randomly assigned to four groups characterized by different types of interaction (responsive, directive, both responsive and directive, and control); the amounts of interaction were constant across the groups. When the infants were observed and tested three months later, the researchers found that infants of mothers who had been encouraged to be responsive showed higher levels of exploratory behavior than any other group and preferred novel to familiar objects. These babies also learned more quickly in a contingency task. Thus, infants randomly assigned to a condition of greater maternal responsiveness showed enhanced cognitive functioning. The conclusion was that different styles of parenting may cause differential cognitive development in children. And there are numerous additional studies that refute Harris's position: Scholars such as Jerome Kagan, who has been an effective critic of Harris's position, have cited a substantial body of research attesting to parents' pivotal roles. Critics have also noted that the measures of parental influence relied on in the studies cited by Harris were not nearly sophisticated enough to depict the subtle, real parental influences that nevertheless exist. They point out that Harris has minimized the fact that even if peer groups are important, parents influence the choice of them.

For all of these reasons, the wide appeal of Harris's book has frustrated many developmental psychologists and others who believe that she took an oversimplified and highly polarized position in the nature-nurture debate to capitalize on the media appeal of a shocking premise ("parents don't matter"). Harris's critics have generally responded by countering her claims with descriptions of empirical research showing parents' impact on child development. Ultimately, however, little real progress toward the truth will result from the piecemeal approach of matching Harris study for study in a stylized nature-nurture poker game. In fact, Harris does the psychological community a service by challenging the assumption that parents can craft their children out of clay. Her assault on closely held beliefs shared by many developmental psychologists forces us all to modify and clarify our thinking about why children turn out the way they do. As the human genome project marches forward, assembling more and more of the puzzle explaining how genes determine who we become, we are reminded that we live in the age of biology, a time when scientists must defend statements about influences on child development that simply used to be assumed to be true. In its role as piquer of interest and an initiator of meaningful argument in the scientific community, then Harris's book is valuable.

Harris's influence is less positive in the popular press and media. One reason for her meteoric ride to prominence is the substantial emotional appeal of her thesis that "parents don't matter as much as peers" to today's parents. The popular press seized on this aspect of the story and took the whole "parents don't matter" ride, giving readers from coast to coast the license they sought to ignore their children and not worry too much about ignoring them. In an era when adolescents premeditate large-scale slayings of classmates and teachers, and teenagers abuse drugs or alcohol and kill behind the wheel, there is little that many modern American readers would rather be told than that they are not to blame for their children's failures. Parents feel guilty about how their kids turned out; Harris's message relieves the guilt. The hopelessness we all share in the face of the Jonesboro slayings—when three-year-old future killers appear on the cover of *Time* wearing army fatigues and clutching rifles—makes us crave the quick and easy answer that someone else must be to blame. Savvy about the media appeal of this message, the press made Harris an overnight celebrity, rarely, if ever, giving equal time to the other side of the debate. What the press did find room for, though, were repeated depictions of Harris as an underdog from suburban New Jersey without any academic affiliation, booted out of Harvard University as a graduate student 40 years ago, and condemned to writing articles and books from her home without access to university facilities.

What will be the legacy of the debate reheated by Harris? One aspect of Harris's story we should all take pride in is the fact that her ideas were given air time despite her lack of academic affiliation. The science of psychology in general—and in particular the editors and reviewers of *Psychological Review* who accepted the article that launched her book and the psychologist who gave this article the prestigious George Miller award—made room for the ruminations of a grandmother from New Jersey without scholarly credentials. Her work was good; she got the recognition. There was no in-group operating to ban outsiders from publishing their ideas in top journals or to guarantee that awards go only to club members. A grandmotherly underdog from outside the system became a top dog and the system permitted her to do it. Media depictions of an invincible underdog denied a place at the (academic) table may appeal to those who harbor delusions about the way science works, but the reality is far more benign: Scientists judged the merits of Harris's ideas, not dissuaded by her failure to graduate from Harvard.

In sum, as is often the case with broad syntheses of literature in an area, when Harris's arguments are examined critically we find that many have been made in the past and that what is compelling about this book is its narrative voice and engaging tone. The actual science has been explored more fully elsewhere, by the researchers doing empirical studies on the individual components of Harris's arguments. So, although *The Nurture Assumption* is a well-written and well-synthesized presentation of the evidence on one side of the issue, it is not the revolutionary portrayal of new data and ultimate answers that so many media outlets and even academic psychologists have touted. Harris is a talented communicator, but she fails to convince us through this book that she is an empirical scientist who impartially evaluates the evidence. Her position is more that of a zealot arguing a side in a court battle than a dispassionate and independent reviewer. (And argue effectively she does—her truly amazing level of success and degree of exposure attest to her ability to command an audience.) Ultimately, *The Nurture Assumption* is worth reading and discussing because it forces every one of us to defend and clarify our thinking about parental influences on child development. However, we must remember that Harris tells only half of a story whose ending was the first part she wrote.

References

Gladwell, M. (1998, August l7). Do parents matter? *The New Yorker*, 55–64.

Hernstein, R.J., & Murray, C. (1995). *The bell curve: Intelligence and class structure in American life*. New York: Free Press.

Riksen-Walraven, J.M. (1978). Effects of caregiver behavior on habituation rate and self-efficacy in humans. *International Journal of Behavioral Development, 1,* 105–103.

Scarr, S. (1985). Constructing psychology: Making facts and fables for our times. *American Psychologist, 40,* 499–512.

Parents and Personality

by Robert Plomin

Source: Plomin, R. (1999). Parents and personality. *Contemporary Psychology: The APA Review of Books, 44,* 269–271.

"Parents Matter Less Than You Think and Peers Matter More." This subtitle on the dust jacket of *The Nurture Assumption* summarizes the book and indicates why it has received so much attention in the media. The nurture assumption is the idea that what shapes children's personalities, apart from their genes, is the way they were treated by their parents. *Newsweek,* in a cover story (Begley, 1998) titled "Who Needs Parents?" seconds Steven Pinker's Foreword to the book that *The Nurture Assumption* "will come to be seen as a turning point in the history of psychology" (p. xiii). The book also received glowing publicity in a lengthy and influential review titled "Do Parents Matter?" in *The New Yorker* (Gladwell, 1998).

However, several newspaper reviews that I have seen have been very negative. "Dumb Book Says What Parents Do or Don't Do Doesn't Matter" is the headline of one newspaper story. Another says, "Quality Time Is Wasted Time." The concern is that if parenting does not shape children's personality, then why bother?

From my perspective as a behavioral geneticist, I see three main messages in *The Nurture Assumption.* Although the first two still have the capacity to shock when put as boldly as Harris does, they are well supported by behavioral genetic research during the past 20 years. Harris refers to these behavioral genetic data but does not review them systematically. The third message is novel and interesting but not yet proven. After reviewing these three issues, I will return to the concern about whether parents matter.

Nonshared Environment

The first message is the importance of nonshared environment for personality. Nonshared environment refers to environmental factors that make children growing up in the same family different. Why do adoptive siblings (genetically unrelated children adopted into the same family) not correlate at all for personality even though they grow up together? That is, if parenting is so important and these children have the same parents, why do they not end up being at all similar in personality? (Note that this question about what makes similar or different is a much narrower issue than asking whether parents matter.) The answer must be that the shared aspects of their family life such as having the same parents is not a potent force in the development of personality. Genetically related siblings correlate more highly (still only about .2) than adoptive siblings, but this resemblance can be attributed to their shared heredity rather than their shared environment.

Why do identical twins growing up in the same family only correlate about .4 for personality? Because identical twins are genetically identical, the answer to the question of why they are so different has to lie with the environment rather than with genes. But it is a particular type of environmental influence—nonshared environment—that makes two children growing up in the same family (even genetically identical clones!) different from one another.

In other words, personality has long been known to run in families and this familial resemblance has reasonably but wrongly been attributed to shared family environment, specifically parenting. This is the nurture assumption. Instead, familial resemblance for personality is largely due to nature, that is, genetics. The environment is important, accounting for more than half of the variance of personality, but these environmental influences are not shared by siblings growing up in the same family. Harris's goal is to specify factors responsible for nonshared environment.

Genetic Mediation

What about the hundreds of studies showing that individual differences in parenting are correlated with individual differences in children's outcomes? Isn't this evidence for shared family environment? This broaches the second message of the book. The nurture assumption assumes that correlations between parenting and children's outcomes are caused environmentally. However, because family members share genes as well as environments (except in the relatively rare case of adoptive families), genetic factors must also be considered as possible mediators of such correlations. Genetically sensitive designs such as twins, adoption, or stepfamilies are needed to test the nurture assumption rigorously.

A surprising finding from such behavioral genetic research is that genetic factors contribute substantially to correlations between parenting and children's outcome (Plomin, 1994; Rowe, 1994). Genetic factors can contribute to individual differences in parenting by way of the parent such as the parents' personality or by way of the child in the sense that parents may respond to genetically instigated propensities in their children. For example, a child's irritability may be directly inherited from parents or parents may respond to this propensity in their child. Both processes are likely to contribute to genetic mediation of relationships between parenting and children's outcomes, which is a type of genotype-environment correlation. Such genetically sensitive designs also provide direct examination of the mediational role of nonshared environment independent of genetic factors. So far, such research finds little evidence for a nonshared environmental role for parenting or other aspects of the family environment independent of genetics (Reiss, Neiderhiser, Hethering-

ton, & Plomin, in press). In other words, attempts to pin personality differences between siblings on differential treatment by parents have come to naught, because the evidence indicates that parents are responding to genetically instigated differences between siblings, rather than producing the sibling differences.

This leads to the third message of *The Nurture Assumption*, which is Harris's novel contribution.

Peers

So far the story is that the environment is important but that the environment works in a nonshared manner making children growing up in the same family different from one another. Although parenting can potentially work in this nonshared manner, there is little evidence for it when genetics is controlled. So what is responsible for the large nonshared environmental chunk of variance for personality and adjustment? There are several possibilities including the scary one of chance (in the sense of idiosyncratic experiences that may be difficult to study systematically: Dunn & Plomin, 1990).

Harris suggests that peers are the answer. She develops a group socialization theory based on an evolutionary argument. She claims that we have evolved to become valued members of a group perceived to be similar to us, which is usually our peers. She emphasizes differences in children's behavior in the home and outside the home—the latter is thought to be the major sphere of influence of peers. Often parents and peers pull in the same direction in terms of norms. But when peers differ from parents, as in the case of immigration to a different culture, the norms of peers rather than parents govern socialization. This is seen most strikingly in language but also in attitudes and values. The bulk of the book expands this group socialization theory with chapters on historical views of parenting, primate and hominid parenting, social psychology, social development, cultural anthropology, gender, schools, adolescence, and dysfunctional families and children.

It is reasonable to look outside the family when trying to explain why children growing up in the same family differ. However, the case for the role of peers as the answer to nonshared environment is far from proven. Her argument for peers primarily involves group norms but this does not explain individual differences. What needs to be identified are the nonshared environmental sources of variance that make children growing up in the same family different. Harris just slips this in by asserting in a single sentence on one of the last pages that "identical twins do not end up with identical personalities, even if they are members of the same peer group, because they have different experiences within the group" (p. 359). From the perspective of nonshared environment, this is the key issue: What we need to know is the extent to which siblings experience different peer groups or have differentiating experiences within peer groups and whether these peer experiences account for sibling differences in personality.

A second problem with the peer hypothesis is that Harris does not follow through the logic of her critique of the nurture assumption. That is, in the rest of the book, she argues forcefully against the nurture assumption—that correlations between parenting and children's outcomes are caused environmentally—because genetic factors mediate these correlations. In turning to peers, however, the possibility of genetic mediation is glossed over, with only a brief mention on page 285. This is not just a debating point: The only relevant study suggests that characteristics of peer groups show strong genetic influence (Manke, McGuire, Reiss, Hetherington, & Plomin, 1995), perhaps because adolescents choose peer groups and are chosen by peer groups on the basis of personality.

Do Parents Matter?

Harris knows that she will be accused of saying that it does not matter how parents treat their children. She declares preemptively that

> I do not say that; nor do I imply it; nor do I believe it. It is *not* all right to be cruel or neglectful to your children...We may not hold their tomorrows in our hands but we surely hold their todays, and we have the power to make their todays very miserable. (p. 291)

She also suggests that parents can pass on information that is not scrutinized by peer groups, such as

religion, cooking, music, interests, and political preferences. And she grudgingly concedes that the extremes of neglectful or abusive parenting might have more of an effect on children's personality, but she calls this "the nurture assumption's last slim hope" (p. 355).

Despite such statements, a confusion develops between the narrow research findings from behavioral genetics and the broad conclusion that parents do not matter. The basic research findings are that shared environment is generally not very important for personality and that parenting-personality correlations are largely mediated genetically. Parents do matter but not in terms of parenting specifically shaping children's personality development. Furthermore, as mentioned earlier, genetic mediation of parenting-personality correlations is a type of genotype-environment correlation. Because this is a correlation between genotypes and environment, parenting is not a genetic main effect nor an environmental main effect. Genotype-environment correlation between parenting and personality can be interpreted to mean that parenting is crucial in mediating these genetic effects. That is, genetic factors might initiate these effects but parenting and other environmental processes are necessary for their expression (Reiss et al., in press).

Harris's basic message for parents is that they should relax and enjoy their children:

> The idea that we can make our children turn out any way we want is an illusion. Give it up. Children are not empty canvases on which parents can paint their dreams. Don't worry about what the advice-givers tell you. Love your kids because kids are lovable, not because you think they need it. Enjoy them. Teach them what you can. Relax. (p. 349)

Even though I have done research in this area, I still find it difficult emotionally to take on board the full implications for parents of this research showing that shared environment is of little importance for personality development when genetics is controlled, but it helps to keep in mind the narrow remit of these findings—parents do matter. I enjoyed Harris's attempt to confront these issues unflinchingly and to force us to face the bête noire that parents may not contribute much to personality development, despite all of our theories to the contrary. For me, it is liberating to think about parents and children in terms of an important relationship that occupies us for the majority of our lives. That is, this relationship is an end in itself, not just a means to an end. Surely it would be good if this relationship were enjoyable both for parents and their children. Harris points out that we do not expect to change our spouse's personality. We need to recognize and respect individual differences in our children as well as in adults. This does not mean that there is nothing we can do as parents. For example, if we recognize that our child is shy, we might arrange to have a friend go with the child to a party so that the child has someone to ease the anxiety of warming up to strangers. We do this not because we think it will make the child less shy but rather because it will help the child sidestep the effects of shyness and thus enjoy the party. This is another way in which parents do matter. We help our children as well as our spouses and friends because we want them to be happy and to enjoy life, not because we want to mold them. Making parents anxious about childrearing is likely to be counterproductive to these goals.

As a behavioral geneticist, I was pleased to see someone coming fresh to this field, looking at the data, and reaching similar conclusions about the importance of nonshared environment and genetic mediation of correlations between parenting and children's outcomes.

For a popular audience, Harris's forceful and provocative yet engaging and humorous writing style is effective (although as a stuffy academic I cringed at some of it). I hope that Harris's hypothesis of peers as the missing source of nonshared environmental influence stimulates research to test it. At the very least, reading Harris's *The Nurture Assumption* will help you think about some big issues in psychology.

References

Begley, S. (1998, August 24). Who needs parents? *Newsweek, 53.*

Dunn, J., & Plomin, R. (1990). *Separate lives: Why siblings are so different.* New York: Basic Books.

Gladwell, M. (1998, August 17). Do parents matter? *The New Yorker,* 54–64.

Manke, B., McGuire, S., Reiss, D., Hetherington, E.M., & Plomin, R. (1995). Genetic contributions to children's extrafamilial social interactions: Teachers, best friends, and peers. *Social Development, 4,* 238–256.

Plomin, R. (1994). *Genetics and experience: The interplay between nature and nurture.* Newbury Park, CA: Sage.

Reiss, D., Neiderhiser, J.M., Hetherington, E.M., & Plomin, R. (in press). *The relationship code: Detecting links between genetic and social influences on psychological development.* Cambridge, MA: Harvard University Press.

Rowe, D.C. (1994). *The limits of family influence: Genes, experience, and behavior.* New York: Guilford Press.

Concluding Comments

How Do the Reviews Help?

The two reviews together provide a great deal of information about the Harris book, the book's thesis, and how it should be regarded. Reviews *do* take away the surprise of opening a book and reading it without any preconceptions. At the same time, in a busy, crowded world with many things to do, reviews such as these provide wise guidance as to what the book might be like. That is a helpful source of information in deciding whether or not to undertake the journey.

Review Questions

1. Why are reviews of psychological books of use to the field?
2. What does Wendy Williams' review tell you factually about Harris' book?
3. What was Williams' evaluation of Harris' book (as opposed to its factual content)?
4. What did Plomin's review tell you about the contents of Harris' book?
5. How did Plomin evaluate Harris' book?

16

A Stage Theory of Development

Help from a Grand Theorist

I use the term *grand theorists* to refer to individuals working in the beginning-to-mid portion of the 20th century who attempted to synthesize information about human nature into broad theories of personality. The grand theorists included Sigmund Freud, Alfred Adler, Carl Jung, Karen Horney, George Kelley, Gordon Allport, Raymond Cattell, Abraham Maslow, and Carl Rogers, among others. These were great thinkers whose ambitious systems were constrained, however, by the lack of empirical evidence at the time. Nonetheless, much of their work remains thought-provoking today.

Grand theorists typically preferred writing books to journal articles; as such their work was not peer-reviewed, but (initially, at least) rather judged on the basis of its persuasiveness and insight, its capacity to generate research and to be of use to clinical psychologists. Reading a grand theorist means examining that individual's way of thinking as much as a specific piece of science. To be sure, general systematizations tend to oversimplify the rich complexity of the real world. Nonetheless, they also provide guideposts that the human mind can use as starting points in approaching a subject.

Significance of the Reading

Erik H. Erikson was one of the grand theorists of personality psychology working in the mid-20th century. His division of the human life cycle into eight stages is regarded as among the most influential schemes for understanding human development during the past century (Welchman, 2000, p. 127). It provides an overall framework that generations of personality and developmental psychologists have employed for categorizing and thinking about the tasks and conflicts facing an individual at a particular stage of life.

Four years before its publication, in 1946, Erikson published an essay called "Ego Development and Historical Change," which was to define a critical new point in his intellectual work. He then completely stopped publishing for four years. During that time he occupied himself as a clinician, but kept one day a week for writing, and described himself to his friends as "working on a book." That book was published in 1950 by W. W. Norton as *Childhood and Society* (Coles, 1970, pp. 113–119).

Upon its completion, *Childhood and Society* was immediately published in England, and was translated into Japanese, Swedish, German, Spanish, French, Hebrew, Finnish, Dutch, Italian, Norwegian, and Danish within several years. It became a familiar sight in many university bookstores.

Chapter 7 of the book is an essay entitled, "The Eight Ages of Man." The chapter presents an example of a "Grand Theorist" writing at the top of his form. In the chapter, Erikson tries to tame the unfathomable complexities of human development by organizing it into eight periods of time (Welchman, 2000, p. 52).

Part of the richness of the chapter comes from Erikson's attempt to synthesize at least four perspectives in looking at the growing person. First, he attends to bodily processes, including the physical development and capacities of the individual, particularly during infancy and childhood. Second, he examines personality processes including wishes, fears, and life tasks. Third, he takes into account his own and others' experiences as practicing psychoanalysts—followers of Freudian psychotherapy—and uses his clinical experience to describe what can go right or wrong in development. Fourth, he focuses on the individual's relation to society.

The Watch List

The introduction to the "Eight Ages of Man" (Chapter 7 of *Childhood and Society*) exists, in a sense, at the conclusion to the chapter before (Chapter 6). There, Erikson remarks, "...the next chapter is a list of ego qualities that emerge from critical periods of development" (Erikson, 1963, p. 246), and says he will provide a timetable of the individual in relation to society. Chapter 7 is divided into an introduction and nine numbered sections thereafter. Erikson jumps into the first stage of development with no further preamble.

In Section I, Erikson ties his essay to advanced psychoanalytic concepts: introjection and projection. Oversimply, introjection as Erikson describes it means identifying a set of qualities with one's self, and projection means not realizing one's own bad qualities—and recognizing them instead only in others. The "ego" is the rational part of the self.

Each of the subsequent numbered sections denotes a new stage. In Section II, Erikson discusses the problem of "too much shaming" by the parents. This attention to the dark side of personality, and its hidden rebelliousness is both a glory and weakness of psychodynamic theory. For, in acknowledging the dark side of human nature, some have said it also has overemphasized the negative. Other psychodynamic terminology that appears here includes *libidinal focus,* by which is meant focusing on the pleasure of a matter. Erikson also refers to "An area of the body which can be magically dominated"—Erikson is probably making reference to diaper-changing, and particularly toilet-training, here.

His Section III refers to childhood sexuality based on clinical observations, making reference to "genitality... phallic-intrusive modes...'catching.'" Such terms are couched in the language common to early-to-mid-20th-century views of sexuality and do not make allowances for the greater flexibility of gender roles far more widely acknowledged by psychologists today. Like other psychodynamic theorists, Erikson believes the young child identifies with the parent and internalizes real or imagined punishments of the parents in the course of developing a superego (or conscience).

The early grand theorists were often somewhat casual in their referencing of others' work. In Section IV a mention of "(Ives Hendrick)" is an incomplete citation to an article appearing in the 1943 volume (#12) of *Psychoanalytic Quarterly* entitled "Work and the pleasure principle."

Erikson brings up a chapter on Native Americans when he says, *"As we saw on the chapter on American Indians...."* Erikson lived amidst and studied two Native American tribes, which considerably broadened his understanding of human development.

Probably the most well-known work of Erikson's today (beyond this stage theory) was the idea of the *identity crisis*. This crisis is introduced and discussed in Section V—and probably more richly so because Erikson lived some of it himself. Erikson had dropped out of school toward the end of (what in the U.S. would be) high school, and drifted along European beaches for an extended time.

Erikson's Section VI discusses the (psychoanalytic term) *object*, which is here used to mean the internal representation of an outside real person. Thus, the love-object is one's internal perception of the person one truly loves. Erikson was writing at a time when homosexuality was still classified as a psychopathology and less was known about same sex relationships. His focus here is almost exclusively on heterosexual love and relationships.

The final section, Section IX, refers not to a new stage, but rather an "Epigenetic Chart" that summarizes the developmental course Erikson has described.

From: Childhood and Society: Chapter 7: Eight Ages of Man

by Erik H. Erikson

Source: Erikson, E. (1950/1963). [Chapter 7, "Eight Ages of Man" (pp. 247–274)]. *Childhood and Society* (2nd ed.). New York: W. W. Norton.

1. Basic Trust vs. Basic Mistrust

The first demonstration of social trust in the baby is the ease of his feeding, the depth of his sleep, the relaxation of his bowels. The experience of a mutual regulation of his increasingly receptive capacities with the maternal techniques of provision gradually helps him to balance the discomfort caused by the immaturity of homeostasis with which he was born. In his gradually increasing waking hours he finds that more and more adventures of the senses arouse a feeling of familiarity, of having coincided with a feeling of inner goodness. Forms of comfort, and people associated with them, become as familiar as the gnawing discomfort of the bowels. The infant's first social achievement, then, is his willingness to let the mother out of sight without undue anxiety or rage, because she has become an inner certainty as well as an outer predictability. Such consistency, continuity, and sameness of experience provide a rudimentary sense of ego identity which depends, I think, on the recognition that there is an inner population of remembered and anticipated sensations and images which are firmly correlated with the outer population of familiar and predictable things and people.

What we here call trust coincides with what Therese Benedek has called confidence. If I prefer the word "trust," it is because there is more naïveté and more mutuality in it; an infant can be said to be trusting where it would go too far to say that he has confidence. The general state of trust, furthermore, implies not only that one has learned to rely on the sameness and continuity of the outer providers, but also that one may trust oneself and the capacity of one's own organs to cope with urges; and that one is able to consider oneself trustworthy enough so that the providers will not need to be on guard lest they be nipped.

The constant tasting and testing of the relationship between inside and outside meets its crucial test during the rages of the biting stage, when the teeth cause pain from within and when outer friends either prove of no avail or withdraw from the only action which promises relief: biting. Not that teething itself seems to cause all the dire consequences sometimes ascribed to it. As outlined earlier, the infant now is driven to "grasp" more, but he is apt to find desired presences elusive: nipple and breast, and the mother's focused attention and care. Teething seems to have a prototypal significance and may well be the model for the masochistic tendency to assure cruel comfort by enjoying one's hurt whenever one is unable to prevent a significant loss.

In psychopathology the absence of basic trust can best be studied in infantile schizophrenia, while lifelong underlying weakness of such trust is apparent in adult personalities in whom withdrawal into schizoid and depressive states is habitual. The re-establishment of a state of trust has been found to be the basic requirement for therapy in these cases. For no matter what conditions may have caused a psychotic break, the bizarreness and withdrawal in the behavior of many very sick individuals hides an attempt to recover social mutuality by testing of the borderlines between senses and physical reality, between words and social meanings.

Psychoanalysis assumes the early process of differentiation between inside and outside to be the origin of projection and introjection which remain some of our deepest and most dangerous defense mechanisms. In introjection we feel and act as if an outer goodness had become an inner certainty. In projection, we experience an inner harm as an outer one: we endow significant people with the evil which actually is in us. These two mechanisms, then, projection and introjection, are assumed to be modeled after whatever goes on in infants when they would like to externalize pain and internalize pleasure, an intent which must yield to the testimony of the maturing senses and ultimately of reason. These mechanisms are, more or less normally, reinstated in acute crises of love, trust, and faith in adulthood and can characterize irrational attitudes toward adversaries and enemies in masses of "mature" individuals.

The firm establishment of enduring patterns for the solution of the nuclear conflict of basic trust versus basic mistrust in mere existence is the first task of the ego, and thus first of all a task for maternal care. But let it be said here that the amount of trust derived from earliest infantile experience does not seem to depend on absolute quantities of food or demonstrations of love, but rather on the quality of the maternal relationship. Mothers create a sense of trust in their children by that kind of administration which in its quality combines sensitive care of the baby's individual needs and a firm sense of personal trustworthiness within the trusted framework of their culture's life style. This forms the basis in the child for a sense of identity, which will later combine a sense of being "all right," of being oneself, and of becoming what other people trust one will become. There are, therefore (within certain limits previously defined as the "musts" of child care), few frustrations in either this or the following stages which the growing child cannot endure if the frustration leads to the ever-renewed experience of greater sameness and stronger continuity of development, toward a final integration of the individual life cycle with some meaningful wider belongingness. Parents must not only have certain ways of guiding by prohibition and permission; they must also be able to represent to the child a deep, an almost somatic conviction that there is a meaning to what they are doing. Ultimately, children become neurotic not from frustrations, but from the lack or loss of societal meaning in these frustrations.

But even under the most favorable circumstances, this stage seems to introduce into psychic life (and become prototypical for) a sense of inner division and universal nostalgia for a paradise forfeited. It is against this powerful combination of a sense of having been deprived, of having been divided, and of having been abandoned—that basic trust must maintain itself throughout life.

Each successive stage and crisis has a special relation to one of the basic elements of society, and this for the simple reason that the human life cycle and man's institutions have evolved together. In this chapter we can do little more than mention, after the description of each stage, what basic element of social organization is related to it. This relation is twofold: man brings to these institutions the remnants of his infantile mentality and his youthful fervor, and receives from them—as long as they manage to maintain their actuality—a reinforcement of his infantile gains.

The parental faith, which supports the trust emerging in the newborn, has throughout history sought its institutional safeguard (and, on occasion, found its greatest enemy) in organized religion. Trust born of care is, in fact, the touchstone of the *actuality* of a given religion. All religions have in common the periodical childlike surrender to a Provider or providers who dispense earthly fortune as well as spiritual health; some demonstration of man's smallness by way of reduced posture and humble gesture; the admission in prayer and song of misdeeds, of mis-thoughts, and of evil intentions; fervent appeal for inner unification by divine guidance; and finally, the insight that individual trust must become a common faith, individual mistrust a commonly formulated evil, while the individual's restoration must become part of the ritual practice of many, and must become a sign of trustworthiness in the community.* We have illustrated how tribes dealing with one segment of nature develop a collective magic which seems to treat the Supernatural Providers of food and fortune as if they were angry and must be appeased by prayer and self-torture. Primitive religions, the most primitive layer in all religions, and the religious layer in each individual,

---

* This is the communal and psychosocial side of religion. Its often paradoxical relation to the spirituality of the individual is a matter not to be treated briefly and in passing (see *Young Man Luther*). (E.H.E.)

abound with efforts at atonement which try to make up for vague deeds against a maternal matrix and try to restore faith in the goodness of one's strivings and in the kindness of the powers of the universe.

Each society and each age must find the institutionalized form of reverence which derives vitality from its world-image—from predestination to indeterminacy. The clinician can only observe that many are proud to be without religion whose children cannot afford their being without it. On the other hand, there are many who seem to derive a vital faith from social action or scientific pursuit. And again, there are many who profess faith, yet in practice breathe mistrust both of life and man.

2. Autonomy vs. Shame and Doubt

In describing the growth and the crises of the human person as a series of alternative basic attitudes such as trust vs. mistrust, we take recourse to the term a "sense of," although, like a "sense of health," or a "sense of being unwell," such "senses" pervade surface and depth, consciousness and the unconscious. They are, then, at the same time, ways of *experiencing* accessible to introspection; ways of *behaving*, observable by others; and unconscious *inner states* determinable by test and analysis. It is important to keep these three dimensions in mind, as we proceed.

Muscular maturation sets the stage for experimentation with two simultaneous sets of social modalities; holding on and letting go. As is the case with all of these modalities, their basic conflicts can lead in the end to either hostile or benign expectations and attitudes. Thus, to hold can become a destructive and cruel retaining or restraining, and it can become a pattern of care: to have and to hold. To let go, too, can turn into an inimical letting loose of destructive forces, or it can become a relaxed "to let pass" and "to let be."

Outer control at this stage, therefore, must be firmly reassuring. The infant must come to feel that the basic faith in existence, which is the lasting treasure saved from the rages of the oral stage, will not be jeopardized by this about-face of his, this sudden violent wish to have a choice, to appropriate demandingly, and to eliminate stubbornly. Firmness must protect him against the potential anarchy of his as yet untrained sense of discrimination, his inability to hold on and to let go with discretion. As his environment encourages him to "stand on his own feet," it must protect him against meaningless and arbitrary experiences of shame and of early doubt.

The latter danger is the one best known to us. For if denied the gradual and well-guided experience of the autonomy of free choice (or if, indeed, weakened by an initial loss of trust) the child will turn against himself all his urge to discriminate and to manipulate. He will overmanipulate himself, he will develop a precocious conscience. Instead of taking possession of things in order to test them by purposeful repetition, he will become obsessed by his own repetitiveness. By such obsessiveness, of course, he then learns to repossess the environment and to gain power by stubborn and minute control, where he could not find large-scale mutual regulation. Such hollow victory is the infantile model for a compulsion neurosis. It is also the infantile source of later attempts in adult life to govern by the letter, rather than by the spirit.

Shame is an emotion insufficiently studied, because in our civilization it is so early and easily absorbed by guilt. Shame supposes that one is completely exposed and conscious of being looked at: in one word, self-conscious. One is visible and not ready to be visible; which is why we dream of shame as a situation in which we are stared at in a condition of incomplete dress, in night attire, "with one's pants down." Shame is early expressed in an impulse to bury one's face, or to sink, right then and there, into the ground. But this, I think, is essentially rage turned against the self. He who is ashamed would like to force the world not to look at him, not to notice his exposure. He would like to destroy the eyes of the world. Instead he must wish for his own invisibility. This potentiality is abundantly used in the educational method of "shaming" used so exclusively by some primitive peoples. Visual shame precedes auditory guilt, which is a sense of badness to be had all by oneself when nobody watches and when everything is quiet—except the voice of the superego. Such shaming exploits an increasing sense of being small, which can develop only as the child stands up and as his awareness permits him to note the relative measures of size and power.

Too much shaming does not lead to genuine propriety but to a secret determination to try to get away with things, unseen—if, indeed, it does not result in defiant shamelessness. There is an impressive American ballad in which a murderer to be hanged on the gallows before the eyes of the community, instead of feeling duly chastened, begins to berate the onlookers, ending every salvo of defiance with the words, "God damn your eyes." Many a small child, shamed beyond endurance, may be in a chronic mood (although not in possession of either the courage or the words) to express defiance in similar terms. What I mean by this sinister reference is that there is a limit to a child's and an adult's endurance in the face of demands to consider himself, his body, and his wishes as evil and dirty, and to his belief in the infallibility of those who pass such judgment. He may be apt to turn things around, and to consider as evil only the fact that they exist: his chance will come when they are gone, or when he will go with them.

Doubt is the brother of shame. Where shame is dependent on the consciousness of being upright and exposed, doubt, so clinical observation leads me to believe, has much to do with a consciousness of having a front and a back—and especially a "behind." For this reverse area of the body, with its aggressive and libidinal focus in the sphincters and in the buttocks, cannot be seen by the child, and yet it can be dominated by the will of others. The "behind" is the small being's dark continent, an area of the body which can be magically dominated and effectively invaded by those who would attack one's power of autonomy and who would designate as evil those products of the bowels which were felt to be all right when they were being passed. This basic sense of doubt in whatever one has left behind forms a substratum for later and more verbal forms of compulsive doubting; this finds its adult expression in paranoiac fears concerning hidden persecutors and secret persecutions threatening from behind (and from within the behind).

This stage, therefore, becomes decisive for the ratio of love and hate, cooperation and willfulness, freedom of self-expression and its suppression. From a sense of self-control without loss of self-esteem comes a lasting sense of good will and pride; from a sense of loss of self-control and of foreign overcontrol comes a lasting propensity for doubt and shame.

If, to some reader, the "negative" potentialities of our stages seem overstated throughout, we must remind him that this is not only the result of a preoccupation with clinical data. Adults, and seemingly mature and unneurotic ones, display a sensitivity concerning a possible shameful "loss of face" and fear of being attacked "from behind" which is not only highly irrational and in contrast to the knowledge available to them, but can be of fateful import if related sentiments influence, for example, interracial and international policies.

We have related basic trust to the institution of religion. The lasting need of the individual to have his will reaffirmed and delineated within an adult order of things which at the same time reaffirms and delineates the will of others has an institutional safeguard in the *principle of law and order*. In daily life as well as in the high courts of law—domestic and international—this principle apportions to each his privileges and his limitations, his obligations and his rights. A sense of rightful dignity and lawful independence on the part of adults around him gives to the child of good will the confident expectation that the kind of autonomy fostered in childhood will not lead to undue doubt or shame in later life. Thus the sense of autonomy fostered in the child and modified as life progresses, serves (and is served by) the preservation in economic and political life of a sense of justice.

3. Initiative vs. Guilt

There is in every child at every stage a new miracle of vigorous unfolding, which constitutes a new hope and a new responsibility for all. Such is the sense and the pervading quality of initiative. The criteria for all these senses and qualities are the same: a crisis, more or less beset with fumbling and fear, is resolved, in that the child suddenly seems to "grow together" both in his person and in his body. He appears "more himself," more loving, relaxed and brighter in his judgment, more activated and activating. He is in free possession of a surplus of energy which permits him to forget failures quickly and approach what seems desirable (even if it also seems uncertain and even dangerous) with undiminished and

---

* See "The Problem of Ego-Identity," J. Amer. Psa. Assoc., 4:56–121.

more accurate direction. Initiative adds to autonomy the quality of undertaking, planning and "attacking" a task for the sake of being active and on the move, where before self-will, more often than not, inspired acts of defiance or, at any rate, protested independence.

I know that the very word "initiative" to many, has an American, and industrial connotation. Yet, initiative is a necessary part of every act, and man needs a sense of initiative for whatever he learns and does, from fruit-gathering to a system of enterprise.

The ambulatory stage and that of infantile, genitality add to the inventory of basic social modalities that of "making," first in the sense of "being on the make." There is no simpler, stronger word for it; it suggests pleasure in attack and conquest. In the boy, the emphasis remains on phallic-intrusive modes; in the girl it turns to modes of "catching" in more aggressive forms of snatching or in the milder form of making oneself attractive and endearing.

The danger of this stage is a sense of guilt over the goals contemplated and the acts initiated in one's exuberant enjoyment of new locomotor and mental power: acts of aggressive manipulation and coercion which soon go far beyond the executive capacity of organism and mind and therefore call for an energetic halt on one's contemplated initiative. While autonomy concentrates on keeping potential rivals out, and therefore can lead to jealous rage most often directed against encroachments by younger siblings, initiative brings with it anticipatory rivalry with those who have been there first and may, therefore, occupy with their superior equipment the field toward which one's initiative is directed. Infantile jealousy and rivalry, those often embittered and yet essentially futile attempts at demarcating a sphere of unquestioned privilege, now come to a climax in a final contest for a favored position with the mother; the usual failure leads to resignation, guilt, and anxiety. The child indulges in fantasies of being a giant and a tiger, but in his dreams he runs in terror for dear life. This, then, is the stage of the "castration complex," the intensified fear of finding the (now energetically eroticized) genitals harmed as a punishment for the fantasies attached to their excitement.

Infantile sexuality and incest taboo, castration complex and superego all unite here to bring about that specifically human crisis during which the child must turn from an exclusive, pregenital attachment to his

parents to the slow process of becoming a parent, a carrier of tradition. Here the most fateful split and transformation in the emotional powerhouse occurs, a split between potential human glory and potential total destruction. For here the child becomes forever divided in himself. The instinct fragments which before had enhanced the growth of his infantile body and mind now become divided into an infantile set which perpetuates the exuberance of growth potentials, and a parental set which supports and increases self-observation, self-guidance, and self-punishment.

The problem, again, is one of mutual regulation. Where the child, now so ready to overmanipulate himself, can gradually develop a sense of moral responsibility, where he can gain some insight into the institutions, functions, and roles which will permit his responsible participation, he will find pleasurable accomplishment in wielding tools and weapons, in manipulating meaningful toys—and in caring for younger children.

Naturally, the parental set is at first infantile in nature: the fact that human conscience remains partially infantile throughout life is the core of human tragedy. For the superego of the child can be primitive, cruel, and uncompromising, as may be observed in instances where children over-control and over-constrict themselves to the point of self-obliteration; where they develop an over-obedience more literal than the one the parent has wished to exact; or where they develop deep regressions and lasting resentments because the parents themselves do not seem to live up to the new conscience. One of the deepest conflicts in life is the hate for a parent who served as the model and the executor of the superego, but who (in some form) was found trying to get away with the very transgressions which the child can no longer tolerate in himself. The suspiciousness and evasiveness which is thus mixed in with the all-or-nothing quality of the superego, this organ of moral tradition, makes moral (in the sense of moralistic) man a great potential danger to his own ego—and to that of his fellow men.

In adult pathology, the residual conflict over initiative is expressed either in hysterical denial, which causes the repression of the wish or the abrogation of its executive organ by paralysis, inhibition, or impotence; or in over-compensatory showing off, in which the scared individual, so eager to "duck," instead "sticks his neck out." Then also a plunge into psychosomatic disease is now common. It is as if the culture had made a man over-advertise himself and so identify with his own advertisement that only disease can offer him escape.

But here, again, we must not think only of individual psychopathology, but of the inner powerhouse of rage which must be submerged at this stage, as some of the fondest hopes and the wildest phantasies are repressed and inhibited. The resulting self-righteousness—often the principal reward for goodness—can later be most intolerantly turned against others in the form of persistent moralistic surveillance, so that the prohibition rather than the guidance of initiative becomes the dominant endeavor. On the other hand, even moral man's initiative is apt to burst the boundaries of self-restriction, permitting him to do to others, in his or in other lands, what he would neither do nor tolerate being done in his own home.

In view of the dangerous potentials of man's long childhood, it is well to look back at the blueprint of the life-stages and to the possibilities of guiding the young of the race while they are young. And here we note that according to the wisdom of the ground plan the child is at no time more ready to learn quickly and avidly, to become bigger in the sense of sharing obligation and performance than during this period of development. He is eager and able to make things cooperatively, to combine with other children for the purpose of constructing and planning, and he is willing to profit from teachers and to emulate ideal prototypes. He remains, of course, identified with the parent of the same sex, but for the present he looks for opportunities where work-identification seems to promise a field of initiative without too much infantile conflict or oedipal guilt and a more realistic identification based on a spirit of equality experienced in doing things together. At any rate, the "oedipal" stage results not only in the oppressive establishment of a moral sense restricting the horizon of the permissible; it also sets the direction toward the possible and the tangible which permits the dreams of early childhood to be attached to the goals of an active adult life. Social institutions, therefore, offer children of this age an *economic ethos,* in the form of ideal adults recognizable by their uniforms and their functions, and fascinating enough to replace, the heroes of picture book and fairy tale.

4. Industry vs. Inferiority

Thus the inner stage seems all set for "entrance into life," except that life must first be school life, whether school is field or jungle or classroom. The child must forget past hopes and wishes, while his exuberant imagination is tamed and harnessed to the laws of impersonal things—even the three R's. For before the child, psychologically already a rudimentary parent, can become a biological parent, he must begin to be a worker and potential provider. With the oncoming latency period, the normally advanced child forgets, or rather sublimates, the necessity to "make" people by direct attack or to become papa and mama in a hurry: he now learns to win recognition by producing things. He has mastered the ambulatory field and the organ modes. He has experienced a sense of finality regarding the fact that there is no workable future within the womb of his family, and thus becomes ready to apply himself to given skills and tasks, which go far beyond the mere playful expression of his organ modes or the pleasure in the function of his limbs. He develops a sense of industry—i.e., he adjusts himself to the inorganic laws of the tool world. He can become an eager and absorbed unit of a productive situation. To bring a productive situation to completion is an aim which gradually supersedes the whims and wishes of play. His ego boundaries include his tools and skills: the work principle (Ives Hendrick) teaches him the pleasure of work completion by steady attention and persevering diligence. In all cultures, at this stage, children receive some *systematic instruction,* although, as we saw in the chapter on American Indians, it is by no means always in the kind of school which literate people must organize around special teachers who have learned how to teach literacy. In preliterate people and in non-literate pursuits much is learned from adults who become teachers by dint of gift and inclination rather than by appointment, and perhaps the greatest amount is learned from older children. Thus the *fundamentals of technology* are developed, as the child becomes ready to handle the utensils, the tools, and the weapons used by the big people. Literate people, with more specialized careers, must prepare the child by teaching him things which first of all make him literate, the widest possible basic education for the greatest number of possible careers. The more confusing specialization becomes, however, the more indistinct are the eventual goals of the initiative; and the more complicated social reality, the vaguer are the father's and mother's role in it. School seems to be a culture all by itself, with its own goals and limits, its achievements and disappointment.

The child's danger, at this stage, lies in a sense of inadequacy and inferiority. If he despairs of his tools and skills or of his status among his tool partners, he may be discouraged from identification with them and with a section of the tool world. To lose the hope of such "industrial" association may pull him back to the more isolated, less tool-conscious familial rivalry of the oedipal time. The child despairs of his equipment in the tool world and in anatomy, and considers himself doomed to mediocrity or inadequacy. It is at this point that wider society becomes significant in its ways of admitting the child to an understanding of meaningful roles in its technology and economy. Many a child's development is disrupted when family life has failed to prepare him for school life, or when school life fails to sustain the promises of earlier stages.

Regarding the period of a developing sense of industry, I have referred to *outer and inner hindrances* in the use of new capacities but not to aggravations of new human drives, nor to submerged rages resulting from their frustration. This stage differs from the earlier ones in that it is not a swing from an inner upheaval to a new mastery. Freud calls it the latency stage because violent drives are normally dormant. But it is only a lull before the storm of puberty, when all the earlier drives reemerge in a new combination, to be brought under the dominance of genitality.

On the other hand, this is socially a most decisive stage: since industry involves doing things beside and with others, a first sense of division of labor and of differential opportunity, that is, a sense of the *technological ethos* of a culture, develops at this time. We have pointed in the last section to the danger threatening individual and society where the schoolchild begins to feel that the color of his skin, the background of his parents, or the fashion of his clothes rather than his wish and his will to learn will decide his worth as an apprentice, and thus his sense of *identity*—to which we must now turn. But there is another, more fundamental danger, namely man's restriction of himself and constriction of his hori-

zons to include only his work to which, so the Book says, he has been sentenced after his expulsion from paradise. If he accepts work as his only obligation, and "what works" as his only criterion of worthwhileness, he may become the conformist and thoughtless slave of his technology and of those who are in a position to exploit it.

5. Identity vs. Role Confusion

With the establishment of a good initial relationship to the world of skills and tools, and with the advent of puberty, childhood proper comes to an end. Youth begins. But in puberty and adolescence all samenesses and continuities relied on earlier are more or less questioned again, because of a rapidity of body growth which equals that of early childhood and because of the new addition of genital maturity. The growing and developing youths, faced with this physiological revolution within them, and with tangible adult tasks ahead of them are now primarily concerned with what they appear to be in the eyes of others as compared with what they feel they are, and with the question of how to connect the roles and skills cultivated earlier with the occupational prototypes of the day. In their search for a new sense of continuity and sameness, adolescents have to refight many of the battles of earlier years, even though to do so they must artificially appoint perfectly well-meaning people to play the roles of adversaries; and they are ever ready to install lasting idols and ideals as guardians of a final identity.

The integration now taking place in the form of ego identity is, as pointed out, more than the sum of the childhood identifications. It is the accrued experience of the ego's ability to integrate all identifications with the vicissitudes of the libido, with the aptitudes developed out of endowment, and with the opportunities offered in social roles. The sense of ego identity, then, is the accrued confidence that the inner sameness and continuity prepared in the past are matched by the sameness and continuity of one's meaning for others, as evidenced in the tangible promise of a "career."

The danger of this stage is role confusion.[*] Where this is based on a strong previous doubt as to one's sexual identity, delinquent and outright psychotic episodes are not uncommon. If diagnosed and treated correctly, these incidents do not have the same fatal significance which they have at other ages. In most instances, however, it is the inability to settle on an occupational identity which disturbs individual young people. To keep themselves together they temporarily overidentify, to the point of apparent complete loss of identity, with the heroes of cliques and crowds. This initiates the stage of "falling in love," which is by no means entirely, or even primarily, a sexual matter—except where the mores demand it. To a considerable extent adolescent love is an attempt to arrive at a definition of one's identity by projecting one's diffused ego image on another and by seeing it thus reflected and gradually clarified. This is why so much of young love is conversation.

Young people can also be remarkably clannish, and cruel in their exclusion of all those who are "different," in skin color or cultural background, in tastes and gifts, and often in such petty aspects of dress and gesture as have been temporarily selected as *the* signs of an in-grouper or out-grouper. It is important to understand (which does not mean condone or participate in) such intolerance as a defense against a sense of identity confusion. For adolescents not only help one another temporarily through much discomfort by forming cliques and by stereotyping themselves, their ideals, and their enemies; they also perversely test each other's capacity to pledge fidelity. The readiness for such testing also explains the appeal which simple and cruel totalitarian doctrines have on the minds of the youth of such countries and classes as have lost or are losing their group identities (feudal, agrarian, tribal, national) and face world-wide industrialization, emancipation, and wider communication.

The adolescent mind is essentially a mind of the *moratorium,* a psychosocial stage between childhood and adulthood, and between the morality learned by the child, and the ethics to be developed by the adult. It is an ideological mind—and, indeed, it is the ideological outlook of a society that speaks most clearly to the adolescent who is eager to be affirmed by his peers, and is ready to be confirmed by rituals, creeds, and programs which at the same time define what is evil, uncanny, and inimical. In searching for the social values which guide identity, one therefore confronts the problems of *ideology* and *aristocracy,* both in their widest possible sense which connotes that within a defined world image and a predestined course of history, the best peo-

ple will come to rule and rule develops the best in people. In order not to become cynically or apathetically lost, young people must somehow be able to convince themselves that those who succeed in their anticipated adult world thereby shoulder the obligation of being the best. We will discuss later the dangers which emanate from human ideals harnessed to the management of super-machines, be they guided by nationalistic or international, communist or capitalist ideologies. In the last part of this book we shall discuss the way in which the revolutions of our day attempt to solve and also to exploit the deep need of youth to redefine its identity in an industrialized world.

6. Intimacy vs. Isolation

The strength acquired at any stage is tested by the necessity to transcend it in such a way that the individual can take chances in the next stage with what was most vulnerably precious in the previous one. Thus, the young adult, emerging from the search for and the insistence on identity, is eager and willing to fuse his identity with that of others. He is ready for intimacy, that is, the capacity to commit himself to concrete affiliations and partnerships and to develop the ethical strength to abide by such commitments, even though they may call for significant sacrifices and compromises. Body and ego must now be masters of the organ modes and of the nuclear conflicts, in order to be able to face the fear of ego loss in situations which call for self-abandon: in the solidarity of close affiliations, in orgasms and sexual unions, in close friendships and in physical combat, in experiences of inspiration by teachers and of intuition from the recesses of the self. The avoidance of such experiences because of a fear of ego loss may lead to a deep sense of isolation and consequent self-absorption.

The counterpart of intimacy is distantiation: the readiness to isolate and, if necessary, to destroy those forces and people whose essence seems dangerous to one's own, and whose "territory" seems to encroach on the extent of one's intimate relations. Prejudices thus developed (and utilized and exploited in politics and in war) are a more mature outgrowth of the blinder repudiations which during the struggle for identity differentiate sharply and cruelly between the familiar and the foreign. The danger of this stage is that intimate, competitive, and combative relations are experienced with and against the selfsame people. But as the areas of adult duty are delineated, and as the competitive encounter, and the sexual embrace, are differentiated, they eventually become subject to that *ethical sense* which is the mark of the adult.

Strictly speaking, it is only now that *true genitality* can fully develop: for much of the sex life preceding these commitments is of the identity-searching kind, or is dominated by phallic or vaginal strivings which make of sex-life a kind of genital combat. On the other hand, genitality is all too often described as a permanent state of reciprocal sexual bliss. This then, may be the place to complete our discussion genitality.

For a basic orientation in the matter I shall quote what has come to me as Freud's shortest saying. It has often been claimed, and bad habits of conversation seem to sustain the claim, that psychoanalysis as a treatment attempts to convince the patient that before God and man he has only one obligation: to have good orgasms, with a fitting "object," and that regularly. This, of course, is not true. Freud was once asked what he thought a normal person should be able to do well. The questioner probably expected a complicated answer. But Freud, in the curt way of his old days, is reported to have said: "Lieben und arbeiten" (to love and to work). It pays to ponder on this simple formula; it gets deeper as you think about it. For when Freud said "love" he meant *genital* love, and genital *love;* when he said love *and* work, he meant a general work-productiveness which would not preoccupy the individual to the extent that he loses his right or capacity to be a genital and a loving being. Thus we may ponder, but we cannot improve on "the professor's" formula.

Genitality, then, consists in the unobstructed capacity to develop an orgastic potency so free of pregenital interferences that genital libido (not just the sex products discharged in Kinsey's "outlets") is expressed in heterosexual mutuality, with full sensitivity of both penis and vagina, and with a convulsion-like discharge of tension from the whole body. This is a rather concrete way of saying something about a process which we really do not understand. To put it more situationally: the total fact of finding, via the climactic turmoil of the orgasm,

a supreme experience of the mutual regulation of two beings in some way takes the edge off the hostilities and potential rages caused by the oppositeness of male and female, of fact and fancy, of love and hate. Satisfactory sex relations thus make sex less obsessive, overcompensation less necessary, sadistic controls superfluous.

Preoccupied as it was with curative aspects, psychoanalysis often failed to formulate the matter of genitality in a way significant for the processes of society in all classes, nations, and levels of culture. The kind of mutuality in orgasm which psychoanalysis has in mind is apparently easily obtained in classes and cultures which happen to make a leisurely institution of it. In more complex societies this mutuality is interfered with by so many factors of health, of tradition, of opportunity, and of temperament, that the proper formulation of sexual health would be rather this: A human being should be potentially able to accomplish mutuality of genital orgasm, but he should also be so constituted as to bear a certain amount of frustration in the matter without undue regression wherever emotional preference or considerations of duty and loyalty call for it.

While psychoanalysis has on occasion gone too far in its emphasis on genitality as a universal cure for society and has thus provided a new addiction and a new commodity for many who wished to so interpret its teachings, it has not always indicated all the goals that genitality actually should and must imply. In order to be of lasting social significance, the utopia of genitality should include:

1. mutality of orgasm
2. with a loved partner
3. of the other sex
4. with whom one is able and willing to share a mutual trust
5. and with whom one is able and willing to regulate the cycles of
   a. work
   b. procreation
   c. recreation
6. so as to secure to the offspring, too, all the stages of a satisfactory development.

It is apparent that such utopian accomplishment on a large scale cannot be an individual or, indeed, a therapeutic task. Nor is it a purely sexual matter by any means. It is integral to a culture's style of sexual selection, cooperation, and competition.

The danger of this stage is isolation, that is the avoidance of contacts which commit to intimacy. In psychopathology, this disturbance can lead to severe "character-problems." On the other hand, there are partnerships which amount to an isolation à deux, protecting both partners from the necessity to face the next critical development—that of generativity.

7. Generativity vs. Stagnation

In this book the emphasis is on the childhood stages, otherwise the section on generativity would of necessity be the central one, for this term encompasses the evolutionary development which has made man the teaching and instituting as well as the learning animal. The fashionable insistence on dramatizing the dependence of children on adults often blinds us to the dependence of the older generation on the younger one. Mature man needs to be needed, and maturity needs guidance as well as encouragement from what has been produced and must be taken care of.

Generativity, then, is primarily the concern in establishing and guiding the next generation, although there are individuals who, through *misfortune* or because of special and genuine gifts in other directions, do not apply this drive to their own offspring. And indeed, the concept generativity is meant to include such more popular synonyms as *productivity* and *creativity*, which, however, cannot replace it.

It has taken psychoanalysis some time to realize that the ability to lose oneself in the meeting of bodies and minds leads to a gradual expansion of ego-interests and to a libidinal investment in that which is being generated. Generativity thus is an essential stage on the psychosexual as well as on the psychosocial schedule. Where such enrichment fails altogether, regression to an obsessive need for pseudo-intimacy takes place, often with a pervading sense of stagnation and personal impoverishment. Individuals, then, often begin to indulge themselves as if they were their own—or one another's—one and only child; and where conditions favor it, early invalidism, physical or psychological, becomes the vehicle of self-concern. The mere fact of having or even wanting children, however, does not "achieve" generativity. In fact, some young parents suffer, it seems, from the retardation of the ability to develop this stage. The reasons are often to be found in early childhood impressions; in excessive self-love based on a too strenuously self-made personality; and finally (and here we return to the beginnings) in the lack of some faith, some "belief in the species," which would make a child appear to be a welcome trust of the community.

As to the institutions which safeguard and reinforce generativity, one can only say that all institutions codify the ethics of generative succession. Even where philosophical and spiritual tradition suggests the renunciation of the right to procreate or to produce, such early turn to "ultimate concerns," wherever instituted in monastic movements, strives to settle at the same time the matter of its relationship to the Care for the creatures of this world and to the Charity which is felt to transcend it.

If this were a book on adulthood, it would be indispensable and profitable at this point to compare economic and psychological theories (beginning with the strange convergencies and divergencies of Marx and Freud) and to proceed to a discussion of man's relationship to his production as well as to his progeny.

8. Ego Integrity vs. Despair

Only in him who in some way has taken care of things and people and has adapted himself to the triumphs and disappointments adherent to being, the originator of others or the generator of products and ideas—only in him may gradually ripen the fruit of these seven stages. I know no better word for it than ego integrity. Lacking a clear definition, I shall point to a few constituents of this state of mind. It is the ego's accrued assurance of its proclivity for order and meaning. It is post-narcissistic love of the human ego—not of the self—as an experience which conveys some world order and spiritual sense, no matter how dearly paid for. It is the acceptance of one's one and only life cycle as something that had to be and that, by necessity, permitted of no substitutions: it thus means a new, a different love of one's parents. It is a comradeship with the ordering ways of distant times and different pursuits, as expressed in the simple products and sayings of such times and pursuits. Although aware of the relativity of all the various life styles which have given meaning to human striving, the possessor of integrity is ready to defend the dignity of his own life style against all physical and economic threats. For he knows that an individual life is the accidental coincidence of but one life cycle with but one segment of history; and that for him all human integrity stands or falls with the one style of integrity of which he partakes. The style of integrity developed by his culture or civilization thus becomes the "patrimony of his soul," the seal of his moral paternity of himself ("...*pero el honor/Es patrimonio del alma*": Calderón). In such final consolidation, death loses its sting.

The lack or loss of this accrued ego integration is signified by fear of death: the one and only life cycle is not accepted as the ultimate of life. Despair expresses the feeling that the time is now short, too short for the attempt to start another life and to try out alternate roads to integrity. Disgust hides despair, if often only in the form of "a thousand little disgusts" which do not add up to one big remorse: *mille petits dégoûts de soi, dont le total ne fait pas un remords, mais un gêne obscure.*" (Rostand)

Each individual, to become a mature adult, must to a sufficient degree develop all the ego qualities mentioned, so that a wise Indian, a true gentleman, and a mature peasant share and recognize in one another the final stage of integrity. But each cultural entity, to develop the particular style of integrity suggested by its historical place, utilizes a particular combination of these conflicts, along with specific provocations and prohibitions of infantile sexuality. Infantile conflicts become creative only if sustained by the firm support of cultural institutions and of the special leader classes representing them. In order to approach or experience integrity, the individual must know how to be a follower of image bearers in religion and in politics, in the economic order and in technology, in aristocratic living and in the arts and sciences. Ego integrity, therefore, implies an emotional integration, which permits participation by followership as well as acceptance of the responsibility of leadership.

Webster's Dictionary is kind enough to help us complete this outline in a circular fashion. Trust (the first of our ego values) is here defined as "the assured reliance on another's integrity," the last of our values. I

suspect that Webster had business in mind rather than babies, credit rather than faith. But the formulation stands. And it seems possible to further paraphrase the relation of adult integrity and infantile trust by saying that healthy children will not fear life if their elders have integrity enough not to fear death.

9. An Epigenetic Chart

In this book the emphasis is on the childhood stages. The foregoing conception of the life cycle, however, awaits systematic treatment. To prepare this, I shall conclude this chapter with a diagram. In this, as in the diagram of pregenital zones and modes, the diagonal represents the normative sequence of psychosocial gains made as at each stage one more nuclear conflict adds a new ego quality, a new criterion of accruing human strength. Below the diagonal there is space for the precursors of each of these solutions, all of which begin with the beginning; above the diagonal there is space for the designation of the derivatives of these gains and their transformations in the maturing and the mature personality.

The underlying assumptions for such charting are (1) that the human personality in principle develops according to steps predetermined in the growing person's readiness to be driven toward, to be aware of, and to interact with, a widening social radius; and (2) that society, in principle, tends to be so constituted as to meet and invite this succession of potentialities for interaction and attempts to safeguard and to encourage the proper rate and the proper sequence of their enfolding. This is the "maintenance of the human world."

But a chart is only a tool to think with, and cannot aspire to be a prescription to abide by, whether in the practice of child-training, in psychotherapy, or in the methodology of child study. In the presentation of the psychosocial stages in the form of an *epigenetic chart* analogous to the one employed in Chapter 2 for analysis of Freud's psychosexual stages, we have definite and delimited methodological steps in mind. It is one purpose of this work to facilitate the comparison of the stages first discerned by Freud as sexual to other schedules of development (physical, cognitive). But any one chart delimits one schedule only, and it must not be

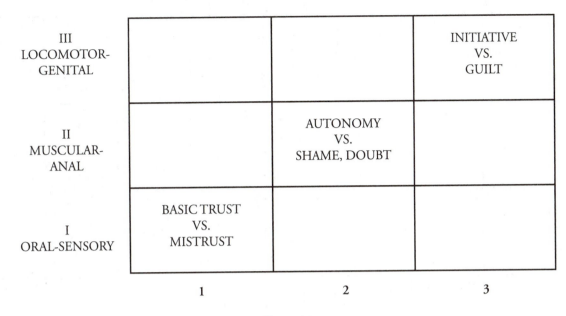

	1	2	3
III LOCOMOTOR-GENITAL			INITIATIVE VS. GUILT
II MUSCULAR-ANAL		AUTONOMY VS. SHAME, DOUBT	
I ORAL-SENSORY	BASIC TRUST VS. MISTRUST		

Figure 11

imputed that our outline of the psychosocial schedule is intended to imply obscure generalities concerning other aspects of development—or, indeed, of existence. If the chart, for example, lists a series of conflicts or crises, we do not consider all development a series of crises: we claim only that psychosocial development proceeds by critical steps—"critical" being a characteristic of turning points, of moments of decision between progress and regression, integration and retardation.

It may be useful at this point to spell out the methodological implications of an epigenetic matrix. The more heavily-lined squares of the diagonal signify both a sequence of stages and a gradual development of component parts: in other words, the chart formalizes a progression through time of a differentiation of parts. This indicates (1) that each critical item of psychosocial strength discussed here is systematically related to all others, and that they all depend on the proper development in the proper sequence of each item; and (2) that each item exists in some form before its critical time normally arrives.

If I say, for example, that a favorable ratio of basic trust over basic mistrust is the first step in psychosocial adaptation, a favorable ratio of autonomous will over shame and doubt, the second, the corresponding diagrammatic statement expresses a number of fundamental relations that exist between the two steps, as well as

some facts fundamental to each. Each comes to its ascendance, meets its crisis, and finds its lasting solution during the stage indicated. But they all must exist from the beginning in some form, for every act calls for an integration of all. Also, an infant may show something like "autonomy" from the beginning in the particular way in which he angrily tries to wriggle himself free when tightly held. However, under normal conditions, it is not until the second year that he begins to experience the whole *critical opposition of being an autonomous creature and being a dependent one;* and it is not until then that he is ready for a decisive encounter with his environment, and environment, which, in turn, feels called upon to convey to him its particular ideas and concepts of autonomy and coercion in ways decisively contributing to the character and the health of his personality in his culture. It is this encounter, together with the resulting crisis, that we have tentatively described for each stage. As to the progression from one stage to the next, the diagonal indicates the sequence to be followed. However, it also makes room for variations in tempo and intensity. An individual or a culture may linger excessively over trust and proceed from I 1 over I 2 to II 2, or an accelerated progression may move from I 1 over II 1 to II 2. Each such acceleration or (relative) retardation, however, is assumed to have a modifying influence on all later stages.

	1	2	3	4	5	6	7	8
VIII MATURITY								EGO INTEGRITY VS. DESPAIR
VII ADULT-HOOD							GENERA-TIVITY VS. STAG-NATION	
VI YOUNG ADULT-HOOD						INTIMACY VS. ISOLATION		
V PUBERTY AND ADOLES-CENCE					IDENTITY VS. ROLE CONFU-SION			
IV LATENCY				INDUSTRY VS. INFERIOR-ITY				
III LOCO-MOTOR-GENITAL			INITIATIVE VS. GUILT					
II MUSCULAR-ANAL		AUTONO-MY VS. SHAME, DOUBT						
I ORAL SENSORY	BASIC TRUST VS. MISTRUST							

Figure 12

188

An epigenetic diagram thus lists a system of stages dependent on each other; and while individual stages may have been explored more or less thoroughly or named more or less fittingly, the diagram suggests that their study be pursued always with the total configuration of stages in mind. The diagram invites, then, a thinking through of all its empty boxes: if we have entered Basic Trust in I 1 and Integrity in VIII 8, we leave the question open, as to what trust might have become in a stage dominated by the need for integrity even as we have left open what it may look like and, indeed, be called in the stage dominated by a striving for autonomy (II 1). All we mean to emphasize is that trust must have developed in its own right, before it becomes something more in the critical encounter in which autonomy develops—and so on, up the vertical. If, in the last stage (VIII 1), we would expect trust to have developed into the most mature *faith* that an aging person can muster in his cultural setting and historical period, the chart permits the consideration not only of what old age can be, but also what its preparatory stages must have been. All of this should make it clear that a chart of epigenesis suggests a global form of thinking and rethinking which leaves details of methodology and terminology to further study.*

---

* To leave this matter truly open, certain misuses of the whole conception would have to be avoided. Among them is the assumption that the sense of trust (and all the other "positive" senses postulated) is an *achievement,* secured once and for all at a given state. In fact, some writers are so intent on making an *achievement scale* out of these stages that they blithely omit all the "negative" senses (basic mistrust, etc.) which are and remain the dynamic counterpart of the "positive" ones throughout life. The assumption that on each stage a goodness is achieved which is impervious to new inner conflicts and to changing conditions is, I believe, a projection on child development of that success ideology which can so dangerously pervade our private and public daydreams and can make us inept in a heightened struggle for a meaningful existence in a new, industrial era of history. The personality is engaged with the hazards of existence continuously, even as the body's metabolism copes with decay. As we come to diagnose a state of relative strength and the symptoms of an impaired one, we face only more clearly the paradoxes and tragic potentials of human life.

The stripping of the stages of everything but their "achievements" has its counterpart in attempts to describe or test them as 'traits' or "aspirations" without first building a systematic bridge between the conception advanced throughout this book and the favorite concepts of other investigators. If the foregoing sounds somewhat plaintive, it is not intended to gloss over the fact that in giving to these strengths the very designations by which in the past they have acquired countless connotations of superficial goodness, affected niceness, and all too strenuous virtue, I invited misunderstandings and misuses. However, I believe that there is an intrinsic relationship between ego and language and that despite passing vicissitudes certain basic words retain essential meanings.

I have since attempted to formulate for Julian Huxley's *Humanist Frame* (Allen and Unwin, 1961; Harper and Brothers, 1962) a blueprint of essential strengths which evolution has built both into the ground plan of the life stages and into that of man's institutions. While I cannot discuss here the methodological problems involved (and aggravated by my use of the term "basic virtues"), I should append the list of these strengths because they are really the lasting outcome of the "favorable ratios" mentioned at every step of the chapter on psychosocial stages. Here they are:

Basic Trust vs. Basic Mistrust: Drive and *Hope*
Autonomy vs. Shame and Doubt: Self-Control and *Willpower*
Initiative vs. Guilt: Direction and *Purpose*
Industry vs. Inferiority: Method and *Competence*
Identity vs. Role Confusion: Devotion and *Fidelity*

The italicized words are called *basic* virtues because without them, and their re-emergence from generation to generation, all other and more changeable systems of human values lose their spirit and their relevance. Of this list, I have been able so far to give a more detailed account only for Fidelity (see *Youth, Change and Challenge,* E.H. Erikson, editor, Basic Books, 1963). But here again, the list represents a total conception within which there is much room for a discussion of terminology and methodology. (E.H.E.)

Concluding Comments

Guideposts in Considering Development

A great deal of what passed for brilliant theory among the grand theorists of the early-20th century turned out to be in error. Sometimes, however, when the theory came out of careful first-hand observation, and stuck close to the clinician's direct observations, it proved helpful, and very readily accessible. Such is the case with Erikson's "Eight Ages," I believe. Over half a century later, personality and developmental psychologists can read it and use it as a first approximation to understanding how personality emerges, grows, and matures across the life span. To be sure, the overall guide can be brought up-to-date here and there (for example, the adult stages can be further refined), but it remains a good first approximation of some important trends in development.

Review Questions

1. How does writing by a grand theorist differ from contemporary journal articles? How is it the same?
2. Erikson talks about eight stages of growth. How many of these occur before identity versus role-diffusion? How many occur after?
3. Erikson is trying to integrate Freud's developmental stages with contemporary thinking. Which of Erikson's stages map onto Freud's oral, anal, phallic, and genital stages (Hint: See Figure 11 for the first three)?
4. One central stage of importance is the third stage. Can you describe the importance of the stage of initiative versus guilt?

17

Re-Envisioning Development: Updating the Grand Theorists

Reading Back to the Future

New grand integrations of research are, in some ways, similar to the kinds of theorizing that the grand theorists of the early to mid-20th century carried out. Contemporary theoretical integrations are, however, different in that they must integrate the more carefully controlled and extensive research of today, relative to the past.

Contemporary theoretical work is only successful when it is closely attuned to the growing research foundations of the field. Empirical research is among the most fundamental activities carried out in a field of science such as personality psychology. The diversity of methods, measures, and findings in the field has led to a richness of knowledge that has not been known before. The field's empirical findings, however, do not make sense all by themselves. Such findings must be interpreted, and that requires theory. Most theories are aimed at a narrow point or two, such as whether a person's extraversion influences whether he or she is more likely to study in groups. At key moments, however, broad collections of empirical findings can reach a critical point at which they can be interpreted in a new and novel fashion. New grand theoretical statements can then integrate contemporary research in exciting new ways. The best of these theories may appear in a number of journals, notably the *American Psychologist, Psychological Review,* and *Psychological Inquiry.*

Such new grand theories are often original, innovative, and based on accumulating evidence from unexpected sources. By their nature, they are different from most other articles. As a consequence there are few rules for presenting a theory—nor perhaps could there be, given the wide range of forms such theories can take. Although there are no rules, there do exist some standards. The theory must be of general interest and, indeed, more interesting than most. It must be persuasive and well supported empirically. It must draw together important research, and be testable. The reading in this chapter is of that sort. Some theories ought to predict things, although other theories simply provide a better description of something that came before. The selection in this chapter is mostly a descriptive theory.

Reading This Specific Article

Since 1950, one of the most influential theories of human growth has been Erikson's model of the life cycle, which divided it into eight parts. Erikson noted that the transition from childhood to adolescence occurred when a growing person faced the conflict of identity versus role-confusion, and this was followed by a transition to young adulthood. That system, however, may be too simple for modern times.

In this reading, Arnett argues that there exists a new phase of life for most young people called *emerging adulthood*. Arnett updates Erikson's view, arguing that a new stage exists that most young people go through in their 20's. Part of the significance here is that this article deals with a time of life that many college students are in or might be about to enter.

Another level of significance relates to the nature of the article itself. It is a theoretical article that attempts to marshal evidence for a new stage in life—one overlooked, or simply not present earlier in history. But Arnett is not writing in 1950, as did Erikson, and this is not a chapter in a book in which he can engage in speculation, but rather a peer-reviewed article that must pass muster across a number of anonymous experts. So part of the fun is watching how Arnett presents his theory, the evidence he marshals, and wondering, for example, if the evidence is enough, and if Erikson were alive now, what sort of evidence he would need to convince people of his vision.

Arguing from a variety of statistical and polling data, Arnett points out that emerging adulthood is a time when many options are available to individuals. At almost no other time in life, he contends, do young people diverge so dramatically from one another in their living arrangements, educational plans, and other life circumstances. Does this make a reason to delineate a new stage of growth? You be the judge.

The Watch List

In the Introduction, Arnett notes that the new stage of life he is describing, *emerging adulthood*, is culturally constructed. By using the term "culturally constructed," Arnett suggests that society and its institutions have created the conditions for a new psychological stage. This is very consistent with Erik Erikson's psychosocial theorizing—the idea that psychological stages and society's cues develop together.

In the "Theoretical Background" section, Arnett looks for past theoretical precedents for his own theory while still distinguishing his approach from those that have come before. Erik Erikson and Daniel Levinson are mentioned. Both are eminent psychologists who developed stage theories of development in the early 1960's and late 1970's, respectively.

Then, consider the juxtaposition of the demographic description of emerging adults in the section "Emerging Adulthood Is Distinct Demographically," and the description of emerging adults' subjective feelings in the section "Emerging Adulthood Is Distinct Subjectively." The combination of these two markedly different sources of information is, in this case, called convergent operations, because both lines of evidence, different as they are, converge on a similar conclusion: that a distinct psychological stage of growth exists.

Lastly, in the section "Emerging Adulthood Is Distinct for Identity Explorations," Arnett uses his new theory to account for previously hard-to-explain findings. For example, Erik Erikson had suggested that identity formation occurs in adolescence. Contemporary research, however, has found that identity formation is incomplete for most college-aged individuals. Whereas Erikson's stages do not accurately mirror this empirical fact, Arnett's new theory includes it.

Emerging Adulthood: A Theory of Development from the Late Teens through the Twenties

by Jeffrey Jensen Arnett

Source: Arnett, J. J. (2000). Emerging adulthood. A theory of development from the late teens through the twenties. *American Psychologist, 55*, 469–480.

When our mothers were our age, they were engaged…They at least had some idea what they were going to do with their lives…I, on the other hand, will have a dual degree in majors that are ambiguous at best and impractical at worst (English and political science), no ring on my finger and no idea who I am, much less what I want to do…Under duress, I will admit that this is a pretty exciting time. Sometimes, when I look out across the wide expanse that is my future, I can see beyond the void. I realize that having nothing ahead to count on means I now have to count on myself; that having no direction means forging one of my own. (Kristen, age 22; Page, 1999, pp. 18, 20)

For most young people in industrialized countries, the years from the late teens through the twenties are years of profound change and importance. During this time, many young people obtain the level of education and training that will provide the foundation for their incomes and occupational achievements for the remainder of their adult work lives (Chisholm & Hurrelmann, 1995; William T. Grant Foundation Commission on Work, Family, and Citizenship, 1988). It is for many people a time of frequent change as various possibilities in love, work, and worldviews are explored (Erikson, 1968; Rindfuss, 1991). By the end of this period, the late twenties, most people have made life choices that have enduring ramifications. When adults later consider the most important events in their lives, they most often name events that took place during this period (Martin & Smyer, 1990).

Sweeping demographic shifts have taken place over the past half century that have made the later teens and early twenties not simply a brief period of transition into adult roles but a distinct period of the life course, characterized by change and exploration of possible life directions. As recently as 1970, the median age of marriage in the United States was about 21 for women and 23 for men; by 1996, it had risen to 25 for women and 27 for men (U.S. Bureau of the Census, 1997). Age of first childbirth followed a similar pattern. Also, since mid-century the proportion of young Americans obtaining higher education after high school has risen steeply from 14% in 1940 to over 60% by the mid-1990s (Arnett & Taber, 1994; Bianchi & Spain, 1996). Similar changes have taken place in other industrialized countries (Chisholm & Hurrelmann, 1995; Noble, Cover, & Yanagishita, 1996).

These changes over the past half-century have altered the nature of development in the late teens and early twenties for young people in industrialized societies. Because marriage and parenthood are delayed until the mid-twenties or late twenties for most people, it is no longer normative for the late teens and early twenties to be a time of entering and settling into long-term adult roles. On the contrary, these years are more typically a period of frequent change and exploration (Arnett, 1998; Rindfuss, 1991).

In this article, I propose a new theory of development from the late teens through the twenties, with a focus on ages 18–25. I argue that this period, emerging adulthood, is neither adolescence nor young adulthood but is theoretically and empirically distinct from them both. Emerging adulthood is distinguished by relative independence from social roles and from normative expectations. Having left the dependency of childhood and adolescence, and having not yet entered the enduring responsibilities that are normative in adulthood, emerging adults often explore a variety of possible life directions in love, work, and worldviews. Emerging adulthood is a time of life when many different directions remain possible, when little about the future has been decided for certain, when the scope of independent exploration of life's possibilities is greater for most people than it will be at any other period of the life course.

For most people, the late teens through the midtwenties are the most *volitional* years of life. However, cultural influences structure and sometimes limit the extent to which emerging adults are able to use their late teens and twenties in this way, and not all young people in this age period are able to use these years for independent exploration. Like adolescence, emerging adulthood is a period of the life course that is culturally constructed, not universal and immutable.

I lay out the theoretical background first and then present evidence to illustrate how emerging adulthood is a distinct period demographically, subjectively, and in terms of identity explorations. Next, I explain how emerging adulthood can be distinguished from adolescence and young adulthood. Finally, I discuss the economic and cultural conditions under which emerging adulthood is most likely to exist as a distinct period of the life course.

The Theoretical Background

There have been a number of important theoretical contributions to the understanding of development from the late teens through the twenties. One early contribution was made by Erik Erikson (1950, 1968). Erikson rarely discussed specific ages in his writings, and in his theory of human development across the life course he did not include a separate stage that could be considered analogous to emerging adulthood as proposed here. Rather, he wrote of development in adolescence and of development in young adulthood. However, he also commented on the *prolonged adolescence* typical of industrialized societies and on the *psychosocial moratori-*

um granted to young people in such societies "during which the young adult through free role experimentation may find a niche in some section of his society" (Erikson, 1968, p. 156). Thus, Erikson seems to have distinguished—without naming—a period that is in some ways adolescence and in some ways young adulthood yet not strictly either one, a period in which adult commitments and responsibilities are delayed while the role experimentation that began in adolescence continues and in fact intensifies.

Another theoretical contribution can be found in the work of Daniel Levinson (1978). Levinson interviewed men at midlife, but he had them describe their earlier years as well, and on the basis of their accounts he developed a theory that included development in the late teens and the twenties. He called ages 17–33 the *novice phase* of development and argued that the overriding task of this phase is to move into the adult world and build a stable life structure. During this process, according to Levinson, the young person experiences a considerable amount of change and instability while sorting through various possibilities in love and work in the course of establishing a life structure. Levinson acknowledged that his conception of the novice phase was similar to Erikson's ideas about the role experimentation that takes place during the psychosocial moratorium (Levinson, 1978, pp. 322–323).

Perhaps the best-known theory of development in the late teens and the twenties is Kenneth Keniston's theory of youth. Like Erikson and Levinson, Keniston (1971) conceptualized youth as a period of continued role experimentation between adolescence and young adulthood. However, Keniston wrote at a time when American society and some Western European societies were convulsed with highly visible youth movements protesting the involvement of the United States in the Vietnam War (among other things). His description of youth as a time of "tension between self and society" (Keniston, 1971, p. 8) and "refusal of socialization" (p. 9) reflects that historical moment rather than any enduring characteristics of the period.

More importantly, Keniston's (1971) application of the term *youth* to this period is problematic. *Youth* has a long history in the English language as a term for childhood generally and for what later became called adolescence (e.g., Ben-Amos, 1994), and it continues to be used popularly and by many social scientists for these purposes (as reflected in terms such as *youth organizations*). Keniston's choice of the ambiguous and confusing term *youth* may explain in part why the idea of the late teens and twenties as a separate period of life never became widely accepted by developmental scientists after his articulation of it. However, as I argue in the following sections, there is good empirical support for conceiving this period—proposed here as emerging adulthood—as a distinct period of life.

Emerging Adulthood Is Distinct Demographically

Although Erikson (1968), Levinson (1978), and Keniston (1971) all contributed to the theoretical groundwork for emerging adulthood, the nature of the period has changed considerably since the time of their writings more than 20 years ago. As noted at the outset of this article, demographic changes in the timing of marriage and parenthood in recent decades have made a period of emerging adulthood typical for young people in industrialized societies. Postponing these transitions until at least the late twenties leaves the late teens and early twenties available for exploring various possible life directions.

An important demographic characteristic of emerging adulthood is that there is a great deal of demographic variability, reflecting the wide scope of individual volition during these years. Emerging adulthood is the only period of life in which nothing is normative demographically (Rindfuss, 1991; Wallace, 1995). During adolescence, up to age 18, a variety of key demographic areas show little variation. Over 95% of American adolescents aged 12–17 live at home with one or more parents, over 98% are unmarried, fewer than 10% have had a child, and over 95% are enrolled in school (U.S. Bureau of the Census, 1997). By age 30, new demographic norms have been established: About 75% of 30-year-olds have married, about 75% have become parents, and fewer than 10% are enrolled in school (U.S. Bureau of the Census, 1997).

In between these two periods, however, and especially from ages 18 to 25, a person's demographic status in these areas is very difficult to predict on the basis of age alone. The demographic diversity and unpre-

dictability of emerging adulthood is a reflection of the experimental and exploratory quality of the period. Talcott Parsons (1942) called adolescence the *roleless role*, but this term applies much better to emerging adulthood. Emerging adults tend to have a wider scope of possible activities than persons in other age periods because they are less likely to be constrained by role requirements and this makes their demographic status unpredictable.

One demographic area that especially reflects the exploratory quality of emerging adulthood is residential status. Most young Americans leave home by age 18 or 19 (Goldscheider & Goldscheider, 1994). In the years that follow, emerging adults' living situations are diverse. About one-third of emerging adults go off to college after high school and spend the next several years in some combination of independent living and continued reliance on adults, for example, in a college dormitory or a fraternity or sorority house (Goldscheider & Goldscheider, 1994). For them, this is a period of semiautonomy (Goldscheider & Davanzo, 1986) as they take on some of the responsibilities of independent living but leave others to their parents, college authorities, or other adults. About 40% move out of their parental home not for college but for independent living and full-time work (Goldscheider & Goldscheider, 1994). About two-thirds experience a period of cohabitation with a romantic partner (Michael, Gagnon, Laumann, & Kolata, 1995). Some remain at home while attending college or working or some combination of the two. Only about 10% of men and 30% of women remain at home until marriage (Goldscheider & Goldscheider, 1994).

Amidst this diversity, perhaps the unifying feature of the residential status of emerging adults is the instability of it. Emerging adults have the highest rates of residential change of any age group. Using data from several cohorts of the National Longitudinal Study, Rindfuss (1991) described how rates of residential mobility peak in the midtwenties (see Figure 1). For about 40% of the current generation of emerging adults, residential changes include moving back into their parents' home and then out again at least once in the course of their late teens and twenties (Goldscheider & Goldscheider, 1994). Frequent residential changes during emerging adulthood reflect its exploratory quality, because these changes often take place at the end of one period of exploration or the beginning of another (e.g., the end of a period of cohabitation, entering or leaving college, or the beginning of a new job in a new place).

School attendance is another area in which there is substantial change and diversity among emerging adults. The proportion of American emerging adults who enter higher education in the year following high school is at its highest level ever, over 60% (Bianchi & Spain, 1996). However, this figure masks the expanding diversity in the years that follow. Only 32% of young people ages 25–29 have completed four years or more of college (U.S. Bureau of the Census, 1997). For emerging adults, college education is often pursued in a nonlinear way, frequently combined with work, and punctuated by periods of nonattendance. For those who do eventually graduate with a four-year degree, college

is increasingly likely to be followed by graduate school. About one-third of those who graduate with a bachelor's degree are enrolled in postgraduate education the following year (Mogelonsky, 1996). In European countries too, the length of education has become extended in recent decades (Chisholm & Hurrelman, 1995).

Overall, then, the years of emerging adulthood are characterized by a high degree of demographic diversity and instability, reflecting the emphasis on change and exploration. It is only in the transition from emerging adulthood to young adulthood in the late twenties that the diversity narrows and the instability eases, as young people make more enduring choices in love and work. Rindfuss (1991) called the period from ages 18 to 30 "demographically dense" (p. 496) because of the many demographic transitions that take place during that time, especially in the late twenties.

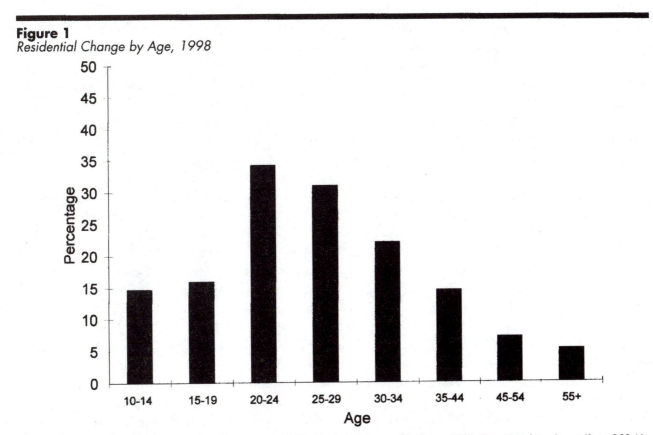

Figure 1
Residential Change by Age, 1998

Note. Data are from "Geographic Mobility: March 1997 to March 1998," by the U.S. Bureau of the Census, 2000, *Current Population Reports* (Series P-20, No. 520), Washington, DC: U.S. Government Printing Office.

Emerging Adulthood Is
Distinct Subjectively

Emerging adults do not see themselves as adolescents, but many of them also do not see themselves entirely as adults. Figure 2 shows that when they are asked whether they feel they have reached adulthood, the majority of Americans in their late teens and early twenties answer neither *no* nor *yes* but the ambiguous *in some respects yes, in some respects no* (Arnett, in press). This reflects a subjective sense on the part of the emerging adults that they have left adolescence but have not yet completely entered young adulthood (Arnett, 1994a, 1997, 1998). They have no name for the period they are in—because the society they live in has no name for it—so they regard themselves as being neither adolescents nor adults, in between the two but not really one or the other. As Figure 2 shows, only in their late twenties and early thirties do a clear majority of people indicate that they feel they have reached adulthood. However, age is only the roughest marker of the subjective transition from emerging adulthood to young adulthood. As illustrated in Figure 2, even in their late twenties and early thirties, nearly one-third did not feel their transition to adulthood was complete.

One might expect emerging adults' subjective sense of ambiguity in attaining full adulthood to arise from the demographic diversity and instability described above. Perhaps it is difficult for young people to feel they have reached adulthood before they have established a stable residence, finished school, settled into a career, and married (or at least committed themselves to a long-term love relationship). However, perhaps surprisingly, the research evidence indicates strongly that these demographic transitions have little to do with emerging adults' conceptions of what it means to reach adulthood. Consistently, in a variety of studies with young people in their teens and twenties, demographic transitions such as finishing education, settling into a career, marriage, and parenthood rank at the *bottom* in importance among possible criteria considered necessary for the attainment of adulthood (Arnett, 1997, 1998, in press; Greene, Wheatley, & Aldava, 1992; Scheer, Unger, & Brown, 1994).

The characteristics that matter most to emerging adults in their subjective sense of attaining adulthood are

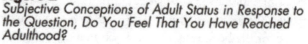

Figure 2
Subjective Conceptions of Adult Status in Response to the Question, Do You Feel That You Have Reached Adulthood?

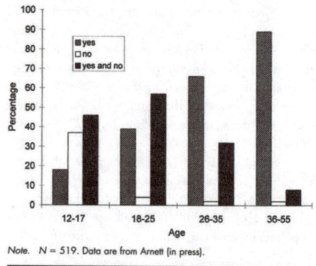

Note. N = 519. Data are from Arnett (in press).

not demographic transitions but individualistic *qualities of character* (Arnett, 1998). Specifically, the two top criteria for the transition to adulthood in a variety of studies have been *accepting responsibility for one's self* and *making independent decisions* (Arnett, 1997, 1998; Greene et al., 1992; Scheer et al., 1994). A third criterion, also individualistic but more tangible, *becoming financially independent*, also ranks consistently near the top.

The prominence of these criteria for the transition to adulthood reflects an emphasis in emerging adulthood on becoming a self-sufficient person (Arnett, 1998). During these years, the character qualities most important to becoming successfully self-sufficient— accepting responsibilities for one's self and making independent decisions—are being developed. Financial independence is also crucial to self-sufficiency, so it is also important in emerging adults' conceptions of what is necessary to become an adult. Only after these character qualities have reached fruition and financial independence has been attained do emerging adults experience a subjective change in their developmental status, as they move out of emerging adulthood and into young adulthood. For most young people in American society, this occurs some time during the twenties and is usually accomplished by the late twenties (Arnett, in press).

Although emerging adults do not view demographic transitions as necessary for attaining adulthood, it should be noted that parenthood in particular is often sufficient for marking a subjective sense of adult status. Parenthood ranks low in young people's views of the essential criteria for adulthood for people in general, but those who have had a child tend to view becoming a parent as the most important marker of the transition to adulthood for themselves (Arnett, 1998). The explorations that occur in emerging adulthood become sharply restricted with parenthood, because it requires taking on the responsibilities of protecting and providing for a young child. With parenthood, the focus of concern shifts inexorably from responsibility for one's self to responsibility for others.

Emerging Adulthood Is Distinct for Identity Explorations

A key feature of emerging adulthood is that it is the period of life that offers the most opportunity for identity explorations in the areas of love, work, and worldviews. Of course, it is adolescence rather than emerging adulthood that has typically been associated with identity formation. Erikson (1950) designated identity versus role confusions as the central crisis of the adolescent stage of life, and in the decades since he articulated this idea the focus of research on identity has been on adolescence (Adams, 1999). However, as noted, Erikson (1950, 1968) clearly believed that industrialized societies allow a prolonged adolescence for extended identity explorations. If adolescence is the period from ages 10 to 18 and emerging adulthood is the period from (roughly) ages 18 to 25, most identity exploration takes place in emerging adulthood rather than adolescence. Although research on identity formation has focused mainly on adolescence, this research has shown that identity achievement has rarely been reached by the end of high school (Montemayor, Brown, & Adams, 1985; Waterman, 1982) and that identity development continues through the late teens and the twenties (Valde, 1996; Whitbourne & Tesch, 1985).

The focus on identity issues in emerging adulthood can be seen in the three main areas of identity exploration: love, work, and worldviews. Identity formation involves trying out various life possibilities and gradually moving toward making enduring decisions. In all three of these areas, this process begins in adolescence but takes place mainly in emerging adulthood. With regard to love, American adolescents typically begin dating around ages 12 to 14 (Padgham & Blyth, 1991). However, because any serious consideration of marriage is a decade or more away for most 12- to 14-year-olds, young people view the early years of dating as primarily recreational (Roscoe, Dian, & Brooks, 1987). For adolescents, dating provides companionship, the first experiences of romantic love, and sexual experimentation; however, their dating relationships typically last only a few weeks or months (Feiring, 1996), and few adolescents expect to remain with their "high school sweetheart" much beyond high school.

In emerging adulthood, explorations in love become more intimate and serious. Dating in adolescence often takes place in groups, as adolescents pursue shared recreation such as parties, dances, and hanging out (Padgham & Blyth, 1991). By emerging adulthood, dating is more likely to take place in couples, and the focus is less on recreation and more on exploring the potential for emotional and physical intimacy. Romantic relationships in emerging adulthood last longer than in adolescence, are more likely to include sexual intercourse, and may include cohabitation (Michael et al., 1995). Thus, in adolescence, explorations in love tend to be tentative and transient; the implicit question is, Who would I enjoy being with, here and now? In contrast, explorations in love in emerging adulthood tend to involve a deeper level of intimacy, and the implicit question is more identity focused: Given the kind of person I am, what kind of person do I wish to have as a partner through life?

With regard to work, a similar contrast exists between the transient and tentative explorations of adolescence and the more serious and focused explorations of emerging adulthood. In the United States, the majority of high school students are employed part-time (Barling & Kelloway, 1999), for the most part their jobs do not provide them with knowledge or experience that will be related to their future occupations (Greenberger & Steinberg, 1986; Steinberg & Cauffman, 1995). Most adolescents are employed in service jobs—at restaurants, retail stores, and so forth—in which the cognitive challenges are minimal and the skills learned are few. Adolescents tend to view their jobs not as occupational preparation but as a way to obtain the money that will support an active leisure life—paying for compact discs, concerts, restaurant meals, clothes, cars, travel, and so forth (Bachman & Schulenberg, 1993; Shanahan, Elder, Burchinal, & Conger, 1996; Steinberg & Cauffman, 1995).

In emerging adulthood work experiences become more focused on preparation for adult work roles. Emerging adults begin to consider how their work experiences will lay the groundwork for the jobs they may have through adulthood. In exploring various work possibilities, they explore identity issues as well: What kind of work am I good at? What kind of work would I find satisfying for the long term? What are my chances of getting a job in the field that seems to suit me best?

Emerging adults' educational choices and experiences explore similar questions. In their educational paths, they try out various possibilities that would prepare them for different kinds of future work. College students often change majors more than once, especially in their first two years, as they try on possible occupational futures, discard them, and pursue others. With graduate school becoming an increasingly common choice after an undergraduate degree is obtained, emerging adults' educational explorations often continue through their early twenties and midtwenties. Graduate school allows emerging adults to switch directions again from the path of occupational preparation they had chosen as undergraduates.

For both love and work, the goals of identity explorations in emerging adulthood are not limited to direct preparation for adult roles. On the contrary, the explorations of emerging adulthood are in part explorations for their own sake, part of obtaining a broad range of life experiences before taking on enduring—and limiting—adult responsibilities. The absence of enduring role commitments in emerging adulthood makes possible a degree of experimentation and exploration that is not likely to be possible during the thirties and beyond. For people who wish to have a variety of romantic and sexual experiences, emerging adulthood is the time for it, because parental surveillance has diminished and there is as yet little normative pressure to

enter marriage. Similarly, emerging adulthood is the time for trying out unusual work and educational possibilities. For this reason, short-term volunteer jobs in programs such as Americorps and the Peace Corps are more popular with emerging adults than with persons in any other age period. Emerging adults may also travel to a different part of the country or the world on their own for a limited period, often in the context of a limited-term work or educational experience. This too can be part of their identity explorations, part of expanding their range of personal experiences prior to making the more enduring choices of adulthood.

With regard to worldviews, the work of William Perry (1970/1999) has shown that changes in worldviews are often a central part of cognitive development during emerging adulthood. According to Perry, emerging adults often enter college with a worldview they have learned in the course of childhood and adolescence. However, a college education leads to exposure to a variety of different worldviews, and in the course of this exposure college students often find themselves questioning the worldviews they brought in. Over the course of their college years, emerging adults examine and consider a variety of possible worldviews. By the end of their college years they have often committed themselves to a worldview different from the one they brought in, while remaining open to further modifications of it.

Most of the research on changes in worldviews during emerging adulthood has involved college students and graduate students, and there is evidence that higher education promotes explorations and reconsiderations of worldviews (Pascarella & Terenzini, 1991). However, it is notable that emerging adults who do not attend college are as likely as college students to indicate that deciding on their own beliefs and values is an essential criterion for attaining adult status (Arnett, 1997). Also, research on emerging adults' religious beliefs suggests that regardless of educational background, they consider it important during emerging adulthood to reexamine the beliefs they have learned in their families and to form a set of beliefs that is the product of their own independent reflections (Arnett & Jensen, 1999; Hoge, Johnson, & Luidens, 1993).

Although the identity explorations of emerging adulthood make it an especially full and intense time of life for many people, these explorations are not always experienced as enjoyable. Explorations in love sometimes result in disappointment, disillusionment, or rejection. Explorations in work sometimes result in a failure to achieve the occupation most desired or in an inability to find work that is satisfying and fulfilling. Explorations in worldviews sometimes lead to rejection of childhood beliefs without the construction of anything more compelling in their place (Arnett & Jensen, 1999). Also, to a large extent, emerging adults pursue their identity explorations on their own, without the daily companionship of either their family of origin or their family to be (Jonsson, 1994; Morch, 1995). Young Americans ages 19–29 spend more of their leisure time alone than any persons except the elderly and spend more of their time in productive activities (school and work) alone than any other age group under 40 (Larson, 1990). Many of them see the condition of the world as grim and are pessimistic about the future of their society (Arnett, 2000b). Nevertheless, for themselves personally, emerging adults are highly optimistic about ultimately achieving their goals. In one national poll of 18- to 24-year olds in the United States (Hornblower, 1997) nearly all—96%—agreed with the statement, "I am very sure that someday I will get to where I want to be in life."

Other Notable Findings on Emerging Adulthood

The three areas outlined above—demographics, subjective perceptions, and identity explorations—provide the most abundant information on the distinctiveness of emerging adulthood. However, evidence is available from other areas that suggests possible lines of inquiry for future research on emerging adulthood. One of these areas is risk behavior. Although there is a voluminous literature on adolescent risk behavior and relatively little research on risk behavior in emerging adulthood (Jessor, Donovan, & Costa, 1991), the prevalence of several types of risk behavior peaks not during adolescence but during emerging adulthood (ages 18–25). These risk behaviors include unprotected sex, most types of substance use, and risky driving behaviors such as driving at high speed or while intoxicated (Arnett,

1992; Bachman, Johnston, O'Malley, & Schulenberg, 1996). Figure 3 shows an example for binge drinking.

What is it about emerging adulthood that lends itself to such high rates of risk behavior? To some degree, emerging adults' risk behaviors can be understood as part of their identity explorations, that is, as one reflection of the desire to obtain a wide range of experiences before settling down into the roles and responsibilities of adult life. One of the motivations consistently found to be related to participation in a variety of types of risk behavior is sensation seeking, which is the desire for novel and intense experiences (Arnett, 1994b). Emerging adults can pursue novel and intense experiences more freely than adolescents because they are less likely to be monitored by parents and can pursue them more freely than adults because they are less constrained by roles. After marriage, adults are constrained from taking part in risk behavior by the responsibilities of the marriage role, and once they have a child, they are constrained by the responsibilities of the parenting role. In one example of this, Bachman et al. (1996) used longitudinal data to show how substance use rises to a peak in the early twenties during the role hiatus of emerging adulthood, declines steeply and sharply following marriage, and declines further following the entry to parenthood. The responsibilities of these roles lead to lower rates of risk behavior as emerging adulthood is succeeded by young adulthood.

Research on family relationships among emerging adults has also been conducted. For American emerging adults in their early twenties, physical proximity to parents has been found to be *inversely* related to the quality of relationships with them. Emerging adults with the most frequent contact with parents, especially emerging adults still living at home, tend to be the least close to their parents and to have the poorest psychological adjustment (Dubas & Petersen, 1996; O'Connor, Allen, Bell, & Hauser, 1996). In European studies, emerging adults who remain at home tend to be happier with their living situations than those who have left home; they continue to rely on their parents as a source of support and comfort, but they also tend to have a great deal of autonomy within their parents' households (Chisholm & Hurrelmann, 1995). Thus, for emerging adults in both the United States and Europe, *autonomy* and *relatedness* are complementary rather than opposing

Figure 3
Rates of Binge Drinking (Five or More Alcoholic Drinks in a Row) in the Past Two Weeks at Various Ages

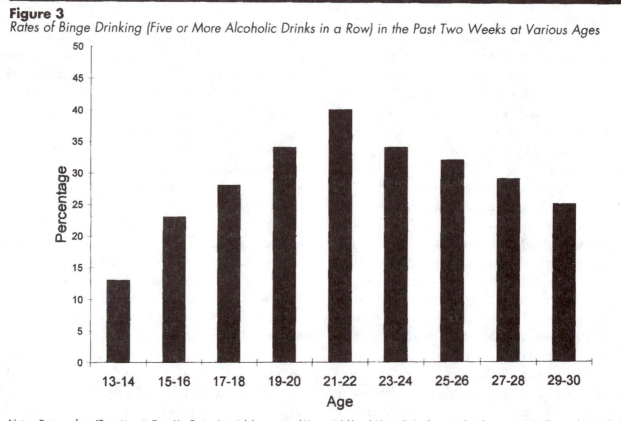

Note. Data are from "Transitions in Drug Use During Late Adolescence and Young Adulthood," by J. G. Bachman, L. D. Johnston, P. O'Malley, and J. Schulenberg, in *Transitions Through Adolescence: Interpersonal Domains and Context* (p. 118), by J. A. Graber, J. Brooks-Gunn, and A. C. Petersen (Eds.), 1996, Mahwah, NJ: Erlbaum. Copyright 1996 by Erlbaum. Used with permission. Data also available at http://www.monitoringthefuture.org/data/99data/pr99t1c.pdf.

dimensions of their relationships with their parents (O'Connor et al., 1996).

These findings provide a foundation for research into development during emerging adulthood. Of course, much more work remains to be done on virtually every aspect of development during this period. To what extent do emerging adults rely on friends for support and companionship, given that this is a period when most young people have left their families of origin but have not yet entered marriage? To what extent are the explorations of emerging adulthood different for men and women? Do emerging adults have especially high rates of media use, given that they spend so much time alone? These and many other questions about the period await investigation. Establishing emerging adulthood as a distinct developmental period may help to promote this research.

Why Emerging Adulthood Is Not Adolescence

It is widely known that the scientific study of adolescence began with the publication of G. Stanley Hall's two-volume magnum opus nearly a century ago (Hall, 1904). What is less widely known, however, is that in Hall's view adolescence extended from age 14 to age 24 (Hall, 1904, p. xix). In contrast, contemporary scholars generally consider adolescence to begin at age 10 or 11 and to end by age 18 or 19. The cover of every issue of the *Journal of Research on Adolescence*, the flagship journal of the Society for Research on Adolescence, proclaims that adolescence is defined as "the second decade of life." What happened between Hall's time and our own to move scholars' conceptions of adolescence earlier in the life course?

Two changes stand out as possible explanations. One is the decline that has taken place during the 20th century in the typical age of the initiation of puberty. At the beginning of the 20th century, the median age of menarche in Western countries was about 15 (Eveleth & Tanner, 1976). Because menarche takes place relatively late in the typical sequence of pubertal changes, this means that the initial changes of puberty would have begun at about ages 13–15 for most people, which is just where Hall designated the beginning of adolescence. However, the median age of menarche (and by implication other pubertal changes) declined steadily between 1900 and 1970 before leveling out, so that now the typical age of menarche in the United States is 12.5 (Brooks-Gunn & Paikoff, 1997). The initial changes of puberty usually begin about 2 years earlier, thus the designation of adolescence as beginning with the entry into the second decade of life.

As for the age when adolescence ends, the change in this age may have been inspired not by a biological change but by a social change: the growth of high school attendance that made high school a normative experience for adolescents in the United States. In 1900, only 10% of persons ages 14–17 were enrolled in high school. However, this proportion rose steeply and steadily over the course of the 20th century to reach 95% by 1985 (Arnett & Taber, 1994). This makes it easy to understand why Hall would not have chosen age 18 as the end of adolescence, because for most adolescents of his time no significant transition took place at that age. Education ended earlier, work began earlier, and leaving home took place later. Marriage and parenthood did not take place for most people until their early twenties or midtwenties (Arnett & Taber, 1994) which may have been why Hall designated age 24 as the end of adolescence. (Hall himself did not explain why he chose this age.)

In our time, it makes sense to define adolescence as ages 10–18. Young people in this age group have in common that they live with their parents, are experiencing the physical changes of puberty, are attending secondary school, and are part of a school-based peer culture. None of this remains normative after age 18, which is why it is not adequate simply to call the late teens and early twenties late adolescence. Age 18 also marks a variety of legal transitions, such as being allowed to vote and sign legal documents.

Although some scholars have suggested that the late teens and early twenties should be considered late adolescence (e.g., Elliott & Feldman, 1990), for the most part scholars on adolescence focus on ages 10–18 as the years of adolescent development. Studies published in the major journals on adolescence rarely include samples with ages higher than 18. For example, in 1997, 90% of the studies published in the *Journal of Research on Adolescence* and the *Journal of Youth & Adolescence* were samples of high school age or younger. College students have been the focus of many research studies, but most often as "adults" in social psychology studies. Sociologists have studied the late teens and the twenties for patterns of demographic events viewed as part of the transition to adulthood (e.g., Hogan & Astone, 1986; Rindfuss, 1991). However, few studies have recognized the late teens through the twenties as a distinct developmental period.

Why the Forgotten Half Remains Forgotten

In 1987, a distinguished panel of scholars and public policy officials was assembled by the William T. Grant Foundation and asked to address the life situations of young people who do not attend college after high school, especially with respect to their economic prospects. They produced an influential and widely read report entitled *The Forgotten Half: Non-College-Bound Youth in America* (William T. Grant Foundation Commission on Work, Family, and Citizenship, 1988), which contained an analysis of the circumstances of the "forgotten half" and a set of policy suggestions for promoting a successful transition from high school to work.

Over a decade later, the forgotten half remains forgotten by scholars, in the sense that studies of young people who do not attend college in the years following high school remain rare. Why did the Grant commission's widely acclaimed report not inspire more enduring scholarly attention to young people not attending college in this age period? One reason is practical. Studies of college students are ubiquitous because college students are so easy to find—most scholars who teach at colleges or universities have ready access to them. Studying young people who are not in college is more difficult because they are not readily accessible in any institutional setting. Other ways of obtaining research participants in this age period must be used, such as contacting community organizations or taking out newspaper ads, and these samples often have the liability of being nonrepresentative. The same conditions apply to research on college students after they leave college. Few studies exist of young people in their midtwenties to late twenties, in part because they are not available in any institutional setting. Notable exceptions to this rule include some excellent longitudinal studies (the National Longitudinal Studies, e.g., Rindfuss, 1991; the Monitoring the Future studies, e.g, Bachman et al., 1996; O'Connor et al., 1996; Offer & Offer, 1975).

However, the dearth of studies on young people in their late teens and twenties is not due only to the difficulty of finding samples in this age group. It also arises from the lack of a clear developmental conception of this age group. Scholars have no clearly articulated way of thinking about development from the late teens through the twenties, no paradigm for this age period, so they may not think about young people at these ages as a focus for developmental research. Emerging adulthood is offered as a new paradigm, a new way of thinking about development from the late teens through the twenties, especially ages 18–25, partly in the hope that a definite conception of this period will lead to an increase in scholarly attention to it.

Why Emerging Adulthood Is Not Young Adulthood

But (some might object) is there not already a paradigm for the years of the late teens and the twenties? Is that not what young adulthood is? The answer is no. There are a number of reasons why *young adulthood* is unsatisfactory as a designation for this developmental period.

One reason is that the use of young adulthood implies that adulthood has been reached at this point. As we have seen, most young people in this age period would disagree that they have reached adulthood. They see themselves as gradually making their way into adulthood, so emerging adulthood seems a better term for their subjective experience. More generally, the term *emerging* captures the dynamic, changeable, fluid quality of the period.

Also, if ages 18–25 are young adulthood, what would that make the thirties? Young adulthood is a term better applied to the thirties, which are still young but are definitely adult in a way that the years 18–25 are not. It makes little sense to lump the late teens, twenties, and thirties together and call the entire period young adulthood. The period from ages 18 to 25 could hardly be more distinct from the thirties. The majority of young people ages 18–25 do not believe they have reached full adulthood, whereas the majority of people in their thirties believe that they have (Arnett, in press). The majority of people ages 18–25 are still in the process of obtaining education and training for a long-term adult occupation, whereas the majority of people in their thirties have settled into a more stable occupational path. The majority of people ages 18–25 are unmarried, whereas the majority of people in their thirties are married. The majority of people ages 18–25 are childless, whereas the majority of people in their thirties have had at least one child. The list could go on. The point should be clear. Emerging adulthood and young adulthood should be distinguished as separate developmental periods.

It should be emphasized, however, that age is only a rough indicator of the transition from emerging adulthood to young adulthood. Eighteen is a good age marker for the end of adolescence and the beginning of emerging adulthood, because it is the age at which most young people finish secondary school, leave their parents' home, and reach the legal age of adult status in a variety of respects. However, the transition from emerging adulthood to young adulthood is much less definite with respect to age. There are 19-year-olds who have reached adulthood—demographically, subjectively, and in terms of identity formation—and 29-year-olds who have not. Nevertheless, for most people, the transition from emerging adulthood to young adulthood intensifies in the late twenties and is reached by age 30 in all of these respects.

Emerging adulthood differs both from adolescence and from young adulthood in that it is, to some extent, defined by its heterogeneity. As noted, in emerging adulthood, there is little that is normative. Emerging adulthood is very much a transitional period leading to adulthood, and different emerging adults reach adulthood at different points. Also, the possibility of devoting the late teens and early twenties to explorations of various kinds is not equally available to all young people, and in any case, people vary in the degree of exploration they choose to pursue.

The heterogeneity of emerging adulthood represents both a warning and an opportunity for those who wish to study this age period. The warning is to be cautious in making sweeping statements about emerging adults. Almost always, such statements need to be qualified by mentioning the heterogeneity of emerging adulthood. The opportunity is that this heterogeneity makes emerging adulthood an especially rich, complex, dynamic period of life to study.

Emerging Adulthood across Cultures

Thus far, the focus of this article has been on emerging adulthood among young people in the West, especially in the United States. Is emerging adulthood a period of life that is restricted to certain cultures and certain times? The answer to this question appears to be *yes*. For example, Schlegel and Barry (1991), in their comprehensive integration of information on adolescence in 186 traditional non-Western cultures, concluded that adolescence as a life stage is virtually universal, but that a further period between adolescence and adulthood (*youth*, in the terminology they used) existed in only 20% of the cultures they studied. In the cultures in their sample, adulthood was typically signified by entry into marriage, and marriage usually took place at ages 16 to 18 for girls and at about ages 18 to 20 for boys. This early timing of marriage allowed for a period of adolescence but not for a period of emerging adulthood.

Emerging adulthood, then, is not a universal period but a period that exists only in cultures that postpone the entry into adult roles and responsibilities until well past the late teens. Thus, emerging adulthood would be most likely to be found in countries that are highly industrialized or postindustrial. Such countries require a high level of education and training for entry into the information-based professions that are the most prestigious and lucrative, so many of their young people remain in school into their early twenties and midtwenties. Marriage and parenthood are typically postponed until well after schooling has ended, which allows for a period of exploration of various relationships before marriage and

for exploration of various jobs before taking on the responsibility of supporting a child financially. Table 1 shows the median ages of marriage in a range of highly industrialized countries, contrasted with the median ages of marriage in selected developing countries.

Although median marriage ages are typically calculated on a countrywide basis, it should be noted that emerging adulthood is best understood as a characteristic of cultures rather than countries. Within some highly industrialized countries, members of minority cultures may have cultural practices that lead to a shortened period of emerging adulthood or no emerging adulthood at all. For example, in the United States, members of the Mormon church tend to have a shortened and highly structured emerging adulthood. Because of cultural beliefs prohibiting premarital sex and emphasizing the desirability of large families, considerable social pressure is placed on young Mormons to marry early and begin having children. Consequently, the median ages of marriage and first childbirth are much lower among Mormons than in the American population as a whole (Heaton, 1992), and young Mormons are likely to have a much briefer period of exploration before taking on adult roles.

Limitations in educational and occupational opportunities also influence the extent to which young people can experience their late teens and twenties as a volitional period. The young woman who has a child out-

Table 1 Median Marriage Age of Women in Selected Countries

Industrialized Countries	Age	Developing Countries	Age
United States	25.2	Egypt	21.9
Canada	26.0	Morocco	22.3
Germany	26.2	Ghana	21.1
France	26.1	Nigeria	18.7
Italy	25.8	India	20.0
Japan	26.9	Indonesia	21.1
Australia	26.0	Brazil	22.6

Note. Data are from *The World's Youth*, by J. Noble, J. Cover and M. Yamagishita, 1996, Washington, DC: Population Reference Bureau. Copyright 1996 by the Population Reference Bureau. Reprinted with permission.

side of marriage at age 16 and spends her late teens and early twenties alternating between welfare and low-paying jobs has little chance for exploration of possible life directions, nor does the young man who drops out of school and spends most of his late teens and early twenties unemployed and looking unsuccessfully for a job (Cote & Allanhar, 1996). Because opportunities tend to be less widely available in minority cultures than in the majority culture in most industrialized countries, members of minority groups may be less likely to experience ages 18–25 as a period of independent exploration of possible life directions (Morch, 1995). However, social class may be more important than ethnicity, with young people in the middle class or above having more opportunities for the explorations of emerging adulthood than young people who are working class or below. Alternatively, it may be that explorations are not fewer in the working class but different, with more emphasis on work explorations and less emphasis on education. These are possibilities to be investigated.

In economically developing countries, there tends to be a distinct cultural split between urban and rural areas. Young people in urban areas of countries such as China and India are more likely to experience emerging adulthood, because they marry later, have children later, obtain more education, and have a greater range of occupational and recreational opportunities than young people in rural areas. In contrast, young people in rural areas of developing countries often receive minimal schooling, marry early, and have little choice of occupations except agricultural work. Thus, in developing countries emerging adulthood is often experienced in urban areas but rarely in rural areas.

However, it should also be noted that emerging adulthood is likely to become more pervasive worldwide in the decades to come, with the increasing globalization of the world economy. Between 1980 and 1995, the proportion of young people in developing countries who attended secondary school rose sharply, and the median ages of marriage and first childbirth rose in these countries as well (Noble et al., 1996). As developing countries are becoming more integrated into a global economy, there is an increasing number of higher-paying jobs in these countries, jobs that require young people to obtain higher education. At the same time, as technology becomes increasingly available in these countries, particularly in agriculture, the labor of young people is becoming less and less necessary for family survival, making it possible for many of them to attend school instead.

These changes open up the possibility for the spread of emerging adulthood in developing countries. Economic development makes possible a period of the independent role exploration that is at the heart of emerging adulthood. As societies become more affluent, they are more likely to grant young people the opportunity for the extended moratorium of emerging adulthood, because they have no urgent need for young people's labor. Similarly, economic development is usually accompanied by increased life expectancy, and devoting years to the explorations of emerging adulthood becomes more feasible and attractive when people can expect to live to be at least 70 or 80 rather than 40 or 50. Thus it seems possible that by the end of the 21st century emerging adulthood will be a normative period for young people worldwide, although it is likely to vary in length and content both within and between countries (Arnett, 2000a). The growth and variability of emerging adulthood in countries and cultures around the world would make an important and fascinating topic for a nascent scholarly field of emerging adulthood.

Conclusion

Emerging adulthood has become a distinct period of the life course for young people in industrialized societies. It is a period characterized by change and exploration for most people, as they examine the life possibilities open to them and gradually arrive at more enduring choices in love, work, and worldviews. Not all young people experience their late teens and twenties as years of change and exploration, even in industrialized societies. Some lack the opportunities to use those years as a volitional period; others may be inclined by personality or circumstances to limit their explorations or to seek a relatively early resolution to them. Nevertheless, as scholars we can characterize emerging adulthood as a period when change and exploration are common, even as we recognize the heterogeneity of the period and investigate this heterogeneity as one of emerging adulthood's distinguishing characteristics.

Emerging adulthood merits scholarly attention as a distinct period of the life course in industrialized societies. It is in many respects the age of possibilities, a period in which many different potential futures remain possible and personal freedom and exploration are higher for most people than at any other time. It is also a period of life that is likely to grow in importance in the coming century, as countries around the world reach a point in their economic development where they may allow the prolonged period of exploration and freedom from roles that constitutes emerging adulthood.

References

Adams, G. R. (1999). *The objective measure of ego identity status: A manual on theory and test construction.* Guelph, Ontario, Canada: Author

Arnett, J. (1992). Reckless behavior in adolescence: A developmental perspective. *Developmental Review, 12,* 339–373.

Arnett, J. J. (1994a). Are college students adults? Their conceptions of the transition to adulthood. *Journal of Adult Development, 1,* 154–168.

Arnett, J. J. (1997). Young people's conceptions of the transition to adulthood. *Youth & Society, 29,* 1–23.

Arnett, J. J. (1998). Learning to stand alone: The contemporary American transition to adulthood in cultural and historical context. *Human Development, 41,* 295–315.

Arnett, J. J. (2000a). *Emerging adulthood: Prospects for the 21st century.* Manuscript submitted for publication.

Arnett, J. J. (2000b). High hopes in a grim world: Emerging adults' view of their futures and of "Generation X." *Youth & Society, 31,* 267–286.

Arnett, J. J. (in press). Conceptions of the transition to adulthood from adolescence through midlife. *Journal of Adult Development.*

Arnett, J. J., & Jensen, L. A. (1999, November). *A congregation of one: The individuation of religious beliefs among people in their twenties.* Paper presented at the annual meeting of the Society for the Scientific Study of Religion, Boston, MA.

Arnett, J., & Taber, S. (1994). Adolescence terminable and interminable: When does adolescence end? *Journal of Youth & Adolescence, 23,* 517–537.

Bachman, J. G., Johnston, L. D., O'Malley, P., & Schulenberg, J. (1996). Transitions in drug use during late adolescence and young adulthood. In J. A. Graber, J. Brooks-Gunn, & A. C. Petersen (Eds.), *Transitions through adolescence: Interpersonal domains and context* (pp. 111–140). Mahwah, NJ: Erlbaum.

Bachman, J. G., & Schulenberg, J. (1993). How part-time work intensity relates to drug use, problem behavior, time use, and satisfaction among high school seniors: Are these consequences or just correlates? *Developmental Psychology, 29,* 22–235.

Barling, J., & Kelloway, E. K. (1999). *Young workers: Varieties of experience.* Washington, DC: American Psychological Association.

Ben-Amos, I. K. (1994). *Adolescence and youth in early modern England.* New Haven, CT: Yale University Press.

Bianchi, S. M., & Spain, D. (1996). Women, work, and family in America. *Population Bulletin, 51(31),* 1–48.

Brooks-Gunn, J., & Paikoff, R. (1997). Sexuality and developmental transitions during adolescence. In J. Schulenberg, J. L. Maggs, & K. Hurrelmann (Eds.), *Health risks and developmental transitions during adolescence* (pp. 190–219). New York: Cambridge University Press.

Chisholm, L., & Hurrelmann, K. (1995). Adolescence in modern Europe: Pluralized transition patterns and their implications for personal and social risks. *Journal of Adolescence, 18,* 129–158.

Cote, J. E., & Allahar, A. L. (1996). *Generation on hold: Coming of age in the late twentieth century.* New York: New York University Press.

Dubas, J. S., & Petersen, A. C. (1996). Geographical distance from parents and adjustment during adolescence and young adulthood. *New Directions for Child Development, 71,* 3–19.

Elliott, G. R., & Feldman, S. S. (1990). Capturing the adolescent experience. In S. S. Feldman & G. R. Elliott (Eds.), *At the threshold: The developing adolescent* (pp. 1–14). Cambridge, MA: Harvard University Press.

Erikson, E. H. (1950). *Childhood and society.* New York: Norton.

Erikson, E. H. (1968). *Identity: Youth and crisis.* New York: Norton.

Eveleth, P., & Tanner, J. (1976). *Worldwide variation in human growth.* New York: Cambridge University Press.

Feiring, C. (1996). Concepts of romance in 15-year-olds. *Journal of Research on Adolescence, 6,* 181–200.

Goldscheider, F., & Davanzo, J. (1986). Semiautonomy and leaving home during early adulthood. *Social Forces, 65,* 187–201.

Goldscheider, F., & Goldscheider, C. (1994). Leaving and returning home in 20th century America. *Population Bulletin, 48(4),* 1–35.

Greenberger, E., & Steinberg, L. (1986). *When teenagers work: The psychological and social costs of adolescent employment.* New York: Basic Books.

Greene, A. L., Wheatley, S. M., & Aldava, J. F., IV. (1992). Stages on life's way: Adolescents' implicit theories of the life course. *Journal of Adolescent Research, 7,* 364–381.

Hall, G. S. (1904). *Adolescence: Its psychology and its relation to physiology, anthropology, sociology, sex, crime, religion, and education* (Vol. 1), Englewood Cliffs, NJ: Prentice-Hall.

Heaton, T. B. (1992). Demographics of the contemporary Mormon family. *Dialogue, 25,* 19–34.

Hogan, D. P., & Astone, N. M. (1986). The transition to adulthood. *Annual Review of Sociology, 12,* 109–130.

Hoge, D. R., Johnson, B., & Luidens, D. A. (1993). Determinants of church involvement of young adults who grew up in Presbyterian churches. *Journal of the Scientific Study of Religion, 32,* 242–255.

Hornblower, M. (1997, June 9). Great Xpectations. *Time, 149*, 58–68.

Jessor, R., Donovan, J. E., & Costa, F. M. (1991). *Beyond adolescence: Problem behavior and young adult development.* New York: Cambridge University Press.

Johnson, B. (1994, March). *Youth life projects and modernization in Sweden: A cross-sectional study.* Paper presented at the biennial meeting of the Society for Research on Adolescence, San Diego, CA.

Keniston, K. (1971). *Youth and dissent: The rise of a new opposition.* New York: Harcourt Brace Jovanovich.

Larson, R. W. (1990). The solitary side of life: An examination of the time people spend alone from childhood to old age. *Developmental Review, 10*, 155–183.

Levinson, D. J. (1978). *The seasons of a man's life.* New York: Ballantine.

Martin, P., & Smyer, M. A. (1990). The experience of micro- and macroevents: A life span analysis. *Research on Aging, 12*, 294–310.

Michael, R. T., Gagnon, J. H., Laumann, E. O., & Kolata, G. (1995). *Sex in America: A definitive survey.* New York: Warner Books.

Mogelonsky, M. (1996, May). The rocky road to adulthood. *American Demographics, 18*, 26–36, 56.

Montemayor, R., Brown, B., & Adams, G. (1985). *Changes in identity status and psychological adjustment after leaving home and entering college.* Paper presented at the biennial meeting of the Society for Research on Child Development, Toronto, Canada.

Morch, S. (1995). Culture and the challenge of adaptation: Foreign youth in Denmark. *International Journal of Comparative Race and Ethnic Studies, 2*, 102–115.

Mortimer, J. T., Harley, C., & Aronson, P. J. (1999). How do prior experiences in the workplace set the stage for transitions to adulthood? In A. Booth, A. C. Crouter, & M. J. Shanahan (Eds.), *Transitions to adulthood in a changing economy: No work, no family, no future?* (pp. 131–159). Westport, CT: Praeger.

Noble, J., Cover, J., & Yanagishita, M. (1996). *The world's youth.* Washington, DC: Population Reference Bureau.

O'Connor, T. G., Allen, J. P., Bell, K. L., & Hauser, S. T. (1996). Adolescent-parent relationships and leaving home in young adulthood. *New Directions in Child Development, 71*, 39–52.

Offer, D., & Offer, J. B. (1975). *From teenage to young manhood.* New York: Basic Books.

Padgham, J. J., & Blyth, D. A. (1991). Dating during adolescence. In R. M. Lerner, A. C. Petersen, & J. Brooks-Gunn (Eds.), *Encyclopedia of adolescence* (pp. 196–198). New York: Garland.

Page, K. (1999, May 16). The graduate. *Washington Post Magazine, 152*, 18, 20.

Parsons, T. (1942). Age and sex in the social structure of the United States. *American Sociological Review, 7*, 604–616.

Pascarella, E., & Terenzini, P. (1991). *How culture affects students: Findings and insights from twenty years of research.* San Francisco: Jossey-Bass.

Perry, W. G. (1999). *Forms of ethical and intellectual development in the college years: A scheme.* San Francisco: Jossey-Bass. (Original work published 1970)

Rindfuss, R. R. (1991). The young adult years: Diversity, structural change, and fertility. *Demography, 28*, 493–512.

Roscoe, B., Dian, M. S., & Brooks, R. H. (1987). Early, middle, and late adolescents' views on dating and the factors influencing partner selection. *Adolescence, 22*, 59–68.

Scheer, S. D., Unger, D. G., & Brown, M. (1994, February). *Adolescents becoming adults: Attributes for adulthood.* Poster presented at the biennial meeting of the Society for Research on Adolescence, San Diego, CA.

Schlegel, A., & Barry, H., III. (1991). *Adolescence: An anthropological inquiry.* New York: Free Press.

Shanahan, M., Elder, G. H., Jr., Burchinal, M., & Conger, R. D. (1996). Adolescent earnings and relationships with parents: The work-family nexus in urban and rural ecologies. In J. T. Mortimer & M. D. Finch (Eds.), *Adolescents, work, and family: An intergenerational developmental analysis* (pp. 97–128). Thousand Oaks, CA: Sage.

Steinberg, L., & Cauffman, E. (1995). The impact on employment on adolescent development. In R. Vasta (Ed.), *Annals of child development* (Vol. 11, pp. 131–166). London: Kingsley.

U.S. Bureau of the Census (1997). *Statistical abstracts of the United States: 1997.* Washington, DC: Author.

U.S. Bureau of the Census (2000). *Geographic mobility: March 1997 to March 1998 (Current Population Reports, Series P-20, No 520).* Washington, DC: U.S. Government Printing Office.

Valde, G. A. (1996). Identity closure: A fifth identity status. *Journal of Genetic Psychology, 157*, 245–254.

Wallace, C. (1995, April). How old is young and young is old? *The restructuring of age and the life course in Europe.* Paper presented at Youth 2000: An International Conference, Middlesborough, UK.

Waterman, A. L. (1982). Identity development from adolescence to adulthood: An extension of theory and a review of research. *Developmental Psychology, 18*, 341–358.

Whitbourne, S. K., & Tesch, S. A. (1985). A comparison of identity and intimacy statuses in college students and alumni. *Developmental Psychology, 21*, 1039–1044.

William T. Grant Foundation Commission on Work, Family, and Citizenship. (1988). *The forgotten half: Non-college-bound youth in America.* Washington, DC: William T. Grant Foundation.

Concluding Comments

Revising Theoretical Approaches to Fit Emerging Facts

In this admirably clear article, Arnett has employed an old theoretical approach: the psychosocial stage theory, to arrive at new insights about current development. He updates prior stage theories to incorporate a new psychological stage of growth: that of emerging adulthood. This newly proposed stage accounts for many young people's sense of not quite having attained adulthood; it integrates those subjective experiences with newly evolved social factors that have led to extended educational periods, delayed career identification, and marriage at a later age. This new stage seems to better capture changes in people's lives than earlier stage theories of the mid-20th century could do, providing psychologists with a better map of a person between the years of 18 and 25.

Review Questions

1. The introduction to this reading noted that there are few specific rules for presenting a theoretical paper, but that a theoretical article must meet standards of plausibility, of high-caliber description, and of information integration. How well did Arnett's paper do this? How would you compare it to Erik Erikson's theoretical work in the prior reading?

2. The author mentions Erikson's stage of identity vs. role confusion. How is his stage of emerging adulthood similar to Erikson's stage? How is it different?

3. Arnett marshals a great deal of evidence for a stage of emerging adulthood—and from a great number of areas of study. What sociological evidence does Arnett draw upon to make his case for emerging adulthood?

4. Arnett also draws on psychological evidence for the existence of a stage of emerging adulthood. What sorts of evidence does he present in this regard?

5. At the end of the article, Arnett points to differences in the emerging adulthood phase that may be present across cultures. Earlier on, he had mentioned that emerging adulthood is socially constructed. What does it mean to say that emerging adulthood is socially constructed in this context? Do cultural differences support his claims for the presence of this stage?

6. Arnett pulled together data from sociological, psychological, and developmental studies to support his position that there exists a period of emerging adulthood. Why did Arnett use information from different sources to do this? Would concentrating on one area of data have been better?

Editor's References

Adair, J. G. & Vohra, N. (2003). The explosion of knowledge, references, and citations: Psychology's unique response to a crisis. *American Psychologist, 58,* 15–23.

Allport, G. W. (1965). *Letters from Jenny.* New York: Harcourt, Brace, & World.

American Psychological Association (2001). *Publication manual of the American Psychological Association (5th ed).* American Psychological Association: Washington, DC.

Aristotle (350 BCE/1961). *The poetics.* [S. H. Butcher, Trans.]. New York: Hill & Wang.

Buros Institute (2005). *The 16th mental measurements yearbook.* Lincoln, NE: University of Nebraska Press.

Cialdini, R. B, Borden, R. J., Thorne, A., Walker, M. R., Freeman, S., & Sloan, L. R. (1976). Basking in reflected glory: Three (football) field studies. *Journal of Personality & Social Psychology, 34,* 366–375.

Coles, R. (1970). *Erik H. Erikson: The growth of his work.* Boston: Little, Brown & Company.

Cozby, P. C. (2004). *Methods in behavioral research (8th ed.).* New York: McGraw-Hill.

Emmons, R. A. (1989). The big three, the big four, or the big five? *Contemporary Psychology, 34,* 644–646.

Endler, N. S., Rushton, J. P., & Roediger, H. L. (1978). Productivity and scholarly impact (citations) of British, Canadian, and U.S. Departments of Psychology. *American Psychologist, 33,* 1064–1082.

Freud, S. (1963). *Dora: An analysis of a case of hysteria.* New York: Macmillan. [Original work published 1905.]

Freud, S. (1961). A seventeenth-century demonological neurosis. In J. Strachey (ed.). *The standard edition of the complete psychological works of Sigmund Freud (Vol. XIX, pp. 72–105).* London: The Hogarth press. [Original work published 1923.]

Freud, S. (1961). Jokes and their relation to the unconscious. In J. Strachey (ed.). *The standard edition of the complete psychological works of Sigmund Freud (Vol. VIII, pp. 9–247).* London: the Hogarth press. [Original work published 1905.]

Greenwald, A. G. (1980). The totalitarian ego. *American Psychologist, 35,* 603–618.

Gudjonsson, G. H., & Sigurdsson, J. F. (2003). The relationship of compliance with coping strategies and self-esteem. *European Journal of Psychological Assessment, 19,* 117–123.

Harris, J. H. (l998). *The nurture assumption: Why children turn out the way they do.* New York: Free Press.

Hogan, J. D. (2003). Anne Anastasi (1908–2001). *American Journal of Psychology, 116,* 649–653.

Holtzman, W. H. (2002). Over half a century of playing with inkblots and other wondrous pursuits. *Journal of Personality Assessment, 79,* 1–18.

Mayer, J. D. (1993–1994). A System-Topics Framework for the study of personality. *Imagination, Cognition, and Personality, 13,* 99–123.

Mayer, J. D. (1998). A systems framework for the field of personality psychology. *Psychological Inquiry, 9,* 118–144.

Mayer, J. D. (2005). A tale of two visions: Can a new view of personality help integrate psychology? *American Psychologist, 60,* 294–307.

McAdams, D. P. (1995). What do we know when we know a person? *Journal of Personality, 63,* 365–396.

McAdams, D. P., & West, S. G. (1997). Introduction: Personality psychology and the case study. *Journal of Personality, 65,* 757–783.

Meehl, P. E. (1973). Why I do not attend case conferences. In P. E. Meehl (ed.). *Psychodiagnosis: Selected papers (pp. 225–302).* New York: W. W. Norton.

Meehl, P. E. (1973). Wanted—a good cookbook. In P. E. Meehl (ed.). *Psychodiagnosis: Selected papers (pp. 63–80).* New York: W. W. Norton. [Original work published 1956.]

Motley, M. T., Camden, C. T., Baars, B. J. (1982). Covert formulation and editing of anomalies in speech production: Evidence from experimentally elicited slips of the tongue. *Journal of Verbal Learning & Verbal Behavior, 21,* 578–594.

Murphy, L. L., Plake, B. S., Impara, J. C., & Spies, R. A. (2002) *Tests in print VI: An index to tests, test reviews, and the literature on specific tests.* Lincoln, NE: University of Nebraska Press.

Over, R. (1982). The durability of scientific reputation. *Journal of the History of the Behavioral Sciences, 18,* 53–61.

Reznikoff, M. & Procidano, M. (2001). Anne Anastasi (1908–2001). *American Psychologist, 56,* 816–817.

Robinson, J. P., Shaver, P. R., & Wrightsman, L. S. (1991). *Measures of personality and social psychological attitudes.* New York: Academic Press.

Rogers, C. R. (1951). *Client-centered therapy.* Boston: Houghton Mifflin.

Skinner, B. F. (1960). Pigeons in a pelican. *American Psychologist, 15,* 28–37.

Smyth, J. M. (1998). Written emotional expression: Effect sizes, outcome types, and moderating variables. *Journal of Consulting & Clinical Psychology, 66,* 174–184.

Sommer, B., & Sommer, R. (1997). *A practical guide to behavioral research: Tools and techniques (4th ed.).* New York: Oxford University Press.

Sternberg, R. J. (1992). *Psychological Bulletin's* Top 10 "Hit Parade." *Psychological Bulletin, 112,* 387–388.

Steuer, F. B. (1996). Reading in the undergraduate curriculum. *Teaching of Psychology, 23,* 226–230.

Thorngate, W. (1990). The economy of attention and the development of psychology. *Canadian Psychology, 31,* 262–271.

Welchman, K. (2000). *Erik Erikson: His life, work, and significance.* Buckingham, PA: Open University Press.

West, S. G. (2003). Towards finding the person in the data of personality. *Journal of Personality, 71,* 299–318.

Westen, D. (1998). The scientific legacy of Sigmund Freud: Toward a psychodynamically informed psychological science. *Psychological Bulletin, 124,* 333–371.

White, M. J. & White, K. G. (1977). Citation analysis of psychology journals. *American Psychologist, 32,* 301–305.

Winter, D. H. (2005). Things I've learned about personality from studying personality at a distance. *Journal of Personality, 73,* 567–584.